Recollections And Essays

OXFORD UNIVERSITY PRESS
AMEN HOUSE, E.C 4
London Edinburgh Glasgow New York
Toronto Melbourne Cape Town Bombay
Calcutta Madras
GEOFFREY CUMBERLEGE
PUBLISHER TO THE UNIVERSITY

RECOLLECTIONS & ESSAYS

By
LEO TOLSTÓY

*Translated
with an Introduction by*
AYLMER MAUD

GEOFFREY CUMBERLEGE
OXFORD UNIVERSITY PRESS
LONDON NEW YORK TORONTO

LEO TOLSTÓY

Born: Yásnaya Polyána, Túla
    August 28 (Old Style) = September 9 (New Style), 1828
Died: Astápovo, Riazán
    November 7 (Old Style) = November 20 (New Style), 1910

The articles, jottings, and letters which comprise 'Recollections and Essays' were written between 1890 and 1910. In the 'World's Classics' 'Recollections and Essays' was first published in 1937 and reprinted in 1946.

PRINTED IN GREAT BRITAIN

CONTENTS

INTRODUCTION, by AYLMER MAUDE	vii
'RECOLLECTIONS.' *Jottings made in 1902 and in 1908*	1
WHY DO MEN STUPEFY THEMSELVES? *1890*	67
THE FIRST STEP. *1892*	90
NON-ACTING. *1893*	136
AN AFTERWORD TO FAMINE ARTICLES. *1893*	171
MODERN SCIENCE. *1898*	176
AN INTRODUCTION TO RUSKIN'S WORKS. *1899*	188
LETTERS ON HENRY GEORGE. *1897*	189
'THOU SHALT NOT KILL.' *1900*	195
BETHINK YOURSELVES! *1904*	204
A GREAT INIQUITY. *1905*	272
SHAKESPEARE AND THE DRAMA. *1906*	307
WHAT'S TO BE DONE? *1906*	384
I CANNOT BE SILENT. *1908*	395
A LETTER TO A HINDU. *1908*	413
GANDHI LETTERS. *1910*	433
LETTER TO A JAPANESE. *1910*	440
THE WISDOM OF CHILDREN. *1910*	446
THOUGHTS FROM PRIVATE LETTERS	494
INDEX TO THIS VOLUME	501
GENERAL INDEXES	

INTRODUCTION

THIS volume is a reproduction of the final volume of the Centenary Edition, which was the first edition of Tolstóy's works in any language so arranged as to show the sequence and development of his views.

From the first, but especially from the time he wrote *Confession*, the censor constantly suppressed or mutilated Tolstóy's works and at times even interpolated sentences he had not written. This occasioned many perplexities. Clandestine hectographed and mimeographed editions of some of his writings began to circulate, and these at times contained errors and omissions which were afterwards reproduced in translations. Tolstóy's wife, wishing to include in her edition any portions of his prohibited works the censor could be induced to pass, introduced these under various headings, and such fragments were often mistaken for fresh works by Tolstóy, thus adding to the confusion which was again increased by the mistakes of careless or incompetent translators. For instance, in an American collected edition which absurdly professed to be 'complete', the editor included three compilations a friend of Tolstóy's had made from undated fragments of private letters and rejected drafts. Against the publication of these Tolstóy issued a protest, saying that he refused to be held responsible for them.

The premature publication of part of a work as though it were complete often placed editors in a difficulty when the rest of the work was subsequently released, and they took little trouble to explain what had happened. The collected editions of Tolstóy's works originally published in

America are therefore far from doing him justice or rendering it easy for readers to understand his works.

Tolstóy once remarked that a chief quality of an artist is to know what to strike out, and said that he wished to be judged only by works he himself had selected for publication and of which he had corrected the proofs. When he died, however, he authorized his friend V. G. Chertkóv to deal with his writings as he thought best, and Chertkóv decided to publish everything, including a mass of posthumous stories and diaries, neither of which were in Tolstóy's opinion worth publishing, as he told me the year before he died.

The collected library Centenary Edition was the first in any language to present his works in due sequence and to assemble in separate volumes what he wrote on various subjects. The same translations are given in the volumes of the World's Classics, but as these are sold separately the reader has not the same guidance as to the sequence and development of Tolstóy's thought.

Considering how previous editions have been arranged, it is scarcely surprising that Mr. Nazaroff's well-written biography of Tolstóy published in 1930 should be entitled *Tolstóy, the Inconstant Genius*. That no doubt represents a very common opinion, but it is really quite wide of the mark for very few men have ever been so consistent as Tolstóy in the pursuit of a single aim: that of uniting all men. He never lost sight of the vision which delighted him in boyhood, when his brother Nicholas told of the 'green stick, the inscription on which would, when disclosed, make all men happy ... no one would be angry with anybody and all would love one another'. And his constant and conscious desire throughout the last thirty years of his life was that all men should be united in such a clear view of truth that all discord, strife, and enmity among them would end.

Every subject he dealt with—whether it was religion, war, art, or anything else—he approached from that one central outlook, and the underlying connexion of them all is easy to perceive. To-day, for instance, when the nations are actively arming against one another, one notes in his *Confession* that a main cause of his questioning the teachings of the Church was the fact that it approved of war or connived at it.

In *What is Art?* he points out that by means of art feelings are transmitted from man to man and thus become general.

For ages much of the world's best art, and not the best art only—Homer's battles, David's rejoicings at the destruction of his enemies, the story of how well Horatius kept the bridge in the brave days of old, Henry V's heroics, *The Battle of the Baltic*, *The Charge of the Light Brigade*, Kipling's *The Soldiers of the Queen*, and similar works in all countries—has caused succeeding generations to regard war as a glorious adventure to be welcomed and enjoyed.

How, then, can we reasonably hope for permanent peace in the atmosphere produced by so potent an organ? Modification or rearrangement of the League of Nations is of minor importance compared with the influence of art, but this is as yet hardly recognized and Tolstóy's works on the subject have been met by ridicule and denunciation, though no one else has so clearly shown how potent is the influence of art on all phases of life, and how necessary for the betterment of human life a due understanding of that influence is.

A curious instance of the difficulties the attempt

to convey Tolstóy's meaning to our public has encountered, occurred in connexion with the book just referred to. Tolstóy entrusted the translation of *What is Art?* to me, but left the arrangements for its publication to his literary factotum, Mr. V. G. Chertkóv. The latter injudiciously entrusted the book to a third-rate publishing house, The Brotherhood Publishing Company. The manager of that firm received the translation in advance of the book's appearance in Russia and before it reached any other country. Noticing that it contained a chapter which mentioned in scathing terms some forty French poets, novelists, and painters of the day, he unscrupulously sold that chapter for publication in a Paris monthly magazine in advance of the book's publication. The other chapters explain Tolstóy's attitude towards the artists he mentioned—symbolists, decadents, and others—but when this chapter appeared by itself in the magazine they took it as a gratuitous, unprovoked, and personal assault, and directly the book came out it was virulently attacked, grossly misrepresented, ridiculed, and denounced by almost the whole literary, artistic, and critical world of Paris.

The excitement aroused in Paris influenced the book's reception in England. Directly it appeared Mr. H. D. Traill, the editor of *Literature* (the forerunner of the *Times Literary Supplement*), had a leading article on it in which he said that 'there never was any reason for inferring . . . that Count Tolstoi's (*sic*) opinions on the philosophy of art would be worth the paper on which they are written'. He added that he held himself absolved from discussing Count Tolstoi's (*sic*) 'fantastic doctrines seriously', but remarked that their expounder 'surpasses all other advocates of this same theory in perverse unreason', and that 'this is Tolstoi's (*sic*) chief distinction among aesthetic circle-squarers. . . . Nobody, however eminent as a novelist, has any business to invite his fellow-men to step with him outside the region of sanity and sit down beside him like Alice beside the Hatter and the March Hare for the solemn examination of so lunatic a thesis as this . . . clotted nonsense.'

Other critics hardly went to such an extreme of ridicule and denunciation, but most of them took more or less the same line of declining to discuss Tolstóy's theory seriously and imputing to him absurdities he had not uttered, so that they practically invited Bernard Shaw's remark that 'the book is a most effective booby-trap. It is written with so utter a contempt for the objections which the routine critic is sure to allege against it, that many a dilettantist reviewer has already accepted it as a butt set up by Providence to show off his own brilliant marksmanship'. Shaw added, of Tolstóy's chief assault on the prevalent aesthetic theory of that day, that 'our generation has not seen a heartier bout of literary fisticuffs, nor one in which the challenger has been more brilliantly victorious'.

One of Tolstóy's opinions that particularly exasperated the professional aestheticians was his statement that since art is the transmission of feeling from man to man, to be susceptible to the influence of art it is essential not to have lost 'that simple feeling familiar to the plainest man and even to a child, the sense of infection with another's feeling—compelling us to rejoice in another's gladness, to sorrow at another's grief, and to mingle souls with another—which is the very essence of art'. They were especially provoked by his saying that many people who have become specialists in one or other branch of art have by this very specialization of their life and occupation perverted that simple feeling, and become immune to art—with which they deal so eruditely—while children, savages, and peasants who are not perverted in that way and have retained their capacity to share the feelings of others, can readily respond to such art as is suitable for them.

What the critics particularly objected to was the statement that for 'a country peasant of unperverted taste' (that is, a man who can share the feelings of his fellow men) 'it is as easy to select the work of art *he* requires (which infects him with the feeling experienced by the artist) as it is for an animal of unspoilt scent to follow the trace he needs among a thousand others in wood or forest'.

This was fantastically misrepresented as claiming for the peasant some peculiar quality making him a touchstone or criterion of art—not only of the work of art *he* requires, but of all art of all ages and all nations and all classes of mankind. In other words it was supposed to show that Tolstóy was a semi-lunatic; whereas what he claimed for the child, the savage, and the peasant, he claimed for every man—namely, that if he has not perverted his capacity to share another's feelings, he will have retained the capacity to respond to the art *he* requires.

Given the personal animosity aroused by the premature publication of a detached chapter of the book, and the readiness of critics at a time of excitement to repeat what someone else has emphatically declared, it is not very strange that the first reception of the book should have been so hostile. What is extraordinary is the tenacity with which this absurd misrepresentation has been repeated during a whole generation and is still kept alive.

INTRODUCTION xiii

What is Art? was published in 1898, and in 1919 George Moore dealt with it in his *Avowals*. He tells us of Tolstóy that

'in imitation of the early hermits he elected to live in a sheeling, but in a sheeling that communicates with folding doors with his wife's apartment. And he will not sleep upon a spring-mattress, he must have a feather-bed, the one he sleeps upon costs more than any spring-mattress. His rooms are quite plain, but to paint and heat them to his liking workmen had to be brought from England.'

All this—the sheeling, the folding doors, the feather-bed, the painting and special heating of his room, as well as the 'workmen brought from England'—is pure invention with no scrap of foundation in fact, and is in flat contradiction to the evidence of those who knew Tolstóy and lived with him. Its apparent object is to prejudice the reader and prepare him to accept the misrepresentation of Tolstóy's works which follows. Moore suggests that Tolstóy's touchstone of art was the peasant, and adds:

'Which peasant, we ask—Russian, English, or French? Is he or she fifteen or sixty? Is he or she the most intelligent in the village? Or is he or she the least intelligent? are the questions put to Tolstóy, and his answer is: The peasant representing the average intelligence of the village. Why should the lowest intelligence be excluded? If the peasant is the best judge of what is art, why should not the best art be produced by peasants?'

Now, it is simply untrue that Tolstóy gave any such answer. Moore invents it to add verisimilitude to the otherwise bald and unconvincing assertion that Tolstóy's touchstone of art is the peasant. He finishes off his remarkable effort in criticism by asking what is

'the value of this exhibition of Tolstóy's hard, isolated,

tenacious apprehensions? It seems,' he says, 'that Nature has answered this question by devising a death for Tolstóy that reads so like an admonition that we cannot but suspect the eternal wisdom of a certain watchfulness over human life. . . . Can we doubt that Saint Helena, with Napoleon gazing blankly at the ocean, carries a meaning, and is not the end that Nature devised for Tolstóy as significant, a flight from his wife and home in his eighty-second year and his death in the waiting-room of a wayside station in the early hours of a March morning?'

Had George Moore lived to read Count Sergius Tolstóy's book, *The Final Struggle*, he might not have been so sure of Nature's purpose. But let it here suffice to notice that, in addition to the other mis-statements of which his article is full, he manages to cram three more into that last sentence. Tolstóy was not in his eighty-second year but in his eighty-third, he died not in a waiting-room but in a house the station-master had vacated for his use, and unless Moore thought it sounded well, I do not know why he should say that Tolstóy died 'in the early hours of a March morning', when he actually died in November.

In fact, George Moore was writing very spitefully about a man of whom he knew very little and about a book he completely misunderstood. It is surprising to find Miss Rebecca West acclaiming his article as 'among the major glories of English criticism', but that, too, is a reminder that the fit of hysteria that affected the literary world when *What is Art?* appeared, with its bold attempt to set art on a new basis, has not yet quite died down, though nearly forty years have passed since its publication.

The survival of the myth of a peasantry that furnishes a touchstone for art is indicated by two recent publications. Gerald Abraham's well-written and generally impartial life of Tolstóy (Duckworth's Great Lives Series, 1935) repeated the statement that Tolstóy considered he had found a 'surer touchstone than his own individual taste in the taste of the ideal peasant, or, as we should say, the plain man who knows what he likes'. And Mr. H. W. Garrod, in a Taylorian Lecture published by the Clarendon Press, says that for Tolstóy 'the judge of art is not the intelligent man; he is in fact the peasant'. In a subsequent letter, however, he made the penetrating remark that when Tolstóy attributes a capacity to recognize art to a peasant whose natural qualities have not been perverted by spurious art or otherwise '... he is saying of the peasant what would be equally true of the nobleman, and in respect of either tautologous'. That hits the nail precisely on the head, and had critics perceived it from the first, all this pother about the peasant's exceptional appreciation of art would never have arisen.

It all shows how badly needed is an edition properly grouping together Tolstóy's articles on kindred subjects. In the Oxford Press editions *What is Art?* is followed by an article by Tolstóy on a German novel he liked. In that article he says:

'To that enormously important question, "What, of all that has been written, is one to read?" only real criticism can furnish a reply: criticism which, as Matthew Arnold says, sets itself the task of bringing to the front and pointing out to people all that is best, both in former and in contemporary writers.

'On whether such disinterested criticism, which understands and loves art and is independent of any party, makes its appearance or not, and on whether its authority becomes sufficiently established for it to be stronger than mercenary advertisement, depends, in my opinion, the decision of the question whether the last rays of enlightenment are to perish in our so-called European society without having reached the masses of the people, or whether they will revive as they did in the Middle Ages, and reach the great mass of the people who are now without any enlightenment.'

That makes it perfectly clear that Tolstóy did not imagine that an unaided peasant would be able to select for himself the best that has been written. But those who attack *What is Art?* have generally not read what else Tolstóy wrote on the subject, and to make it appear that Tolstóy was talking nonsense have selected a single line detached from the main argument.

It is probably due to the abuse with which *What is Art?* was originally received that it has been generally ignored by writers on aesthetics—despite its originality and the great practical importance of an understanding of the relation in which art stands to the rest of life.

Bosanquet's *Aesthetics*, for instance, does not even mention it, and Croce dismisses it in two slighting sentences.

The article on Famine Relief in this volume is the last one of a series written during the two years that Tolstóy and his daughters devoted to the arduous task of organizing relief on a large scale in the famine district. The Government wished it not to be known that there was a famine, and Tolstóy's articles were forbidden by the censor. But when a translation of some of them appeared in the *Daily Telegraph* in January 1892, one was promptly and inexactly retranslated by the reactionary *Moscow Gazette*, which supplemented it by extracts from other writings of Tolstóy's so arranged as to suggest that he was inciting the peasants to revolt. The *Gazette* added a demand that he should be suppressed as a dangerous revolutionary, and that cry was taken up by other reactionary papers. Matters went so far that

Durnovó, the Minister of the Interior, submitted a proposal to the Tsar that Tolstóy should be confined in Súzdal Monastery prison (where two Uniate Bishops, after twenty-three years' confinement, had been forgotten by the authorities who had had them arrested). The Tsar rejected the proposal, but that was far from being the end of the attacks upon Tolstóy.

He was reproached with having published abuse of Russia in the English papers, and while he was engaged in the famine district of Riazán his wife sent a letter to the papers denying that he had sent anything to any English paper. This was verbally correct, but was misleading in its suggestion that the translation of his Famine Article in the *Daily Telegraph* was a fabrication. Dr. Dillon (who had translated it for the *Daily Telegraph*, but whose name had not appeared there) saw a first-rate opportunity to advertise himself and establish connexion with influential individuals and groups in Church and State who were bent on Tolstóy's destruction. Though Tolstóy gave him a written acknowledgement that the article in question was genuine, this did not prevent Dillon from insinuating that Tolstóy had equivocated, treated him badly, and failed to stick to his guns. These insinuations were eagerly taken up by the reactionary Russian press, and complications and misunderstandings were piled one on another. As it happens, a prolonged examination of Dr. Dillon's accusation is rendered unnecessary by his posthumous volume which appeared in 1934, having for frontispiece a facsimile of part of a letter written by Tolstóy in Russian, to which is appended the underline: 'Tolstóy's letter of apology to Dillon for repudiation of his word.' This is evidently intended to impress readers with the reliability and authenticity of Dillon's book. But fortunately the letter of which he reproduced a portion has been published in full in Russia, and proves not to be what Dr. Dillon represents it as being, but merely to contain an expression of Tolstóy's regret for having omitted to answer a letter.

That discreditable trick is characteristic of Dr. Dillon's tactics throughout the affair, as well as of the tactics pursued by the *Moscow Gazette* and the reactionary press generally.

During Tolstóy's absence in the famine district pressure was brought to bear on his family by the Governor-General of Moscow, who wanted them to secure from Tolstóy a substantiation of his wife's published suggestion that he had not written the articles attributed to him. His wife accordingly tried to get him to write something to placate the authorities and lessen the danger he was in. But he would do nothing of the kind, and in his reply to her said:

'I write what I think and what cannot please the Government or the wealthy classes. I have been doing this for the last twelve years not casually but deliberately, and do not intend to justify myself for so doing. . . . Only ignorant people—of whom the most ignorant are those who form the Court—reading what I have written can suppose that views such as mine can suddenly change one fine day and become revolutionary.'

Though Tolstóy was not physically molested he was persistently harassed and persecuted. During his famine work he was repeatedly denounced from the pulpit as Antichrist, and later on he was excommunicated by the Holy Synod. His secretary and several of his friends were banished and his life repeatedly threatened by reactionary patriots who were exasperated by his exposure of governmental abuses and his condemnation of prepara-

INTRODUCTION

tions for war, the persecution of dissenters, and the discovery and announcement by the Church of the 'incorruptible' bodies of newly devised saints.

Surrounded as Tolstóy was by obstacles, discouragements, and dangers during those years of strenuous famine-relief work, it is wonderful that he found time and energy to write *The Kingdom of God is Within You*, the twelfth chapter of which is an artistic gem comparable to his other autobiographical masterpieces in *Confession* and *What Then Must We Do?*

It was with reference especially to this period of Tolstóy's life that Bernard Shaw (after making a passing reference to the Russian saying that 'nothing matters provided the baby is not crying') wrote:

'If you have a baby who can speak with Tsars in the gate, who can make Europe and America stop and listen when he opens his mouth, who can smite with unerring aim straight at the sorest spots in the world's conscience, who can break through all censorships and all barriers of language, who can thunder on the gates of the most terrible prisons in the world and place his neck under the keenest and bloodiest axes only to find that for him the gates dare not open and the axes dare not fall, then indeed you have a baby that must be nursed and coddled and petted and let go his own way.'

It remains to say something about the other articles in this volume.

Most of the *Recollections* appear now for the first time in English. No precise date can be given to them, for they are a collection of rough, unrevised notes jotted down by Tolstóy at various times, not for publication but for the information of friends and biographers who asked for them. They are, however, so characteristic of Tolstóy and show so keenly treasured a memory of his happy boyhood, that though they are disjointed it seemed a pity to omit them. They do not provide a connected narrative of his early years, but I have brought them together in what seems a natural sequence. Some of them have already been given in vol. i of my *Life of Tolstóy* in this edition, and wherever such citations are of any length I have, to avoid repetition, referred to the page where they can be found. When, owing to the disjointed nature of these recollections, it seemed desirable to insert some comment of my own, this has been done in square brackets.

The other contents of the volume are chiefly essays dealing in Tolstóy's masterly manner with important subjects, and it is remarkable to note how fresh and topical they still are some forty years after they were written.

Why Do Men Stupefy Themselves? is probably as powerful and persuasive an essay as was ever written on the evils of drink. Tolstóy was as keen on that subject as any Prohibitionist in the United States, but his non-resistant views saved him from the error of wishing to invoke the aid of physical force and Prohibition Laws to combat the evil he deplored.

The First Step, the best vegetarian essay I ever read, is still as applicable and persuasive as when it was penned.

Non-Acting, apart from the interest of juxtaposing Zola's speech and Dumas's article, presents Tolstóy's view of a question the understanding of which is as necessary for the welfare of mankind now as it was then.

Modern Science, Tolstóy's introduction to an essay of Edward Carpenter's, deals with a matter on which his views (not always expressed with due moderation) have often been misunderstood. It may be considered a companion article to his reply to Thomas Huxley's Romanes Lecture of 1894 (given in the essay *Religion and Morality* in the volume *On Life and Essays on Religion*), which goes to the root of a matter of vital importance that still sorely perplexes many minds.

The *Introduction to Ruskin* is a note Tolstóy contributed to a booklet of extracts from Ruskin issued by the Posrédnik firm that did so much to make first-rate literature accessible to the Russian people.

Letters on Henry George and *A Great Iniquity* deal with a matter on which Tolstóy felt very strongly. He sympathized with the peasants' grievance at having to go short of land while men who did not work on it owned large estates which some of them had never even seen. Henry George's plan for the taxation of land-values seemed to him by far the most just and practicable way of dealing with the matter; and looking back now, one can see how much the adoption of that plan would have done to mitigate the worst evils of the Revolution that was then approaching.

Allowing the peasants' grievances to rankle enabled the Revolutionaries to set them against the landed proprietors and created the confusion amid which it was possible for a small group of men to seize absolute power. Had the Henry George system been adopted, not only could the peasants' taxation have been greatly lightened but the peasants would have seen that the possession of land carried with it an obligation to contribute to the public expenditure and would therefore have been less eager to seize it and less credulous of the promises made by the Revolutionaries.

The introduction of that system would also have done much to save the landowners from the wholesale expropriation they had to endure in 1917 and 1918. This was one of many instances in which

Tolstóy saw further and more clearly into a complex problem than the 'practical' men who refused to listen to his advice.

Thou Shalt Not Kill relates to the assassination of King Humbert of Italy by an anarchist in 1900. It forcibly expresses Tolstóy's conviction that it is an evil thing whether for private individuals or for kings to kill their fellow men.

Bethink Yourselves!, written at the time of the Japanese war, was once more a dangerous article for Tolstóy to write while efforts were being made to arouse patriotic enthusiasm among the people. His fearlessness in uttering what no one else could say with such power was one of the qualities that marked him out as standing head and shoulders above any of his contemporaries. He appeared as a hero and a prophet and not merely a great writer. What is said in *Bethink Yourselves!* had to a large extent been said before in *The Kingdom of God is Within You* and *Christianity and Patriotism*, but its immediate application to the facts of the Russo-Japanese war and to the state of Russia at that preliminary stage of the Revolution added to the significance of a message that was equally applicable ten years later at the time of the Great War and will still be as applicable when the next war comes.

The long article on *Shakespeare and the Drama* would have placed me in a dilemma had it not fortunately happened that Professor G. Wilson Knight, an ardent admirer of the English dramatist and an acknowledged authority on his works, has dealt very ably with it in his article *Shakespeare and Tolstóy*, published by the English Association. Few readers of Shakespeare would fail to benefit by a careful perusal of Tolstóy's attack and Wilson Knight's defence. The professor is so sure of his

INTRODUCTION

ground that he can afford to be just to Tolstóy, and in the course of his article he says:

'We find "characterization" not only not the Shakespearian essence, but actually the most penetrable spot to adverse criticism that may be discovered in his technique. Thence two great minds have directed their hostility— Tolstóy and Bridges. I shall show that those attacks on Shakespeare, often perfectly justifiable within limits, are yet based on a fundamental misunderstanding of his art; but that such misunderstanding is nevertheless extremely significant and valuable, since it forces our appreciation and interpretation from excessive psychologies of "character" . . . into the true substance and solidity of Shakespeare's dramatic poetry.'

In another passage he speaks of Tolstóy's *Essays on Art* as

'a massive collection of some of the most masculine, incisive, and important criticism that exists: all, whether we agree or disagree, of so rock-like an integrity and simplicity that its effect is invariably tonic and invigorating, and often points us directly, as in this essay on Shakespeare, to facts before unobserved, yet both obvious and extremely significant.'

What's to be Done?, written amid the strikes and disturbances of the first revolution (in 1905-6), was a fresh statement of Tolstóy's conviction that no good would result from men killing one another. For much more than a thousand years physical force has been relied on to secure peace and harmony among mankind. But an increasingly large number of men now seem to object to being killed or even to preparing to kill other people. The progress of science in the preparation of deadly bacterial bombs and poison gases and improved flying-machines has brought us within easy reach of utter destruction; but Tolstóy thought that it was not too much to hope that, before we all perish, we may have time to face the fundamental question whether reliance on wholesale or retail murder does afford the best hope for the physical and spiritual salvation of mankind. Man's body must in any case perish, and to imperil his soul by relying on murder to safeguard his life and property seemed to Tolstóy both senseless and wicked.

Of all that Tolstóy wrote in his last year, *I Cannot Be Silent* produced the greatest sensation in Russia. Its occasion was the introduction by Stolýpin, the Prime Minister, of field courts-martial which hanged many revolutionaries, or people accused of being such. This outraged Tolstóy's profoundest feelings. Since the time of Catherine the Great the death penalty had, at least theoretically, been abolished in Russia; and though men had not infrequently been done to death in the army and in prisons, the idea of formally, deliberately, and publicly putting them to death outraged Tolstóy's soul, and gave an incisive vigour to his protest which aroused a responsive thrill from one end of the country to the other. Specially moving was his wish that if 'these inhuman deeds' were not stopped '. . . they may put on me, as on those twelve or twenty persons, a shroud and a cap, and may push me too off a bench, so that by my own weight I may tighten the well-soaped noose round my old throat'.

His protest was against the taking of human life whether by the government or by the revolutionaries, but the sensation the article occasioned was increased by the fact that the anti-governmental parties found it a convenient instrument wherewith to discredit the Tsardom.

The English Labour Party published it as a penny pamphlet under the quite misleading title of *The Hanging Tsar*, though its argument was no

INTRODUCTION xxv

more directed against the one side than the other, and if any one man was indicated as the chief culprit it was Stolýpin and not the Tsar. Such attempts to make party capital out of Tolstóy's moral appeal largely defeated his purpose, and when the Revolution came those who seized the dictatorship slew many tens of thousands where Stolýpin had only slain hundreds.

The *Letter to a Hindu* and the *Gandhi Letters* deal with a matter which may become of great importance in the future. Tolstóy not only thought that wars and all violence between man and man should cease, but he sought for practical means towards furthering that end. One of the most potent of these seemed to him to be passive resistance which, if practised by a whole population refusing to serve or in any way assist those who rule over them, would render such rule impossible. The chief example of such an attempt to get rid of a foreign domination has been the Non-cooperation movement Gandhi formulated ten years after Tolstóy's death. That movement failed partly because there were some among the Hindus who still relied on violence, and partly because the Mohammedan section of the population of India were not at one with the Hindus. But the strength the movement attained made it a serious challenge to British rule in India at that time, and indicated that under other circumstances Non-cooperation may some day play a decisive role in deciding the fate of a nation or a government.

As disapproval of war spreads among mankind, more and more people will seek practical means of preventing it, and even from that practical side it would be unwise to leave what Tolstóy wrote on the subject unconsidered.

Another practical movement of which Tolstóy

was a main instigator was the migration of over seven thousand Doukhobors from the Caucasus to Canada in 1898. They had refused military service and suffered severe persecution which caused many deaths among them. An arrangement was made with the Canadian government that they might settle in Canada under an agreement exempting them from any form of conscription or military service. Their number has now, I believe, more than doubled, and comparing their fate with that of other inhabitants of the Caucasus during the Great War and the subsequent Civil War in Russia, there is no room to doubt that they have benefited by the migration Tolstóy made possible for them. Some among them have shown themselves fanatics, unreasonably suspicious of and hostile to the Canadian (or any other) government, and that renders their example less attractive than it otherwise would be, but the main fact stands out clearly. Several thousand men by steadfastly withstanding conscription in their own country secured exemption from military service in the country to which they migrated, and thereby escaped the dreadful suffering and disasters that would have befallen them had they been willing to be trained to slay their fellow men. If, as seems probable, the objection to war many people feel is to take practical form in the future, the Doukhobórs and Gandhi's Non-co-operation movement deserve to be kept in remembrance, adding as they do a note of actuality and practicality to what Tolstóy has written against war and the use of physical violence.

In the *Letter to a Japanese* Tolstóy gives his unknown correspondent a summary of what he considered to be 'the truth that has been preached by all the great thinkers of the world', and applies it to the question of military service. It was written in the year that Tolstóy died, and when quoting from the book *For Every Day* which he was then engaged on compiling he made a slip which can surprise no one who has read *The Final Struggle* and realizes the very trying conditions under which he was then living.

The Wisdom of Children is in a style Tolstóy only tried experimentally and during the last months of his life. He left it unfinished and unrevised, and there are signs of the off-hand method of its composition. In it he broke fresh ground at the very end of his life when living under conditions which would have rendered literary work impossible to almost anyone else.

Tolstóy is a foreign writer who died a quarter of a century ago, of whose works two collected editions were entrenched in our public libraries and served as a hindrance to the recognition of his calibre as a great thinker, as well as a novelist, dramatist, autobiographer, and critic. It was therefore a doubtful venture for any publisher to undertake a new edition of his works—the success of which would depend largely on whether librarians and library committees could be brought to realize that Tolstóy's works are valuable and that those previous editions conceal their value.

For a long time no one was ready to undertake so large and doubtful a venture, and everyone who values Tolstóy's works and thinks that a readable and reliable version of them is worth having owes a debt of gratitude to Sir Humphrey Milford for undertaking the publication of the Centenary Edition, the translations of which (minus the frontispieces and the special introductions) are reproduced in the volumes of the World's Classics series. While matters hung in the balance the publication of the Centenary Edition was encouraged by the generosity of more than twenty distinguished English and American writers in contributing Introductions for its volumes. They nearly all did so gratuitously—a noteworthy testimony to the esteem in which Tolstóy was held. The American contingent, consisting of Jane Addams, Hamlin Garland, Madeline Mason-Manheim, Professors G. R. Noyes and W. Lyon Phelps, and the Hon. Brand Whitlock, contributed particularly helpful and suitable articles which well match those provided by John Galsworthy, Harley Granville-Barker, Hugh Walpole, and the best of the other English contributors.

The General Index prepared for that edition is reprinted at the end of this volume, as it provides readers with a classified list of Tolstóy's works.

In conclusion, let me acknowledge an obligation to Mr. H. W. Garrod, who has drawn my attention to the obscurity of a passage on p. 12 of *Tolstóy on Art and its Critics*. I there said that Tolstóy was 'not speaking of the mass of the peasantry, but of a not very common individual . . .'. That is misleading, for the claim Tolstóy makes for the peasant he makes for all men—namely that if they are capable of sharing another's feelings, they can be reached by the influence of art that is suitable for them.

AYLMER MAUDE.

INTRODUCTION

By LEO TOLSTÓY *to his 'Recollections'*

This and the *'Recollections'* that follow are rough uncorrected drafts Tolstóy never revised or prepared for the press. They include what he gave to Birukóv, to Lowenfeld his German biographer, to Paul Boyer, and others who wrote about him.

Some earlier autobiographical recollections, published in 1878, have been given on pp. 10 to 15 of vol. i of the *Life of Tolstóy* in this edition.

My friend P. Birukóv having undertaken to write my biography for a French edition of my works asked me to supply him with some biographical information.

I wanted to do what he asked and began mentally to plan my biography. Involuntarily at first I began to recall only the good in my life, merely adding what was dark and bad in my conduct and actions like shades in a picture. Reflecting more seriously on the events of my life, however, I saw that such a biography, though not absolutely false, would be false by reason of its incorrect illumination—its presentation of what was good and its silence as to, or smoothing over of, all that was bad. But when I thought of writing the whole sincere truth, not hiding anything that was bad in my life, I was horrified at the impression such a biography must produce. Just at that time I fell ill.[1] And during the involuntary idleness caused by my illness my thoughts constantly turned to recollections, and those recollections were terrifying.

[1] This was written in 1902, when Tolstóy was recovering from a prolonged and very severe illness.—A. M.

I experienced profoundly what Púshkin speaks of in his poem *Remembrance*:

> 'When for us mortals silent grows the noisy day
> And on the hushed streets of the city
> Descend the night's semi-translucent shadows grey
> And sleep, reward of day-time labour,—
> Then comes the time for me when in the silence deep,
> All through the night's enforcèd leisure
> Long dismal hours of sleepless torment slowly creep.
> Remorse within my heart burns fiercely,
> My mind is seething and my weary aching brain
> With hosts of bitter thoughts is crowded,
> And old disgraceful memories of shame, with pain
> Unwind their heavy roll in silence.
> As with disgust the record of my life I face,
> I curse, chastise myself and shudder,
> And bitter tears I shed, but never can efface
> The lines of my unhappy story.'

The only change I would make would be in the last line, where I would put 'disgraceful' instead of 'unhappy'.

Under the influence of this impression I wrote as follows in my Diary.

'January 6th 1903.

'I am now experiencing the torments of hell: I remember all the vileness of my former life and those recollections poison my life and do not leave me. People often express regret that man's memory will not survive death. But how fortunate that it does not! What torture it would be if in a future life I remembered all the bad things I have done in this life and that now torment my conscience. But if I am to remember the good I must also remember all the bad. How fortunate it is that memory disappears with death and only consciousness remains—consciousness which presents as it were the common resultant of the good and the bad like a complex equation reduced to its

INTRODUCTION TO 'RECOLLECTIONS'

simplest form: $x =$ a quantity which may be large or small, positive or negative.

'Yes, the destruction of memories is a great happiness. With memory it would be impossible to live joyfully. But with the destruction of memories we can enter into a life with clean white slates on which we can write afresh, good and bad.

'It is true that not all my life was so terribly bad. Only twenty years of it was that. And it is true that during that period it was not the continuous evil it appeared to me to be during my illness, and that during that period, too, good impulses arose in me though they did not long prevail but were soon overwhelmed by passions. But still that effort of reflection—especially during my illness—showed me clearly that a biography written as biographies usually are and passing in silence over all the nastiness and guilt of my life, would be false, and that if a biography is to be written the whole real truth must be told. Only a biography of that kind —however ashamed one may be to write it—can be of any real benefit to its readers. Reflecting on it in that way, regarding it, that is, from the standpoint of good and evil, I saw that my whole long life falls into four periods: that wonderful period (especially in comparison with what followed) of innocent, joyful, poetic childhood up to fourteen; then the terrible twenty years that followed—a period of coarse dissoluteness, employed in the service of ambition, vanity, and above all of lust; then the eighteen-year period from my marriage to my spiritual birth—which from a worldly point of view may be called moral, that is to say, that during those eighteen years I lived a correct, honest, family life, not practising any vices condemned by social opinion, though all the interests of that period were limited to egotistic cares for the family, the increase of our property, the attainment of literary success, and pleasures of all kinds: and finally the fourth, twenty-year, period in which I am now living and in which I hope to die, from the standpoint of which I see the meaning of my past life, and which I should not wish to alter in any respect except for the effects of the evil habits to which I grew accustomed in the former periods.

'I should like to write a perfectly truthful story of those four periods if God grants me the life and strength to do it. I think my biography written in such a manner would be of more use to people, in spite of its great defects, than all the artistic chatter that fills the twelve volumes of my works[1] and to which people of our day attribute more importance than they deserve.

'I now wish to do that. I will first tell of the joyful period of my childhood, which attracts me particularly; then, however shameful it may be, I will recount the terrible twenty years of the next period without concealing anything. Then I will deal with the third period, which is of less interest than the others, and finally will tell of the last period of my awakening to the truth which has given me the highest good in life and a joyful tranquillity in regard to my approaching death.

'In order not to repeat myself when describing the period of childhood, I have re-read what I wrote under that title, and felt regret that I wrote it; so ill and (in a literary sense) insincerely is it written. Nor could it be otherwise, for in the first place my plan was to relate not my own story but

---

[1] At that time, January 1903, those of Tolstóy's works allowed in Russia were published in a collected edition of twelve volumes. His works on religion, social problems, war, and violence were generally suppressed by the Censor.—A. M.

that of my childhood's friends, and as a result there is an ill-proportioned mixture of the events of their childhood and my own,[1] and in the second place I was far from being independent in my forms of expression at the time it was written, but was much under the influence of two writers—Sterne (the *Sentimental Journey*) and Töpffer[2] (*La Bibliothèque de mon oncle*).

'In particular the last two parts, *Boyhood* and *Youth*, now displeased me. In them, besides an ill-proportioned mixture of fact and fiction, there is insincerity—a wish to present as good and important what I did not then consider good and important, namely, my democratic tendency. I hope that what I shall now write will be better, and particularly that it will be of more use to other people.'

[*Tolstóy never carried out the project of writing an autobiography, and all he left besides the recollections published in 1878 are the following highly characteristic fragments.—A. M.*]

'RECOLLECTIONS'

My grandmother, Pelagéya Nikoláevna (Tolstóy), was the daughter of the blind Prince Nicholas Ivánovich Gorchakóv, who had accumulated a large fortune. As far as I can form an opinion of her she was a woman of limited intellect and education. Like all her set, she knew French better than Russian (that was the extent of her education), and was very much spoilt—first by her father, then by her husband, and afterwards, within my memory, by her son. Moreover, as the daughter of

---

[1] Yet in some English editions *Childhood, Boyhood, and Youth* is presented as a reliable autobiography.—A. M.
[2] Rodolphe Töpffer (1799-1846), Swiss novelist and artist.—A. M.

the senior member of the family she was highly respected by all the Gorchakóvs: Alexéy Ivánovich, the former Minister of War, Andrew Ivánovich, and the sons of the freethinking Dmítri Petróvich—Peter, Sergéy, and Michael[1] who served at the siege of Sevastopol.

My grandfather (her husband) also exists in my memory as a man of limited intelligence, very gentle and merry, and not only generous but senselessly prodigal, and above all very confiding. On his estate in the Belévski district, Polyány (not Yásnaya Polyána, but Polyány), there was for a long time a continuous round of feasting, theatrical performances, balls, dinners, and outings, which, with his fondness for playing lombard and whist for high stakes (though he was a poor player) and his readiness to give to everyone who asked either for a loan or a free gift, and above all by becoming entangled in affairs—ended by his wife's large estate becoming so involved in debts that they had nothing to live on, and my grandfather had to apply for and accept the Governorship of Kazán—a post easily obtainable with such connexions as his.

I have been told that he never accepted bribes (except from the spirit-monopolist) though it was then the generally accepted practice to do so, and that he was angry when any were offered him. But I have been told that my grandmother accepted contributions without her husband's knowledge.

In Kazán my grandmother married off her younger daughter, Pelagéya, to Yúshkov. Her elder daughter, Alexándra, had already been married in Petersburg to Count Osten-Saken.

After the death of her husband at Kazán and my father's marriage, my grandmother settled with

[1] He was commander-in-chief of the Russian forces in the Crimea during the siege of Sevastopol.—A. M.

my father at Yásnaya Polyána, where I well remember her as an old woman.

My grandmother loved my father and us, her grandsons, amusing herself with us. She loved my aunts but I fancy she did not love my mother much, considering her to be not good enough for my father and feeling jealous of his affection for her. With the servants she could not be exacting for everyone knew that she was the chief person in the house and sought to please her; but with her maid Gásha she gave way to caprice and tormented her, calling her: 'You . . . my dear,'[1] expecting of her things that she had not asked for, and tormenting her in all sorts of ways. And curiously enough Gásha (Agáfya Mikháylovna),[2] whom I knew well, was infected by my grandmother's capriciousness, and with the girl in attendance on her and with her cat, and in general with all with whom she could be exacting, she was as capricious as my grandmother was with her.

My earliest recollections of my grandmother, before we moved to Moscow and lived there, are three vivid ones. The first is the way in which she washed, making, with some special soap, wonderful bubbles on her hands which it seemed to me she alone could produce. We were taken specially to see her when she washed—probably our delight and astonishment at her soap-bubbles amused her. I remember her white cap, her dressing jacket, her white old hands, and the immense bubbles that rose on them, and her white face with its satisfied smile.

The second is of how she was drawn by my

[1] This sounded ironical, for a mistress in the ordinary course of things would never say 'You' but always 'Thou' to a servant.—A. M.

[2] Agáfya Mikháylovna lived to be quite an old woman at Yásnaya Polyána.—A. M.

father's footmen, without a horse, in a well-sprung yellow cabriolet (in which we used to go driving with our tutor, Fëdor Ivánovich) to the Little Forest to gather nuts, of which there were a great many that year. I remember the thick, close-growing hazel-bushes into the midst of which Petrúshka and Matyúsha (the footmen) drew the yellow cabriolet in which my grandmother was seated, and how they bent down to her the boughs with clusters of ripe nuts, some of which were already falling out of their husks. I remember how grandmother herself plucked them and put them into a bag, and how we children bent down some branches, as did Fëdor Ivánovich, surprising us by his strength in bending down thick ones. We gathered the nuts from all sides and when Fëdor Ivánovich let go of them the bushes, slowly disentangling themselves, resumed their proper shape, and still others remained that we had overlooked. I remember how hot it was in the glades, how pleasant was the coolness in the shade, and I remember the pungent scent of the nut-leaves and how the maids who were with us cracked and ate the nuts, and how we ourselves unceasingly chewed the fresh, full, white kernels.

We filled our pockets and skirts and the cabriolet, and grandmother took us in and praised us. How we returned home and what followed I do not at all remember. I only remember that grandmamma, the nut-glade, the pungent scent of the leaves of the nut-trees, the footmen, the yellow cabriolet, and the sun, all merged into one joyful impression. It seemed to me that as the soap-bubbles could only exist with grandmamma, so the thicket, the nuts, the sun, and the other things, could only be where grandmamma was, in the yellow cabriolet drawn by Petrúshka and Matyúsha.

But the strongest recollection I have of my grandmother is of a night passed in her bedroom with Lév Stepánich. He was a blind story-teller (already an old man when I knew him)—a relic of the old-time *bárstvo*[1] of my grandfather. He was a serf who had been bought simply that he might tell stories which, with the remarkable memory characteristic of the blind, he could repeat word for word after having had them read to him once or twice.

He lived somewhere in the house and was not seen all day. But in the evening he would come upstairs to grandmamma's bedroom (her bedroom was a low, little room which one had to enter by two steps) and sit down on a low window-sill where supper was brought him from the master's table. There he would await my grandmother, who had no need to hesitate about undressing in the presence of a blind man. On that day, when it was my turn to spend the night with grandmamma, the blind Lev Stepánich, in a long, dark-blue coat with puffs at the shoulders, was already sitting on the window-sill eating his supper. I do not remember where my grandmother undressed, whether in that room or another, or how they put me to bed. I only remember the moment when the candle was extinguished and just a small lamp remained burning before the gilt icons. Grandmamma, that same wonderful grandmamma who produced those extraordinary soap-bubbles, all white—in white, on white, and covered with white—a white night-cap on her head, lay raised high on pillows, and from the window-sill came the even, tranquil voice of

---

[1] *Bárstvo*, though a characteristic and almost indispensable word in dealing with the old order of things in Russia, is difficult to translate. It is something like 'seigniorality', 'grandeur', or 'lordliness'.—A. M.

Lëv Stepánich: 'Do you wish me to continue?' 'Yes, continue.' 'Dear sister, said she—' Lëv Stepánich's quiet, smooth, elderly voice went on, 'tell us one of those interesting stories which you can tell so well. Willingly, replied Sheherazade, I will tell the remarkable story of Prince Camaralzaman, if your ruler will express his consent to that. Having received the Sultan's consent, Sheherazade began as follows: A certain ruling King had an only son' ... and Lëv Stepánich began the story of Camaralzaman, evidently word for word as it was in the book. I neither listened nor understood, so absorbed was I by the mysterious appearance of my white grandmother, her wavering shadow on the wall, and the old man with his white, sightless eyes, whom I did not now see but whom I remembered sitting on the window-sill, slowly uttering some strange, and as it seemed to me solemn, words, which sounded monotonous in the dim room, lit only by the flickering light of the little lamp. Probably I fell asleep at once, for I remember nothing more, but in the morning was again surprised and delighted by the soap-bubbles grandmamma made on her hands while washing.

Of his maternal grandfather Tolstóy tells us:

Of my grandfather I know that having attained the high position of *Général en Chef*, he lost it suddenly by refusing to marry Potëmkin's niece and mistress, Varvára Engelhardt. To Potëmkin's suggestion that he should do so, he replied: 'What makes him think I would marry his strumpet?'

Having married a Princess Catherine Dmítrievna Trubetskóy he settled on the estate of Yásnaya Polyána inherited from her father, Sergéy Fëdorovich.

The Princess soon died, leaving my grandfather

an only daughter, Márya. With that much-loved daughter and her French girl-companion my grandfather lived till his death, about the year 1821. He was regarded as a very exacting master but I never heard any instance of his being cruel or inflicting the severe punishments common in those days. I believe such things did happen on his estate, but the enthusiastic respect for his importance and cleverness was so great among the household and agricultural serfs whom I have often questioned about him, that though I have heard my father condemned, I have heard only praise of my grandfather's intelligence, capacity for management, and interest both in the affairs of the serfs on the land and more particularly of those of his great number of domestic serfs. He built admirable accommodation for the latter and was careful to see that they always had enough to eat and were well clothed and had recreation. On holidays he arranged amusements for them—swings and village dances.

Like all wise landowners of that day he was extremely concerned as to the well-being of his agricultural serfs, who flourished the more because grandfather's high rank inspired respect among the local police and enabled the serfs to escape the exactions of the authorities.

He probably had an acute appreciation of beauty, for all his buildings were not only well built and convenient but exceedingly elegant. So, too, was the park he laid out in front of the house. Probably he was also very fond of music, for he kept a good though small orchestra of his own, merely for himself and my mother. I remember an immense elm which stood where the lime avenues converged. Round its trunk—which was so large that it took three men to span it—were placed benches and stands for the musicians. Of a morning my grandfather would walk in the avenue and listen to the music. He could not endure hunting, but was fond of flowers and the plants in his greenhouses.

A strange fate brought him again in touch with that same Varvára Engelhardt for refusing to marry whom his army career had suffered. She had married Prince Sergéy Fëdorovich Golítsin, who in consequence had received all sorts of dignities, Orders, and rewards. My grandfather came so closely in touch with Sergéy Fëdorovich and his family, and consequently with Varvára also, that my mother in childhood was engaged to one of Golítsin's ten sons, and the two old princes exchanged family portraits (that is, copies painted of course by their own serfs). All those portraits of the Golítsins are now in our house, including Sergéy Fëdorovich wearing the ribbon of the Order of Saint Andrew, and the stout, red-haired Varvára Vasílevna as a Lady of the Order of Knighthood. My mother's engagement was, however, not destined to be fulfilled, for her fiancé died of high fever before the marriage.

My mother I do not at all remember. I was a year-and-a-half old when she died, and by some strange chance no portrait of her has been preserved, so that as an actual physical being I cannot picture her to myself. In a way I am glad of this, for my conception of her is thus purely spiritual and all I know about her is beautiful. I think this has come about not merely because all who told me of her tried to say only what was good, but because that good was actually in her.

My mother was not beautiful, but was very well educated for her time. Besides Russian (which, contrary to the prevailing custom, she wrote correctly) she knew four languages: French, German, English, and Italian, and she must have had a fine feeling for art. She played the piano well, and women of her own age have told me that she was very clever at telling interesting stories, inventing them as she went along. But her most precious quality, according to her servants, was that, though quick tempered, she was self-restrained. 'She would go quite red in the face and even begin to cry,' her maid told me, 'but would never say a rude word—she did not even know any.'

I have some letters of hers to my father and aunts, and her diary of my eldest brother Nikólenka's behaviour. He was six years old when she died and was, I think, more like her than the rest of us. They both had a characteristic very dear to me—at least from her letters I assume my mother had it, and I knew it in my brother. This was an indifference to what others thought about them, and a modesty which went to the length of trying to hide their mental, educational, and moral superiority. They seemed to be almost ashamed of those superiorities.

In my brother—of whom Turgénev very truly said that he lacked the defects necessary to become a great writer—I knew that last trait very well.

I remember how a very stupid and bad man, an adjutant to the Governor, who was hunting with my brother, ridiculed him in my presence, and how my brother, glancing at me, smiled good-humouredly, evidently finding pleasure in it.

I notice the same trait in my mother's letters. She was evidently morally superior to my father and his family, except perhaps Tatiána Alexándrovna Érgolski, with whom I lived half my life and who was a woman of remarkable moral qualities.

Besides that they both had another trait which I think accounts for their indifference to people's disapproval. It was that they never blamed anyone. I knew that certainly of my brother, with whom I spent half my life. His most pronouncedly negative relation to any man was expressed by a delicate, good-natured humour and a similar smile. I notice the same in my mother's letters and have heard it spoken of by those who knew her.

A third trait which distinguished my mother from others of her circle was the sincerity and simplicity of her letters. In those days exaggerated expressions were exceedingly common. 'Incomparable', 'adored', 'joy of my life', 'inestimable', and the like, were very customary epithets among intimates, and the more high-flown they were the less were they sincere.

That trait showed itself also in my father's letters, though not in any marked degree. He writes: '*Ma bien douce amie, je ne pense qu'au bonheur d'être auprès de toi.*'[1] That was hardly quite sincere. But her mode of address was always the same: '*Mon bon ami*,'[2] and in one of her letters she says plainly: '*Le temps me paraît long sans toi, quoiqu'à dire vrai, nous ne jouissons pas beaucoup de la société quand tu es ici*,'[3] and she always signed herself in the same way: '*Ta dévouée Marie.*'[4]

My mother passed her childhood partly in Moscow and partly in the country with that very able, proud, and gifted man, my grandfather Volkónski. I have been told that she was very fond of me, and called me: '*mon petit Benjamin*'.

[1] My very sweet friend, I think only of the happiness of being with you.
[2] My good friend.
[3] The time seems long without you, though to tell the truth we do not enjoy much of your company when you are here.
[4] Your devoted Marie.

I think that her love for her deceased betrothed, just because the engagement ended in his death, was that poetic love which girls experience only once. Her marriage with my father was arranged by her relatives and his. She was wealthy, no longer in her first youth, and an orphan, and my father was a gay, brilliant young man of good family and connexions, but whose fortune had been utterly ruined by his father Ilyá Tolstóy—ruined to such a degree that my father refused even to take over the inheritance. I think that my mother was not in love with my father, but loved him as a husband and chiefly as the father of her children. Her real loves, as I understand it, were three or four: the love of her deceased fiancé; then a passionate friendship for her French companion Mademoiselle Hénissienne, of which I heard from my aunts, and which, it seems, ended in disillusion. Mademoiselle Hénissienne married my mother's cousin, Prince Michael Alexándrovich Volkónski, grandfather of the present Volkónski, the writer.

Her third and perhaps most passionate love was for my eldest brother Koko [Nicholas], a diary of whose conduct she kept in Russian, writing down what he did and reading it to him. That diary portrays her passionate wish to do everything to educate Koko in the best possible way, and at the same time how very obscure a perception she had of what such an education should be. She reproves him, for instance, for being too sensitive, and crying over the sufferings of animals when he witnessed them. A man, in her view, had to be firm. Another defect she tried to correct in him was that he was absent-minded and said '*je vous remercie*' to grand-mamma instead of saying '*Bonsoir*' or '*Bonjour*'.

My aunts told me, I hope correctly, that a fourth strong feeling was her love for me, replacing her love for Koko, who from the time of my birth became detached from her and was handed over into masculine hands. She had to love someone, and the one love replaced the other.

Such was my mother as her portrait exists in my imagination.

She appeared to me a creature so elevated, pure, and spiritual, that often in the middle period of my life when I was struggling with overwhelming temptations, I prayed to her spirit, begging her to aid me, and those prayers always helped me a great deal.

Altogether I conclude from letters and reports that my mother's life in my father's family was a very good and happy one.

That family consisted of his mother, her daughters, one of whom was Countess Alexándra Ilínishna Osten-Saken, and her ward Páshenka; another 'aunt' as we called her, though she was really a much more distant relation, Tatiána Alexándrovna Érgolski, who had been brought up in my grandfather's house and lived the remainder of her life with us, my father, and our tutor Fèdor Ivánovich Ressel, who is described correctly enough in *Childhood*. There were five of us children: Nicholas, Sergéy, Dmítri, myself, and my sister Máshenka (Márya), in consequence of whose birth my mother died. My mother's short married life—hardly more than nine years—was a good and happy one. It was a very full one and adorned by her love of all who lived with her and by everyone's love of her. Judging by her letters, she lived at that time in great isolation. Hardly anyone except our close acquaintances, the Ogarëvs, and relatives casually travelling along the high road and who turned aside to visit us, ever came to Yásnaya Polyána.

My mother's life was spent in care for her children, in managing the household, in walks, reading novels aloud to my grandmother in the evening, in serious reading such as Rousseau's *Émile*, and in discussing what had been read, in playing the piano, and in teaching Italian to one of my aunts.

In all families there are periods when they all live peacefully and sickness and death are as yet absent. Such a period, I think, was experienced by my family till my mother's death. No one died, no one was seriously ill, and my father's disorganized affairs improved. Everyone was well, cheerful, and friendly. My father amused us all by his stories and jests. I do not remember that time. By the time my recollections begin my mother's death had already put its seal on the life of our family.

I have described all this from hearsay and letters. Now I will tell of what I myself experienced and remember. I will not mention confused, infantile, obscure recollections in which I cannot distinguish reality from dreams, but will begin with what I clearly remember—the place and the people that surrounded me from my first years. The first place among those people is naturally occupied by my father—not by his influence on me, but by my feeling for him.

In his early years he had been left an only son. His younger brother Ílenka, who had injured his spine, became hunchbacked, and died in childhood. In 1812[1] my father was seventeen years old, and in spite of his parents' remonstrances, fears, and horror, entered the military service. At that time Prince Alexéy Ivánovich Gorchakóv, a near relation of my grandmother's (who was by birth a Princess Gorchakóv) was Minister of War. His brother, Andrew Ivánovich, was a general com-

[1] When Napoleon invaded Russia.—A. M.

manding part of the active army, and my father was appointed adjutant to him. He served through the campaign of 1813–14, and in 1814, being sent somewhere in France with dispatches, was taken prisoner by the French and only liberated when our army entered Paris.

At the age of twenty my father was no longer an innocent youngster, for at the age of sixteen, before he entered the army, his parents had arranged a liaison between him and a serf-girl—such connexions being then considered desirable for the health of young men. That union resulted in the birth of a son, Míshenka, who became a postilion and who, while my father was alive, lived steadily, but afterwards went to pieces and often when we brothers were grown up used to come to us begging for help. I remember the strange feeling of perplexity I experienced when this brother of mine, who was very much like my father (more so than any of us), having fallen into destitution, was grateful for the ten or fifteen rubles we would give him.

After the war was over my father, disenchanted with army service—as is apparent from his letters—left it and returned to Kazán, where my grandfather (already completely ruined) was Governor, and where my father's sister, Pelagéya Ilínishna, who was married to Yúshkov, also lived. My grandfather died in Kazán soon after this, leaving on my father's hands an estate encumbered with debts which exceeded its value, and an old mother accustomed to luxury, as well as a sister and another relative. His marriage with my mother was arranged at that time, and he moved to Yásnaya Polyána, where after nine years he became a widower.

Returning to what I knew of my father and how I picture his life to myself: he was of medium height, well built, an active, sanguine man with a pleasant face, but with eyes that were always sad. His occupations were farming and lawsuits, chiefly the latter. Everybody at that time had many lawsuits, but my father, I think, had particularly many, as he had to disentangle my grandfather's affairs. These lawsuits frequently obliged him to leave home, and besides that he used often to go off hunting and shooting. His chief companions when hunting were his friends, a rich old bachelor Kiréevsky, Yazýkov, Glébov, and Islénev. My father shared a characteristic common among landed proprietors of having certain favourites among his household serfs. His chief favourites were two brothers, Petrúshka and Matyúsha, both handsome, dexterous fellows and clever huntsmen. When at home my father read a good deal, besides occupying himself with farming and with his children. He collected a library consisting of the French classics of that period, historical works, and works on natural history—Buffon and Cuvier. My aunt told me that my father made it a rule not to buy new books until he had read the old ones, but though he read a great deal it is difficult to believe that he got through all those *Histoires des Croisades* and *des Papes* which he acquired for his library.

As far as I can judge he was not fond of science, but was on the ordinary educational level of people of his day. Like most of the men of Alexander I's early years and of the campaigns of 1813, 1814, and 1815, he was not what is now called a Liberal, but simply from a feeling of self-respect did not consider it possible to serve either during Alexander's later reactionary period or under Nicholas I. And not only he but all his friends similarly held themselves aloof from government service and were rather Frondeurs in regard to Nicholas I's rule.

Throughout my childhood and even my youth our family were neither acquainted with nor had close intercourse with a single official. Of course I did not understand the significance of this in my childhood. All I then understood was that my father never humbled himself before anyone and never changed his debonair, gay, and often ironical tone. And this sense of personal dignity which I noticed in him increased my love for and my delight in him.

I remember him in his study when we went to say 'good night', or sometimes simply to play. There he sat on the leather divan smoking a pipe and petted us, and sometimes to our intense joy let us climb onto the back of the divan while he continued to read or talked to the clerk standing at the door, or to S. I. Yazýkov, my godfather, who often stayed with us. I remember how he came downstairs and drew pictures for us which seemed to us the height of perfection. I remember, too, how he once made me read him Púshkin's poems, which had pleased me and which I had learnt by heart: 'To the Sea', 'Farewell, free element!', and 'To Napoleon'—

> The wondrous fate has been fulfilled,
> The great man is no more.

—and so on. He was evidently struck by the pathos with which I spoke those verses, and having listened to me, exchanged significant looks with Yazýkov, who was present. I understood that he saw something good in that reading of mine and I was very happy about it.

I remember his merry jests and stories at dinner and supper, and how grandmamma and my aunts and we children laughed, listening to him. I also remember his journeys to town, and how wonderfully handsome he looked when he wore his frock-coat and narrow trousers. But my most vivid recollections of him are in connexion with hunting and dogs. I remember his setting off for the hunt ... I remember our going to walk with him and how the young borzois following him grew excited as the high grass whipped them and tickled their stomachs, and how they flew around with their tails bent over their backs, and how he admired them. I remember how on September 1st, the hunting holiday, we all set out in a *linéyka*[1] to a wood where a fox had been brought, and how the hounds chased it and how it was caught somewhere—though we did not see it—by the borzois. I also remember with particular clearness the taking of a wolf quite near home, and how we all went out on foot to see it. The big grey wolf was brought in a cart, trussed up and with his legs bound. He lay there quietly but glancing askance at those who approached him. Having reached a place behind the garden, they took the wolf out of the cart and held him down to the ground with pitchforks while they unbound his legs. He began to struggle and jerk and gnaw angrily at the cord. At last they loosed the cord from behind and someone shouted: 'Let him go!' The pitchforks were lifted and the wolf got up. He stood still for some ten seconds, but they shouted at him and let loose the dogs; and wolf, dogs, horsemen, and hunters flew downhill across the field. And the wolf got away. I remember my father scolding and gesticulating angrily when he returned home.[2]

[1] A four-wheeled vehicle rather like an Irish jaunting car, but longer, and seating more people.—A. M.
[2] Here evidently is part of the material from which the famous hunting scenes in *War and Peace* (Book VII, Chs. 4 to 6) were produced.—A. M.

But I liked my father best when he sat on the divan with grandmother and helped her lay out her cards for patience. He was always polite and affable with everyone, but for grandmother he had a special kind of amiable humility. Grandmother, with her long chin, and a cap with frills and a bow on her head, would sit on the divan and lay out the cards, occasionally taking a pinch of snuff from her gold snuff-box.

In an arm-chair beside the divan would sit the Túla gunsmith, Petróvna, in her short, cartridge-studded jacket. She would be spinning, sometimes knocking the clew against the wall which was already indented by such knocks. This Petróvna was a tradeswoman to whom my grandmother had taken a fancy, and she often stayed with us and always sat near the divan beside grandmamma. My aunts would be sitting in arm-chairs, one of them reading aloud. On another arm-chair, where she had made a place for herself, would be Mílka, my father's favourite dog, high-spirited and pie-bald, with beautiful black eyes. We would come in to say good night and would sometimes stay a while.

[A paragraph beginning on p. 20 of vol. i of the *Life of Tolstóy* and continuing at the top of p. 21 should follow on here.]

I loved my father very much, but only realized how strong that love was when he died.

[Tolstóy's earliest recollections (of being swaddled and bathed) are given on pp. 10 to 13 of the first volume of the *Life of Tolstóy* in this edition, and are therefore not repeated here. He goes on to say:]

After my recollections of being swaddled and tubbed I have no others up to the age of four or five, or very few of them, and not one of them relates to life out of doors. Up to the age of five nature did not exist for me. All that I remember happened in bed or in a room. Neither grass, nor leaves, nor sky, nor sun existed for me. It cannot be that no one gave me flowers and leaves to play with, or that I did not see the grass and was not sheltered from the sun, but up to the age of five or six I have no recollection of what is called 'nature'. Probably it is necessary to be separate from it in order to see it, and I was then part of nature.

It is strange and frightening to realize that from my birth and up to the age of three—when I was being fed at the breast, when I was weaned, when I first began to crawl about, to walk, and to speak—I cannot find a single recollection except those two, however much I search my memory. When did I begin to be? When did I begin to live? And why is it pleasant to imagine myself as I then was, but frightening—as it used to be to me and as it still is to many people—to imagine entering a similar condition at death, where there will be no recollections expressible in words? Was I not alive when I was learning to look, to hear, to understand, to speak, to take the breast and kiss it, and to laugh and delight my mother? I was alive and lived blissfully! Did I not then become possessed of everything by which I now live? Did I not then acquire so much and so rapidly that in all the rest of my life I have not acquired a one-hundredth part as much? From a five-year-old boy to me is only a step, from a new-born babe to a five-year-old boy there is an immense distance, from an embryo to a new-born babe there is an enormous chasm, while between non-existence and an embryo there is not merely a chasm but incomprehensibility. Not only are space and time and cause forms of thought, and the essence of life is beyond those forms, but our whole life is a greater and greater subjection of ourselves to those forms and then again a liberation from them.

[After this should follow the paragraph on p. 11 of vol. i of the *Life of Tolstóy* beginning with the words: 'My next recollections belong to the time when I was five or six', and continuing to 'a serious matter' at the end of the quotation on p. 13. Tolstóy goes on to tell us that:]

The third person after my father and mother who had the most important influence on my life was 'Auntie', as we called Tatiána Alexándrovna Érgolski. She was a very distant relation of my grandmother's on the Gorchakóv side. She and her sister Lisa, who afterwards married Count Peter Ivánovich Tolstóy, were left as poor unprotected little orphans when their parents died. They had some brothers whom relations managed somehow to place. But the imperious and important Tatiána Semënovna Skurátov, famous in her circle in the Chern district, and my grandmother, decided to take the girls to educate. They put folded pieces of paper bearing their names before an icon, prayed, and drew lots. Lisa fell to Tatiána Semënovna and the dark one to grandmamma. Tánichka, as we called her, was of the same age as my father, being born in 1795. She was educated on an exact equality with my aunts and was tenderly loved by us all, as could not be otherwise with her firm, energetic, and yet self-sacrificing character. Her character is well shown by an occurrence about which she told us, showing the large scar, almost the size of one's palm, left by the burn on her forearm. They children were reading the story of Mucius Scaevola, and argued that no one of them could do such a thing. 'I will do it,' said Tánichka. 'You won't!' said Yazýkov, my godfather, and characteristically enough heated a ruler over the candle till it bent and smoked. 'There, lay that on your arm!' said he. Tánichka stretched out her bare arm (all girls wore short sleeves then) and Yazýkov pressed the charred ruler against it. She frowned but did not withdraw her arm, and only groaned when the ruler was pulled away, taking the skin with it. When the grown-ups saw her wound and asked her how it had happened, she said she had done it herself, wishing to experience the same thing as Mucius Scaevola.[1]

She was like that in everything, determined yet self-sacrificing.

She must have been very attractive with her enormous plait of crisp black curly hair, her jet-black eyes and vivacious energetic expression. V. I. Yúshov, Pelagéya Ilýnichna's husband, a great lady-killer, when he was already old used to say of her (with the feeling lovers exhibit when speaking of former objects of their love)—'*Toinette, oh, elle était charmante!*'

When I first remember her she was already over forty and I never thought of whether she was beautiful or not. I simply loved her, loved her eyes, her smile, and her dusky broad little hand with its energetic cross-vein.

Probably she loved my father and he loved her, but she did not marry him when they were young because she thought he had better marry my wealthy mother, and she did not marry him subsequently because she did not wish to spoil her pure

[1] Readers will remember the use Tolstóy makes of this recollection in Chapter I of Book IV of *War and Peace*, where Sónya shows the scar on her arm.—A. M.

poetic relations with him and with us. Among her papers in a small beaded portfolio lies the following note, written in 1836, six years after the death of my mother:

'*16 août 1836. Nicholas m'a fait aujourd'hui une étrange proposition — celle de l'épouser — de servir de mère à ses enfants et de ne jamais les quitter. J'ai refusé la première proposition, j'ai promis de remplir l'autre tant que je vivrai.*'[1]

So she wrote, but never did she speak of that to us or to anyone. After my father's death she fulfilled his second request. We had two aunts and a grandmother who all had more claim on us than Tatiána Alexándrovna, whom we called 'auntie' only by habit, for our kinship was so distant that I could never remember what it was, but she held the first place in our upbringing by right of love to us—like Buddha in the story of the wounded swan—and we felt that.

I had fits of passionately tender love for her. I remember how once when I was about five, I squeezed in behind her on the divan in the drawing-room, and how, caressing me, she touched my hand. I caught her hand and began to kiss it and to cry from tender love of her.

She had been educated like the daughter of a wealthy family and spoke and wrote French better than Russian. She played the piano admirably, but had not touched it for some thirty years. She resumed playing only when I was grown up and was learning to play; and sometimes, when playing duets together, she surprised me by the correctness and elegance of her execution.

---

[1] 16th August 1836. Nicholas has to-day made me a strange proposal—that I should marry him, to act as mother to his children and never leave them. I have refused the first proposal, but have promised to fulfil the other as long as I live.

To her servants she was kind, never spoke to them angrily and could not endure the idea of beating or whipping; but she considered that the serfs were serfs, and behaved to them as a mistress. But in spite of that they regarded her as different from other people, and everybody loved her. When she died and was being borne through the village, peasants came out of all the huts and ordered requiems for her.[1] Her chief characteristic was love, but—much as I could wish that it had not been so—love of one man, my father. Only from that centre did her love radiate to everyone. We felt that she loved us for his sake. Through him she loved everyone, for her whole life was made up of love.

Though she had the greatest right to us by her love, our own aunts, especially Pelagéya Ilýnichna when she took us away to Kazán, had a prior legal right and Tatiána Alexándrovna submitted to it, but her love did not weaken because of it. She lived with her sister, Countess E. A. Tolstóy, but in spirit she lived with us, and she returned to us as soon as possible. That she lived her last years (about twenty) with me at Yásnaya Polyána was a great happiness for me. But how unable we were to value our happiness, for true happiness is always quiet and unnoticed! I valued it, but far from sufficiently. She was fond of keeping sweets, figs, gingerbreads, and dates, in various jars in her room, giving them me as a special treat. I cannot forget, or remember without a cruel pang of remorse, that I repeatedly refused her the money she wanted for such things and how, with a sad

---

[1] It was customary to get the priests to say prayers for the dead for a certain fee, but it was unusual for peasants to have such prayers said for a lady, especially for one who was not even the owner of the estate.—A. M.

sigh, she remained silent. It is true that I was myself in need of money, but I cannot now remember without horror that I refused her.

When I was already married and she had begun to grow feeble, one day when we were in her room, having awaited her opportunity, she said to us—turning away (I saw that she was ready to cry)—'Look here, *mes chers amis*, my room is a good one and you will want it. If I die in it,' and her voice trembled, 'the recollection will be unpleasant for you, so move me somewhere else that I may not die here.' Such she always was from my earliest childhood, when I did not yet understand her.

I have said that Auntie Tatiána Alexándrovna had a great influence on my life. That influence consisted first of all in teaching me from childhood the spiritual delight of love. She did not teach me that by words, but by her whole being she filled me with love.

I saw and felt how she enjoyed loving, and I understood the joy of love. That was the first thing. And the second was that she taught me the charm of an unhurried, tranquil life.

[Of the half-crazy saints who wandered from one holy place to another and were then common in Russia, and some of whom used to visit at the Tolstóys' house, he writes:]

Grísha [who figures in *Childhood*] was an invented character. Many of these *yurodívy* of various kinds used to come to our house and I was accustomed to regard them with profound respect, for which I am deeply grateful to those who brought me up. If there were some among them who were insincere or had periods of weakness and insincerity in their lives, the aim of their life, though practically absurd, was so lofty that I am glad I learned unconsciously in childhood to understand the height of their achievement. They practised what Marcus Aurelius speaks of when he says: 'There is nothing higher than to endure contempt for a good life.' The temptation to win human praise that mingles with good actions is so harmful and so unavoidable that one must sympathize with efforts to avoid praise and even to evoke contempt. Such a *yurodívy* was Márya Gerásimovna, my sister's godmother, and the semi-idiot Evdokímushka, and some others who used to come to our house.

And we children overheard the prayer not of a *yurodívy* but of a fool, the gardener's assistant Akím, who was praying in the large room between the two hothouses that was used in summer, and who really amazed and touched me by his prayer, in which he spoke to God as to a living person: 'You are my healer. You are my dispenser,'[1] said he with impressive conviction. And then he sang a verse about the Day of Judgement and how God would separate the just from the unjust and close the eyes of sinners with yellow sand.

Besides my brothers and sister we had with us from the time I was five Dúnechka Temyashóv, a girl of my own age, and I must tell who she was and how she happened to come among us. One of the visitors I remember in childhood was the husband of my aunt Yúshkov, whose appearance with his black moustache, whiskers, and spectacles, surprised us children, and another was my godfather S. I. Yazýkov, smelling of tobacco and remarkably

[1] *Léka*, a doctor or healer, and *aptéka*, an apothecary or dispenser, are so similar in sound and so akin in suggestion that having uttered the one word Akím could automatically follow it up with the other.—A. M.

ugly with loose skin on his large face which he constantly twitched into the strangest grimaces. Besides these and two neighbours, Ogarev and Islénev, there was on the Gorchakóv side of the family a distant relation who came to see us. This was the wealthy bachelor Temyashóv, who called my father 'brother' and cherished a kind of ecstatic liking for him. He lived forty versts from Yásnaya Polyána at the village of Pirogóva, and brought from there on one occasion sucking-pigs with tails twisted into rings, which were spread out on a large dish in the servants' quarters. Temyashóv, Pirogóva, and the sucking-pigs became merged into one in my imagination.

Besides that, Temyashóv was memorable for us children by the fact that he played on the piano in the large living-room a dance-tune (the only one he could play) and made us dance to it. When we asked him what dance it was, he said that one could dance all dances to that tune. And we enjoyed availing ourselves of such an opportunity.

It was a winter's evening, tea had been drunk and we were soon to be taken up to bed. I could hardly keep my eyes open, when suddenly from the servants' quarters, through the large open door into the drawing-room where we were all sitting in semi-darkness with only two candles burning, a man in soft boots entered with rapid strides and reaching the middle of the room fell on his knees. The lighted pipe he held in his hand struck the floor with its long stem and sparks flew about, lighting up the face of the kneeling man. It was Temyashóv. He said something to my father before whom he was kneeling. I do not remember what, and did not even hear. I only knew later that he had fallen on his knees before my father because he had brought his illegitimate daughter,

Dúnechka, about whom he had previously spoken to my father, asking him to take her to be educated with his own children. From that time there appeared among us a broad-faced little girl of my own age, Dúnechka, with her nurse Evpráxia, a tall wrinkled old woman with a pendulous jowl like a turkey-cock's in which was a ball she allowed us to feel.

The appearance in our house of Dúnechka was connected with a complicated transaction between my father and Temyashóv.

Temyashóv was very wealthy. He had no legitimate children, but there were two girls, Dúnechka and Vérochka, a hunchbacked girl whose mother Marfúsha had been a serf-girl. Temyashóv's heirs were his two sisters. He was leaving them all his other properties, but wished to transfer Pirogóva, where he lived, to my father, on condition that my father should hand over the value of the estate, 300,000 rubles (it was always said that Pirogóva was a gold-mine and worth much more than that), to the two girls. To arrange this the following plan was devised: Temyashóv drew up a bill of sale by which he sold Pirogóva to my father for 300,000 rubles, and my father gave notes-of-hand for 100,000 rubles each to three other people—Islénev, Yazýkov, and Glébov. In the event of Temyashóv's death my father was to receive the estate and (it having been explained to Glébov, Islénev, and Yazýkov with what object the notes-of-hand had been made out in their names) he was to pay the 300,000 rubles which were to go to the two girls.

Perhaps I may not have stated the whole plan correctly, but I know for certain that the estate of Pirogóva passed to us after my father's death and that there were three notes-of-hand in Islénev's,

Glébov's, and Yazýkov's names, and that our guardian redeemed these notes-of-hand and the two first-named each gave 100,000 rubles to the girls. But Yazýkov appropriated the money which did not belong to him.

Dúnechka lived with us and was a dear, simple, quiet girl, but not clever, and a great cry-baby. I remember that I, who had already been taught to read French, was set to teach her the letters. At first matters went well (she and I were both five years old) but afterwards she probably grew tired and no longer named correctly the letter I pointed to. I insisted. She began to cry and so did I. And when they came for us, our desperate tears prevented our uttering a word.

Another thing I remember about her is that when it appeared that one plum had been stolen from the plate and the culprit could not be discovered, Fëdor Ivánovich with a serious mien, not looking at us, said that it did not matter having eaten it, but if the stone had been swallowed one might die of it. Dúnechka could not endure that terror and exclaimed that she had spat out the stone. I also remember her desperate tears when she and my brother Mítenka (Dmítri) had started a game of spitting a little brass chain into one another's mouths, and she spat it out so forcibly and Mítenka had opened his mouth so wide, that he swallowed the chain. She wept inconsolably till the doctor came and tranquillized us all.

She was not clever, but was a good simple-minded girl, and above all was so chaste that between us boys and her there were never any but brotherly relations.

[Of the servants Tolstóy tells us:]
Praskóvya Isáevna I have described fairly

accurately in *Childhood* under the name of Natálya Sávishna. All that I wrote about her was taken from life. Praskóvya Isáevna was a respected person, the housekeeper, yet our, the children's, little trunk stood in her little room. One of the pleasantest impressions I have is of sitting in her little room and talking or listening to her after our lesson, or even in the middle of lesson-time. Probably she liked to see us at that time of particularly happy and tender expansiveness. 'Praskóvya Isáevna, how did grandpapa make war? On horseback?' one would ask her with a grunt, just to start her off on a conversation.

'He fought in every way, on horse and on foot. That's why he became a *Général en chef*,' she would reply, and opening a cupboard would get out some resin which she called 'Ochákov fumigation'. It seemed from what she said that grandfather had brought it back from the siege of Ochákov. She would light a bit of paper at the little lamp burning before the icon, and light the resin, which would smoke with a pleasant aroma.

Besides an indignity she inflicted on me by beating me with a wet napkin (as I have described in *Childhood*) she also offended me on another occasion. Among her duties was that of administering enemas to us when necessary. One morning, after I had already ceased to live in the women's quarters and had been moved downstairs to Theodore Ivánovich's, we had just got up and my elder brothers had already dressed. I however had been slow and was only just taking off my dressing-gown preparatory to putting on my clothes, when Praskóvya Isáevna, with an old woman's quick steps, entered with her instruments. They consisted of a tube wrapped for some reason in a napkin so that only the yellow horn nozzle was visible, and a small dish of olive oil in which the horn nozzle was dipped. Seeing me, Praskóvya Isáevna decided that I must be the one Auntie intended the operation to be performed on. Really it was Mítenka who, either by accident or guile, knowing that he was threatened with an operation which we all greatly disliked, had dressed quickly and left the bedroom. And despite my sworn assurance that the operation was not ordered for me, Praskóvya Isáevna administered it to me.

Besides loving her for her faithfulness and honesty I loved her even more because she and old Anna Ivánovna seemed to me to be representatives of the mysterious side of grandfather's life connected with the 'Ochákov fumigation'.

Anna Ivánovna was no longer in service but I saw her once or twice at our house. They said she was a hundred years old, and she remembered Pugachèv. She had very black eyes and one tooth, and her extreme age was frightening to us children.

Nurse Tatiána Filíppovna, a small dusky young woman with small plump hands, assisted old nurse Ánnushka. I hardly remember Ánnushka herself, simply because I was not conscious of myself except with her, and as I did not observe or remember myself so I did not observe and do not remember her.

But I remember the new arrival, Dúnechka's nurse Evpráxia with the ball in her neck, extremely well. I remember how we took turns to feel that ball, and how I understood, as something new, that Nurse Ánnushka did not belong to everybody but that Dúnechka had a quite special nurse of her own from Pirogóva.

I remember Nurse Tatiána Filíppovna because later on she was nurse to my nieces and my eldest son. She was one of those touching creatures from among the people who become so attached to their foster-children that all their interests become centred on them, and their own relations have nothing but the possibility of wheedling out of them, or inheriting, the money they earn.

Such people always seem to have spendthrift brothers, husbands, and sons. And Tatiána Filíppovna, as far as I remember, had such a husband and son. I remember her dying, quietly and meekly though painfully, in our house on the very spot on which I am now sitting and writing these recollections.

Her brother Nicholas Filíppovich was our coachman, whom we not only loved, but for whom—like the majority of landowners' children—we nursed a great respect. He had particularly thick boots and there was always a pleasant smell of the stables about him and his voice was deep-toned and affable. . . .

Vasíli Trubetskóy, our butler, must be mentioned. He was an affable and kindly man who was evidently fond of children, particularly of Sergéy in whose service he afterwards lived and died. I remember how he sat us on a tray (that was one of our great delights—'Me too! My turn!') and carried us up and down the pantry, which seemed to us a mysterious place with its entrance from the basement. I remember his kindly crooked smile and how closely one saw his shaven wrinkled face and neck when he took us up in his arms. There was also a particular smell I connect with him. Another vivid recollection relates to his departure for Shcherbachevka, an estate in Kursk province that my father received as an inheritance from Petróvsky. Vasíli Trubetskóy's departure took place during the Christmas holidays when we children and some of the household serfs were playing 'Go, little ruble!' in the big room.

Something should also be told of those Christmas amusements. All the household serfs—there were perhaps thirty of them—came into the house in fancy dress, played various games, and danced to the music of old Gregory who appeared in the house only at such times. This was very amusing. The costumes were generally the same from year to year: a bear with a leader, and a goat, Turks and Turkish women, robbers, and peasant men and women. I remember how handsome some of those in costume seemed to me, particularly Másha the Turk-girl. Sometimes Auntie dressed us up, too. A certain belt with stones was specially coveted and a piece of net embroidered with silver and gold, and I thought myself very handsome with a burnt-cork moustache. I remember looking at myself in the glass with a black moustache and eyebrows, and how though I ought to have assumed the face of a majestic Turk I could not restrain a smile of pleasure. The mummers walked through all the rooms and were treated to various dainties.

At one of the Christmas holidays of my early childhood the Islénevs all came to us in fancy dress: the father (my wife's grandfather), his three sons, and three daughters. They all wore wonderful costumes. One represented a dressing-table, another a boot, another a cardboard buffoon, and a fourth something else. Having come thirty miles and dressed themselves up in the village, they entered our big room, and Islénev sat down to the piano and sang verses of his own composition in a voice I still remember.

The lines were:

> To salute you at the New Year
> We have come here for a spree.
> If we can at all amuse you
> We ourselves shall happy be.

All this was very surprising and probably pleased the grown-ups, but we children were best pleased by the house serfs.

These festivities occurred between Christmas and New Year, sometimes lasting even up to Twelfth Night. But after New Year few people came and the amusements flagged. So it was on the day that Vasíli started for Shcherbachévka. I remember that we were sitting in a circle in a corner of the large, dimly lighted room on home-made imitation-mahogany chairs with leather cushions, and were playing 'Little Ruble'. The ruble was passed from hand to hand while we sang: 'Go, little ruble! Go, little ruble!' and one of us went round and had to find it. I remember that one of the domestic serf-girls sang those words over and over again in a particularly pleasant and true voice. Suddenly the pantry door opened and Vasíli, unusually buttoned up and without his tray and dishes, passed along the side of the room into the study. Only then did I learn that he was going away to be steward at Shcherbachévka. I understood that this was a promotion for him and I was glad for his sake. At the same time I was sorry to part from him and to know that he would not be in the pantry again and would no longer carry us on his tray. Indeed, I could not even understand, and did not believe, that such a change could take place. I became terribly and mysteriously sad, and the refrain: 'Go, little ruble!' seemed tenderly touching. And when Vasíli returned from saying good-bye to our aunts, and came up to us with his kindly crooked smile, kissing us on the shoulder, I for the first time experienced horror and fear at the instability of life, and pity and love for dear Vasíli.

When later on I met Vasíli, and saw him as my brother's good or bad steward who was under suspicion, there was no longer any trace of that former sacred, brotherly, human feeling.

[The next passage to this in the *Recollections* relates to Nicholas, Tolstóy's eldest brother, and to the 'Ant-brothers' and the Fanfarónov Hill. It is given in full on pp. 17 to 19 of vol. i of the *Life of Tolstóy*.]

[Of his other brothers Tolstóy tells us:]

Dmítri was my comrade, Nicholas I respected, but I was enraptured by Sergéy, imitated him, loved him, and wished I were he. I was enraptured by his handsome exterior, his voice (he was always singing), his drawing, his gaiety, and in particular (strange as it seems to say so), the spontaneity of his egotism. I was always conscious of myself, always felt, mistakenly or not, what other people thought and felt about me, and this spoilt the joy of life for me. That is probably why I particularly liked the opposite in others—a spontaneous egotism. And for that in particular I loved Sergéy—though the word 'loved' is incorrect. I loved Nicholas, but I was enraptured by Sergéy as by something quite different from and incomprehensible to me. His was a human life, very beautiful but quite incomprehensible to me, mysterious and on that account particularly attractive.

He died just the other day,[1] and in his last illness and on his death-bed he was as inscrutable to me and as dear as in the far-off days of childhood. Latterly, in his old age, he loved me more, valued my attachment to him, was proud of me, and wished to agree with me, but could not. He remained what he had always been: himself, quite singular, handsome, thoroughbred, proud, and above all such a truthful and sincere man as I have never met elsewhere. He was what he was, hid nothing, and did not wish to appear anything else.

[1] In August 1904.—A. M.

With Nicholas I wished to be, to talk, and to think. Sergéy I simply wished to imitate. That imitation began in early childhood. He started keeping hens and chickens of his own, and I did the same. That was almost my first insight into animal life. I remember the different breeds of chickens—grey, speckled, and crested. I remember how they ran to our call, how we fed them, and how we hated the big Dutch cock that ill-treated them. It was Sergéy who asked for the chickens and started keeping them. I did the same merely to imitate him. Sergéy drew and coloured (wonderfully well as it seemed to me) a series of different cocks and hens on a long sheet of paper, and I did the same, but worse. (I hoped to perfect myself in this by means of the Fanfarónov Hill.) When the double windows were put in for the winter, Sergéy invented a way of feeding his chickens through the key-hole by means of long sausages of white and black bread—and I did the same.

One insignificant occurrence left a strong impression on my childish mind. I remember it now as if it had just happened. Temyashóv was sitting in our nursery upstairs and talking to Fédor Ivánovich. I do not remember why, but the conversation touched on the observance of fasts, and Temyashóv—good-natured Temyashóv—remarked quite simply: 'I had a man-cook who took it into his head to eat meat during a fast and I sent him to serve as a soldier.' I remember it now because it then seemed to me strange and unintelligible.

There was another occurrence—the Peróvskoe inheritance.[1] There was a memorable file of horses and carts with high-piled loads which

[1] The Peróvskoe inheritance consisted of two estates: Shcherbachevka and Nerúch in the Kursk province.

arrived from Nerúch when the lawsuit about the inheritance had been won thanks to Ilyá Mitrofánych, who was a tall old man with white hair, a former serf on the Peróvskoe estate, a hard drinker, and a great adept in all sorts of chicanery, such as used to go on in the old days. He managed the affair of that inheritance, and on that account was allowed to live and was provided for at Yásnaya Polyána till his death.

I also remember the arrival of the famous 'American' Theodore Tolstóy, an uncle of Valerian, my sister's husband. I remember that he drove up in a *calèche* with post-horses, went into my father's study, and demanded that they should bring him some special dry French bread. He ate no other. My brother Sergéy had bad toothache at the time. Theodore asked what was the matter with him, and on hearing what it was said that he could stop the pain by magnetism. He went into the study, closing the door behind him. A few minutes later he came out with two lawn handkerchiefs which I remember had borders with a lilac design. He gave these to my aunt and said: 'When this one is applied the pain will pass, and with this one he will go to sleep.' She took the handkerchiefs, put them on Sergéy, and we retained the impression that everything happened as he had said.

I remember his handsome face, bronzed and shaven, with thick white whiskers down to the corners of his mouth and similarly white curly hair. There is much I should like to tell about that extraordinary, criminal, and attractive man.[1]

A third impression was that of the visit of an

[1] He was in part the original of Dólokhov in *War and Peace*, though Davýdov, a guerilla leader in the war of independence, furnished some of Dólokhov's characteristics.—A. M.

Hussar, Prince Volkónski, some sort of a cousin of my mother's. He wished to caress me and sat me on his knee, and as often happens went on talking to the grown-ups while holding me. I struggled, but he only held me the tighter. This continued for a couple of minutes. But that feeling of imprisonment, loss of freedom, and use of force, made me so indignant that I suddenly began to struggle violently, cry, and hit out at him.

Two miles from Yásnaya Polyána lies the village of Grumond (so named by my grandfather who had been Military Governor of Archangel where there is an island called Grumond). [At Grumond, Tolstóy tells us, there was a very good cattle-yard and a small but excellently built house for occasional use. It was a great treat for the Tolstóy children to spend the day at Grumond, where there was a spring of excellent water and a pond full of fish. He adds:]

But I remember that on one occasion our delight was infringed by an occurrence which made us—or at least Dmítri and me—cry bitterly. Bertha, Fëdor Ivánovich's dear brown dog, who had beautiful eyes and soft curly hair, was as usual running now in front and now behind our cabriolet as we were returning home, when as we drove away from the Grumond garden a peasant dog flew at her. She rushed to the cabriolet. Fëdor Ivánovich, who was driving, could not stop the horses and drove over her paw. When we had returned home—poor Bertha running on three legs—Fëdor Ivánovich and Nikíta Dmítrich (our male nurse who was also a huntsman) examined her and decided that her leg was broken and she would never be of any use for hunting. I listened to what they were saying in the little room upstairs and could not believe my ears when I heard Fedor Ivánovich say, in a sort of swaggering tone of decision: 'She's no more good. There's only one way—to hang her!'

The dog was suffering, was ill, and was to be hung for it! I felt that it was wrong and ought not to be done, but Fédor Ivánovich's tone and that of Nikíta Dmítrich who approved the decision, were so decided that, as on the occasion when Kuzmá was being taken to be flogged,[1] and when Temyashóv related how he had sent a man to be a soldier for having eaten meat during a fast, though I felt there was something wrong I did not dare to trust my feeling in face of the firm decision of older people whom I respected.

I will not recount all my joyful childish memories because there would be no end to them and because, though to me they are dear and important, I could not make them seem important to others.

I will only tell of one spiritual condition which I experienced several times in my early childhood, and which I think was more important than very many feelings experienced later. It was important because it was my first experience of love, not love of some one person, but love of love, the love of God, a feeling I subsequently experienced only occasionally, but still did experience, thanks it seems to me to the fact that its seed was sown in earliest childhood. That condition manifested itself in this way: we, especially Dmítri and I and the girls, used to seat ourselves under chairs as close to one another as possible. These chairs were draped with shawls and barricaded with cushions and we said we were 'ant brothers', and thereupon felt a particular tenderness for one another. Some-

---

[1] This incident is given in the *Life of Tolstóy*, vol. i, p. 14.— A. M.

times this tenderness passed into caresses, stroking one another or pressing against one another, but that seldom happened and we ourselves felt it was not the thing, and checked ourselves immediately. To be 'ant brothers' as we called it (probably this came from some stories of the Moravian Brothers¹ which reached us through brother Nicholas's Fanfarónov Hill) meant only to screen ourselves from everybody, separate ourselves from everyone and everything, and love one another.

Sometimes when under the chairs we talked of what and whom each of us loved, of what is necessary for happiness, and how we should live and love everybody.

It began, I remember, from a game of travelling. We seated ourselves on chairs, harnessed other chairs, arranged a carriage or a cabriolet, and then having settled down in the carriage we changed from travellers into 'ant brothers'. To them other people were joined up. It was very, very good, and I thank God that I played it. We called it a game, but really everything in the world is a game except that.

[This repeated reference by Tolstóy to the 'ant brotherhood' shows how much importance he attributed to that game, full as it was of profound human meaning.]

At the beginning of our life in Moscow when my father was still alive, we had a pair of very fiery horses bred in our own stables. My father's coachman, Mítka Konýlov, also acted as his groom, and was a very clever rider and huntsman besides being an excellent coachman and above all an invaluable postilion—invaluable because a boy could not manage such fiery horses, and an old man would

¹ In Russian 'ant' is *muravéy*.

be heavy and unsuitable, whereas Mítka united the rare qualities a postilion requires: he was small, light, and had strength and agility. I remember that once when the carriage was brought for my father, the horses bolted, dashing through the gate. Someone cried out: 'The Count's horses have bolted!' Páshenka fainted, and my aunts rushed to grandmamma to calm her, but it turned out that my father had not yet got into the carriage and that Mítka dexterously held the horses in and brought them back into the yard.

After my father's death when our expenses had to be cut down, that same Mítka was released to work on his own account on payment of a quit-rent. Rich merchants competed for his service and would have engaged him at a high salary, for Mítka already swaggered about in silk shirts and velvet coats. But it happened that his brother was chosen to go as a soldier, and his father, who was already an old man, called Mítka home to do the statutory field labour. And within a month our small, smart Mítka turned himself into a rough bast-shod peasant, fulfilling the corvée and cultivating his two allotments of land, mowing, ploughing, and in general bearing the heavy burden of those days. And he did all this without the least protest, feeling conscious that it should be so and could not be otherwise.

[In reply to an inquiry from his German biographer Löwenfeld as to how it was that Tolstóy with his insatiable thirst for knowledge, left the University without taking his degree, Tolstóy said:]

Yes, that was perhaps the chief cause of my leaving the University. What our teachers at Kazán lectured on interested me but little. At first I studied Oriental languages for a year, but made very little progress. I devoted myself ardently to everything and read an endless quantity of books, but always in one and the same direction. When any subject interested me I did not turn from it either to the right or to the left but tried to acquaint myself with all that could throw light on it alone. That was how it was with me in Kazán.

[On another occasion he said:]

The causes of my leaving the University were two: (1) That my brother Sergéy had finished the course and left. (2) Strangely enough my work on Catherine's *Nakaz* and the *Esprit des lois* (which I still have) opened up for me a new sphere of independent mental work, but the University with its demands not only did not assist such work but hindered it.

My brother Dmítri was a year older than I. He had large dark, serious eyes. I hardly remember him when little and only know by hearsay that as a child he was very capricious. It was said that he had such fits of caprice that he grew angry and cried because our nurse did not look at him, and then grew angry and cried in the same way because she did look at him. I know by hearsay that mamma was much troubled about him. He was nearest to me in age and we played more together, and though I did not love him as much as I loved Sergéy or as I loved and respected Nicholas, he and I were friendly together and I do not remember that we quarrelled. We may have done so and may even have fought, but the quarrels did not leave the least trace and I loved him with a simple, equable, natural love which I did not notice and do not remember. I think and even know, for I have experienced it especially in childhood, that the love of others is a natural state of the soul, or rather a natural relation to people, and when that state exists one does not notice it. It is noticed only when one does not love—no, not 'does not love' but fears—someone (in that way I feared beggars and also one of the Volkónskis who used to pinch me, but I think I feared no one else), or when one loves someone particularly, as I loved Auntie Tatiána Alexándrovna, my brothers Sergéy and Nicholas, Vasíli, Nurse Isáevna, and Páshenka.

As a child I remember nothing about Dmítri except his childish gaiety. His peculiarities showed themselves and impressed themselves on me only from the time we lived at Kazán, where we went in the year eighteen forty, when he was thirteen. Before that I only remember that he did not fall in love as Sergéy and I did, and in particular did not like dances and military pageants, but that he studied well and diligently. I remember that our teacher, an undergraduate named Poplónsky who gave lessons, summed us up thus: 'Sergéy both wishes to and can, Dmítri wishes to but can't (that was not true) and Leo neither wishes to nor can' (that I think was perfectly correct).[1]

So that my real recollections of Dmítri begin in Kazán. There, always imitating Sergéy, I began to grow depraved. There too, and even earlier, I became concerned about my appearance. I tried to be elegant and *comme il faut*. There was not a trace of that in Dmítri. I think he never suffered from the usual vices of youth. He was always serious, thoughtful, pure, and resolute though hot-tempered, and whatever he did he did to the utmost of his strength. When he swallowed the little chain he was not, as far as I remember, particularly uneasy about it, whereas I remember what terror

[1] In another place Tolstóy has told this differently, and found a place to include Nicholas.—A. M.

I experienced when I swallowed the stone of a French plum that auntie gave me, and how I solemnly announced that calamity to her as if certain death awaited me. I also remember how we little ones tobogganed down a steep hill past a shed: what fun it was, and how some passer-by drove up that hill in a troyka instead of going along the road. I think it was Sergéy and a village boy who were coming down and, unable to stop the toboggan, fell under the horses' feet. They scrambled out unhurt, and the troyka went on up the hill. We were all preoccupied with the occurrence—how they got out from under the trace-horse, how the shaft-horse shied, and so on. But Dmítri (then about nine) went up to the man in the sledge and began to scold him. I remember how surprised I was and how it displeased me when he said that for such a thing—for daring to drive where there was no road—he ought to be sent to the stable, which in the language of those days meant that he ought to be flogged.

His peculiarities first appeared at Kazán. He learnt well and steadily and wrote verses with great facility. (I remember how admirably he translated Schiller's *Der Jüngling am Bache*) but he did not devote himself to that occupation. I remember how he once began playing pranks, and how this delighted the girls and I felt jealous and thought they were so delighted because he was always serious, and I wished to imitate him in that. The aunt who was our guardian (Pelagéya Ilýnishna) had the very stupid idea of giving each of us a serf-boy who should later on become our devoted body-servant. To Dmítri she gave Vanyúsha who is still living. Dmítri often treated him badly and I think even beat him. I say 'I think' because I do not remember his doing so but only remember his penitence addressed to Vanyúsha for something he had done to him, and his humble appeal for forgiveness.

So he grew up unnoticed, having little intercourse with others, and except at moments of anger quiet and serious, with pensive, serious, large brown eyes. He was tall, rather thin, not very strong, with large long hands and round shoulders. He was a year younger than Sergéy but entered the University at the same time, in the Mathematical Faculty merely because his elder brother was a mathematician.

I do not know how or by what he was at so early an age attracted towards a religious life, but it began in the first year of his life at the University. His religious aspirations naturally directed him to the Church, and he devoted himself to this with his usual thoroughness. He began to eat Lenten food, went to all the Church services, and became even stricter in his life.

Dmítri must have had that valuable characteristic which I believe my mother had and which I knew in Nicholas but which I entirely lacked—namely, complete indifference as to what other people thought of him. Until quite lately, in old age, I have never been able to divest myself of concern about other people's opinion, but Dmítri was quite free from this. I never remember seeing that restrained smile on his face which involuntarily appears when one is being praised. I always remember his large, serious, quiet, sad, almond-shaped hazel eyes. Only in our Kazán days did we begin to pay particular attention to him and then only because, while Sergéy and I attributed great importance to what was *comme il faut*—to externals—he was untidy and dirty and we condemned him for that. He did not dance and did not wish to learn to, did not as a student go out into society, wore only a student's coat with a narrow cravat, and from his youth had a twitching of the face—he twisted his head as if to free himself from the narrowness of his cravat.

His peculiarity first showed itself during his first fasting in preparation for communion. He prepared not at the fashionable University Church but at the Prison Church. We were living in Gortálov's house opposite the prison. At this church there was a particularly pious and strict priest who, as something unusual, used during Holy Week to read through the whole of the Gospels as is prescribed but seldom done, and so the services lasted particularly long. Dmítri stood through them all and made acquaintance with the priest. The church was so built that the place where the prisoners stood was only separated by a glass partition with a door in it. Once one of the prisoners wished to pass something to the deacons —either a taper or money for a taper. No one in the church wished to undertake that commission, but Dmítri with his serious face promptly took it and handed it over. It appeared that this was not allowed and he received a reprimand, but considering that it ought to be done, he continued to act in the same way on similar occasions.

I remember a certain incident after we had moved to another lodging . . . our upstairs rooms were separated into two parts. In the first part lived Dmítri, and in the further part Sergéy and I. Sergéy and I were fond of having ornaments to put on our little tables, like grown-up people, and such things were given to us as presents. Dmítri had nothing of the sort. The only thing he took of our father's possessions was a collection of minerals.

He arranged them, labelled them, and put them in a glass-covered case. As we brothers and our aunt regarded Dmítri with some contempt for his low tastes and acquaintances, our frivolous friends adopted a similar tone. One of them, a very limited fellow (an engineer, Es, who was our friend not so much by our choice as because he attached himself to us), passing through Dmítri's room on one occasion, noticed the minerals and put a question to Dmítri. Es was unsympathetic and unnatural. Dmítri answered him reluctantly. Es moved the case and shook it. Dmítri said: 'Leave it alone!' Es did not obey and made some jest, calling him, if I remember right, 'Noah.'[1] Dmítri flew into a rage and hit Es in the face with his enormous hand. Es took to flight and Dmítri after him. When they reached our domain we shut the door on Dmítri, but he announced that he would beat Es when the latter went back. Sergéy and, I think, Shuválov went to persuade Dmítri to let Es pass, but he took up a broom and announced that he would certainly give him a thrashing. I don't know what would have happened had Es gone through his room, but the latter asked us to find a way out for him, and we got him out as best we could, almost crawling through a dusty attic.

Such was Dmítri in his moments of anger. But this is what he was like when no one drew him out of himself. In our family a very strange and pitiful creature, a certain Lyubóv Sergéevna, an old maid, had found a place for herself, or had been taken in out of pity. I do not know her surname. She was the offspring of the incestuous relations of some Protásovs (the Protásovs to whom Zhukóvski the poet belonged). How she came to us I do not

[1] This reference to Noah is explained in Tolstóy's *Confession*, p. 3.—A. M.

know. I heard that they pitied her, petted her, and had even wished to marry her to Fëdor Ivánovich, but that all came to nothing. She lived with us for a while at Yásnaya Polyána (I do not remember it) but afterwards she was taken to Kazán by my aunt Pelagéya Ilýnishna and lived with her. I came to know her there. She was a pitiable, meek, down-trodden creature. They let her have a little room, and a girl to look after her. When I knew her she was not only pitiable but hideous. I do not know what her illness was, but her face was swollen as if it had been stung by bees. Her eyes were just narrow slits between two swollen shiny cushions without eyebrows. Similarly swollen, shiny, and yellow were her cheeks, nose, lips, and mouth. She spoke with difficulty (having probably a similar swelling in her mouth). In summer, flies used to settle on her face and she did not feel them, which was particularly unpleasant to witness. Her hair was still black but scanty, and did not hide her scalp. Vasíli Ivánovich Yúshkov, our aunt's husband, who was an ill-natured jester, did not conceal the repulsion he felt for her. A bad smell always came from her, and in her little room, the windows of which were never opened, the odour was stifling. And this Lyubóv Sergéevna became Dmítri's friend. He began to go to see her, to listen to her, to talk to her, and to read to her. And we were morally so dense that we only laughed at it, while Dmítri was morally so superior, so free from caring about people's opinion, that he never by word or hint showed that he considered that what he was doing was good. He simply did it. And it was not a momentary impulse but continued all the time we lived in Kazán.

How clear it is to me now that Dmítri's death did not annihilate him, that he existed before I knew him, before he was born, and that he exists now after his death!

[The account of Nicholas Lévin's last illness and death, told in *Anna Karénina*, Part III, chapters 31 and 32, and in Part IV, chapters 17 to 20 inclusive, is closely drawn from Dmítri's illness and death, which occurred in January 1857. The following notes which Tolstóy gave to Birukóv complete what he wrote about Dmítri.]

When our inheritance was divided up, the estate of Yásnaya Polyána where we were living was allotted to me, the youngest son, as was customary. Sergéy, as there was a horse-stud at Pirogóvo and he was very fond of horses, received that estate, which was what he wanted. The two remaining estates went to Nicholas and Dmítri—Nicholas receiving Nikólskoe and Dmítri receiving Shcherbachévka (in Kursk province) which we had inherited from Peróvsky. I still have a memorandum of Dmítri's regarding the ownership of serfs. The idea that such ownership should not exist, and that serfs should be liberated, was quite unknown in our circle in the eighteen forties. The ownership of serfs by inheritance seemed a necessary condition, and all that could be done to ensure that such ownership should not be an evil, was to attend not only to the material but also to the moral condition of the serfs. And in that sense Dmítri's memorandum was written, very seriously, naively, and sincerely. He, a lad of twenty (when he took his degree), took on himself the duty, and considered that he could not but undertake the duty, of morally guiding hundreds of peasant families, and guiding them by threats and punishments in the manner Gógol recommends in his *Letter to a Landowner*. I remember that Dmítri had read that letter which was pointed out to him by the prison priest. So Dmítri took up his duties as a landowner. But besides those obligations of a landowner to his serfs, there was at that time another obligation, neglect of which was unthinkable, namely, the Military or Civil Service. And Dmítri, having taken his degree, decided to take up the Civil Service. In order to decide which branch to select he bought a directory and, having considered all the various branches, decided that the most important was the legislative. Having decided that, he went to Petersburg and called on the Secretary of State of the Second Department at the hour when he received petitioners. I can imagine Tanéev's amazement when among the petitioners he stopped before a tall, round-shouldered, badly-dressed young man (Dmítri always dressed merely to cover his body) with beautiful tranquil eyes and face, and on asking what he wanted received the reply that he was a Russian nobleman who had finished his course at the University and wishing to be of use to his fatherland had chosen legislation for his sphere of activity.

'Your name?'

'Count Tolstóy.'

'You have not served anywhere?'

'I have only just finished my course and I only wish to be useful.'

'What post do you want?'

'It is all the same to me—one in which I can be useful.'

Dmítri's serious sincerity so impressed Tanéev that he took him into the Second Department and there handed him over to an official.

Probably that official's attitude towards him, and still more his attitude towards the business of the Department, repelled Dmítri, for he did not enter the Second Department. He had no acquaintance in Petersburg except D. A. Obolénski, the jurist, who had been a lawyer in Kazán when we lived there. Dmítri went to see Obolénski at his *dácha* [country house for summer use] and Obolénski laughingly told me about it.

Obolénski was a very ambitious, fashionable, and tactful man. He related how while he was entertaining guests (probably of high rank, such as he always cultivated) Dmítri came to him through the garden in a cap and a nankeen overcoat. 'At first I did not recognize him, but when I did so I tried to *le mettre à son aise*, introduced him to the guests, and asked him to take off his overcoat, but it appeared that he had nothing on under it.' (He considered that unnecessary.) Dmítri sat down and unembarrassed by the presence of the guests immediately turned to Obolénski with the same question he had put to Tanéev—where it would be best to serve so as to be of most use? To Obolénski, who looked on the Service merely as a means of satisfying his ambition, such a question had probably never presented itself. But with the tact and superficial amiability natural to him he replied by indicating various positions and offering his services. But Dmítri was evidently dissatisfied with Obolénski as well as with Tanéev, for he left Petersburg without entering the Service there. He went to his own place in the country, and at Súdzha, I think it was, took up some post in the nobility's organization and concerned himself with farming, principally peasant-farming.

After we left the University I lost sight of him, but I know that he continued to live the same strict, abstemious life as before, not touching wine, tobacco, or women till the age of twenty-six—which was a very rare thing at that period. I know that he associated with monks and pilgrims and became closely associated with a very original man who lived with our guardian Voékov, and whose origin no one knew. He was called Father Luke, and went about in a sort of cassock. He was very hideous: short, crooked, dark, but very clean and extraordinarily strong. He pressed one's hands as with pincers, and always spoke in a significant and mysterious way. He lived with Voékov by the mill, where he built a small house and arranged a remarkable parterre. Dmítri used to take this Father Luke about with him. I have heard that he also went about with a landowning house-grabber of the old sort, a neighbour of Samóylov's.

I had, I believe, already gone to the Caucasus when an extraordinary change came over Dmítri. He suddenly began to drink, smoke, squander money, and go about with women. How it happened I do not know, and I did not see him at that period. I only know that the man who led him astray was Islénev's youngest son, externally very attractive but also profoundly immoral. In this life Dmítri was still the same serious, religious man he had always been. He bought the prostitute Másha, the woman he first knew, out of the brothel and took her to live with him. But this new life did not endure long. I think it was not so much the bad, unwholesome life he led for some months in Moscow, as the inward struggle caused by reproaches of conscience, that suddenly ruined his powerful constitution. He fell ill with consumption, went back to the country, underwent treatment in towns, and collapsed in Orèl, where I saw him for the last time, after the Crimean War. His appearance then was terrible. His enormous hands just hung onto the two bones of his arms, and his face seemed all eyes—the same beautiful, serious eyes, but now they had a questioning look. He coughed continually and spat, and did not wish to die or to believe that he was dying. Pock-marked Másha whom he had bought out was with him and tended him, her head bound in a kerchief. When I was there a wonder-working icon was brought to the house at his wish and I remember the expression on his face as he prayed to it.

I was particularly detestable at that time. I was full of conceit and had come to Orèl from Petersburg, where I had been going out into society. I pitied Dmítri, but not very much. I went to Orel and returned to Petersburg, and he died a few days later.

It really seems to me now that his death troubled me chiefly because it prevented me from taking part in a Court spectacle that was then being arranged and to which I had been invited.

[When dealing in his biography of L. N. Tolstóy with the incident of Tolstóy's defence of a soldier on trial for his life for striking an officer, Birukóv asked Tolstóy to tell him something more than had been previously published about it, and Tolstoy wrote him the following letter:]

Dear friend Pável Ivánovich,

I am very glad to fulfil your wish and tell you more fully of what I thought and felt in connexion with my defence of the soldier about which you write in your book. That incident had much more influence on my life than all the apparently more important events—the loss or recovery of my fortune, my success or non-success in literature, and even the loss of people near to me.

I will tell how it all happened, and will then try to express the thoughts and feelings aroused in me by the occurrence at the time, and by the recollection of it now.

I do not remember what I was specially occupied with or absorbed in at the time—you will know that better than I. I only know that I was living a tranquil, self-satisfied, and thoroughly egotistic life. In the summer of 1866 we were quite unexpectedly visited by Grísha Kolokóltsev, a cadet who used to know the Behrs and was an acquaintance of my wife's. It turned out that he was serving in an infantry regiment stationed in our vicinity. He was a gay, good-natured lad, specially preoccupied at that time by his small Cossack horse on which he liked to prance, and he often rode over to see us.

Thanks to him we also made acquaintance with his commanding officer, Colonel Yu..., and with A. M. Stasyulévich who had either been reduced to the ranks or sent to serve as a soldier for some political affair (I don't remember which), and who was a brother of the well-known editor. Stasyulévich was no longer a young man. He had then recently been promoted from the ranks and made an ensign, and had joined the regiment of his former comrade Yu..., who was now his colonel. Both Yu... and Stasyulévich rode over to see us occasionally. Yu... was a stout, red-faced, good-natured bachelor of a type one often meets, in whom human nature is entirely subordinated to the conventional position in which they are placed, and the retention of which is the chief aim of their life. For Colonel Yu... that conventional position was his status as a regimental commander. From a human standpoint it is impossible to say of such a man whether he is good or reasonable, for one does not know what he would be like if he ceased to be a colonel, a professor, a minister, a judge, or a journalist, and were to become a human being. So it was with Colonel Yu... He was an acting regimental commander, but what sort of *man* he was it was impossible to tell. I think he did not know himself and was not even interested in it. But Stasyulévich was a live man, though mutilated in various ways and most of all by the misfortunes and humiliations which he, an ambitious and egotistic man, had so painfully endured. So it seemed to me, but I did not know him sufficiently to penetrate more deeply into his mental condition. I only know that intercourse with him was pleasant and evoked a mingled feeling of compassion and respect. Later on I lost sight of him, and not long afterwards, when their regiment was already stationed elsewhere, I heard that he had taken his own life in the strangest manner, and without, it was said, any personal reasons. Early one morning he put on a heavy wadded military overcoat and walked into the river where, as he could not swim, he sank on reaching a deep place.

I do not remember whether it was Kolokóltsev or Stasyulévich who, having come to us one day in summer, told of something that had occurred—a most terrible and unusual event for military men. A soldier had struck a company commander, a captain from the Academy. Stasyulévich spoke of the affair with particular warmth and with feeling for the fate that awaited the soldier, namely, the death-sentence, and asked me to plead his cause before the military tribunal.

I should mention that I was always not merely shocked by the fact that some men should sentence others to death and that yet others should perform the execution, but it appeared to me an impossible, invented thing—one of those deeds in the performance of which one refuses to believe though one knows quite well that such actions have been and are performed. Capital punishment has been and remains for me one of those human actions the actual performance of which does not infringe in me the consciousness of their impossibility.

I understand that under the influence of momentary irritation, hatred, revenge, or loss of consciousness of his humanity, a man may kill another in his own defence or in defence of a friend; or that under the influence of patriotic mass-hypnotism and while exposing himself to death he may take part in collective murder in war. But that men in full control of their human attributes can quietly and deliberately admit the necessity of killing a fellow man, and can oblige others to perform that action so contrary to human nature, I never can understand. Nor did I understand it then when I was living my limited egotistical life in 1866, and so, strange as it may have been, I undertook the man's defence with some hope of success.

I remember that arriving at the village of Ózerki where the prisoner was kept (I don't quite remember whether it was in a special building or the one in which the deed had been committed) I entered the low brick hut and was met by a small man with high cheek-bones who was stout rather than thin, which is very rare among soldiers, and who had a very simple, unchanging expression of face. I don't remember who was with me, but I think it was Kolokóltsev. When we entered the man rose in military fashion. I explained to him that I wished to be his advocate and asked him to tell me how the affair had occurred. He said little, and answered my questions reluctantly with 'just so'. The sense of his replies was that it had been very dull and the captain had been very exacting. 'He pressed me very hard,' said he. . . .

As I understood, the reason of his action was that the captain—a man always apparently calm—had for some months brought him to the last degree of exasperation by his quiet monotonous voice, demanding implicit obedience and the rewriting of work which the man (an office orderly) considered he had done correctly. The essence of the matter, as I then understood it, was that besides the official relations between the two, a painful relation of mutual hatred had established itself between them. The company commander, as often happens, felt an antipathy to the man, which was increased by a suspicion that the man in his turn hated him for being a Pole; and availing himself of his position he took pleasure in being always dissatisfied with whatever the man did, and repeatedly obliged him to rewrite what the man himself considered to be faultlessly done. The man for his part hated the captain both for being a Pole and for not acknowledging his competence, and most of all for his calmness and the unapproachability of his position. That hatred finding no vent burnt up more fiercely with each new reproach that was uttered, and on reaching its zenith burst out in a way he did not himself at all anticipate. In your Biography it is said that the explosion was evoked by the captain saying he would have the man flogged. That is a mistake. The captain gave him back a paper and ordered him to correct it and rewrite it.

The Court was soon set up. The President was Yu... and the two assistant members were Kolokóltsev and Stasyulévich. The prisoner was brought in. After I forget what formalities, I read my speech, which now not only seems to me strange but fills me with shame. The judges, their weariness evidently only concealed by propriety, listened to all the futilities I uttered referring to such-and-such an article of volume so-and-so, and, when it had all been heard, went out to consult together.

At that consultation, as I subsequently learnt, only Stasyulévich was in favour of the application of the stupid paragraph of the law that I had cited, namely, that the prisoner should be acquitted on the ground of his irresponsibility for the action. Kolokóltsev, good kindly lad, though he certainly would have liked to do what I wanted, nevertheless submitted to Yu..., and his vote decided the matter. Sentence of death by being shot was read. Immediately after the trial I wrote to a near friend of mine, Alexándra Andréevna Tolstáya, a Maid of Honour and in favour at Court, asking her to intercede with the Emperor (Alexander II) for a pardon for Shibúnin. I wrote to her, but distractedly omitted to give the name of the regiment in which the case had occurred. She addressed herself to Milyútin, the Minister of War, but he said it was impossible to petition the Emperor without indicating the prisoner's regiment. She wrote that to me and I hastened to reply, but the regimental commander also hastened, and by the time the petition was ready for presentation to the Emperor the execution had already taken place....

Yes, it is horribly revolting to me now to re-read my pitiful, repulsive speech for the defence, which you have printed. Speaking of the most evident infringement of all laws human and divine, which some men were preparing to perpetrate against their brother-man, I did nothing better than cite some stupid words written by somebody and entitled laws.

Yes, I am ashamed now to have uttered that wretched and stupid defence. If a man understands what people have assembled to do—sitting in their uniforms on three sides of a table and imagining that, because they are so sitting, and because certain words are written in certain books and on certain sheets of paper with printed headings, they may infringe the eternal, general law written not in books but in every human heart—then the one thing that may and should be said to such men is to beseech them to remember who they are and what they propose to do, and certainly not to prove astutely by false and stupid words called laws, that it is possible not to kill the man before them. All men know that the life of every man is sacred and that no man has a right to deprive another of life, and it cannot be proved because it needs no proof. Only one thing is possible, necessary, and right: to try to free men—judges—from the stupefaction that leads them to such a wild and inhuman intention. To prove that one should not sentence a man to death is the same as to prove that a man should not do what is repellant and contrary to his nature: that he should not go naked in winter, should not feed himself on the contents of cesspools, and should not walk on all fours. That it is discordant with, and contrary to, human nature was proved long ago by the story of the woman who was to be stoned to death.

Is it possible that people are now so just—Colonel Yu... and Grísha Kolokóltsev with his little horse—that they no longer fear to cast the first stone?

I did not then understand this, and did not understand it when, through my cousin Tolstáya, I petitioned for a pardon for Shibúnin. I cannot but feel amazed at the delusion I then was in that all that was done to Shibúnin was quite normal.

I did not then understand anything of this. I only dimly felt that something had happened that should not have happened, and that this affair was not a casual occurrence but had a profound connexion with all the other errors and sufferings of mankind and that it lies indeed at the root of all of them.

Even then I felt dimly that the death penalty, a conscious, deliberate, and premeditated murder, is an action directly contrary to the Christian law which we, it would seem, profess, and is an action obviously infringing the possibility both of a reasonable life and of any morality. For it is evident that if one man, or an assembly of men, may decide that it is necessary to kill one man or many men, there is nothing to prevent another man or other men from finding a similar necessity for the murder of others. And what reasonable life or morality can there be among people who may kill one another when they please to do so?

I dimly felt even then that the justification of murder that is put forward by the Church and by science, instead of attaining its object of justifying the use of violence, proved on the contrary the falsity of the Church and of science. I had felt that dimly for the first time in Paris when I was a far-off witness of an execution,[1] and I felt it more clearly—far more clearly—now when I took part in this affair. But I still feared to trust myself and sunder myself from the judgement of the whole world. Only much later was I brought to the necessity of believing my own convictions and denying those two terrible deceptions that hold the people of our day in their power and produce all those misfortunes from which mankind suffers: the deception of the Church and the deception of science.

Only much later when I began to examine attentively the arguments by which the Church and science try to support and justify the existing

[1] In 1857. See *Confession*, p. 12.—A. M.

State, did I see through the obvious and coarse deceptions by which they both try to hide from men the evil deeds the State commits. I saw those disquisitions in the catechism and in scientific books circulated by millions, in which the rightness and necessity of the murder of some people at the will of others is explained. . . .

In scientific works of two kinds—those called jurisprudence with their criminal law, and in works of what is called pure science—the same thing is argued with even more narrowness and confidence. About criminal law there is nothing to be said: it is all a series of most evident sophistries aiming at the justification of all sorts of violence done by man to man, as well as of murder itself. And in the scientific works, beginning with Darwin who puts the law of the struggle for existence at the basis of the progress of life, the same is implied. Some *enfants terribles* of that doctrine, like the celebrated professor Ernst Haeckel of Jena University in his famous work *Natürliche Schöpfungsgeschichte* (the gospel of sceptics), state it plainly:

'Artificial selection exerts a very beneficial influence on the cultural life of humanity. How great in the complex advance of civilization is, for instance, a good school education and upbringing! Like artificial selection, capital punishment also renders a similarly beneficial influence, though at the present day many people ardently advocate its abolition as a 'liberal measure', and produce a series of absurd arguments in the name of a false humanitarianism.

'In fact, however, capital punishment, for the enormous majority of incorrigible criminals and scoundrels, is not only a just retribution but also a great benefit for the better part of mankind, just as for the successful cultivation of a well-tended garden the destruction of harmful weeds is necessary. And just as the careful removal of the weedy overgrowth gives more light, air, and room to plants, the unremitting extinction of all hardened criminals will not merely lighten the "struggle for existence" for the better part of humanity, but will produce an artificial selection advantageous for it, since in that way those degenerate dregs of humanity will be deprived of the possibility of passing on their bad qualities to the rest of mankind.'

And people read that, teach it, call it science, and it enters no one's head to put the question that naturally presents itself, as to who—if it is useful to kill the harmful people—is to decide who is harmful? I, for instance, consider that I do not know anyone worse and more harmful than Mr. Haeckel. Am I and others of my opinion really to sentence Mr. Haeckel to be hanged? On the contrary, the more profound his error the more I should wish him to become reasonable, and in no case should I wish to deprive him of the possibility of becoming so.

It is Church lies and scientific lies such as these that have brought us to the position we are now in. Not months but years have now passed during which there has not been a day without executions and murders. Some people are glad when there are more murders by the government than by the revolutionaries, and others are glad when more generals, landowners, merchants, and policemen are killed. On the one hand, rewards of ten and twenty-five rubles are paid out for murders, and on the other the revolutionists honour murderers and expropriators and extol them as heroic martyrs. . . . 'Fear not them which kill the body, but those that destroy both soul and body. . . .'

All this I understood much later, but dimly felt even when I so stupidly and shamefully defended that unfortunate soldier. That is why I say that that incident has had a very strong and important influence on my life.

Yes, that incident had an enormous and beneficial influence on me. On that occasion I felt for the first time, primarily that all violence presupposes for its accomplishment murder, or a threat of murder, and that therefore all violence is inevitably connected with murder; secondly that the organization of government is unimaginable without murders and is therefore incompatible with Christianity; and thirdly that what among us is called science is only a lying justification of existing evils, just as the Church teaching used to be.

That is clear to me now, but then it was only a dim recognition of the falsehood amid which my life was passing.

LEO TOLSTÓY.

YÁSNAYA POLYÁNA.
24th May 1908.

WHY DO MEN STUPEFY THEMSELVES?

I

WHAT is the explanation of the fact that people use things that stupefy them: vódka, wine, beer, hashish, opium, tobacco, and other things less common: ether, morphia, fly-agaric, &c.? Why did the practice begin? Why has it spread so rapidly, and why is it still spreading among all sorts of people, savage and civilized? How is it that where there is no vódka, wine or beer, we find opium, hashish, fly-agaric, and the like, and that tobacco is used everywhere?

Why do people wish to stupefy themselves?

Ask anyone why he began drinking wine and why he now drinks it. He will reply, 'Oh, I like it, and everybody drinks,' and he may add, 'it cheers me up.' Some—those who have never once taken the trouble to consider whether they do well or ill to drink wine—may add that wine is good for the health and adds to one's strength; that is to say, will make a statement long since proved baseless.

Ask a smoker why he began to use tobacco and why he now smokes, and he also will reply: 'To while away the time; everybody smokes.'

Similar answers would probably be given by those who use opium, hashish, morphia, or fly-agaric.

'To while away time, to cheer oneself up; everybody does it.' But it might be excusable to twiddle one's thumbs, to whistle, to hum tunes, to play a fife or to do something of that sort 'to while away the time,' 'to cheer oneself up,' or 'because everybody does it'—that is to say, it might be excusable to do something which does not involve wasting Nature's wealth, or spending what has cost great labour to produce, or doing what brings evident harm to oneself and to others. But to produce tobacco, wine, hashish, and opium, the labour of millions of men is spent, and millions and millions of acres of the best land (often amid a population that is short of land) are employed to grow potatoes, hemp, poppies, vines, and tobacco. Moreover, the use of these evidently harmful things produces terrible evils known and admitted by everyone, and destroys more people than all the wars and contagious diseases added together. And people know this, so that they cannot really use these things 'to while away time,' 'to cheer themselves up,' or because 'everybody does it.'

There must be some other reason. Continually and everywhere one meets people who love their children and are ready to make all kinds of sacrifices for them, but who yet spend on vódka, wine and beer, or on opium, hashish, or even tobacco, as much as would quite suffice to feed their hungry and poverty-stricken children, or at least as much as would suffice to save them from misery. Evidently if a man who has to choose between the want and sufferings of a family he loves on the one hand, and abstinence from stupefying things on the other, chooses the former—he must be induced thereto by something more potent than the consideration that everybody does it, or that it is pleasant. Evidently it is done not 'to while away time,' nor merely 'to cheer himself up.' He is actuated by some more powerful cause.

This cause—as far as I have detected it by reading about this subject and by observing other people, and particularly by observing my own case when I used to drink wine and smoke tobacco—this cause, I think, may be explained as follows:

When observing his own life, a man may often notice in himself two different beings: the one is blind and physical, the other sees and is spiritual. The blind animal being eats, drinks, rests, sleeps, propagates, and moves, like a wound-up machine. The seeing, spiritual being that is bound up with the animal does nothing of itself, but only appraises the activity of the animal being; coinciding with it when approving its activity, and diverging from it when disapproving.

This observing being may be compared to the needle of a compass, pointing with one end to the north and with the other to the south, but screened along its whole length by something not noticeable so long as it and the needle both point the same way; but which becomes obvious as soon as they point different ways.

In the same manner the seeing, spiritual being, whose manifestation we commonly call conscience, always points with one end towards right and with the other towards wrong, and we do not notice it while we follow the course it shows: the course from wrong to right. But one need only do something contrary to the indication of conscience to become aware of this spiritual being, which then shows how the animal activity has diverged from the direction indicated by conscience. And as a navigator conscious that he is on the wrong track cannot continue to work the oars, engine, or sails, till he has adjusted his course to the indications of the compass, or has obliterated his consciousness of this divergence—each man who has felt the duality of his animal activity and his conscience can continue his activity only by adjusting that activity to the demands of conscience, or by hiding from himself the indications conscience gives him of the wrongness of his animal life.

All human life, we may say, consists solely of these two activities: (1) bringing one's activities into harmony with conscience, or (2) hiding from oneself the indications of conscience in order to be able to continue to live as before.

Some do the first, others the second. To attain the first there is but one means: moral enlightenment—the increase of light in oneself and attention to what it shows. To attain the second—to hide from oneself the indications of conscience—there are two means: one external and the other internal. The external means consists in occupations that divert one's attention from the indications given by conscience; the internal method consists in darkening conscience itself.

As a man has two ways of avoiding seeing an object that is before him: either by diverting his sight to other more striking objects, or by obstructing the sight of his own eyes—just so a man can hide from himself the indications of conscience in two ways: either by the external method of diverting his attention to various occupations, cares, amusements, or games; or by the internal method of obstructing the organ of attention itself. For people of dull, limited moral feeling, the external diversions are often quite sufficient to enable them not to perceive the indications conscience gives of the wrongness of their lives. But for morally sensitive people those means are often insufficient.

The external means do not quite divert attention from the consciousness of discord between one's life and the demands of conscience. This consciousness hampers one's life: and in order to be able to go on living as before people have recourse to the reliable, internal method, which is that of darkening conscience itself by poisoning the brain with stupefying substances.

One is not living as conscience demands, yet lacks the strength to reshape one's life in accord with its demands. The diversions which might distract attention from the consciousness of this discord are insufficient, or have become stale, and so—in order to be able to live on, disregarding the indications conscience gives of the wrongness of their life—people (by poisoning it temporarily) stop the activity of the organ through which conscience manifests itself, as a man by covering his eyes hides from himself what he does not wish to see.

II

The cause of the world-wide consumption of hashish, opium, wine, and tobacco, lies not in the taste, nor in any pleasure, recreation, or mirth they afford, but simply in man's need to hide from himself the demands of conscience.

I was going along the street one day, and passing some cabmen who were talking, I heard one of them say: 'Of course when a man's sober he's ashamed to do it!'

When a man is sober he is ashamed of what seems all right when he is drunk. In these words we have the essential underlying cause prompting men to resort to stupefiers. People resort to them either to escape feeling ashamed after having done something contrary to their consciences, or to bring themselves beforehand into a state in which they can commit actions contrary to conscience, but to which their animal nature prompts them.

A man when sober is ashamed to go after a prostitute, ashamed to steal, ashamed to kill. A drunken man is ashamed of none of these things, and therefore if a man wishes to do something his conscience condemns he stupefies himself.

I remember being struck by the evidence of a man-cook who was tried for murdering a relation of mine, an old lady in whose service he lived. He related that when he had sent away his paramour, the servant-girl, and the time had come to act, he wished to go into the bedroom with a knife, but felt that while sober he could not commit the deed he had planned . . . 'when a man's sober he's ashamed.' He turned back, drank two tumblers of vódka he had prepared beforehand, and only then felt himself ready, and committed the crime.

Nine-tenths of the crimes are committed in that way: 'Drink to keep up your courage.'

Half the women who fall do so under the influence of wine. Nearly all visits to disorderly houses are paid by men who are intoxicated. People know this capacity of wine to stifle the voice of conscience, and intentionally use it for that purpose.

Not only do people stupefy themselves to stifle their own consciences, but, knowing how wine acts, they intentionally stupefy others when they wish to make them commit actions contrary to conscience—that is, they arrange to stupefy people in order to deprive them of conscience. In war, soldiers are usually intoxicated before a hand-to-hand fight. All the French soldiers in the assaults on Sevastopol were drunk.

When a fortified place has been captured but the soldiers do not sack it and slay the defenceless old men and children, orders are often given to make them drunk and then they do what is expected of them.[1]

[1] See the allusion to Skóbelev's conduct at Geok-Tepe on the last page of *Tales of Army Life*.—A. M.

Everyone knows people who have taken to drink in consequence of some wrong-doing that has tormented their conscience. Anyone can notice that those who lead immoral lives are more attracted than others by stupefying substances. Bands of robbers or thieves, and prostitutes, cannot live without intoxicants.

Everyone knows and admits that the use of stupefying substances is a consequence of the pangs of conscience, and that in certain immoral ways of life stupefying substances are employed to stifle conscience. Everyone knows and admits also that the use of stupefiers does stifle conscience: that a drunken man is capable of deeds of which when sober he would not think for a moment. Everyone agrees to this, but strange to say when the use of stupefiers does not result in such deeds as thefts, murders, violations, and so forth—when stupefiers are taken not after some terrible crimes, but by men following professions which we do not consider criminal, and when the substances are consumed not in large quantities at once but continually in moderate doses—then (for some reason) it is assumed that stupefying substances have no tendency to stifle conscience.

Thus it is supposed that a well-to-do Russian's glass of vódka before each meal and tumbler of wine with the meal, or a Frenchman's absinthe, or an Englishman's port wine and porter, or a German's lager-beer, or a well-to-do Chinaman's moderate dose of opium, and the smoking of tobacco with them—is done only for pleasure and has no effect whatever on these people's consciences.

It is supposed that if after this customary stupefaction no crime is committed—no theft or murder, but only customary bad and stupid actions —then these actions have occurred of themselves and are not evoked by the stupefaction. It is supposed that if these people have not committed offences against the criminal law they have no need to stifle the voice of conscience, and that the life led by people who habitually stupefy themselves is quite a good life, and would be precisely the same if they did not stupefy themselves. It is supposed that the constant use of stupefiers does not in the least darken their consciences.

Though everybody knows by experience that a man's frame of mind is altered by the use of wine or tobacco, that he is not ashamed of things which but for the stimulant he would be ashamed of, that after each twinge of conscience, however slight, he is inclined to have recourse to some stupefier, and that under the influence of stupefiers it is difficult to reflect on his life and position, and that the constant and regular use of stupefiers produces the same physiological effect as its occasional immoderate use does—yet in spite of all this it seems to men who drink and smoke moderately that they use stupefiers not at all to stifle conscience, but only for the flavour or for pleasure.

But one need only think of the matter seriously and impartially—not trying to excuse oneself—to understand, first, that if the use of stupefiers in large occasional doses stifles man's conscience, their regular use must have a like effect (always first intensifying and then dulling the activity of the brain) whether they are taken in large or small doses. Secondly, that all stupefiers have the quality of stifling conscience, and have this always —both when under their influence murders, robberies, and violations are committed, and when under their influence words are spoken which would not have been spoken, or things are thought and felt which but for them would not have been thought and felt; and, thirdly, that if the use of stupefiers is needed to pacify and stifle the consciences of thieves, robbers, and prostitutes, it is also wanted by people engaged in occupations condemned by their own consciences, even though these occupations may be considered proper and honourable by other people.

In a word, it is impossible to avoid understanding that the use of stupefiers, in large or small amounts, occasionally or regularly, in the higher or lower circles of society, is evoked by one and the same cause, the need to stifle the voice of conscience in order not to be aware of the discord existing between one's way of life and the demands of one's conscience.

III

In that alone lies the reason of the widespread use of all stupefying substances, and among the rest of tobacco—probably the most generally used and most harmful.

It is supposed that tobacco cheers one up, clears the thoughts, and attracts one merely like any other habit—without at all producing the deadening of conscience produced by wine. But you need only observe attentively the conditions under which a special desire to smoke arises, and you will be convinced that stupefying with tobacco acts on the conscience as wine does, and that people consciously have recourse to this method of stupefaction just when they require it for that purpose. If tobacco merely cleared the thoughts and cheered one up there would not be such a passionate craving for it, a craving showing itself just on certain definite occasions. People would not say that they would rather go without bread than without tobacco, and would not often actually prefer tobacco to food.

That man-cook who murdered his mistress said that when he entered the bedroom and had gashed her throat with his knife and she had fallen with a rattle in her throat and the blood had gushed out in a torrent—he lost his courage. 'I could not finish her off,' he said, 'but I went back from the bedroom to the sitting-room and sat down there and smoked a cigarette.' Only after stupefying himself with tobacco was he able to return to the bedroom, finish cutting the old lady's throat, and begin examining her things.

Evidently the desire to smoke at that moment was evoked in him, not by a wish to clear his thoughts or be merry, but by the need to stifle something that prevented him from completing what he had planned to do.

Any smoker may detect in himself the same definite desire to stupefy himself with tobacco at certain specially difficult moments. I look back at the days when I used to smoke: when was it that I felt a special need of tobacco? It was always at moments when I did not wish to remember certain things that presented themselves to my recollection, when I wished to forget—not to think. I sit by myself doing nothing and know I ought to set to work, but I don't feel inclined to, so I smoke and go on sitting. I have promised to be at someone's house by five o'clock, but I have stayed too long somewhere else. I remember that I have missed the appointment, but I do not like to remember it, so I smoke. I get vexed and say unpleasant things to someone, and know I am doing wrong and see that I ought to stop, but I want to give vent to my irritability—so I smoke and continue to be irritable. I play at cards and lose more than I intended to risk—so I smoke. I have placed myself in an awkward position, have acted badly, have made a mistake, and ought to acknowledge the mess I am in and thus escape from it, but I do not like to acknowledge it, so I accuse others—and smoke. I write something and am not quite satisfied with what I have written. I ought to abandon it, but I wish to finish what I have planned to do—so I smoke. I dispute, and see that my opponent and I do not understand and cannot understand one another, but I wish to express my opinion, so I continue to talk—and I smoke.

What distinguishes tobacco from most other stupefiers, besides the ease with which one can stupefy oneself with it and its apparent harmlessness, is its portability and the possibility of applying it to meet small, isolated occurrences that disturb one. Not to mention that the use of opium, wine, and hashish involves the use of certain appliances not always at hand, while one can always carry tobacco and paper with one; and that the opium-smoker and the drunkard evoke horror while a tobacco-smoker does not seem at all repulsive—the advantage of tobacco over other stupefiers is, that the stupefaction of opium, hashish, or wine extends to all the sensations and acts received or produced during a certain somewhat extended period of time—while the stupefaction from tobacco can be directed to each moment. You wish to do what you ought not—you smoke a cigarette and stupefy yourself sufficiently to enable you to do what should not be done, and then you are all right again; you can think and speak clearly; or you have done what you should not—again you smoke a cigarette and the unpleasant consciousness of the wrong or awkward action is obliterated, and you can occupy yourself with other things and forget it.

But apart from individual cases in which every

smoker has recourse to smoking, not to satisfy a habit or while away time but as a means of stifling his conscience with reference to acts he is about to commit or has already committed, is it not quite evident that there is a strict and definite relation between men's way of life and their passion for smoking?

When do lads begin to smoke? Usually when they lose their childish innocence. How is it that smokers can abandon smoking when they come among more moral conditions of life, and again start smoking as soon as they fall among a depraved set? Why do gamblers almost all smoke? Why among women do those who lead a regular life smoke least? Why do prostitutes and madmen *all* smoke? Habit is habit, but evidently smoking stands in some definite connexion with the craving to stifle conscience, and achieves the end required of it.

One may observe in the case of almost every smoker to what an extent smoking drowns the voice of conscience. Every smoker when yielding to his desire forgets, or sets at naught, the very first demands of social life—demands he expects others to observe, and which he observes in all other cases until his conscience is stifled by tobacco. Everyone of average education considers it inadmissible, ill-bred, and inhumane to infringe the peace, comfort, and still more the health of others for his own pleasure. No one would allow himself to wet a room in which people are sitting, or to make a noise, shout, let in cold, hot, or ill-smelling air, or commit acts that incommode or harm others. But out of a thousand smokers not one will shrink from producing unwholesome smoke in a room where the air is breathed by non-smoking women and children.

If smokers do usually say to those present: 'You don't object?' everyone knows that the customary answer is: 'Not at all' (although it cannot be pleasant to a non-smoker to breathe tainted air, and to find stinking cigar-ends in glasses and cups or on plates and candlesticks, or even in ashpans).[1] But even if non-smoking adults did not object to tobacco-smoke, it could not be pleasant or good for the children whose consent no one asks. Yet people who are honourable and humane in all other respects smoke in the presence of children at dinner in small rooms, vitiating the air with tobacco-smoke, without feeling the slightest twinge of conscience.

It is usually said (and I used to say) that smoking facilitates mental work. And that is undoubtedly true if one considers only the quantity of one's mental output. To a man who smokes, and who consequently ceases strictly to appraise and weigh his thoughts, it seems as if he suddenly had many thoughts. But this is not because he really has many thoughts, but only because he has lost control of his thoughts.

When a man works he is always conscious of two beings in himself: the one works, the other appraises the work. The stricter the appraisement the slower and the better is the work; and vice versa, when the appraiser is under the influence of something that stupefies him, more work gets done, but its quality is poorer.

'If I do not smoke I cannot write. I cannot get on; I begin and cannot continue,' is what is usually said, and what I used to say. What does it really

[1] In the matters alluded to the Russian customs are worse than the English, partly perhaps because in Russia the smell of stale tobacco in the rooms is less offensive than in England owing to a drier climate.—A. M.

mean? It means either that you have nothing to write, or that what you wish to write has not yet matured in your consciousness but is only beginning dimly to present itself to you, and the appraising critic within, when not stupefied with tobacco, tells you so. If you did not smoke you would either abandon what you have begun, or you would wait until your thought has cleared itself in your mind; you would try to penetrate into what presents itself dimly to you, would consider the objections that offer themselves, and would turn all your attention to the elucidation of the thought. But you smoke, the critic within you is stupefied, and the hindrance to your work is removed. What seemed insignificant to you when not inebriated by tobacco, again seems important; what seemed obscure no longer seems so; the objections that presented themselves vanish and you continue to write, and write much and rapidly.

IV

But can such a small—such a trifling—alteration as the slight intoxication produced by the moderate use of wine or tobacco produce important consequences? 'If a man smokes opium or hashish, or intoxicates himself with wine till he falls down and loses his senses, of course the consequences may be very serious; but it surely cannot have any serious consequences if a man merely comes slightly under the influence of hops or tobacco,' is what is usually said. It seems to people that a slight stupefaction, a little darkening of the judgement, cannot have any important influence. But to think so is like supposing that it may harm a watch to be struck against a stone, but that a little dirt introduced into it cannot be harmful.

Remember, however, that the chief work actuating man's whole life is not done by his hands, his feet, or his back, but by his consciousness. Before a man can do anything with his feet or hands, a certain alteration has first to take place in his consciousness. And this alteration defines all the subsequent movements of the man. Yet these alterations are always minute and almost imperceptible.

Bryullóv[1] one day corrected a pupil's study. The pupil, having glanced at the altered drawing, exclaimed: 'Why, you only touched it a tiny bit, but it is quite another thing.' Bryullóv replied: 'Art begins where the tiny bit begins.'

That saying is strikingly true not only of art but of all life. One may say that true life begins where the tiny bit begins—where what seem to us minute and infinitely small alterations take place. True life is not lived where great external changes take place—where people move about, clash, fight, and slay one another—it is lived only where these tiny, tiny, infinitesimally small changes occur.

Raskólnikov[2] did not live his true life when he murdered the old woman or her sister. When murdering the old woman herself, and still more when murdering her sister, he did not live his true life, but acted like a machine, doing what he could not help doing—discharging the cartridge with which he had long been loaded. One old woman was killed, another stood before him, the axe was in his hand.

Raskólnikov lived his true life not when he met the old woman's sister, but at the time when he had not yet killed any old woman, nor entered a stranger's lodging with intent to kill, nor held the axe in his hand, nor had the loop in his overcoat by which the axe hung. He lived his true life when

[1] K. P. Bryullóv, a celebrated Russian painter (1799–1852).
[2] The hero of Dostoévski's novel, *Crime and Punishment*.

he was lying on the sofa in his room, deliberating not at all about the old woman, nor even as to whether it is or is not permissible at the will of one man to wipe from the face of the earth another, unnecessary and harmful, man, but whether he ought to live in Petersburg or not, whether he ought to accept money from his mother or not, and on other questions not at all relating to the old woman. And then— in that region quite independent of animal activities—the question whether he would or would not kill the old woman was decided. That question was decided—not when, having killed one old woman, he stood before another, axe in hand—but when he was doing nothing and was only thinking, when only his consciousness was active: and in that consciousness tiny, tiny alterations were taking place. It is at such times that one needs the greatest clearness to decide correctly the questions that have arisen, and it is just then that one glass of beer, or one cigarette, may prevent the solution of the question, may postpone the decision, stifle the voice of conscience and prompt a decision of the question in favour of the lower, animal nature—as was the case with Raskólnikov.

Tiny, tiny alterations—but on them depend the most immense and terrible consequences. Many material changes may result from what happens when a man has taken a decision and begun to act: houses, riches, and people's bodies may perish, but nothing more important can happen than what was hidden in the man's consciousness. The limits of what can happen are set by consciousness.

And boundless results of unimaginable importance may follow from most minute alterations occurring in the domain of consciousness.

Do not let it be supposed that what I am saying

has anything to do with the question of free will or determinism. Discussion on that question is superfluous for my purpose, or for any other for that matter. Without deciding the question whether a man can, or cannot, act as he wishes (a question in my opinion not correctly stated), I am merely saying that since human activity is conditioned by infinitesimal alterations in consciousness, it follows (no matter whether we admit the existence of free will or not) that we must pay particular attention to the condition in which these minute alterations take place, just as one must be specially attentive to the condition of scales on which other things are to be weighed. We must, as far as it depends on us, try to put ourselves and others in conditions which will not disturb the clearness and delicacy of thought necessary for the correct working of conscience, and must not act in the contrary manner—trying to hinder and confuse the work of conscience by the use of stupefying substances.

For man is a spiritual as well as an animal being. He may be moved by things that influence his spiritual nature, or by things that influence his animal nature, as a clock may be moved by its hands or by its main wheel. And just as it is best to regulate the movement of a clock by means of its inner mechanism, so a man—oneself or another—is best regulated by means of his consciousness. And as with a clock one has to take special care of that part by means of which one can best move the inner mechanism, so with a man one must take special care of the cleanness and clearness of consciousness which is the thing that best moves the whole man. To doubt this is impossible; everyone knows it. But a need to deceive oneself arises. People are not as anxious that consciousness should work correctly as they are that it should seem to them that what they are doing is right, and they deliberately make use of substances that disturb the proper working of their consciousness.

V

People drink and smoke, not casually, not from dulness, not to cheer themselves up, not because it is pleasant, but in order to drown the voice of conscience in themselves. And in that case, how terrible must be the consequences! Think what a building would be like erected by people who did not use a straight plumb-rule to get the walls perpendicular, nor right-angled squares to get the corners correct, but used a soft rule which would bend to suit all irregularities in the walls, and a square that expanded to fit any angle, acute or obtuse.

Yet, thanks to self-stupefaction, that is just what is being done in life. Life does not accord with conscience, so conscience is made to bend to life.

This is done in the life of individuals, and it is done in the life of humanity as a whole, which consists of the lives of individuals.

To grasp the full significance of such stupefying of one's consciousness, let each one carefully recall the spiritual conditions he has passed through at each period of his life. Everyone will find that at each period of his life certain moral questions confronted him which he ought to solve, and on the solution of which the whole welfare of his life depended. For the solution of these questions great concentration of attention was needful. Such concentration of attention is a labour. In every labour, especially at the beginning, there is a time when the work seems difficult and painful, and when human weakness prompts a desire to abandon it.

Physical work seems painful at first; mental work still more so. As Lessing says: people are inclined to cease to think at the point at which thought begins to be difficult; but it is just there, I would add, that thinking begins to be fruitful. A man feels that to decide the questions confronting him needs labour—often painful labour—and he wishes to evade this. If he had no means of stupefying his faculties he could not expel from his consciousness the questions that confront him, and the necessity of solving them would be forced upon him. But man finds that there exists a means to drive off these questions whenever they present themselves —and he uses it. As soon as the questions awaiting solution begin to torment him he has recourse to these means, and avoids the disquietude evoked by the troublesome questions. Consciousness ceases to demand their solution, and the unsolved questions remain unsolved till his next period of enlightenment. But when that period comes the same thing is repeated, and the man goes on for months, years, or even for his whole life, standing before those same moral questions and not moving a step towards their solution. Yet it is in the solution of moral questions that life's whole movement consists.

What occurs is as if a man who needs to see to the bottom of some muddy water to obtain a precious pearl, but who dislikes entering the water, should stir it up each time it begins to settle and become clear. Many a man continues to stupefy himself all his life long, and remains immovable at the same once-accepted, obscure, self-contradictory view of life—pressing, as each period of enlightenment approaches, ever at one and the same wall against which he pressed ten or twenty years ago, and which he cannot break through because he intentionally blunts that sharp point of thought which alone could pierce it.

Let each man remember himself as he has been during the years of his drinking or smoking, and let him test the matter in his experience of other people, and everyone will see a definite constant line dividing those who are addicted to stupefiers from those who are free from them. The more a man stupefies himself the more he is morally immovable.

VI

Terrible, as they are described to us, are the consequences of opium and hashish on individuals; terrible, as we know them, are the consequences of alcohol to flagrant drunkards; but incomparably more terrible to our whole society are the consequences of what is considered the harmless, moderate use of spirits, wine, beer, and tobacco, to which the majority of men, and especially our so-called cultured classes, are addicted.

The consequences must naturally be terrible, admitting the fact, which must be admitted, that the guiding activities of society—political, official, scientific, literary, and artistic—are carried on for the most part by people in an abnormal state: by people who are drunk.

It is generally supposed that a man who, like most people of our well-to-do classes, takes alcoholic drink almost every time he eats, is in a perfectly normal and sober condition next day, during working hours. But this is quite an error. A man who drank a bottle of wine, a glass of spirits, or two glasses of ale, yesterday, is now in the usual state of drowsiness or depression which follows excitement, and is therefore in a condition of mental prostration, which is increased by smoking.

For a man who habitually smokes and drinks in moderation, to bring his brain into a normal condition would require at least a week or more of abstinence from wine and tobacco. But that hardly ever occurs.[1]

So that most of what goes on among us, whether done by people who rule and teach others, or by those who are ruled and taught, is done when the doers are not sober.

And let not this be taken as a joke or an exaggeration. The confusion, and above all the imbecility, of our lives, arises chiefly from the constant state of intoxication in which most people live. Could people who are not drunk possibly do all that is being done around us—from building the Eiffel Tower to accepting military service?

Without any need whatever, a company is formed, capital collected, men labour, make calculations, and draw plans; millions of working days and thousands of tons of iron are spent to

[1] But how is it that people who do not drink or smoke are often morally on an incomparably lower plane than others who drink and smoke? And why do people who drink and smoke often manifest very high qualities both mentally and morally?

The answer is, first, that we do not know the height that those who drink and smoke would have attained had they not drunk and smoked. And secondly, from the fact that morally gifted people achieve great things in spite of the deteriorating effect of stupefying substances, we can but conclude that they would have produced yet greater things had they not stupefied themselves. It is very probable, as a friend remarked to me, that Kant's works would not have been written in such a curious and bad style had he not smoked so much. Lastly, the lower a man's mental and moral plane the less does he feel the discord between his conscience and his life, and therefore the less does he feel a craving to stupefy himself; and on the other hand a parallel reason explains why the most sensitive natures—those which immediately and morbidly feel the discord between life and conscience—so often indulge in narcotics and perish by them.—L. T.

build a tower; and millions of people consider it their duty to climb up it, stop awhile on it, and then climb down again; and the building and visiting of this tower evoke no other reflection than a wish and intention to build other towers, in other places, still bigger. Could sober people act like that? Or take another case. For dozens of years past all the European peoples have been busy devising the very best ways of killing people, and teaching as many young men as possible, as soon as they reach manhood, how to murder. Everyone knows that there can be no invasion by barbarians, but that these preparations made by the different civilized and Christian nations are directed against one another; everyone knows that this is burdensome, painful, inconvenient, ruinous, immoral, impious, and irrational—but everyone continues to prepare for mutual murder. Some devise political combinations to decide who is to kill whom and with what allies, others direct those who are being taught to murder, and others again yield —against their will, against their conscience, against their reason—to these preparations for murder. Could sober people do these things? Only drunkards who never reach a state of sobriety could do them and live on in the horrible state of discord between life and conscience in which, not only in this but in all other respects, the people of our society are now living.

Never before, I suppose, have people lived with the demands of their conscience so evidently in contradiction to their actions.

Humanity to-day has as it were stuck fast. It is as though some external cause hindered it from occupying a position in natural accord with its perceptions. And the cause—if not the only one, then certainly the greatest—is this physical condition of stupefaction induced by wine and tobacco to which the great majority of people in our society reduce themselves.

Emancipation from this terrible evil will be an epoch in the life of humanity; and that epoch seems to be at hand. The evil is recognized. An alteration has already taken place in our perception concerning the use of stupefying substances. People have understood the terrible harm of these things and are beginning to point them out, and this almost unnoticed alteration in perception will inevitably bring about the emancipation of men from the use of stupefying things—will enable them to open their eyes to the demands of their consciences, and they will begin to order their lives in accord with their perceptions.

And this seems to be already beginning. But as always it is beginning among the upper classes only after all the lower classes have already been infected.

[*June 10, o.s., 1890.*]

The above essay was written by Leo Tolstóy as a preface to a book on *Drunkenness* written by my brother-in-law, Dr. P. S. Alexéyev.—A. M.

THE FIRST STEP
I

IF a man is working in order to accomplish whatever he has in hand and not merely making a pretence of work, his actions will necessarily follow one another in a certain sequence determined by the nature of the work. If he postpones to a later time what from the nature of the work should be done first, or if he altogether omits some essential part, he is certainly not working seriously but only pretending. This rule holds unalterably true whether the work be physical or not. As a man seriously wishing to bake bread first kneads the flour and then heats the brick-oven, sweeps out the ashes, and so on, so also a man seriously wishing to lead a good life adopts a certain order of succession in the attainment of the necessary qualities.

This rule is especially important in regard to right living; for whereas in the case of physical work, such as making bread, it is easy to discover by the result whether a man is seriously engaged in work or only pretending, no such verification is possible in regard to goodness of life. If without kneading the dough or heating the oven people merely pretend to make bread—as they do in the theatre—then the absence of bread makes it obvious that they were only pretending; but when a man pretends to be leading a good life we have no such direct indications that he is not striving seriously but only pretending, for not only are the results of a good life not always evident and palpable to those around, but very often such results even appear to them harmful. Respect for a man's activity and the acknowledgement of its utility and pleasantness by his contemporaries, furnish no proof of the real goodness of his life.

Therefore, to distinguish the reality from the mere appearance of a good life, the indication given by a regular order of succession in the acquirement of the essential qualities is especially valuable. And this indication is valuable, not so much to enable us to discover the seriousness of other men's strivings after goodness as to test this sincerity in ourselves, for in this respect we are liable to deceive ourselves even more than we deceive others.

A correct order of succession in the attainment of virtues is an indispensable condition of advance towards a good life, and consequently the teachers of mankind have always prescribed a certain invariable order for their attainment.

All moral teachings set up that ladder which, as the Chinese wisdom has it, reaches from earth to heaven, and the ascent of which can only be accomplished by starting from the lowest step. As in the teaching of the Brahmins, Buddhists, Confucians, so also in the teaching of the Greek sages, steps were fixed, and a superior step could not be attained without the lower one having been previously taken. All the moral teachers of mankind, religious and non-religious alike, have admitted the necessity of a definite order of succession in the attainment of the qualities essential to a righteous life. The necessity for this sequence lies in the very essence of things, and therefore, it would seem, ought to be recognized by everyone.

But, strange to say, from the time Church-Christianity spread widely, the consciousness of this necessary order appears to have been more and more lost, and is now retained only among ascetics and monks. Among worldly Christians it is taken for granted that the higher virtues may be attained not only in the absence of the lower ones, which are a necessary condition of the higher, but even in company with the greatest vices; and consequently the very conception of what constitutes a good life has reached a state of the greatest confusion in the minds of the majority of worldly people to-day.

II

In our times people have quite lost consciousness of the necessity of a sequence in the qualities a man must have to enable him to live a good life, and in consequence have lost the very conception of what constitutes a good life. This it seems to me has come about in the following way.

When Christianity replaced paganism it put forth moral demands superior to the heathen ones, and at the same time (as was also the case with pagan morality) it necessarily laid down an indispensable order for the attainment of virtues—certain steps to the attainment of a righteous life.

Plato's virtues, beginning with self-control, advanced through courage and wisdom to justice; the Christian virtues, commencing with self-renunciation, rise, through devotion to the will of God, to love.

Those who accepted Christianity seriously and strove to live righteous Christian lives, understood Christianity in this way, and always began living rightly by renouncing their lusts; which renunciation included the self-control of the pagans.

But let it not be supposed that Christianity in this matter was only echoing the teachings of paganism; let me not be accused of degrading Christianity from its lofty place to the level of heathenism. Such an accusation would be unjust, for I regard the Christian teaching as the highest the world has known, and as quite different from heathenism. Christian teaching replaced pagan teaching simply because the former was different from and superior to the latter. But both Christian and pagan teaching alike lead men toward truth and goodness; and as these are always the same, the way to them must also be the same, and the *first steps* on this way must inevitably be the same for Christian as for heathen.

The difference between the Christian and pagan teaching of goodness lies in this: that the heathen teaching is one of final perfection, while the Christian is one of infinite perfecting. Every heathen, non-Christian, teaching sets before men a model of final perfection; but the Christian teaching sets before them a model of infinite perfection. Plato, for instance, makes justice the model of perfection, whereas Christ's model is the infinite perfection of love. '*Be ye perfect, even as your Father in heaven is perfect.*' In this lies the difference, and from this results the different relation of pagan and Christian teaching towards different grades of virtue. According to the former the attainment of the highest virtue was possible, and each step towards this attainment had its comparative merit—the higher the step the greater the merit; so that from the pagan point of view men may be divided into moral and immoral, into more or less immoral—whereas according to the Christian teaching, which sets up the ideal of infinite perfection, this division is impossible. There can be neither higher nor lower grades. In the Christian teaching, which shows the infinity of perfection, all steps are equal in relation to the infinite ideal.

Among the pagans the plane of virtue attained by a man constituted his merit; in Christianity merit consists only in the process of attaining, in the greater or lesser speed of attainment. From the pagan point of view a man who possessed the virtue of reasonableness stood morally higher than one deficient in that virtue, a man who in addition to reasonableness possessed courage stood higher still, a man who to reasonableness and courage added justice stood yet higher. But one Christian cannot be regarded as morally either higher or lower than another. A man is more or less of a Christian only in proportion to the speed with which he advances towards infinite perfection, irrespective of the stage he may have reached at a given moment. Hence the stationary righteousness of the Pharisee was worth less than the progress of the repentant thief on the cross.

Such is the difference between the Christian and the pagan teachings. Consequently the stages of virtue, as for instance self-control and courage, which in paganism constitute merit, constitute none whatever in Christianity. In this respect the teachings differ. But with regard to the fact that there can be no advance towards virtue, towards perfection, except by mounting the lowest steps, paganism and Christianity are alike: here there can be no difference.

The Christian, like the pagan, must commence the work of perfecting himself from the beginning—at the same step at which the heathen begins it, namely, self-control; just as a man who wishes to ascend a flight of stairs cannot avoid beginning at the first step. The only difference is that for the pagan, self-control itself constitutes a virtue; whereas for the Christian it is only part of that self-abnegation which is itself but an indispensable condition of all aspiration after perfection. Therefore the manifestation of true Christianity could not but follow the same path that had been indicated and followed by paganism.

But not all men have understood Christianity as an aspiration towards the perfection of the heavenly Father. The majority of people have regarded it as a teaching about salvation—that is, deliverance from sin by grace transmitted through the Church according to the Catholics and Greek Orthodox; by faith in the Redemption according to the Protestants, the Reformed Church, and the Calvinists; or by means of the two combined according to others.

And it is precisely this teaching that has destroyed the sincerity and seriousness of men's relation to the moral teaching of Christianity. However much the representatives of these faiths may preach that these means of salvation do not hinder man in his aspiration after a righteous life but on the contrary contribute towards it—still, from certain assertions certain deductions necessarily follow, and no arguments can prevent men from making these deductions when once they have accepted the assertions from which they flow. If a man believes that he can be saved through grace transmitted by the Church, or through the sacrifice of the Redemption, it is natural for him to think that efforts of his own to live a right life are unnecessary—the more so when he is told that even the hope that his efforts will make him better is a sin. Consequently a man who believes that there are means other than personal effort by which he may escape sin or its results, cannot strive with the same energy and seriousness as the man who knows no other means. And not striving with perfect seriousness, and knowing of other means besides personal effort, a man will inevitably neglect the unalterable order of succession for the attainment of the good qualities necessary to a good life. And this has happened with the majority of those who profess Christianity.

III

The doctrine that personal effort is not necessary for the attainment of spiritual perfection by man, but that there are other means of acquiring it, caused a relaxation of efforts to live a good life and a neglect of the consecutiveness indispensable for such a life.

The great mass of those who accepted Christianity, accepting it only externally, took advantage of the substitution of Christianity for paganism to free themselves from the demands of the heathen virtues—no longer imposed on them as Christians—and to free themselves from all conflict with their animal nature.

The same thing happens with those who cease to believe in the teaching of the Church. They are like the believers just mentioned, only—instead of grace bestowed by the Church or through Redemption—they put forward some imaginary good work approved of by the majority of men, such as the service of science, art, or humanity; and in the name of this imaginary good work they liberate themselves from the consecutive attainment of the qualities necessary for a good life, and are satisfied with pretending, like men on the stage, to live a good life.

Those who fell away from paganism without embracing Christianity in its true significance, began to preach love for God and man apart from self-renunciation, and justice without self-control; that is to say, they preached the higher virtues while omitting the lower ones: they preached not the virtues themselves, but their semblance.

Some preach love of God and man without self-renunciation, and others preach humaneness—the service of humanity—without self-control. And as this teaching, while pretending to introduce man into higher moral regions, encourages his animal nature by liberating him from the most elementary demands of morality—long ago acknowledged by the heathens and not only not rejected but strengthened by true Christianity—it was readily accepted both by believers and unbelievers.

Only the other day the Pope's Encyclical[1] on Socialism was published, in which, after a pretended refutation of the Socialist view of the wrongfulness of private property, it was plainly said: '*No one is commanded to distribute to others that which is required for his own necessities and those of his household; nor even to give away what is reasonably required to keep up becomingly his condition in life; for no one ought to live unbecomingly.*' (This is from St. Thomas Aquinas, who says, *Nullus enim inconvenienter vivere debet.*) '*But when necessity has been fairly supplied, and one's position fairly considered, it is a duty to give to the indigent out of that which is over. That which remaineth give alms.*'

Thus now preaches the head of the most widespread Church. Thus have preached all the Church teachers who considered salvation by works as insufficient. And together with this teaching of selfishness, which prescribes that you shall give to your neighbours only what you do not want yourself, they preach love, and recall with pathos Paul's celebrated words about love in the thirteenth chapter of the First Epistle to the Corinthians.

[1] This refers to the Encyclical of Pope Leo XIII. In the passage quoted the official English translation of the Encyclical has been followed. See the *Tablet*, 1891.—A. M.

Notwithstanding that the Gospels overflow with demands for self-renunciation, with indications that self-renunciation is the first condition of Christian perfection; notwithstanding such clear expressions as: 'Whosoever will not take up his cross . . .' 'Whosoever hath not forsaken father and mother . . .' 'Whosoever shall lose his life . . .'—people assure themselves and others that it is possible to love men without renouncing that to which one is accustomed, or even what one pleases to consider becoming for oneself.

So speak the Church people; and Freethinkers who reject not only the Church but also the Christian teaching, think, speak, write, and act, in just the same way. These men assure themselves and others that they can serve mankind and lead a good life without in the least diminishing their needs and without overcoming their lusts.

Men have thrown aside the pagan sequence of virtues; but, not assimilating the Christian teaching in its true significance, they have not accepted the Christian sequence and are left quite without guidance.

IV

In olden times, when there was no Christian teaching, all the teachers of life, beginning with Socrates, regarded self-control—$\dot{\epsilon}\gamma\kappa\rho\acute{a}\tau\epsilon\iota a$ or $\sigma\omega\phi\rho\sigma\sigma\acute{v}\nu\eta$—as the first virtue of life; and it was understood that every virtue must begin with and pass through this one. It was clear that a man who had no self-control, who had developed an immense number of desires and had yielded himself up to them, could not lead a good life. It was evident that before a man could even think of disinterestedness and justice—to say nothing of generosity or love—he must learn to exercise control over himself. According to our present ideas nothing of the sort is necessary. We are convinced that a man who has developed his desires to the climax reached in our society, a man who cannot live without satisfying the hundred unnecessary habits that enslave him, can yet lead an altogether moral and good life. Looked at from any point of view: the lowest, utilitarian; the higher, pagan, which demands justice; and especially the highest, Christian, which demands love—it should surely be clear to everyone that a man who uses for his own pleasure (which he might easily forgo) the labour, often the painful labour, of others, behaves wrongly; and that this is the very first wrong he must cease to commit if he wishes to live a good life.

From the utilitarian point of view such conduct is bad, because as long as he forces others to work for him a man is always in an unstable position; he accustoms himself to the satisfaction of his desires and becomes enslaved by them, while those who work for him do so with hatred and envy and only await an opportunity to free themselves from the necessity of so working. Consequently such a man is always in danger of being left with deeply rooted habits which create demands he cannot satisfy.

From the point of view of justice such conduct is bad, because it is not well to employ for one's own pleasure the labour of other men who themselves cannot afford a hundredth part of the pleasures enjoyed by him for whom they labour.

From the point of view of Christian love it can hardly be necessary to prove that a man who loves others will give them his own labour rather than take the fruit of their labour from them for his own pleasure.

But these demands of utility, justice, and love, are altogether ignored by our modern society. With us the effort to limit our desires is regarded as neither the first nor even the last condition of a good life, but as altogether unnecessary.

On the contrary, according to the prevailing and most widely spread teaching of life to-day, the augmentation of one's wants is regarded as a desirable condition; as a sign of development, civilization, culture, and perfection. So-called educated people regard habits of comfort, that is, of effeminacy, as not only harmless but even good, indicating a certain moral elevation—as almost a virtue.

It is thought that the more the wants, and the more refined these wants, the better.

This is shown very clearly by the descriptive poetry, and even more so by the novels, of the last two centuries.

How are the heroes and heroines who represent the ideals of virtue portrayed?

In most cases the men who are meant to represent something noble and lofty—from Childe Harold down to the latest heroes of Feuillet, Trollope, or Maupassant—are simply depraved sluggards, consuming in luxury the labour of thousands, and themselves doing nothing useful for anybody. The heroines—the mistresses who in one way or another afford more or less delight to these men—are as idle as they, and are equally ready to consume the labour of others by their luxury.

I do not refer to the representations of really abstemious and industrious people one occasionally meets with in literature. I am speaking of the usual type that serves as an ideal to the masses: of the character that the majority of men and women are trying to resemble. I remember the difficulty (inexplicable to me at the time) that I experienced when I wrote novels, a difficulty with which I contended and with which I know all novelists

THE FIRST STEP

now contend who have even the dimmest conception of what constitutes real moral beauty—the difficulty of portraying a type taken from the upper classes as ideally good and kind, and at the same time true to life. To be true to life, a description of a man or woman of the upper, educated classes must show him in his usual surroundings—that is, in luxury, physical idleness, and demanding much. From a moral point of view such a person is undoubtedly objectionable. But it is necessary to represent this person in such a way that he may appear attractive. And novelists try to do so. I also tried. And, strange to say, such a representation, making an immoral fornicator and murderer (duellist or soldier), an utterly useless, idly drifting, fashionable buffoon, appear attractive, does not require much art or effort. The readers of novels are for the most part exactly such men, and therefore readily believe that these Childe Harolds, Onégins, Messieurs de Camors,[1] &c., are very excellent people.

V

Clear proof that the men of our time really do not admit pagan self-control and Christian self-renunciation to be good and desirable qualities, but on the contrary regard the augmentation of wants as good and elevated, is to be found in the education given to the vast majority of children in our society. Not only are they not trained to self-control, as among the pagans, or to the self-renunciation proper to Christians, but they are deliberately inoculated with habits of effeminacy, physical idleness, and luxury.

[1] Onégin is the hero of a famous Russian poem by Púshkin. M. de Camors is the hero of a French novel by Octave Feuillet.—A. M.

I have long wished to write a fairy-tale of this kind: A woman, wishing to revenge herself on one who has injured her, carries off her enemy's child, and going to a sorcerer asks him to teach her how she can most cruelly wreak her vengeance on the stolen infant, the only child of her enemy. The sorcerer bids her carry the child to a place he indicates, and assures her that a most terrible vengeance will result. The wicked woman follows his advice; but, keeping an eye upon the child, is astonished to see that it is found and adopted by a wealthy, childless man. She goes to the sorcerer and reproaches him, but he bids her wait. The child grows up in luxury and effeminacy. The woman is perplexed, but again the sorcerer bids her wait. And at length the time comes when the wicked woman is not only satisfied but has even to pity her victim. He grows up in the effeminacy and dissoluteness of wealth, and owing to his good nature is ruined. Then begins a sequence of physical sufferings, poverty, and humiliation, to which he is especially sensitive and against which he knows not how to contend. Aspirations towards a moral life—and the weakness of his effeminate body accustomed to luxury and idleness; vain struggles; lower and still lower decline; drunkenness to drown thought, then crime and insanity or suicide.

And, indeed, one cannot regard without terror the education of the children of the wealthy class in our day. Only the cruellest foe could, one would think, inoculate a child with those defects and vices which are now instilled into him by his parents, especially by mothers. One is awestruck at the sight, and still more at the results of this, if only one knows how to discern what is taking place in the souls of the best of these children, so carefully ruined by their parents. Habits of effeminacy are instilled into them at a time when they do not yet understand their moral significance. Not only is the habit of temperance and self-control neglected, but, contrary to the educational practice of Sparta and of the ancient world in general, this quality is altogether atrophied. Not only is man not trained to work, and to all the qualities essential to fruitful labour—concentration of mind, strenuousness, endurance, enthusiasm for work, ability to repair what is spoiled, familiarity with fatigue, joy in attainment—but he is habituated to idleness and to contempt for all the products of labour: is taught to spoil, throw away, and again procure for money anything he fancies, without a thought of how things are made. Man is deprived of the power of acquiring the primary virtue of reasonableness, indispensable for the attainment of all the others, and is let loose in a world where people preach and praise the lofty virtues of justice, the service of man, and love.

It is well if the youth be endowed with a morally feeble and obtuse nature, which does not detect the difference between make-believe and genuine goodness of life, and is satisfied with the prevailing mutual deception. If this be the case all goes apparently well, and such a man will sometimes quietly live on with his moral consciousness unawakened till death.

But it is not always thus, especially of late, now that the consciousness of the immorality of such life fills the air and penetrates the heart unsought. Frequently, and ever more frequently, it happens that there awakens a demand for real, unfeigned morality; and then begin a painful inner struggle and suffering which end but rarely in the triumph of the moral sentiment.

A man feels that his life is bad, that he must reform it from the very roots, and he tries to do so; but he is then attacked on all sides by those who have passed through a similar struggle and have been vanquished. They endeavour by every means to convince him that this reform is quite unnecessary: that goodness does not at all depend upon self-control and self-renunciation, that it is possible while addicting himself to gluttony, personal adornment, physical idleness, and even fornication, to be a perfectly good and useful man. And the struggle in most cases terminates lamentably. Either the man, overcome by his weakness, yields to the general opinion, stifles the voice of conscience, distorts his reason to justify himself, and continues to lead the old dissipated life, assuring himself that it is redeemed by faith in the Redemption or the Sacraments, or by service to science, to the State, or to art; or else he struggles, suffers, and finally becomes insane or shoots himself.

It seldom happens, amid all the temptations that surround him, that a man of our society understands what was thousands of years ago, and still is, an elementary truth for all reasonable people: namely, that for the attainment of a good life it is necessary first of all to cease to live an evil life; that for the attainment of the higher virtues it is needful first of all to acquire the virtue of abstinence or self-control as the pagans called it, or of self-renunciation as Christianity has it, and therefore it seldom happens that he succeeds in attaining this primary virtue by gradual efforts.

VI

I have just been reading the letters of one of our highly educated and advanced men of the eighteen-forties, the exile Ogaryëv, to another yet more highly educated and gifted man, Herzen. In these letters Ogaryev gives expression to his sincere thoughts and highest aspirations, and one cannot fail to see that—as was natural to a young man—he rather shows off before his friend. He talks of self-perfecting, of sacred friendship, love, the service of science, of humanity, and the like. And at the same time he calmly writes that he often irritates the companion of his life by 'returning home in an unsober state, or disappearing for many hours with a fallen, but dear creature. . . .' as he expresses it.

Evidently it never even occurred to this remarkably kind-hearted, talented, and well-educated man that there was anything at all objectionable in the fact that he, a married man awaiting the confinement of his wife (in his next letter he writes that his wife has given birth to a child), returned home intoxicated and disappeared with dissolute women. It did not enter his head that until he had commenced the struggle and had at least to some extent conquered his inclination to drunkenness and fornication, he could not think of friendship and love and still less of serving anyone or anything. But he not only did not struggle against these vices—he evidently thought there was something very nice in them, and that they did not in the least hinder the struggle for perfection; and therefore instead of hiding them from the friend in whose eyes he wishes to appear in a good light, he exhibits them.

Thus it was half a century ago. I was contemporary with such men. I knew Ogaryèv and Herzen themselves, and others of that stamp, and men educated in the same traditions. There was a remarkable absence of consistency in the lives of all these men. Together with a sincere and ardent wish for good there was an utter looseness of personal desire, which they thought could not hinder the living of a good life nor the performance of good and even great deeds. They put unkneaded loaves into a cold oven and believed that bread would be baked. And then, when with advancing years they began to notice that the bread did not bake—i.e. that no good came of their lives—they saw in this something peculiarly tragic.

And the tragedy of such lives is indeed terrible. And this same tragedy apparent in the lives of Herzen, Ogaryev, and others of their time, exists to-day in the lives of very many so-called educated people who hold the same views. A man desires to lead a good life, but the consecutiveness which is indispensable for this is lost in the society in which he lives. The majority of men of the present day, like Ogaryév, Herzen and others fifty years ago, are persuaded that to lead an effeminate life, to eat sweet and rich foods, to delight themselves in every way and satisfy all their desires, does not hinder them from living a good life. But as it is evident that a good life in their case does not result, they give themselves up to pessimism, and say, 'Such is the tragedy of human life.'

It is strange too that these people, who know that the distribution of pleasures among men is unequal and regard this inequality as an evil and wish to correct it, yet do not cease to strive to augment their own pleasures—that is, to augment inequality in the distribution of pleasures. In acting thus, these people are like men who being the first to enter an orchard hasten to gather all the fruit they can lay their hands on, and while professing a wish to organize a more equal distribution of the fruit of the orchard between themselves and later comers, continue to pluck all they can reach.

VII

The delusion that men while addicting themselves to their desires and regarding this life of desire as good, can yet lead a good, useful, just, and loving life, is so astonishing that men of later generations will, I should think, simply fail to understand what the men of our time meant by the words 'good life', when they said that the gluttons—the effeminate, lustful sluggards—of our wealthy classes led good lives. Indeed, one need only put aside for a moment the customary view of the life of our wealthy classes, and look at it, I do not say from the Christian point of view, but from the pagan standpoint, from the standpoint of the very lowest demands of justice, to be convinced that, living amidst the violation of the plainest laws of justice or fairness, such as even children in their games think it wrong to violate, we men of the wealthy classes have no right even to talk about a good life.

Any man of our society who would, I do not say begin a good life but even begin to make some little approach towards it, must first of all cease to lead a bad life, must begin to destroy those conditions of an evil life with which he finds himself surrounded.

How often one hears, as an excuse for not reforming our lives, the argument that any act that is contrary to the usual mode of life would be unnatural, ludicrous—would look like a desire to show off, and would therefore not be a good action. This argument seems expressly framed to prevent people from ever changing their evil lives. If all our life were good, just, kind, then and only then would an action in conformity with the usual mode of life be good. If half our life were good and the other half bad, then there would be as much chance of an action not in conformity with the usual mode of life being good as of its being bad. But when life is altogether bad and wrong, as is the case in our upper classes, then a man cannot perform a single good action without disturbing the usual current of life. He can do a bad action without disturbing this current, but not a good one.

A man accustomed to the life of our well-to-do classes cannot lead a righteous life without first coming out of those conditions of evil in which he is immersed—he cannot begin to do good until he has ceased to do evil. It is impossible for a man living in luxury to lead a righteous life. All his efforts after goodness will be in vain until he changes his life, until he performs that work which stands first in sequence before him. A good life according to the pagan view, and still more according to the Christian view, is, and can be, measured in no other way than by the mathematical relation between love of self and love of others. The less there is of love of self with all the ensuing care about self and the selfish demands made upon the labour of others, and the more there is of love of others with the resultant care for and labour bestowed upon others, the better is the life.

Thus has goodness of life been understood by all the sages of the world and by all true Christians, and in exactly the same way do all plain men understand it now. The more a man gives to others and the less he demands for himself, the better he is: the less he gives to others and the more he demands for himself, the worse he is.

And not only does a man become morally better the more love he has for others and the less for himself, but the less he loves himself the easier it becomes for him to be better, and contrariwise.

The more a man loves himself, and consequently the more he demands labour from others, the less possibility is there for him to love and to work for others; less not only by as much as the increase of his love for himself, but less in an enormously greater degree—just as when we move the fulcrum of a lever from the long end towards the short end, we not only increase the long arm but also reduce the short one. Therefore if a man possessing a certain faculty (love) augments his love and care for himself, he thereby diminishes his power of loving and caring for others not only in proportion to the love he has transferred to himself but in a much greater degree. Instead of feeding others a man eats too much himself; by so doing he not only diminishes the possibility of giving away the surplus, but by overeating deprives himself of power to help others.

In order to love others in reality and not in word only, one must cease to love oneself also in reality and not merely in word. In most cases it happens thus: we think we love others, we assure ourselves and others that it is so, but we love them only in words while we love ourselves in reality. We forget to feed and put others to bed, ourselves—never. Therefore, in order really to love others in deed, we must learn not to love ourselves in deed, learn to forget to feed ourselves and put ourselves to bed, exactly as we forget to do these things for others.

We say of a self-indulgent person accustomed to lead a luxurious life, that he is a 'good man' and 'leads a good life'. But such a person—whether man or woman—although he may possess the most amiable traits of character, meekness, good nature, &c., cannot be good and lead a good life, any more than a knife of the very best workmanship and steel can be sharp and cut well unless it is sharpened.

To be good and lead a good life means to give to others more than one takes from them. But a self-indulgent man accustomed to a luxurious life cannot do this, first because he himself always needs a great deal (and this not because he is selfish, but because he is accustomed to luxury and finds it painful to be deprived of that to which he is accustomed); and secondly, because by consuming all that he receives from others he weakens himself and renders himself unfit for labour, and therefore unfit to serve others. A self-indulgent man who sleeps long upon a soft bed and consumes an abundance of rich, sweet food, who always wears clean clothes and such as are suited to the temperature, who has never accustomed himself to the effort of laborious work, can do very little.

We are so accustomed to our own lies and the lies of others, and it is so convenient for us not to see through the lies of others that they may not see through ours, that we are not in the least astonished at, and do not doubt the truth of, the assertion of the virtue, sometimes even the sanctity, of people who are leading a perfectly unrestrained life.

A person, man or woman, sleeps on a spring bed with two mattresses, two smooth clean sheets, and feather pillows in pillow-cases. By the bedside is a rug that the feet may not get cold on stepping out of bed, though slippers also lie near. Here also are the necessary utensils so that he need not leave the house—whatever uncleanliness he may produce will be carried away and all made tidy. The windows are covered with curtains that the daylight may not awaken him, and he sleeps as long as he is inclined. Besides all this, measures are taken that the room may be warm in winter and cool in summer, and that he may not be disturbed by the noise of flies or other insects. While he sleeps hot and cold water for his ablutions, and sometimes baths and preparations for shaving, are provided. Tea and coffee are also prepared, stimulating drinks to be taken immediately upon rising. Boots, shoes, galoshes—several pairs dirtied the previous day—are already being cleaned, freed from every speck of dust, and made to shine like glass. Other various garments soiled on the preceding day are similarly cleaned, and these differ in texture to suit not only summer and winter, but also spring, autumn, rainy, damp, and warm weather. Clean linen, washed, starched, and ironed, is being made ready, with studs, shirt buttons, and button-holes, all carefully inspected by specially appointed people.

If the person be active he rises early—at seven o'clock—but still a couple of hours later than those who are making all these preparations for him. And besides clothes for the day and covering for the night there is also a special costume and footgear for him while he is dressing—dressing-gown and slippers. And now he undertakes his washing, cleaning, brushing, for which several kinds of brushes are used as well as soap and a great quantity of water. (Many English men and women, for some reason or other, are specially proud of using a great deal of soap and pouring a large quantity of water over themselves.) Then he dresses, brushes his hair before a special kind of looking-glass (different from those that hang in almost every room in the house), takes the things he needs, such as spectacles or eyeglasses, and then distributes in different pockets a clean pocket-handkerchief to blow his nose on; a watch with a chain, though in almost every room he goes to there will be a clock; money of various kinds, small change (often in a specially contrived case which saves him the trouble of looking for the required coin) and bank-notes; also visiting cards on which his name is printed (saving him the trouble of saying or writing it); pocket-book and pencil. In the case of women, the toilet is still more complicated: corsets, arranging of long hair, adornments, laces, elastics, ribbons, ties, hairpins, pins, brooches.

But at last all is complete and the day commences, generally with eating: tea and coffee are drunk with a great quantity of sugar; bread made of the finest white flour is eaten with large quantities of butter, and sometimes the flesh of pigs. The men for the most part smoke cigars or cigarettes meanwhile, and read fresh papers which have just been brought. Then, leaving to others the task of setting right the soiled and disordered room, they go to their office or business, or drive in carriages produced specially to move such people about. Then comes a luncheon of slain beasts, birds, and fish, followed by a dinner consisting, if it be very modest, of three courses, dessert, and coffee. Then playing at cards and playing music—or the theatre, reading, and conversation in soft spring armchairs by the intensified and shaded light of candles, gas, or electricity. After this, more tea, more eating—supper—and to bed again, the bed shaken up and prepared with clean linen, and the utensils washed to be made foul again.

Thus pass the days of a man of modest life, of whom, if he is good-natured and does not possess any habits specially obnoxious to those about him, it is said that he leads a good and virtuous life.

But a good life is the life of a man who does good to others; and can a man accustomed to live thus do good to others? Before he can do good to men he must cease to do evil. Reckon up all the harm such a man, often unconsciously, does to others, and you will see that he is far indeed from doing good. He would have to perform many acts of heroism to redeem the evil he commits, but he is too much enfeebled by his self-created needs to perform any such acts. He might sleep with more advantage, both physical and moral, lying on the floor wrapped in his cloak as Marcus Aurelius did; thus saving all the labour and trouble involved in the manufacture of mattresses, springs, and pillows, as well as the daily labour of the laundress—one of the weaker sex burdened by the bearing and nursing of children—who washes linen for this strong man. By going to bed earlier and getting up earlier he might save window-curtains and the evening lamp. He might sleep in the same shirt he wears during the day, might step barefooted upon the floor, and go out into the yard; he might wash at the pump. In a word, he might live like those who work for him, and thus save all this work that is done for him. He might save all the labour expended upon his clothing, his refined food, his recreations. And he knows under what conditions all these labours are performed: how men perish and suffer in performing them, and how they often hate those who take advantage of their poverty to force them to do it.

How then can such a man do good to others and lead a righteous life, without abandoning this self-indulgence and luxury?

But we need not speak of how other people appear in our eyes—every one must see and feel this concerning himself.

I cannot but repeat this same thing again and again, notwithstanding the cold and hostile silence with which my words are received. A moral man, living a life of comfort, a man even of the middle class (I will not speak of the upper classes, who daily consume the results of hundreds of working days to satisfy their caprices), cannot live quietly, knowing that all he is using is produced by the labour of working people whose lives are crushed, who are dying without hope—ignorant, drunken, dissolute, semi-savage creatures employed in mines, factories, and in agricultural labour, producing the things that he uses.

At the present moment I who am writing this and you who will read it, whoever you may be—have wholesome, sufficient, perhaps abundant and luxurious food, pure warm air to breathe, winter and summer clothing, various recreations, and, most important of all, leisure by day and undisturbed repose at night. And here by our side live the working people, who have neither wholesome food nor healthy lodgings nor sufficient clothing nor recreations, and who above all are deprived not only of leisure but even of rest: old men, children, women, worn out by labour, by sleepless nights, by disease, who spend their whole lives providing for us those articles of comfort and luxury which they do not possess, and which are for us not necessities but superfluities. Therefore a moral man (I do not say a Christian, but simply a man professing humane views or merely esteeming justice) cannot but wish to change his life and to cease to use articles of luxury produced under such conditions.

If a man really pities those who manufacture tobacco, then the first thing he will naturally do will be to cease smoking, because by continuing to buy and smoke tobacco he encourages the preparation of tobacco by which men's health is destroyed. And so with every other article of luxury. If a man can still continue to eat bread notwithstanding the hard work by which it is produced, this is because he cannot forgo what is indispensable while waiting for the present conditions of labour to be altered. But with regard to things which are not only unnecessary but are even superfluous there can be no other conclusion than this: that if I pity men engaged in the manufacture of certain articles, then I must on no account accustom myself to require such articles.

But nowadays men argue otherwise. They invent the most varied and intricate arguments, but never say what naturally occurs to every plain man. According to them, it is not at all necessary to abstain from luxuries. One can sympathize with the condition of the working men, deliver speeches and write books on their behalf, and at the same time continue to profit by the labour that one sees to be ruinous to them.

According to one argument, I may profit by labour that is harmful to the workers because if I do not another will. Which is something like the argument that I must drink wine that is injurious to me because it has been bought and if I do not drink it others will.

According to another argument, it is even beneficial to the workers to be allowed to produce luxuries, for in this way we provide them with money—that is with the means of subsistence: as if we could not provide them with the means of subsistence in any other way than by making them produce articles injurious to them and superfluous to us.

But according to a third argument, now most popular, it seems that, since there is such a thing as division of labour, any work upon which a man is engaged—whether he be a Government official, priest, landowner, manufacturer, or merchant—is so useful that it fully compensates for the labour of the working classes by which he profits. One serves the State, another the Church, a third science, a fourth art, and a fifth serves those who serve the State, science, and art; and all are firmly convinced that what they give to mankind certainly compensates for all they take. And it is astonishing how, while continually augmenting their luxurious requirements without increasing their activity, these people continue to be certain that their activity compensates for all they consume.

Whereas if you listen to these people's judgement of one another it appears that each individual is far from being worth what he consumes. Government officials say that the work of the landlords is not worth what they spend, landlords say the same about merchants, and merchants about Government officials, and so on. But this does not disconcert them, and they continue to assure people that they (each of them) profit by the labours of others exactly in proportion to the service they render to others. So that the payment is not determined by the work, but the value of the imaginary work is determined by the payment. Thus they assure one another, but they know perfectly well in the depth of their souls that all their arguments do not justify them; that they are not necessary to the working men, and that they profit by the labour of those men not on account of any division of labour but simply because they have the power to do so, and because they are so spoiled that they cannot do without it.

And all this arises from people imagining that it is possible to lead a good life without first acquiring the primary quality necessary for a good life.

And that first quality is self-control.

VIII

There never has been and cannot be a good life without self-control. Apart from self-control no good life is imaginable. The attainment of goodness must begin with that.

There is a scale of virtues, and if one would mount the higher steps it is necessary to begin with the lowest; and the first virtue a man must acquire if he wishes to acquire the others is that which the ancients called ἐγκράτεια or σωφροσύνη—that is, self-control or moderation.

If in the Christian teaching self-control was included in the conception of self-renunciation, still the order of succession remained the same, and the acquirement of any Christian virtue is impossible without self-control—and this not because such a rule has been invented, but because it is the essential nature of the case.

But even self-control, the first step in every righteous life, is not attainable all at once but only by degrees.

Self-control is the liberation of man from desires —their subordination to moderation, σωφροσύνη. But a man's desires are many and various, and in order to contend with them successfully he must begin with the fundamental ones—those upon which the more complex ones have grown up—and not with those complex lusts which have grown up upon the fundamental ones. There are complex lusts like that of the adornment of the body, sports, amusements, idle talk, inquisitiveness, and many others; and there are also fundamental lusts—gluttony, idleness, sexual love. And one must begin to contend with these lusts from the beginning: not with the complex but with the fundamental ones, and that also in a definite order.

And this order is determined both by the nature of things and by the tradition of human wisdom.

A man who eats too much cannot strive against laziness, while a gluttonous and idle man will never be able to contend with sexual lust. Therefore, according to all moral teachings, the effort towards self-control commences with a struggle against the lust of gluttony—commences with fasting. In our time, however, every serious relation to the attainment of a good life has been so long and so completely lost that not only is the very first virtue—self-control—without which the others are unattainable, regarded as superfluous, but the order of succession necessary for the attainment of this first virtue is also disregarded, and fasting is quite forgotten, or is looked upon as a silly superstition, utterly unnecessary.

And yet, just as the first condition of a good life is self-control, so the first condition of a life of self-control is fasting.

One may wish to be good, one may dream of goodness, without fasting; but to *be* good without fasting is as impossible as it is to advance without getting up on one's feet.

Fasting is an indispensable condition of a good life, whereas gluttony is and always has been the first sign of the opposite; and unfortunately this vice is in the highest degree characteristic of the life of the majority of the men of our time.

Look at the faces and figures of the men of our circle and day. On all those faces with pendent cheeks and chins, those corpulent limbs and prominent stomachs, lies the indelible seal of a dissolute life. Nor can it be otherwise. Consider our life and the actuating motive of the majority of men in our society, and then ask yourself, What is the chief interest of this majority? And, strange as it may appear to us who are accustomed to hide our real interests and to profess false, artificial ones, you will find that the chief interest of their life is the satisfaction of the palate, the pleasure of eating—gluttony. From the poorest to the richest, eating is, I think, the chief aim, the chief pleasure, of our life. Poor working people form an exception, but only inasmuch as want prevents their addicting themselves to this passion. No sooner have they the time and the means, than, in imitation of the higher classes, they procure rich and tasty foods, and eat and drink as much as they can. The more they eat the more do they deem themselves not only happy, but also strong and healthy. And in this conviction they are encouraged by the upper classes, who regard food in precisely the same way. The educated classes (following the medical men who assure them that the most expensive food, flesh, is the most wholesome) imagine that happiness and health consist in tasty, nourishing, easily digested food—in gorging—though they try to conceal this.

Look at rich people's lives, listen to their conversation. What lofty subjects seem to occupy them: philosophy, science, art, poetry, the distribution of wealth, the welfare of the people, and the education of the young! But all this is, for the immense majority, a sham. All this occupies them only in the intervals of business, real business: in the intervals, that is, between lunch and dinner, while the stomach is full and it is impossible to eat more. The only real living interest of the majority both of men and women, especially after early youth, is eating—How to eat, what to eat, where to eat, and when to eat.

No solemnity, no rejoicing, no consecration, on opening of anything, can dispense with eating.

Watch people travelling. In their case the thing is specially evident. 'Museums, libraries, Parliament—how very interesting! But where shall we dine? Where is one best fed?' Look at people when they come together for dinner, dressed up, perfumed, around a table decorated with flowers—how joyfully they rub their hands and smile!

If we could look into the hearts of the majority of people what should we find they most desire? Appetite for breakfast and for dinner. What is the severest punishment from infancy upwards? To be put on bread and water. What artisans get the highest wages? Cooks. What is the chief interest of the mistress of the house? To what subject does the conversation of middle-class housewives generally tend? If the conversation of the members of the higher classes does not tend in the same direction it is not because they are better educated or are occupied with higher interests, but simply because they have a housekeeper or a steward who relieves them of all anxiety about their dinner. But once deprive them of this convenience and you will see what causes them most anxiety. It all comes round to the subject of eating: the price of grouse, the best way of making coffee, of baking sweet cakes, and so on. People come together whatever the occasion—a christening, a funeral, a wedding, the consecration of a church, the departure or arrival of a friend, the consecration of regimental colours, the celebration of a memorable day, the death or birth of a great scientist, philosopher, or teacher of morality—men come together as if occupied by the most lofty interests. But it is only a pretence: they all know that there will be eating—good tasty food—and drinking, and it is chiefly this that brings them together. To this end, for several days before, animals have been slaughtered, baskets of provisions brought from gastronomic shops, cooks and their helpers, kitchen boys and maids, specially attired in clean, starched frocks and caps, have been 'at work'. Chefs, receiving £50 a month and more, have been occupied in giving directions. Cooks have been chopping, kneading, roasting, arranging, adorning. With like solemnity and importance a master of the ceremonies has been working, calculating, pondering, adjusting with his eye, like an artist. A gardener has been employed upon the flowers. Scullery-maids. . . . An army of men has been at work, the result of thousands of working days are being swallowed up, and all this that people may come together to talk about some great teacher of science or morality, or to recall the memory of a deceased friend, or to greet a young couple just entering upon a new life.

In the middle and lower classes it is perfectly evident that every festivity, every funeral or wedding, means gluttony. There the matter is so understood. To such an extent is gluttony the motive of the assembly that in Greek and in French the same word means both 'wedding' and 'feast'. But in the upper classes of the rich, especially among the refined who have long possessed wealth, great skill is used to conceal this and to make it appear that eating is a secondary matter necessary only for appearance. And this pretence is easy, for in the majority of cases the guests are satiated in the true sense of the word—they are never hungry.

They pretend that dinner, eating, is not necessary to them, is even a burden; but this is a lie. Try giving them—instead of the refined dishes they expect—I do not say bread and water, but porridge or gruel or something of that kind, and see what a storm it will call forth and how evident will become the real truth, namely, that the chief interest of the assembly is not the ostensible one but—gluttony.

Look at what men sell. Go through a town and see what men buy—articles of adornment and things to devour. And indeed this must be so, it cannot be otherwise. It is only possible not to think about eating, to keep this lust under control, when a man does not eat except in obedience to necessity. If a man *ceases* to eat only in obedience to necessity—if, that is, he eats when the stomach is full—then the state of things cannot but be what it actually is. If men love the pleasure of eating, if they allow themselves to love this pleasure, if they find it good (as is the case with the vast majority of men in our time, and with educated men quite as much as with uneducated, though they pretend that it is not so), there is no limit to the augmentation of this pleasure, no limit beyond which it may not grow. The satisfaction of a *need* has limits, but pleasure has none. For the satisfaction of our needs it is necessary and sufficient to eat bread, porridge, or rice; for the augmentation of pleasure there is no end to the possible flavourings and seasonings.

Bread is a necessary and sufficient food. (This is proved by the millions of men who are strong, active, healthy, and hard-working on rye bread alone.) But it is pleasanter to eat bread with some flavouring. It is well to soak the bread in water boiled with meat. Still better to put into this water some vegetable or, even better, several vegetables. It is well to eat flesh. And flesh is better not stewed, but roasted. It is better still with butter, and underdone, and choosing out certain special parts of the meat. But add to this vegetables and mustard. And drink wine with it, red wine for preference. One does not need any more, but one can still eat some fish if it is well flavoured with sauces and swallowed down with white wine. It would seem as if one could get through nothing more, either rich or tasty, but a sweet dish can still be managed: in summer ices, in winter stewed fruits, preserves, and the like. And thus we have a dinner, a modest dinner. The pleasure of such a dinner can be greatly augmented. And it is augmented, and there is no limit to this augmentation: stimulating snacks, *hors-d'œuvres* before dinner, and *entremets* and desserts, and various combinations of tasty things, and flowers and decorations and music during dinner.

And strange to say, men who daily overeat themselves at such dinners—in comparison with which the feast of Belshazzar that evoked the prophetic warning was nothing—are naively persuaded that they may yet be leading a moral life.

IX

Fasting is an indispensable condition of a good life; but in fasting, as in self-control in general, the question arises, what shall we begin with?—How to fast, how often to eat, what to eat, what to avoid eating? And as we can do no work seriously without regarding the necessary order of sequence, so also we cannot fast without knowing where to begin—with what to commence self-control in food.

Fasting! And even an analysis of how to fast and where to begin! The notion seems ridiculous and wild to the majority of men.

I remember how an Evangelical preacher who was attacking monastic asceticism once said to me with pride at his own originality, 'Ours is not a Christianity of fasting and privations, but of beefsteaks.' Christianity, or virtue in general—and beefsteaks!

During a long period of darkness and lack of all guidance, Pagan or Christian, so many wild, immoral ideas have made their way into our life (especially into that lower region of the first steps towards a good life—our relation to food to which no one paid any attention), that it is difficult for us in our days even to understand the audacity and senselessness of upholding Christianity or virtue with beefsteaks.

We are not horrified by this association simply because a strange thing has befallen us. We look and see not: listen and hear not. There is no bad odour, no sound, no monstrosity, to which man cannot become so accustomed that he ceases to remark what would strike a man unaccustomed to it. And it is precisely the same in the moral region. Christianity and morality with beefsteaks!

A few days ago I visited the slaughter-house in our town of Túla. It is built on the new and improved system practised in large towns, with a view to causing the animals as little suffering as possible. It was on a Friday, two days before Trinity Sunday. There were many cattle there.

Long before this, when reading that excellent book, *The Ethics of Diet*, I had wished to visit a slaughter-house in order to see with my own eyes the reality of the question raised when vegetarianism is discussed. But at first I felt ashamed to do so, as one is always ashamed of going to look at suffering which one knows is about to take place but which one cannot avert; and so I kept putting off my visit.

But a little while ago I met on the road a butcher returning to Túla after a visit to his home. He is not yet an experienced butcher, and his duty is to stab with a knife. I asked him whether he did not feel sorry for the animals that he killed. He gave me the usual answer: 'Why should I feel sorry? It is necessary.' But when I told him that eating flesh is not necessary, but is only a luxury, he agreed; and then he admitted that he was sorry for the animals. 'But what can I do?' he said, 'I must earn my bread. At first I was *afraid* to kill. My father, he never even killed a chicken in all his life.' The majority of Russians cannot kill: they feel pity, and express the feeling by the word *'fear'*. This man had also been 'afraid', but he was so no longer. He told me that most of the work was done on Fridays, when it continues until the evening.

Not long ago I also had a talk with a retired soldier, a butcher, and he too was surprised at my assertion that it was a pity to kill, and said the usual things about its being ordained. But afterwards he agreed with me: 'Especially when they are quiet, tame cattle. They come, poor things! trusting you. It is very pitiful.'

This is dreadful! Not the suffering and death of the animals, but that man suppresses in himself, unnecessarily, the highest spiritual capacity—that of sympathy and pity towards living creatures like himself—and by violating his own feelings becomes cruel. And how deeply seated in the human heart is the injunction not to take life!

Once, when walking from Moscow,[1] I was offered a lift by some carters who were going from Sérpukhov to a neighbouring forest to fetch wood.

---

[1] When returning to Yásnaya Polyána in spring after his winter's residence in Moscow, Tolstóy repeatedly chose to walk the distance (something over 130 miles) instead of going by rail. Sérpukhov is a town he had to pass on the way.—A. M.

It was the Thursday before Easter. I was seated in the first cart with a strong, red, coarse carman, who evidently drank. On entering a village we saw a well-fed, naked, pink pig being dragged out of the first yard to be slaughtered. It squealed in a dreadful voice, resembling the shriek of a man. Just as we were passing they began to kill it. A man gashed its throat with a knife. The pig squealed still more loudly and piercingly, broke away from the men, and ran off covered with blood. Being near-sighted I did not see all the details. I saw only the human-looking pink body of the pig and heard its desperate squeal, but the carter saw all the details and watched closely. They caught the pig, knocked it down, and finished cutting its throat. When its squeals ceased the carter sighed heavily. 'Do men really not have to answer for such things?' he said.

So strong is man's aversion to all killing. But by example, by encouraging greediness, by the assertion that God has allowed it, and above all by habit, people entirely lose this natural feeling.

On Friday I decided to go to Túla, and, meeting a meek, kind acquaintance of mine, I invited him to accompany me.

'Yes, I have heard that the arrangements are good, and have been wishing to go and see it; but if they are slaughtering I will not go in.'

'Why not? That's just what I want to see! If we eat flesh it must be killed.'

'No, no, I cannot!'

It is worth remarking that this man is a sportsman and himself kills animals and birds.

So we went to the slaughter-house. Even at the entrance one noticed the heavy, disgusting, fetid smell, as of carpenter's glue, or paint on glue. The nearer we approached the stronger became the smell. The building is of red brick, very large, with vaults and high chimneys. We entered the gates. To the right was a spacious enclosed yard, three-quarters of an acre in extent—twice a week cattle are driven in here for sale—and adjoining this enclosure was the porter's lodge. To the left were the chambers, as they are called—i.e. rooms with arched entrances, sloping asphalt floors, and contrivances for moving and hanging up the carcasses. On a bench against the wall of the porter's lodge were seated half a dozen butchers, in aprons covered with blood, their tucked-up sleeves disclosing their muscular arms also besmeared with blood. They had finished their work half an hour before, so that day we could only see the empty chambers. Though these chambers were open on both sides, there was an oppressive smell of warm blood; the floor was brown and shining, with congealed black blood in the cavities.

One of the butchers described the process of slaughtering, and showed us the place where it was done. I did not quite understand him, and formed a wrong, but very horrible, idea of the way the animals are slaughtered; and I fancied that, as is often the case, the reality would very likely produce upon me a weaker impression than the imagination. But in this I was mistaken.

The next time I visited the slaughter-house I went in good time. It was the Friday before Trinity—a warm day in June. The smell of glue and blood was even stronger and more penetrating than on my first visit. The work was at its height. The dusty yard was full of cattle, and animals had been driven into all the enclosures beside the chambers.

In the street before the entrance stood carts to which oxen, calves, and cows were tied. Other carts drawn by good horses and filled with live calves, whose heads hung down and swayed about, drew up and were unloaded; and similar carts containing the carcasses of oxen, with trembling legs sticking out, with heads and bright red lungs and brown livers, drove away from the slaughter-house. By the fence stood the cattle-dealers' horses. The dealers themselves, in their long coats, with their whips and knouts in their hands, were walking about the yard, either marking with tar cattle belonging to the same owner, or bargaining, or else guiding oxen and bulls from the great yard into the enclosures which lead into the chambers. These men were evidently all preoccupied with money matters and calculations, and any thought as to whether it was right or wrong to kill these animals was as far from their minds as were questions about the chemical composition of the blood that covered the floor of the chambers.

No butchers were to be seen in the yard; they were all in the chambers at work. That day about a hundred head of cattle were slaughtered. I was on the point of entering one of the chambers, but stopped short at the door. I stopped both because the chamber was crowded with carcasses which were being moved about, and also because blood was flowing on the floor and dripping from above. All the butchers present were besmeared with blood, and had I entered I, too, should certainly have been covered with it. One suspended carcass was being taken down, another was being moved towards the door, a third, a slaughtered ox, was lying with its white legs raised, while a butcher with strong hand was ripping up its tight-stretched hide.

Through the door opposite the one at which I was standing, a big, red, well-fed ox was led in.

Two men were dragging it, and hardly had it entered when I saw a butcher raise a knife above its neck and stab it. The ox, as if all four legs had suddenly given way, fell heavily on its belly, immediately turned over on one side, and began to work its legs and its whole hind-quarters. Another butcher at once threw himself upon the ox from the side opposite to the twitching legs, caught its horns and twisted its head down to the ground, while another butcher cut its throat with a knife. From beneath the head there flowed a stream of blackish-red blood, which a besmeared boy caught in a tin basin. All the time this was going on the ox kept incessantly twitching its head as if trying to get up, and waved its four legs in the air. The basin was quickly filling, but the ox still lived, and, its stomach heaving heavily, both hind and fore legs worked so violently that the butchers held aloof. When one basin was full the boy carried it away on his head to the albumen factory, while another boy placed a fresh basin, which also soon began to fill up. But still the ox heaved its body and worked its hind legs.

When the blood ceased to flow the butcher raised the animal's head and began to skin it. The ox continued to writhe. The head, stripped of its skin, showed red with white veins, and kept the position given it by the butcher; the skin hung on both sides. Still the animal did not cease to writhe. Then another butcher caught hold of one of the legs, broke it, and cut it off. In the remaining legs and the stomach the convulsions still continued. The other legs were cut off and thrown aside, together with those of other oxen belonging to the same owner. Then the carcass was dragged to the hoist and hung up and the convulsions were over.

Thus I looked on from the door at the second,

third, and fourth ox. It was the same with each: the same cutting off of the head with bitten tongue, and the same convulsive members. The only difference was that the butcher did not always strike at once so as to cause the animal's fall. Sometimes he missed his aim, whereupon the ox leaped up, bellowed, and, covered with blood, tried to escape. But then his head was pulled under a bar, struck a second time, and he fell.

I afterwards entered by the door at which the oxen were led in. Here I saw the same thing, only nearer, and therefore more plainly. But chiefly I saw here, what I had not seen before, how the oxen were forced to enter this door. Each time an ox was seized in the enclosure and pulled forward by a rope tied to its horns, the animal, smelling blood, refused to advance, and sometimes bellowed and drew back. It would have been beyond the strength of two men to drag it in by force, so one of the butchers went round each time, grasped the animal's tail, and twisted it so violently that the gristle crackled, and the ox advanced.

When they had finished with the cattle of one owner they brought in those of another. The first animal of this next lot was not an ox but a bull—a fine, well-bred creature, black, with white spots on its legs, young, muscular, full of energy. He was dragged forward, but he lowered his head and resisted sturdily. Then the butcher who followed behind seized the tail like an engine-driver grasping the handle of a whistle, twisted it, the gristle crackled, and the bull rushed forward, upsetting the men who held the rope. Then it stopped, looking sideways with its black eyes, the whites of which had filled with blood. But again the tail crackled, and the bull sprang forward and reached the required spot. The striker approached, took aim, and struck. But the blow missed the mark. The bull leaped up, shook his head, bellowed, and, covered with blood, broke free and rushed back. The men at the doorway all sprang aside; but the experienced butchers, with the dash of men inured to danger, quickly caught the rope; again the tail operation was repeated, and again the bull was in the chamber, where he was dragged under the bar, from which he did not again escape. The striker quickly took aim at the spot where the hair divides like a star, and, notwithstanding the blood, found it, struck, and the fine animal, full of life, collapsed, its head and legs writhing while it was bled and the head skinned.

'There, the cursèd devil hasn't even fallen the right way!' grumbled the butcher as he cut the skin from the head.

Five minutes later the head was stuck up, red instead of black, without skin; the eyes, that had shone with such splendid colour five minutes before, fixed and glassy.

Afterwards I went into the compartment where small animals are slaughtered—a very large chamber with asphalt floor, and tables with backs, on which sheep and calves are killed. Here the work was already finished; in the long room, impregnated with the smell of blood, were only two butchers. One was blowing into the leg of a dead lamb and patting the swollen stomach with his hand; the other, a young fellow in an apron besmeared with blood, was smoking a bent cigarette. There was no one else in the long dark chamber, filled with a heavy smell. After me there entered a man, apparently an ex-soldier, bringing in a young yearling ram, black with a white mark on its neck, and its legs tied. This animal he placed upon one of the tables as if upon a bed. The old soldier greeted the butchers, with whom he was evidently acquainted, and began to ask when their master allowed them leave. The fellow with the cigarette approached with a knife, sharpened it on the edge of the table, and answered that they were free on holidays. The live ram was lying as quietly as the dead inflated one, except that it was briskly wagging its short little tail and its sides were heaving more quickly than usual. The soldier pressed down its uplifted head gently, without effort; the butcher, still continuing the conversation, grasped with his left hand the head of the ram and cut its throat. The ram quivered, and the little tail stiffened and ceased to wave. The fellow, while waiting for the blood to flow, began to relight his cigarette which had gone out. The blood flowed and the ram began to writhe. The conversation continued without the slightest interruption. It was horribly revolting.

* * * * * * *

And how about those hens and chickens which daily, in thousands of kitchens, with heads cut off and streaming with blood, comically, dreadfully, flop about, jerking their wings?

And see, a kind, refined lady will devour the carcasses of these animals with full assurance that she is doing right, at the same time asserting two contradictory propositions:

First, that she is, as her doctor assures her, so delicate that she cannot be sustained by vegetable food alone and that for her feeble organism flesh is indispensable; and secondly, that she is so sensitive that she is unable, not only herself to inflict suffering on animals, but even to bear the sight of suffering.

Whereas the poor lady is weak precisely because she has been taught to live upon food unnatural to man; and she cannot avoid causing suffering to animals—for she eats them.

We cannot pretend that we do not know this. We are not ostriches, and cannot believe that if we refuse to look at what we do not wish to see, it will not exist. This is especially the case when what we do not wish to see is what we wish to eat. If it were really indispensable, or if not indispensable, at least in some way useful! But it is quite unnecessary,[1] and only serves to develop animal feelings, to excite desire, and to promote fornication and drunkenness. And this is continually being confirmed by the fact that young, kind, undepraved people—especially women and girls—without knowing how it logically follows, feel that virtue is incompatible with beefsteaks, and, as soon as they wish to be good, give up eating flesh.

What, then, do I wish to say? That in order to be moral people must cease to eat meat? Not at all.

I only wish to say that for a good life a certain order of good actions is indispensable; that if a man's aspirations toward right living be serious they will inevitably follow one definite sequence; and that in this sequence the first virtue a man will strive after will be self-control, self-restraint. And in seeking for self-control a man will inevitably follow one definite sequence, and in this sequence the

[1] Let those who doubt this read the numerous books upon the subject, written by scientists and doctors, in which it is proved that flesh is not necessary for the nourishment of man. And let them not listen to those old-fashioned doctors who defend the assertion that flesh is necessary, merely because it has long been so regarded by their predecessors and by themselves; and who defend their opinion with tenacity and malevolence, as all that is old and traditional always is defended.—L. T.

first thing will be self-control in food—fasting. And in fasting, if he be really and seriously seeking to live a good life, the first thing from which he will abstain will always be the use of animal food, because, to say nothing of the excitation of the passions caused by such food, its use is simply immoral, as it involves the performance of an act which is contrary to moral feeling—killing; and is called forth only by greediness and the desire for tasty food.

The precise reason why abstinence from animal food will be the first act of fasting and of a moral life is admirably explained in the book, *The Ethics of Diet*; and not by one man only, but by all mankind in the persons of its best representatives during all the conscious life of humanity.

But why, if the wrongfulness—i.e. the immorality—of animal food was known to humanity so long ago, have people not yet come to acknowledge this law? will be asked by those who are accustomed to be led by public opinion rather than by reason.

The answer to this question is that the moral progress of humanity—which is the foundation of every other kind of progress—is always slow; but that the sign of true, not casual, progress is its uninterruptedness and its continual acceleration.

And the progress of vegetarianism is of this kind. That progress is expressed both in the words of the writers cited in the above-mentioned book and in the actual life of mankind, which from many causes is involuntarily passing more and more from carnivorous habits to vegetable food, and is also deliberately following the same path in a movement which shows evident strength, and which is growing larger and larger—viz. vegetarianism. That movement has during the last ten years advanced more and more rapidly. More and more books and periodicals on this subject appear every year; one meets more and more people who have given up meat; and abroad, especially in Germany, England, and America, the number of vegetarian hotels and restaurants increases year by year.

This movement should cause especial joy to those whose life lies in the effort to bring about the kingdom of God on earth, not because vegetarianism is in itself an important step towards that kingdom (all true steps are both important and unimportant), but because it is a sign that the aspiration of mankind towards moral perfection is serious and sincere, for it has taken the one unalterable order of succession natural to it, beginning with the first step.

One cannot fail to rejoice at this, as people could not fail to rejoice who, after striving to reach the upper story of a house by trying vainly and at random to climb the walls from different points, should at last assemble at the first step of the staircase and crowd towards it, convinced that there can be no way up except by mounting this first step of the stairs.

[*1892.*]

[The above essay was written as Preface to a Russian translation of Howard Williams's *The Ethics of Diet.*]

NON-ACTING

THE editor of a Paris review, thinking that the opinions of two celebrated writers on the state of mind that is common to-day would interest me, has sent me two extracts from French newspapers—one containing Zola's speech delivered at the banquet of the General Association of Students, the other containing a letter from Dumas to the editor of the *Gaulois*.

These documents interested me profoundly, both on account of their timeliness and the celebrity of their authors, and also because it would be difficult to find so concisely, vigorously, and brilliantly expressed in present-day literature the two fundamental forces that move humanity. The one is the force of routine, tending to keep humanity in its accustomed path; the other is the force of reason and love, drawing humanity towards the light.

The following is Zola's speech *in extenso*:

'GENTLEMEN,

'You have paid me a great honour and conferred on me a great pleasure by choosing me to preside at this Annual Banquet. There is no better or more charming society than that of the young. There is no audience more sympathetic, or before whom one's heart opens more freely with the wish to be loved and listened to.

'I, alas! have reached an age at which we begin to regret our departed youth, and to pay attention to the efforts of the rising generation that is climbing up behind us. It is they who will both judge us and carry on our work. In them I feel the future coming to birth, and at times I ask myself, not without some anxiety, What of all our efforts will they reject and what will they retain? What will happen to our work when it has passed into their hands? For it cannot last except through them, and it will disappear unless they accept it, to enlarge it and bring it to completion.

'That is why I eagerly watch the movement of ideas among the youth of to-day, and read the advanced papers and reviews, endeavouring to keep in touch with the new spirit that animates our schools and striving vainly to know whither you are all wending your way—you, who represent the intelligence and the will of to-morrow.

'Certainly, gentlemen, egotism plays its part in the matter; I do not hide it. I am somewhat like a workman who, finishing a house which he hopes will shelter his old age, is anxious concerning the weather he has to expect. Will the rain damage his walls? May not a sudden wind from the north tear the roof off? Above all, has he built strongly enough to resist the storm? Has he spared neither durable material nor irksome labour? It is not that I think our work eternal or final. The greatest must resign themselves to the thought that they represent but a moment in the ever-continuing development of the human spirit: it will be more than sufficient to have been for one hour the mouthpiece of a generation! And since one cannot keep a literature stationary but all things continually evolve and recommence, one must expect to see younger men born and grow up who will, perhaps, in their turn cause you to be forgotten. I do not say that the old warrior in me does not at times desire to resist when he feels his work attacked. But in truth I face the approaching century with more of curiosity than of revolt, and more of ardent sympathy than of personal anxiety; let me perish, and let all my generation perish with me if indeed we are good for nothing but to fill up the ditch for those who follow us in the march towards the light.

'Gentlemen, I constantly hear it said that Positivism is at its last gasp, that Naturalism is dead, that Science has reached the point of bankruptcy, having failed to supply either the moral peace or the human happiness it promised. You will well understand that I do not here undertake to solve the great problems raised by these questions. I am an ignoramus and have no authority to speak in the name of science or philosophy. I am, if you please, simply a novelist, a writer who has at times seen a little way into the heart of things, and whose competence consists only in having observed much and worked much. And it is only as a witness that I allow myself to speak of what my generation—the men who are now fifty years old and whom your generation will soon regard as ancestors—has been, or at least has wished to be.

'I was much struck, a few days ago, at the opening of the *Salon du Champ-de-Mars,* by the characteristic appearance of the rooms. It is thought that the pictures are always much the same. That is an error. The evolution is slow, but how astonished one would be to-day were it possible to revert to the *Salons* of some former years! For my part, I well remember the last academic and romantic exhibitions about 1863. Work in the open air (*le plein air*) had not yet triumphed; there was a general tone of bitumen, a smudging of canvas, a prevalence of burnt colours, the semi-darkness of studios. Then some fifteen years later, after the victorious and much-contested influence of Manet, I can recall quite other exhibitions where the clear tone of full sunlight shone; it was as it were an inundation of light, a care for truth which made each picture-frame a window opened upon Nature bathed in light. And yesterday, after another fifteen years, I could discern amid the fresh limpidity of the productions the rising of a kind of mystic fog. There was the same care for clear painting, but the reality was changing, the figures were more elongated, the need of originality and novelty carried the artists over into the land of dreams.

'If I have dwelt on these three stages of contemporary painting, I have done so because it seems to me that they correspond very strikingly to the contemporary movements of thought. My generation indeed, following illustrious predecessors of whom we were but the successors, strove to open the windows wide to Nature, in order to see all and to say all. In our generation, even among those least conscious of it, the long efforts of positive philosophy and of analytical and experimental science came to fruition. Our fealty was to Science, which surrounded us on all sides; in her we lived, breathing the air of the epoch. I am free to confess that personally I was even a sectarian who lived to transport the rigid methods of Science into the domain of Literature. But where can the man be found who in the stress of strife does not exceed what is necessary, and is content to conquer without compromising his victory? On the whole I have nothing to regret, and I continue to believe in the passion which wills and acts. What enthusiasm, what hope, were ours! To know all, to prevail in all, and to conquer all! By means of truth to make humanity more noble and more happy!

'And it is at this point, gentlemen, that you, the

young, appear upon the scene. I say the young, but the term is vague, distant, and deep as the sea, for where are the young? What will it—the young generation—really become? Who has a right to speak in its name? I must of necessity deal with the ideas attributed to it, but if these ideas are not at all those held by many of you, I ask pardon in advance, and refer you to the men who have misled us by untrustworthy information, more in accord no doubt with their own wishes than with reality.

'At any rate, gentlemen, we are assured that your generation is parting company with ours, that you will no longer put all your hope in Science, that you have perceived so great a social and moral danger in trusting fully to her that you are determined to throw yourselves back upon the past in order to construct a living faith from the debris of dead ones.

'Of course there is no question of a complete divorce from Science; it is understood that you accept her latest conquests and mean to extend them. It is agreed that you will admit demonstrated truths, and efforts are even being made to fit them to ancient dogmas. But at bottom Science is to stand out of the road of faith—it is thrust back to its ancient rank as a simple exercise of the intelligence, an inquiry permitted so long as it does not infringe on the supernatural and the hereafter. It is said that the experiment has been made, and that Science can neither repeople the heavens she has emptied nor restore happiness to souls whose naïve peace she has destroyed. The day of her mendacious triumph is over; she must be modest since she cannot immediately know everything, enrich everything, and heal everything. And if they dare not yet bid intelligent youth throw away its books and desert its masters, there are already saints and prophets to be found going about to exalt the virtue of ignorance, the serenity of simplicity, and to proclaim the need a too-learned and decrepit humanity has of recuperating itself in the depths of a prehistoric village, among ancestors hardly detached from the earth, anteceding all society and all knowledge.

'I do not at all deny the crisis we are passing through—this lassitude and revolt at the end of the century, after such feverish and colossal labour, whose ambition it was to know all and to say all. It seemed that Science, which had just overthrown the old order, would promptly reconstruct it in accord with our ideal of justice and of happiness. Twenty, fifty, even a hundred years passed. And then, when it was seen that justice did not reign, that happiness did not come, many people yielded to a growing impatience, falling into despair and denying that by knowledge one can ever reach the happy land. It is a common occurrence; there can be no action without reaction, and we are witnessing the fatigue inevitably incidental to long journeys: people sit down by the roadside—seeing the interminable plain of another century stretch before them, they despair of ever reaching their destination, and they finish by even doubting the road they have travelled and regretting not to have reposed in a field to sleep for ever under the stars. What is the good of advancing if the goal is ever further removed? What is the use of knowing, if one may not know everything? As well let us keep our unsullied simplicity, the ignorant happiness of a child.

'And thus it seemed that Science, which was supposed to have promised happiness, had reached bankruptcy.

'But did Science promise happiness? I do not

believe it. She promised truth, and the question is whether one will ever reach happiness by way of truth. In order to content oneself with what truth gives, much stoicism will certainly be needed: absolute self-abnegation and a serenity of the satisfied intelligence which seems to be discoverable only among the chosen few. But meanwhile what a cry of despair rises from suffering humanity! How can life be lived without lies and illusions? If there is no other world—where justice reigns, where the wicked are punished and the good are recompensed—how are we to live through this abominable human life without revolting? Nature is unjust and cruel. Science seems to lead us to the monstrous law of the strongest—so that all morality crumbles away and every society makes for despotism. And in the reaction which results—in that lassitude from too much knowledge of which I have spoken—there comes a recoil from the truth which is as yet but poorly explained, and seems cruel to our feeble eyes that are unable to penetrate into and to seize all its laws. No, no! Lead us back to the peaceful slumber of ignorance! Reality is a school of perversion which must be killed and denied, since it will lead to nothing but ugliness and crime. So one plunges into dreamland as the only salvation, the only way to escape from the earth, to feel confidence in the hereafter and hope that there, at last, we shall find happiness and the satisfaction of our desire for fraternity and justice.

'That is the despairing cry for happiness which we hear to-day. It touches me exceedingly. And notice that it rises from all sides like a cry of lamentation amid the re-echoing of advancing Science, who checks not the march of her waggons and her engines. Enough of truth; give us chimeras! We shall find rest only in dreams of the Non-existent, only by losing ourselves in the Unknown. There only bloom the mystic flowers whose perfume lulls our sufferings to sleep. Music has already responded to the call, literature strives to satisfy this new thirst, and painting follows the same way. I have spoken to you of the exhibition at the *Champ-de-Mars*; there you may see the bloom of all this flora of our ancient windows—lank, emaciated virgins, apparitions in twilight tints, stiff figures with the rigid gestures of the Primitivists. It is a reaction against Naturalism which we are told is dead and buried. In any case the movement is undeniable, for it manifests itself in all modes of expression, and one must pay great attention to the study and the explanation of it if one does not wish to despair of to-morrow.

'For my part, gentlemen, I, who am an old and hardened Positivist, see in it but an inevitable halt in the forward march. It is not really even a halt, for our libraries, our laboratories, our lecture-halls and our schools, are not deserted. What also reassures me is that the social soil has undergone no change, it is still the democratic soil from which our century sprang. For a new art to flourish or a new faith to change the direction in which humanity is travelling—that faith would need a new soil which would allow it to germinate and grow: for there can be no new society without a new soil. Faith does not rise from the dead, and one can make nothing but mythologies out of dead religions. Therefore the coming century will but continue our own in the democratic and scientific rush forward which has swept us along, and which still continues. What I can concede is that in literature we limited our horizon too much. Personally I have already regretted that I was a sectarian in that I wished art to confine itself to proven verities. Later comers have extended the horizon by reconquering the region of the unknown and the mysterious; and they have done well. Between the truths fixed by science, which are henceforth immovable, and the truths Science will to-morrow seize from the region of the unknown to fix in their turn, there lies an undefined borderland of doubt and inquiry, which it seems to me belongs to literature as much as to science. It is there we may go as pioneers, doing our work as forerunners, and interpreting the action of unknown forces according to our characters and minds. The ideal—what is it but the unexplained: those forces of the infinite world in which we are plunged without knowing them? But if it be permissible to invent solutions of what is unknown, dare we therefore call in question ascertained laws, imagining them other than they are and thereby denying them? As science advances it is certain that the ideal recedes: and it seems to me that the only meaning of life, the only joy we ought to attribute to life, lies in this gradual conquest, even if one has the melancholy assurance that we never shall know everything.

'In the unquiet times in which we live, gentlemen,—in our day so satiated and so irresolute—shepherds of the soul have arisen who are troubled in mind and ardently offer a faith to the rising generation. The offer is generous, but unfortunately the faith changes and deteriorates according to the personality of the prophet who supplies it. There are several kinds, but none of them appear to me to be very clear or very well defined.

'You are asked to believe, but are not told precisely what you should believe. Perhaps it cannot be told, or perhaps they dare not tell it.

'You are to believe for the pleasure of believing, and especially that you may learn to believe. The

NON-ACTING

advice is not bad in itself—it is certainly a great happiness to rest in the certainty of a faith, no matter what it may be—but the worst of it is that one is not master of this virtue: it bloweth where it listeth.

'I am therefore also going to finish by proposing to you a faith, and by beseeching you to have faith in work. Work, young people! I well know how trivial such advice appears: no speech-day passes at which it is not repeated amid the general indifference of the scholars. But I ask you to reflect on it, and I—who have been nothing but a worker—will permit myself to speak of all the benefit I have derived from the long task that has filled my life. I had no easy start in life; I have known want and despair. Later on I lived in strife and I live in it still—discussed, denied, covered with abuse. Well, I have had but one faith, one strength—work! What has sustained me was the enormous labour I set myself. Before me stood always in the distance the goal towards which I was marching, and when life's hardships had cast me down, that sufficed to set me on my feet and to give me courage to advance in spite of all. The work of which I speak to you is the regular work, the daily task, the duty one has undertaken to advance one step each day towards the fulfilment of one's engagement. How often in the morning have I sat down to my table—my head in confusion—a bitter taste in my mouth—tortured by some great sorrow, physical or moral! And each time—in spite of the revolt my suffering has caused—after the first moments of agony my task has been to me an alleviation and a comfort. I have always come from my daily task consoled—with a broken heart perhaps, but erect and able to live on till the morrow.

'Work! Remember, gentlemen, that it is the sole

law of the world, the regulator bringing organic matter to its unknown goal! Life has no other meaning, no other *raison d'être*; we each of us appear but to perform our allotted task and to disappear. One cannot define life otherwise than by the movement it receives and bequeaths, and which is in reality nothing but work, work at the final achievement accomplished by all the ages. How, therefore, can we be other than modest? How can we do other than accept the individual task given to each of us, and accept it without rebellion and without yielding to the pride of that personal "I", which considers itself a centre and does not wish to take its place in the ranks?

'From the time one accepts that task and begins to fulfil it, it seems to me tranquillity should come even to those most tormented. I know that there are minds tortured by thoughts of the Infinite, minds that suffer from the presence of mystery, and it is to them I address myself as a brother, advising them to occupy their lives with some immense labour, of which it were even well that they should never see the completion. It will be the balance enabling them to march straight; it will be a continual diversion—grain thrown to their intelligence that it may grind and convert it into daily bread, with the satisfaction that comes of duty accomplished.

'It is true this solves no metaphysical problems; it is but an empirical recipe enabling one to live one's life honestly and more or less tranquilly; but is it a small thing to obtain a sound state of moral and physical health and to escape the danger of dreams, while solving by work the question of finding the greatest happiness possible on this earth?

'I have always, I admit, distrusted chimeras. Nothing is less wholesome for men and nations than illusion; it stifles effort, it blinds, it is the vanity of the weak. To repose on legends, to be mistaken about all realities, to believe that it is enough to dream of force in order to be strong—we have seen well enough to what terrible disasters such things lead. The people are told to look on high, to believe in a Higher Power, and to exalt themselves to the ideal. No, no! That is language which at times seems to me impious. The only strong people are those who work, and it is only work that gives courage and faith. To conquer it is necessary that the arsenals should be full, that one should have the strongest and the most perfect armament, that the army should be trained, should have confidence in its chiefs and in itself. All this can be acquired; it needs but the will and the right method. You may be well assured that the coming century and the illimitable future belong to work. And in the rising force of Socialism does one not already see the rough sketch of the social law of to-morrow, the law of work for all—liberating and pacifying work?

'Young men, young men, take up your duties! Let each one accept his task, a task which should fill his life. It may be very humble, it will not be the less useful. Never mind what it is so long as it exists and keeps you erect! When you have regulated it, without excess—just the quantity you are able to accomplish each day—it will cause you to live in health and in joy: it will save you from the torments of the Infinite. What a healthy and great society that will be—a society each member of which will bear his reasonable share of work! A man who works is always kind. So I am convinced that the only faith that can save us is a belief in the efficacy of accomplished toil. Certainly it is pleasant to dream of eternity. But for an honest man it is enough to have lived his life doing his work.   **EMILE ZOLA.**'

M. Zola does not approve of this faith in something vague and ill-defined, which is recommended to French youth by its new guides; yet he himself advises belief in something which is neither clearer nor better defined—namely, science and work.

A little-known Chinese philosopher named Lao-Tsze, who founded a religion (the first and best translation of his book, 'Of the Way of Virtue', is that by Stanislaus Julien), takes as the foundation of his doctrine the *Tao*—a word that is translated as 'reason, way, and virtue'. If men follow the law of *Tao* they will be happy. But the *Tao*, according to M. Julien's translation, can only be reached by *non-acting*.

The ills of humanity arise, according to Lao-Tsze, not because men neglect to do things that are necessary, but because they do things that are unnecessary. If men would, as he says, but practise *non-acting*, they would be relieved not merely from their personal calamities, but also from those inherent in all forms of government, which is the subject specially dealt with by the Chinese philosopher.

M. Zola tells us that everyone should work persistently; work will make life healthy and joyous, and will save us from the torment of the Infinite. Work! But what are we to work at? The manufacturers of and the dealers in opium or tobacco or brandy, all the speculators on the Stock Exchange, the inventors and manufacturers of weapons of destruction, the military, the gaolers and executioners—all work: but it is obvious that mankind would be better off were these workers to cease working.

But perhaps M. Zola's advice refers only to those whose work is inspired by science. The greater part of his speech is in fact designed to uphold science, which he thinks is being attacked. Well, it so happens that I am continually receiving from various unappreciated authors the outcome of their scientific labours—pamphlets, manuscripts, treatises, and printed books.

One of them has finally solved, so he says, the question of Christian gnosiology; another has written a book on the cosmic ether; a third has settled the social question; a fourth is editing a theosophical review; a fifth (in a thick volume) has solved the problem of the knight's tour in chess.

All these people work assiduously and work in the name of science, but I do not think I am mistaken in saying that my correspondents' time and work, and the time and work of many other such people, have been spent in a way not merely useless but even harmful; for thousands of men are engaged in making the paper, casting the type, and manufacturing the presses needed to print their books, and in feeding, clothing, and housing all these scientific workers.

Work for science? But the word 'science' has so large and so ill-defined a meaning that what some consider science others consider futile folly; and this is so not merely among the profane, but even among men who are themselves priests of science. While one set of the learned esteem jurisprudence, philosophy, and even theology, to be the most necessary and important of sciences, the Positivists consider those very sciences to be childish twaddle devoid of scientific value. And, vice versa, what the Positivists hold to be the science of sciences—sociology—is regarded by the theologians, philosophers, and spiritualists as a collection of arbitrary and useless observations and assertions. Moreover even in one and the same branch, whether it be philosophy or natural science, each system has its ardent defenders and opponents, just as ardent and equally competent, though maintaining diametrically opposite views.

Lastly, does not each year produce its new scientific discoveries, which after astonishing the boobies of the whole world and bringing fame and fortune to the inventors, are eventually admitted to be ridiculous mistakes even by those who promulgated them?

We all know that what the Romans valued as the greatest science and the most important occupation that distinguished them from the barbarians was rhetoric, which does not now rank as a science at all. It is equally difficult to-day to understand the state of mind of the learned men of the Middle Ages who were fully convinced that all science was concentrated in scholasticism.

Unless then our century forms an exception (which is a supposition we have no right to make), it needs no great boldness to conclude by analogy that among the kinds of knowledge occupying the attention of our learned men and called science, there must necessarily be some which will be regarded by our descendants much as we now regard the rhetoric of the ancients and the scholasticism of the Middle Ages.

II

M. Zola's speech is chiefly directed against certain leaders who are persuading the young generation to return to religious beliefs, for M. Zola, as a champion of science, considers himself an adversary of theirs. Really he is nothing of the sort, for his reasoning rests on the same basis as that of his opponents, namely (as he himself admits), on faith.

It is a generally accepted opinion that religion and science are opposed to one another. And they really are so, but only in point of time; that is to say, what is considered science by one generation often becomes religion for their descendants. What is usually spoken of as religion is generally the science of the past, while what is called science is to a great extent the religion of the present.

We say that the assertions of the Hebrews that the world was created in six days, that sons would be punished for their father's sins, and that certain diseases could be cured by the sight of a serpent, were religious statements; while the assertions of our contemporaries that the world created itself by turning round a centre which is everywhere, that all the different species arose from the struggle for existence, that criminals are the product of heredity, and that micro-organisms, shaped like commas, exist which cause certain diseases—we call scientific statements. By reverting in imagination to the state of mind of an ancient Hebrew it becomes easy to see that for him the creation of the world in six days, the serpent that cured diseases, and the like, were scientific statements in accord with its highest stage of development, just as the Darwinian law, Koch's commas, heredity, &c., are for a man of our day.

And just as the Hebrew believed not so much in the creation of the world in six days, in the serpent that healed certain diseases, and so on, as in the infallibility of his priests and therefore in all that they told him—so to-day the great majority of cultured people believe, not in the formation of the world by rotation, or in heredity, or in the comma bacilli, but in the infallibility of the secular priests called scientists who, with a assurance equal to that of the Hebrew priests, assert whatever they pretend to know.

I will even go so far as to say that if the ancient priests, controlled by none but their own colleagues, allowed themselves at times to diverge from the path of truth merely for the pleasure of astonishing and mystifying their public, our modern priests of science do much the same thing and do it with equal effrontery.

The greater part of what is called religion is simply the superstition of past ages; the greater part of what is called science is simply the superstition of to-day. And I suppose that the proportion of error and truth is much about the same in the one as in the other. Consequently to work in the name of a faith, whether religious or scientific, is not merely a doubtful method of helping humanity but is a dangerous method which may do more harm than good.

To consecrate one's life to the fulfilment of duties imposed by religion—prayers, communions, alms—or on the other hand to devote it to some scientific work as M. Zola advises, is to run too great a risk: for on the brink of death one may find that the religious or scientific principle to whose service one has consecrated one's whole life was all a ridiculous error!

Even before reading the speech in which M. Zola extols work of any kind as a merit, I was always surprised by the opinion, especially prevalent in Western Europe that work is a kind of virtue. It always seemed to me that only an irrational being, like the ant of the fable, could be excused for exalting work to the rank of a virtue and boasting of it. M. Zola assures us that work makes men kind; I have always observed the contrary. Not to speak of selfish work aiming at the profit or fame of the worker, which is always bad, self-conscious work, the pride of work, makes not only ants but men cruel. Who does not know those men, inaccessible to truth or to kindliness, who are always so busy that they never have time either to do good or even to ask themselves whether their work is not harmful? You say to such people, 'Your work is useless, perhaps even harmful. Here are the reasons. Pause awhile and let us examine the matter.' They will not listen to you, but scornfully reply: 'It's all very well for you to argue. You have nothing to do. But what time have I for discussions? I have worked all my life, and work does not wait; I have to edit a daily paper with half a million subscribers; I have to organize the army; I have to build the Eiffel Tower, to arrange the Chicago Exhibition, to pierce the Isthmus of Panama, to investigate the problem of heredity or of telepathy, or of how many times this classical author has used such and such words.'

The most cruel of men—the Neros, the Peter the Greats—were constantly occupied, never remaining for a moment at their own disposal without activity or amusement.

If work be not actually a vice, it can from no point of view be considered a virtue.

It can no more be considered a virtue than nutrition. Work is a necessity, to be deprived of which involves suffering, and to raise it to the rank of a merit is as monstrous as it would be to do the same for nutrition. The strange value our society attaches to work can only be explained as a reaction from the view held by our ancestors, who thought idleness an attribute of nobility and almost a merit, as indeed it is still regarded by some rich and uneducated people to-day.

Work, the exercise of our organs, cannot be a merit, because it is a necessity for every man and every animal—as is shown alike by the capers of a tethered calf and by the silly exercises to which rich and well-fed people among ourselves are addicted, who find no more reasonable or useful employment for their mental faculties than reading newspapers and novels or playing chess or cards, or for their muscles than gymnastics, fencing, lawn-tennis, and racing.

In my opinion not only is work not a virtue, but in our ill-organized society it is often a moral anaesthetic, like tobacco, wine, and other means of stupefying and blinding oneself to the disorder and emptiness of our lives. And it is just as such that M. Zola recommends it to young people.

Dumas says something quite different.

III

The following is the letter he sent to the editor of the *Gaulois*:

'Dear Sir,

'You ask my opinion of the aspirations which seem to be arising among the students in the schools, and of the polemics which preceded and followed the incidents at the Sorbonne.

'I should prefer not to express my opinion further on any matter whatever. Those who were of our opinion will continue to be so for some time yet; those who held other views will cling to them more and more tenaciously. It would be better to have no discussions. "Opinions are like nails," said a moralist, a friend of mine: "the more one hits them the more one drives them in."

'It is not that I have no opinion on what one calls the great questions of life, and on the diverse forms in which the mind of man momentarily clothes the subjects of which it treats. Rather, that opinion is so correct and absolute that I prefer to keep it for my own guidance, having no ambition to create anything or to destroy anything. I should have to go back to great political, social, philosophical and religious problems, and that would take us too far, were I to follow you in the study you are commencing of the small external occurrences they have lately aroused, and that they arouse in each new generation. Each new generation indeed comes with ideas and passions old as life itself, which it believes no one has ever had before, for it finds itself subject to their influence for the first time and is convinced it is about to change the aspect of everything.

'Humanity for thousands of years has been trying to solve that great problem of cause and effect which will perhaps take thousands of years yet to settle, if indeed it ever is settled (as I think it should be). Of this problem children of twenty declare that they have an irrefutable solution in their quite young heads. And as a first argument, at the first discussion, one sees them hitting those who do not share their opinions. Are we to conclude that this is a sign that a whole society is readopting the religious ideal which has been temporarily obscured and abandoned? Or is it not, with all these young apostles, simply a physiological question of warm blood and vigorous muscles, such as threw the young generation of twenty years ago into the opposite movement? I incline to the latter supposition.

'He would indeed be foolish who in these manifestations of an exuberant period of life found proof of development that was final or even durable. There is in it nothing more than an attack of growing fever. Whatever the ideas may be for the sake of which these young people have been hitting one another, we may safely wager that they will resist them at some future day if their own children reproduce them. Age and experience will have come by that time.

'Sooner or later many of these combatants and adversaries of to-day will meet on the cross-roads of life, somewhat wearied, somewhat dispirited by their struggle with realities, and hand-in-hand will find their way back to the main road, regretfully acknowledging that, in spite of all their early convictions, the world remains round and continues always turning in one and the same direction, and that the same horizons ever reappear under the same infinite and fixed sky. After having disputed and fought to their hearts' content, some in the name of faith, others in the name of science, both to prove there is a God, and to prove there is no God (two propositions about which one might fight for ever should it be decided not to disarm till the case was proven), they will finally discover that the one knows no more about it than the other, but that what they may all be sure of is, that man needs hope as much if not more than he needs knowledge—that he suffers abominably from the uncertainty he is in concerning the things of most interest to him, that he is ever in quest of a better state than that in which he now exists, and that he should be left at full liberty, especially in the realms of philosophy, to seek this happier condition.

'He sees around him a universe which existed before he did and will last after he is gone; he feels and knows it to be eternal and he would like to share in its duration. From the moment he was called to life he demanded his share of the permanent life that surrounds him, raises him, mocks him, and destroys him. Now that he has begun he does not wish to end. He now loudly demands, now in low tones pleads for, a certainty which ever evades him—fortunately, since certain knowledge would mean for him immobility and death, for the most powerful motor of human energy is uncertainty. And as he cannot reach certainty he wanders to and fro in the vague ideal; and whatever excursions he may make into scepticism and negation, whether from pride, curiosity, anger, or for fashion's sake, he ever returns to the hope he certainly cannot forgo. Like lovers' quarrels, it is not for long.

'So there are at times obscurations, but never any complete obliteration of the human ideal. Philosophical mists pass over it like clouds that pass before the moon; but the white orb, continuing its course, suddenly reappears from behind them intact and shining. Man's irresistible need of an ideal explains why he has accepted with such confidence, such rapture, and without reason's control, the various religious formulas which, while promising him the Infinite, have presented it to him conformably with his nature, enclosing it in the limits always necessary even to the ideal.

'But for centuries past, and especially during the last hundred years, at each new stage new men, more and more numerous, emerge from the darkness, and in the name of reason, science, or observation, dispute the old truths, declare them to be relative, and wish to destroy the formulas which contain them.

'Who is in the right in this dispute? All are right while they seek; none are right when they begin to threaten. Between truth which is the aim, and free inquiry to which all have a right, force is quite out of place notwithstanding celebrated examples to the contrary. Force merely drives farther back that at which we aim. It is not merely cruel, it is also useless, and that is the worst of faults in all that concerns civilization. No blows, however forcibly delivered, will ever prove the existence or the non-existence of God.

'To conclude, or rather to come to an end—seeing that the Power, whatever it be, that created the world (which, I think, certainly cannot have created itself) while using us as its instruments has for the present reserved to itself the privilege of knowing why it has made us and whither it is leading us—seeing that this Power (in spite of all the intentions attributed to it and all the demands made upon it) appears ever more and more determined to guard its own secret—I believe, if I may say all I think, that mankind is beginning to cease to try to penetrate that eternal mystery. Mankind went to religions, which proved nothing for they differed among themselves; it went to philosophies, which revealed no more for they contradicted one another; and it will now try to find its way out of the difficulty by itself, trusting to its own instinct and its own simple good sense; and since mankind finds itself here on earth without knowing why or how, it is going to try to be as happy as it can with just those means the earth supplies.

'Zola recently, in a remarkable address to students, recommended to them work as a remedy and even as a panacea for all the ills of life. *Labor improbus omnia vincit.* The remedy is familiar, nor is it less good on that account; but it is not, never has been, and never will be, sufficient. Whether he works with limbs or brain, man must have some other aim than that of gaining his bread, making a fortune, or becoming famous. Those who confine themselves to such aims feel, even when they have gained their object, that something is still lacking, for no matter what we may say or what we may be told, man has not only a body to be nourished, an intelligence to be cultivated and developed, but also assuredly a soul to be satisfied. That soul, too, is incessantly at work, ever evolving towards light and truth. And as long as it has not reached full light and conquered the whole truth it will continue to torment man.

'Well! The soul never so harassed man, never so dominated him, as it does to-day. It is as though it were in the air we all breathe. The few isolated souls that had separately desired the regeneration of society have little by little sought one another out, beckoned one another, drawn nearer, united, comprehended one another, and formed a group, a centre of attraction, towards which others now fly from the four quarters of the globe like larks towards a mirror. They have as it were formed one collective soul, so that men in future may realize together, consciously and irresistibly, the approaching union and steady progress of nations that were but recently hostile to one another. This new soul I find and recognize in events seemingly most calculated to deny it.

'These armaments of all nations, these threats their representatives address to one another, this recrudescence of race persecutions, these hostilities among compatriots, and even these youthful escapades at the Sorbonne, are all things of evil aspect but not of evil augury. They are the last convulsions of that which is about to disappear. The social body is like the human body. Disease is but a violent effort of the organism to throw off a morbid and harmful element.

'Those who have profited, and expect for long or for ever to continue to profit by the mistakes of the past, are uniting to prevent any modification of existing conditions. Hence these armaments and threats and persecutions; but look carefully and you will see that all this is quite superficial. It is colossal but hollow. There is no longer any soul in it—the soul has gone elsewhere; these millions of armed men who are daily drilled to prepare for a general war of extermination no longer hate the men they are expected to fight, and none of their leaders dares to proclaim this war. As for the appeals, and even the threatening claims, that rise from the suffering and the oppressed—a great and sincere pity, recognizing their justice, begins at last to respond from above.

'Agreement is inevitable, and will come at an appointed time, nearer than is expected. I know not if it be because I shall soon leave this earth and the rays that are already reaching me from below the horizon have disturbed my sight, but I believe our world is about to begin to realize the words, "Love one another," without however being concerned whether a man or a God uttered them.

'The spiritual movement one recognizes on all sides and which so many naive and ambitious men expect to be able to direct, will be absolutely humanitarian. Mankind, which does nothing moderately, is about to be seized with a frenzy, a madness, of love. This will not of course happen smoothly or all at once; it will involve misunderstandings—even sanguinary ones perchance—so trained and so accustomed have we been to hatred, sometimes even by those whose mission it was to teach us to love one another. But it is evident that this great law of brotherhood must be accomplished some day, and I am convinced that the time is commencing when our desire for its accomplishment will become irresistible.   A. DUMAS.

'*June 1, 1893.*'

There is a great difference between Dumas's letter and Zola's speech, not to mention the fact that Zola seems to court the approval of the youths he addresses, whereas Dumas's letter does not flatter them or tell them they are important people and that everything depends on them (which they should never believe if they wish to be good for anything); on the contrary, it points out to them their habitual faults: their presumption and their levity. The chief difference between these two writings consists in the fact that Zola's speech aims at keeping men in the path they are travelling, by making them believe that what they know is just what they need to know, and that what they are doing is just what they ought to be doing—whereas Dumas's letter shows them that they ignore what is essential for them to know and do *not* live as they ought to live.

The more fully men believe that humanity can be led in spite of itself to a beneficial change in its existence by some external self-acting force (whether religion or science)—and that they need only work in the established order of things—the more difficult will it be to accomplish any beneficial change, and it is chiefly in this respect that Zola's speech errs.

On the contrary, the more fully men believe that it depends on themselves to modify their mutual relations, and that they can do this when they like by loving each other instead of tearing each other to pieces as they do at present—the more possible will a change become. The more fully men let themselves be influenced by this suggestion the more will they be drawn to realize Dumas's prediction. That is the great merit of his letter.

Dumas belongs to no party and to no religion: he has as little faith in the superstitions of the past as in those of to-day, and that is why he observes and thinks and sees not only the present but the future —as those did who in ancient times were called *seers.* It will seem strange to those who in reading a writer's works see only the contents of the book and not the soul of the writer, that Dumas—the author of *La Dame aux Camélias*, and of *L'Affaire Clémenceau*—that this same Dumas should see into the future and should prophesy. But however strange it may seem, prophecy making itself heard not in the desert or on the banks of the Jordan from the mouth of a hermit clothed in skins of beasts — but published in a daily paper on the banks of the Seine, remains none the less prophecy.

And Dumas's letter has all the characteristics of prophecy: First, like all prophecy, it runs quite counter to the general disposition of the people among whom it makes itself heard; secondly, those who hear it feel its truth they know not why; and thirdly and chiefly it moves men to the realization of what it foretells.

Dumas predicts that after having tried everything else men will seriously apply to life the law of brotherly love, and that this change will take place much sooner than we expect. One may question the nearness of this change or even its possibility, but it is plain that should it take place it will solve all contradictions and all difficulties, and will divert all the evils with which the end of the century sees us threatened.

The only objection, or rather the only question, one can put to Dumas is this: 'If the love of one's neighbour is possible and is inherent in human nature, why have so many thousand years elapsed (for the command to love God and one's neighbour did not begin with Christ but had been given already by Moses) without men who knew this means of happiness having practised it? What prevents the manifestation of a sentiment so natural and so helpful to humanity? It is evidently not

NON-ACTING

enough to say, 'Love one another.' That has been said for three thousand years past: it is incessantly repeated from all pulpits, religious and even secular; yet, instead of loving one another as they have been bidden to do for so many centuries, men continue to exterminate each other just the same. In our day no one any longer doubts that if men would help one another instead of tearing one another to pieces—each seeking his own welfare, that of his family, or that of his country—if they would replace egotism by love, if they would organize their life on collectivist instead of individualist principles (as the socialists express it in their wretched jargon), if they loved one another as they love themselves, or if they even refrained from doing to others what they do not wish to have done to themselves (as has been well expressed for two thousand years past) the share of personal happiness gained by each man would be greater and human life in general would be reasonable and happy instead of being what it now is, a succession of contradictions and sufferings.

No one doubts that if men continue to snatch from one another the ownership of the soil and the products of their labour, the revenge of those who are deprived of the right to till the soil will not much longer be delayed, but the oppressed will retake with violence and vengeance all that of which they have been robbed. No one doubts that the arming of the nations will lead to terrible massacres and the ruin and degeneration of all the peoples enchained in the circle of armaments. No one doubts that if the present order of things continues for some dozens of years longer it will lead to a general breakdown. We have but to open our eyes to see the abyss towards which we are advancing. But the saying cited by Jesus seems realized among the men of to-day: they have ears that hear not, eyes that see not, and an intelligence that does not understand.

Men of our day continue to live as they have lived, and do not cease to do things that must inevitably lead to their destruction. Moreover, men of our world recognize if not the religious law of love at least the moral rule of that Christian principle: not to do to others what one does not wish done to oneself; but they do not practise it. Evidently there is some greater reason that prevents their doing what is to their advantage, what would save them from menacing dangers, and what is dictated by the law of their God and by their conscience. Must it be said that love applied to life is a chimera? If so, how is it that for so many centuries men have allowed themselves to be deceived by this unrealizable dream? It were time to see through it. But mankind can neither decide to follow the law of love in daily life nor to abandon the idea. How is this to be explained? What is the reason of this contradiction lasting through centuries? It is not that the men of our time neither wish to, nor can, do what is dictated alike by their good sense, by the dangers of their situation, and above all by the law of him whom they call God, and by their conscience—but it is because they act just as M. Zola advises: they are busy, they all labour at some work commenced long ago and in which it is impossible to pause to concentrate their thoughts or to consider what they ought to be. All the great revolutions in men's lives are made in thought. When a change takes place in man's thought, action follows the direction of thought as inevitably as a ship follows the direction given by its rudder.

IV

When he first preached, Jesus did not say, 'Love one another' (he taught love later on to his disciples—men who had understood his teaching), but he said what John the Baptist had preached before: repentance, μετάνοια—that is to say, a change in the conception of life. Μετανοεῖτε—change your view of life or you will all perish, said he. The meaning of your life cannot consist in the pursuit of your personal well-being, or in that of your family or of your nation, for such happiness can be obtained only at the expense of others. Realize that the meaning of your life can consist only in accomplishing the will of him that sent you into this life and who demands of you not the pursuit of your personal interests but the accomplishment of his aims—the establishment of the Kingdom of Heaven, as Jesus expressed it.

Μετανοεῖτε, said he, 1,900 years ago—change your way of understanding life, or you will all perish; and he continues to repeat this to-day by all the contradictions and woes of our time, which all come from the fact that men have not listened to him and have not accepted the understanding of life he offered them. Μετανοεῖτε, said he, or you will all perish, and the alternative remains the same to-day. The only difference is that now it is more pressing. If it were possible 2,000 years ago, in the time of the Roman Empire, in the days of Charles V, or even before the Revolution and the Napoleonic wars, not to see the vanity—I will even say the absurdity—of attempts made to obtain personal happiness, family happiness, or national happiness, by struggling against all those who sought the same personal, family, or national happiness—that illusion has become quite impossible in our time for anyone who will pause if but for a moment from his occupations, and will reflect on what he is, on what the world around him is, and on what he ought to be. So if I were called on to give one single piece of advice, the one I considered most useful for men of our century, I should say this to them: 'For God's sake pause a moment, cease your work, look around you, think of what you are and of what you ought to be—think of the ideal.'

M. Zola says that people should not look on high, or believe in a Higher Power, or exalt themselves to the ideal. Probably M. Zola understands by the word 'ideal' either the supernatural—that is to say, the theological rubbish about the Trinity, the Church, the Pope, &c.—or else the *unexplained*, as he calls the forces of the vast world in which we are plunged. And in that case men would do well to follow M. Zola's advice. But the fact is that the ideal is neither supernatural nor 'unexplained'. On the contrary the ideal is the most natural of things; I will not say it is the most 'explained', but it is that of which man is most sure.

An ideal in geometry is the perfectly straight line or the circle whose radii are all equal; in science it is exact truth; in morals it is perfect virtue. Though these things—the straight line, the exact truth, and perfect virtue—have never existed, they are not only more natural to us, more known and more explicable than all our other knowledge, but they are the only things we know truly and with complete certainty.

It is commonly said that reality is that which exists, or that only what exists is real. Just the contrary is the case: true reality, that which we really know, is what has never existed. The ideal is the only thing we know with certainty, and it has never existed. It is only thanks to the ideal that we know anything at all; and that is why the ideal alone can guide us in our lives either individually or collectively. The Christian ideal has stood before us for nineteen centuries. It shines to-day with such intensity that it needs great effort to avoid seeing that all our woes arise from the fact that we do not accept its guidance. But the more difficult it becomes to avoid seeing this, the more some people increase their efforts to persuade us to do as they do: to close our eyes in order not to see. To be quite sure to reach port, they say, the first thing to do is to throw the compass overboard and forge ahead. Men of our Christian world are like people who strain themselves in the effort to get rid of some object that spoils life for them, but who in their hurry have no time to agree, and all pull in different directions. It would be enough to-day for man to pause in his activity and to reflect—comparing the demands of his reason and his heart with the actual conditions of life—in order to perceive that his whole life and all his actions are in incessant and glaring contradiction to his reason and his heart. Ask each man of our time separately what are the moral bases of his conduct, and he will almost always tell you that they are the principles of Christianity or at least of justice. And in saying so he will be sincere. According to their consciences all men should live as Christians; but see how they behave: they behave like wild beasts. So that for the great majority of men in our Christian world the organization of their life corresponds not to their way of perceiving or feeling, but to certain forms once necessary for other people with quite different perceptions of life, and now existing merely because the constant bustle men live in allows them no time for reflection.

V

If in former times (when the evils produced by pagan life were not so evident, and especially when Christian principles were not yet so generally accepted) men were able conscientiously to uphold the servitude of the workers, the oppression of man by man, penal law, and, above all, war—it has now become quite impossible to explain the *raison d'être* of such institutions. In our time men may continue to live a pagan life but they cannot excuse it.

In order to change their way of living and feeling, men must first of all change their way of thinking; and that such a change may take place they must pause and attend to the things they ought to understand. To hear what is shouted to them by those who wish to save them, men who run towards a precipice singing must cease their clamour and must stop.

Let men of our Christian world only stop their work and reflect for a moment on their condition, and they will involuntarily be led to accept the conception of life given by Christianity—a conception so natural, so simple, and responding so completely to the needs of the mind and the heart of humanity that it will arise, almost of itself, in the understanding of anyone who has freed himself were it but for a moment from the entanglements in which he is held by the complications of work—his own and that of others.

The feast has been ready for nineteen centuries; but one will not come because he has just bought some land, another because he has married, a third because he has to try his oxen, a fourth because he is building a railway, a factory, is engaged on missionary service, is busy in Parliament, in a bank, or on some scientific, artistic, or literary work. During 2,000 years no one has had leisure to do what Jesus advised at the beginning of his ministry: to look round him, think of the results of his work, and ask himself: What am I? Why do I live? Is it possible that the power that has produced me, a reasoning being with a desire to love and be loved, has done this only to deceive me, so that having imagined the aim of life to be my personal well-being—that my life belonged to me and that I had the right to dispose of it, as well as of the lives of others, as seemed best to me—I come at last to the conviction that this well-being that I aimed at (personal, family, or national) cannot be attained, and that the more I strive to reach it the more I find myself in conflict with my reason and my wish to love and be loved, and the more I experience disenchantment and suffering?

Is it not more probable that, having come into the world not by my own will but by the will of him who sent me, my reason and my wish to love and be loved were given to guide me in doing that will?

Once this μετάνοια is accomplished in men's thought and the pagan and egotistic conception of life has been replaced by the Christian conception, the love of one's neighbour will become more natural than struggle and egotism now are. And once the love of one's neighbour becomes natural to man the new conditions of Christian life will come about spontaneously, just as the crystals begin to form in a liquid saturated with salt as soon as one ceases to stir it.

And for this to result, and that men may organize their life in conformity with their consciences, they need expend no positive effort; they need only pause in what they are now doing. If men spent but a hundredth part of the energy they now devote to material activities—disapproved of by their own consciences—to elucidating as completely as possible the demands of that conscience, expressing them clearly, spreading them abroad, and above all putting them in practice, the change which M. Dumas and all the prophets have foretold would be accomplished among us much sooner and more easily than we suppose, and men would acquire the good that Jesus promised them in his glad tidings: 'Seek the Kingdom of Heaven, and all these things shall be added unto you.'

[*August 9, o.s., 1893.*]

Tolstóy wrote this essay first in Russian, and then (after a misleading translation had appeared in France) in French also. The second version differed in arrangement from the first, and has, at Tolstóy's own request, been relied upon in preparing the present translation. In a few places, however—and especially by including Zola's speech and Dumas's letter in full—the earlier version has been followed.—A. M.

AFTERWORD TO AN ACCOUNT OF RELIEF TO THE FAMINE-STRICKEN IN THE GOVERNMENT OF TÚLA IN 1891 AND 1892

Our two years' experience in distributing among a suffering population contributions that passed through our hands have quite confirmed our long-established conviction that most of the want and destitution—and the suffering and grief that go with them—which we have tried almost in vain to counteract by external means in one small corner of Russia, has arisen not from some exceptional, temporary cause independent of us, but from general permanent causes quite dependent on us and consisting entirely in the antichristian, unbrotherly relations maintained by us educated people towards the poor simple labourers who constantly endure distress and want and the accompanying bitterness and suffering—things that have merely been more conspicuous than usual during the past two years. If this year we do not hear of want, cold, and hunger—of the dying-off by hundreds of thousands of adults worn out with overwork, and of underfed old people and children—this is not because these things will not occur, but only because we shall not see them—shall forget about them, shall assure ourselves that they do not exist, or that if they do they are inevitable and cannot be helped.

But such assurances are untrue: not only is it possible for these things not to exist, but they ought not to exist, and the time is coming when they will not exist—and that time is near.

However well the wine cup may seem to us to be hidden from the labouring classes—however artful, ancient, and generally accepted may be the excuses wherewith we justify our life of luxury amid a working folk who, crushed with toil and underfed, supply our luxury—the light is penetrating more and more into our relations with the people, and we shall soon appear in the shameful and dangerous position of a criminal whom the unexpected dawn of day exposes on the scene of his crime. If a dealer disposing of harmful or worthless goods among the working folk and trying to charge as much as possible —or disposing even of good and needful bread, but bread which he had bought cheap and was selling dear—could formerly have said he was serving the needs of the people by honest trade; or if a manufacturer of cotton prints, looking-glasses, cigarettes, spirits, or beer could say that he was feeding his workmen by giving them employment; or if an official receiving hundreds of pounds a year salary collected in taxes from the people's last pence, could assure himself that he was working for the people's good; or (a thing specially noticeable these last years in the famine-stricken districts) if formerly a landlord could say (to peasants who worked his land for less pay than would buy them bread, or to those who hired land of him at rack-rent) that by introducing improved methods of agriculture he was promoting the prosperity of the rural population: if all this were formerly possible, now at least, when people are dying of hunger for lack of bread amid wide acres belonging to landlords and planted with potatoes intended for distilling spirits or making starch—these things can no longer be said. It has become impossible, surrounded by people who are dying out for want of food and from excess of work, not to see that all we consume of the product of their work, on the one hand deprives them of what they need for food and on the other hand

AN AFTERWORD

increases the work which already taxes their strength to the utmost. Not to speak of the insensate luxury of parks, conservatories, and hunting, every glass of wine, every bit of sugar, butter, or meat is so much food taken from the people and so much labour added to their task.

We Russians are specially well situated for seeing our position clearly. I remember, long before these famine years, how a young and morally sensitive savant from Prague who visited me in the country in winter—on coming out of the hut of a comparatively well-to-do peasant at which we had called and in which, as everywhere, there was an overworked, prematurely aged woman in rags, a sick child who had ruptured itself while screaming, and, as everywhere in spring, a tethered calf and a ewe that had lambed, and dirt and damp, and foul air, and a dejected, careworn peasant—I remember how, on coming out of the hut, my young acquaintance began to say something to me, when suddenly his voice broke and he wept. For the first time, after some months spent in Moscow and Petersburg—where he had walked along asphalted pavements, past luxurious shops, from one rich house to another, and from one rich museum, library, or palace to other similar grand buildings—he saw for the first time those whose labour supplies all that luxury, and he was amazed and horrified. To him, in rich and educated Bohemia (as to every man of Western Europe, especially to a Swede, a Swiss, or a Belgian), it might seem (though incorrectly) that where comparative liberty exists—where education is general, where everyone has a chance to enter the ranks of the educated—luxury is a legitimate reward of labour and does not destroy human life. He might manage to forget the successive generations of men who mine the coal by the use of which most of the articles of our luxury are produced, he might forget—since they are out of sight—the men of other races in the colonies, who die out working to satisfy our whims; but we Russians cannot share such thoughts: the connexion between our luxury and the sufferings and deprivations of men of the same race as ourselves is too evident. We cannot avoid seeing the price paid in human lives for our comfort and our luxury.

For us the sun has risen and we cannot hide what is obvious. We can no longer hide behind government, behind the necessity of ruling the people, behind science, or art—said to be necessary for the people—or behind the sacred rights of property or the necessity of upholding the traditions of our forefathers, and so forth. The sun has risen, and these transparent veils no longer hide anything from anyone. Everyone sees and knows that those who serve the government do so not for the welfare of the people (who never asked for their service), but simply because they want their salaries; and that people engaged on science and art are so engaged not to enlighten the people but for pay and pensions: and that those who withhold land from the people and raise its price, do this not to maintain any sacred rights but to increase the incomes they require to satisfy their own caprices. To hide this and to lie is no longer possible.

Only two paths are open to the governing classes—the rich and the non-workers: one way is to repudiate not only Christianity in its true meaning, but humanitarianism, justice, and everything like them, and to say: 'I hold these privileges and advantages and come what may I mean to keep them. Whoever wishes to take them from me will have me to reckon with. The power is in my hands:

the soldiers, the gallows, the prisons, the scourge, and the courts.'

The other way is to confess our fault, to cease to lie, to repent, and to go to the assistance of the people not with words only, or—as has been done during these last two years—with pence that have first been wrung from them at the cost of pain and suffering, but by breaking down the artificial barrier existing between us and the working people and acknowledging them to be our brothers not in words but in deeds: altering our way of life, renouncing the advantages and privileges we possess, and, having renounced them, standing on an equal footing with the people, and together with them obtaining those blessings of government, science, and civilization which we now seek to supply them with from outside without consulting their wishes.

We stand at the parting of the ways and a choice must be made.

The first path involves condemning oneself to perpetual falsehood, to continual fear that our lies may be exposed, and to the consciousness that sooner or later we shall inevitably be ousted from the position to which we have so obstinately clung.

The second path involves the voluntary acceptance and practice of what we already profess and of what is demanded by our heart and our reason—of what sooner or later will be accomplished if not by us then by others—for in this renunciation of their power by the powerful lies the only possible escape from the ills our pseudo-Christian world is enduring. Escape lies only through the renunciation of a false and the confession of a true Christianity.

[*October 28, o.s., 1893.*]

This *Afterword*, written by Tolstóy as a conclusion to his *Account* relating to the famine of 1891 and 1892, was suppressed in Russia at that time.—A. M.

MODERN SCIENCE[1]

παντὶ λόγῳ λόγος ἴσος ἀντίκειται.[2]

I THINK this article of Carpenter's on Modern Science should be particularly useful in Russian society, where more than anywhere else in Europe, there is a prevalent and deeply rooted superstition which considers that humanity does not need the diffusion of true religious and moral knowledge for its welfare, but only the study of experimental science, and that such science will satisfy all the spiritual demands of mankind.

It is evident how harmful an influence (quite like that of religious superstition) so gross a superstition must have on man's moral life. And therefore the publication of the thoughts of writers who treat experimental science and its method critically is specially desirable in our society.

Carpenter shows that neither astronomy, nor physics, nor chemistry, nor biology, nor sociology supplies us with true knowledge of actual facts; that all the laws discovered by those sciences are merely generalizations having but an approximate value as laws, and *that* only as long as we do not know, or leave out of account, certain other factors; and that even these laws seem laws to us only because we discover them in a region so far away from us in time and space that we cannot detect their non-correspondence with actual fact.

Moreover Carpenter points out that the method of science which consists in explaining things near

[1] Written as preface to a Russian translation, by Count Sergius Tolstóy, of Edward Carpenter's essay, *Modern Science: a Criticism*, which forms part of *Civilization: its Cause and Cure*.—A. M.

[2] To every argument an equal argument is matched.

and important to us by things more remote and indifferent, is a false method which can never bring us to the desired result.

He says that every science tries to explain the facts it is investigating by means of conceptions of a lower order. 'Each science has been as far as possible reduced to its lowest terms. Ethics has been made a question of utility and inherited experience. Political economy has been exhausted of all conceptions of justice between man and man, of charity, affection, and the instinct of solidarity, and has been founded on its lowest discoverable factor, namely, self-interest. Biology has been denuded of the force of personality in plants, animals, and men; the "self" here has been set aside and an attempt made to reduce the science to a question of chemical and cellular affinities, protoplasm, and the laws of osmose. Chemical affinities again, and all the wonderful phenomena of physics are reduced to a flight of atoms; and the flight of atoms (and of astronomic orbs as well) is reduced to the laws of dynamics.'

It is supposed that the reduction of questions of a higher order to questions of a lower order will explain the former. But an explanation is never obtained in this way. What happens is merely that, descending ever lower and lower in one's investigations, from the most important questions to less important ones, science reaches at last a sphere quite foreign to man, with which he is barely in touch, and confines its attention to that sphere, leaving all unsolved the questions most important to him.

It is as if a man, wishing to understand the use of an object lying before him—instead of coming close to it, examining it from all sides and handling it—were to retire farther and farther from it until he was at such a distance that all its peculiarities of colour and inequalities of surface had disappeared and only its outline was still visible against the horizon; and as if from there he were to begin writing a minute description of the object, imagining that now at last he clearly understood it, and that this understanding, formed at such a distance, would assist a complete comprehension of it. It is this self-deception that is partly exposed by Carpenter's criticism, which shows first that the knowledge afforded us by the natural sciences amounts merely to convenient generalizations which certainly do not express actual facts; and secondly that facts of a higher order will never be explained by reducing them to facts of a lower order.

But without predetermining the question whether experimental science will, or will not, by its methods, ever bring us to the solution of the most serious problems of human life, the activity of experimental science itself, in its relation to the eternal and most reasonable demands of man, is so anomalous as to be amazing.

People must live. But in order to live they must know how to live. And men have always obtained this knowledge—well or ill—and in conformity with it have lived and progressed. And this knowledge of how men should live has—from the days of Moses, Solon, and Confucius—always been considered a science, the very essence of science. Only in our time has it come to be considered that the science telling us how to live is not a science at all, but that the only real science is experimental science —commencing with mathematics and ending in sociology.

And a strange misunderstanding results.

A plain reasonable working man supposes, in the

old way which is also the common-sense way, that if there are people who spend their lives in study, whom he feeds and keeps while they think for him—then no doubt these men are engaged in studying things men need to know; and he expects science to solve for him the questions on which his welfare and that of all men depends. He expects science to tell him how he ought to live: how to treat his family, his neighbours and the men of other tribes, how to restrain his passions, what to believe in and what not to believe in, and much else. But what does our science say to him on these matters?

It triumphantly tells him how many million miles it is from the earth to the sun; at what rate light travels through space; how many million vibrations of ether per second are caused by light, and how many vibrations of air by sound; it tells of the chemical components of the Milky Way, of a new element—helium—of micro-organisms and their excrements, of the points on the hand at which electricity collects, of X-rays, and similar things.

'But I don't want any of those things,' says a plain and reasonable man—'I want to know how to live.'

'What does it matter what you want?' replies science. 'What you are asking about relates to sociology. Before replying to sociological questions, we have yet to solve questions of zoology, botany, physiology, and biology in general; but to solve those questions we have first to solve questions of physics, and then of chemistry, and have also to agree as to the shape of the infinitesimal atoms, and how it is that imponderable and incompressible ether transmits energy.'

And people—chiefly those who sit on the backs of others, and to whom it is therefore convenient to wait—are content with such replies, and sit blinking and awaiting the fulfilment of these promises; but plain and reasonable working men —such as those on whose backs these others sit while occupying themselves with science—the whole great mass of men, the whole of humanity, cannot be satisfied by such answers, but naturally ask in perplexity: 'But when will this be done? We cannot wait. You say that you will discover these things after some generations. But we are alive now—alive to-day and dead to-morrow—and we want to know how to live our life while we have it. So teach us!'

'What a stupid and ignorant man!' replies science. 'He does not understand that science exists not for use, but for *science*. Science studies whatever presents itself for study, and cannot select the subjects to be studied. Science studies *everything*. That is the characteristic of science.'

And scientists are really convinced that to be occupied with trifles, while neglecting what is more essential and important, is a characteristic not of themselves but of science. The plain, reasonable man, however, begins to suspect that this characteristic pertains not to science, but to men who are inclined to occupy themselves with trifles and to attach great importance to those trifles.

'Science studies *everything*,' say the scientists. But, really, *everything* is too much. Everything is an infinite quantity of objects; it is impossible at one and the same time to study *everything*. As a lantern cannot light up everything, but only lights up the place on which it is turned or the direction in which the man carrying it is walking, so also science cannot study everything, but inevitably only studies that to which its attention is directed. And as a lantern lights up most strongly the things nearest to it, and less and less strongly the things that are more and more remote from it, and does not light up at all those things beyond its reach, so also human science of whatever kind has always studied and still studies most carefully what seems most important to the investigators, less carefully what seems to them less important, and quite neglects the whole remaining infinite quantity of objects. And what has defined and still defines for men the subjects they are to consider most important, less important, and unimportant, is the general understanding of the meaning and purpose of life (that is to say, the religion) possessed by those who occupy themselves with science. But men of science to-day—not acknowledging any religion, and having therefore no standard by which to choose the subjects most important for study, or to discriminate them from less important subjects and, ultimately, from that infinite quantity of objects which the limitations of the human mind, and the infinity of the number of those objects, will always cause to remain uninvestigated—have formed for themselves a theory of 'science for science's sake', according to which science is to study not what mankind needs, but *everything*.

And indeed experimental science studies everything, not in the sense of the totality of objects, but in the sense of disorder—chaos in the arrangement of the objects studied. That is to say, science does not devote most attention to what people most need, less to what they need less, and none at all to what is quite useless; it studies anything that happens to come to hand. Though Comte's and other classifications of the sciences exist, these classifications do not govern the selection of subjects for study; that selection is dependent on the human weaknesses common to men of science as well as to the rest of mankind. So that in reality scientists do not study *everything*, as they imagine and declare; they study what is more profitable and easier to study. And it is more profitable to study things that conduce to the well-being of the upper classes, with whom the men of science are connected; and it is easier to study things that lack life. Accordingly, many men of science study books, monuments, and inanimate bodies.

Such study is considered the most real 'science'. So that in our day what is considered to be the most real 'science', the only one (as the Bible was considered the only book worthy of the name), is not the contemplation and investigation of how to make the life of man more kindly and more happy, but the compilation and copying from many books into one, of all that our predecessors wrote on a certain subject, the pouring of liquids out of one glass bottle into another, the skilful slicing of microscopic preparations, the cultivation of bacteria, the cutting up of frogs and dogs, the investigation of X-rays, the theory of numbers, the chemical composition of the stars, &c.

Meanwhile all those sciences which aim at making human life kindlier and happier—religious, moral, and social science—are considered by the dominant science to be unscientific, and are abandoned to the theologians, philosophers, jurists, historians, and political economists, who under the guise of scientific investigation are chiefly occupied in demonstrating that the existing order of society (the advantages of which they enjoy) is the very one which ought to exist, and that therefore it must not only not be changed, but must be maintained by all means.

Not to mention theology and jurisprudence, political economy—the most advanced of the sciences of this group—is remarkable in this respect. The most prevalent political economy (that of Karl Marx),[1] accepting the existing order of life as though it were what it ought to be, not only does not call on men to alter that order—that is to say, does not point out to them how they ought to live that their condition may improve—but on the contrary demands an increase in the cruelty of the existing order of things, that its more-than-questionable predictions concerning what will happen if people continue to live as badly as they are now living may be fulfilled.

And as always occurs, the lower a human activity descends—the more widely it diverges from what it should be—the more its self-confidence increases. That is just what has happened with the science of to-day. True science is never appreciated by its contemporaries, but on the contrary is usually persecuted. Nor can this be otherwise. True science shows men their mistakes, and points to new, unaccustomed ways of life. And both these services are unpleasant to the ruling section of society. But present-day science not only does not run counter to the tastes and demands of the ruling section of society; it quite complies with them. It satisfies idle curiosity, excites people's wonder, and promises them increase of pleasure. And so, whereas all that is truly great is calm, modest, and unnoticed, the science of to-day knows no limits to its self-laudation.

'All former methods were erroneous, and all that

[1] From the Marxian point of view improvement can be inflicted on a people by external pressure, and there are witnesses to say that this has been accomplished in Russia. But it remains to be proved whether mankind can be made better or happier without freedom of thought or a religious understanding of life. 'For the things which are seen are temporal, but the things that are not seen are eternal.'—A. M.

used to be considered science was an imposture, a blunder, and of no account. Only our method is true, and the only true science is ours. The success of our science is such that thousands of years have not done what we have accomplished in the last century. In the future, travelling the same path, our science will solve all questions and make all mankind happy. Our science is the most important activity in the world, and we men of science are the most important and necessary people in the world.'

So think and say the scientists of to-day, and the cultured crowd echo it, but really at no previous time and among no people has science—the whole of science with all its knowledge—stood on so low a level as at present. One part of it, which should study the things that make human life kind and happy, is occupied in justifying the existing evil order of society; another part is engaged in solving questions of idle curiosity.

'What?—Idle curiosity?' I hear voices ask in indignation at such blasphemy. 'What about steam and electricity and telephones, and all our technical improvements? Not to speak of their scientific importance, see what practical results they have produced! Man has conquered Nature and subjugated its forces' . . . with more to the same effect.

'But all the practical results of the victories over Nature have till now—for a considerable time past—gone to factories that injure the workmen's health, have produced weapons to kill men with, and increased luxury and corruption'—replies a plain, reasonable man—'and therefore the victory of man over Nature has not only failed to increase the welfare of human beings, but has on the contrary made their condition worse.'

If the arrangement of society is bad (as ours is), and a small number of people have power over the majority and oppress it, every victory over Nature will inevitably serve only to increase that power and that oppression. That is what is actually happening.

With a science which aims not at studying how people ought to live, but at studying whatever exists—and which is therefore occupied chiefly in investigating inanimate things while allowing the order of human society to remain as it is—no improvements, no victories over Nature, can better the state of humanity.

'But medical science? You are forgetting the beneficent progress made by medicine. And bacteriological inoculations? And recent surgical operations?' exclaim the defenders of science—adducing as a last resource the success of medical science to prove the utility of all science. 'By inoculations we can prevent illness, or can cure it; we can perform painless operations: cut open a man's inside and clean it out, and can straighten hunchbacks,' is what is usually said by the defenders of present-day science, who seem to think that the curing of one child from diphtheria, among those Russian children of whom 50 per cent. (and even 80 per cent. in the Foundling Hospitals) die as a regular thing apart from diphtheria—must convince anyone of the beneficence of science in general.

Our life is so arranged that not children only but a majority of people die from bad food, excessive and harmful work, bad dwellings and clothes, or want, before they have lived half the years that should be theirs. The order of things is such that children's illnesses, consumption, syphilis, and alcoholism, seize an ever-increasing number of victims, while a great part of men's labour is taken from them to prepare for wars, and every ten or twenty years millions of men are slaughtered in wars; and all this because science, instead of supplying correct religious, moral, and social ideas which would cause these ills to disappear of themselves, is occupied on the one hand in justifying the existing order, and on the other hand with toys. And in proof of the fruitfulness of science we are told that it cures one in a thousand of the sick, who are sick only because science has neglected its proper business.

Yes, if science would devote but a small part of those efforts and that attention and labour which it now spends on trifles, to supplying men with correct religious, moral, social, or even hygienic ideas, there would not be a one-hundredth part of the diphtheria, the diseases of the womb, or the deformities, the occasional cure of which now makes science so proud, though such cures are effected in clinical hospitals the cost of whose luxurious appointments is too great for them to be at the service of all who need them.

It is as though men who had ploughed badly, and sown badly with poor seeds, were to go over the ground tending some broken ears of corn and trampling on others that grew alongside, and were then to exhibit their skill in healing the injured ears as a proof of their knowledge of agriculture.

Our science, in order to become science and to be really useful and not harmful to humanity, must first of all renounce its experimental method, which causes it to consider as its duty the study merely of what exists, and must return to the only reasonable and fruitful conception of science, which is that the object of science is to show how people ought to live. Therein lies the aim and importance of science; and the study of things as they exist can only be a subject for science in so far as that study helps towards the knowledge of how men should live.

It is just to the admission by experimental science of its own bankruptcy, and to the need of adopting another method, that Carpenter draws attention in this article.

[*1898.*]

Chapter XX of *What is Art?* forms a companion article to the above essay. They were both written at the same period and deal with the same topic.—A. M.

AN INTRODUCTION TO RUSKIN'S WORKS

JOHN RUSKIN is one of the most remarkable men not only of England and of our generation, but of all countries and times. He is one of those rare men who think with their hearts (*'les grandes pensées viennent du cœur'*), and so he thinks and says what he has himself seen and felt, and what everyone will think and say in the future.

Ruskin is recognized in England as a writer and art-critic, but he is not spoken of as a philosopher, political economist, and Christian moralist—just as Matthew Arnold and Henry George are not so spoken of either in England or America. Ruskin's power of thought and expression is, however, such that—in spite of the unanimous opposition he met with and still meets with, especially among the orthodox economists (even the most radical of them) who cannot but attack him since he destroys their teaching at its very roots—his fame grows and his thoughts penetrate among the public. Epigraphs of striking force taken from his works are to be found more and more often in English books.

[*1899.*]

LETTERS ON HENRY GEORGE

I

To T. M. Bóndarev, who had written from Siberia asking for information about the Single-Tax.

THIS is Henry George's plan:
The advantage and convenience of using land is not everywhere the same; there will always be many applicants for land that is fertile, well situated, or near a populous place; and the better and more profitable the land the more people will wish to have it. All such land should therefore be valued according to its advantages: the more profitable—dearer; the less profitable—cheaper. Land for which there are few applicants should not be valued at all, but allotted gratuitously to those who wish to work it themselves.

With such a valuation of the land—here in the Túla Government, for instance good arable land might be estimated at about 5 or 6 rubles[1] the desyatín;[2] kitchen-gardens in the villages at about 10 rubles the desyatín; meadows that are fertilized by spring floods at about 15 rubles, and so on. In towns the valuation would be 100 to 500 rubles the desyatín, and in crowded parts of Moscow or Petersburg, or at the landing-places of navigable rivers, it would amount to several thousands or even tens of thousands of rubles the desyatín.

When all the land in the country has been valued in this way, Henry George proposes that a law should be made by which, after a certain date in a certain year, the land should no longer belong to any one individual, but to the whole nation—

---
[1] The ruble was then a little more than 25 pence.
[2] The desyatín is nearly 2¾ acres.

the whole people; and that everyone holding land should therefore pay to the nation (that is, to the whole people) the yearly value at which it has been assessed. This payment should be used to meet all public or national expenses, and should replace all other rates, taxes, or customs dues.

The result of this would be that a landed proprietor who now holds, say, 2,000 desyatíns, might continue to hold them if he liked, but he would have to pay to the treasury—here in the Túla Government for instance (as his holding would include both meadow-land and homestead)—12,000 or 15,000 rubles a year; and, as no large landowners could stand such a payment, they would all abandon their land. But it would mean that a Túla peasant in the same district would pay a couple of rubles per desyatín less than he pays now, and could have plenty of available land near by which he could take up at 5 or 6 rubles per desyatín. Besides this, he would have no other rates or taxes to pay, and would be able to buy all the things he requires, foreign or Russian, free of duty. In towns, the owners of houses and factories might continue to own them, but would have to pay to the public treasury the amount of the assessment on their land.

The advantages of such an arrangement would be:

1. That no one would be unable to get land for use.

2. That there would be no idle people owning land and making others work for them in return for permission to use that land.

3. That the land would be in the possession of those who use it, and not of those who do not use it.

4. That as the land would be available for people who wished to work on it, they would cease to

enslave themselves as hands in factories and workshops, or as servants in towns, and would settle in the country districts.

5. That there would be no more inspectors and collectors of taxes in mills, factories, refineries, and workshops, but there would only be collectors of the tax on land, which cannot be stolen, and from which a tax can be most easily collected.

6 (and most important). That the non-workers would be saved from the sin of exploiting other people's labour (in doing which they are often not the guilty parties, for they have from childhood been educated in idleness and do not know how to work), and from the still greater sin of all kinds of shuffling and lying to justify themselves in committing that sin; and the workers would be saved from the temptation and sin of envying, condemning, and being exasperated with the non-workers, so that one cause of separation among men would be destroyed.

II

To a German Propagandist of Henry George's Views.

It is with particular pleasure that I hasten to answer your letter, and say that I have known of Henry George since the appearance of his *Social Problems*. I read that book and was struck by the justice of his main thought—by the exceptional manner (unparalleled in scientific literature), clear, popular, and forcible, in which he stated his case—and especially by (what is also exceptional in scientific literature) the Christian spirit that permeates the whole work. After reading it I went back to his earlier *Progress and Poverty*, and still more deeply appreciated the importance of its author's activity.

You ask what I think of Henry George's activity, and of his system of Taxation of Land Values. My opinion is this:

Humanity constantly advances: on the one hand elucidating its consciousness and conscience, and on the other hand rearranging its modes of life to suit this changing consciousness. Thus at each period of the life of humanity the double process goes on: the clearing up of conscience, and the incorporation into life of what has been made clear to conscience.

At the end of the eighteenth century and the beginning of the nineteenth, a clearing up of consciences took place in Christendom with reference to the labouring classes, who lived under various forms of slavery, and this was followed by a corresponding readjustment of the forms of social life to match this clearer consciousness. Slavery was abolished, and free wage-labour took its place. At the present time an enlightenment of man's conscience in relation to the way land is used is going on, and it seems to me a practical application of this new consciousness must soon follow.

And in this process (the enlightenment of conscience as to the utilization of land, and the practical application of that new consciousness), which is one of the chief problems of our time, the leader and organizer of the movement was and is Henry George. In this lies his immense, his pre-eminent, importance. By his excellent books he has helped both to clear men's minds and consciences on this question, and to place it on a practical footing.

But in relation to the abolition of the shameful right to own landed estates, something is occurring similar to what happened within our own recollection with reference to the abolition of serfdom. The government and the governing classes—

knowing that their position and privileges are bound up with the land question—pretend that they are preoccupied with the welfare of the people, organizing savings banks for workmen, factory inspection, income taxes, even eight-hour working days—and carefully ignore the land question, or even (aided by compliant science, which will demonstrate anything they like) declare that the expropriation of the land is useless, harmful, and impossible.

Just the same thing occurs as occurred in connexion with slavery. At the end of the eighteenth and the beginning of the nineteenth centuries, men had long felt that slavery was a terrible anachronism, revolting to the human soul; but pseudo-religion and pseudo-science demonstrated that slavery was not wrong and that it was necessary, or at least that it was premature to abolish it. The same thing is now being repeated with reference to landed property. As before, pseudo-religion and pseudo-science demonstrate that there is nothing wrong in the private ownership of landed estates, and that there is no need to abolish the present system.

One would think it should be plain to every educated man of our time that an exclusive control of land by people who do not work on it, but who prevent hundreds and thousands of poor families from using it, is a thing as plainly bad and shameful as it was to own slaves; yet we see educated, refined aristocrats—English, Austrian, Prussian, and Russian—making use of this cruel and shameful right, and not only not feeling ashamed but feeling proud of it.

Religion blesses such possessions, and the science of political economy demonstrates that the present state of things is the one that should exist for the greatest benefit of mankind.

The service rendered by Henry George is that he has not only mastered the sophistries by which religion and science try to justify private ownership of land, and simplified the question to the uttermost so that it is impossible not to admit the wrongfulness of land-ownership unless one simply stops one's ears, but he was also the first to show how the question can be solved in a practical way. He first gave a clear and direct reply to those excuses used by the enemies of every reform, to the effect that the demands of progress are unpractical and inapplicable dreams.

Henry George's plan destroys that excuse by putting the question in such a form that a committee might be assembled to-morrow to discuss the project and convert it into law. In Russia, for instance, the discussion of land purchase, or of nationalizing the land without compensation, could begin to-morrow, and the project might after undergoing various vicissitudes be put into operation, as occurred thirty-three years ago[1] with the project for the emancipation of the serfs.

The need of altering the present system has been explained, and the possibility of the change has been shown (there may be alterations and amendments of the Single-Tax system, but its fundamental idea is practicable); and therefore it will be impossible for people not to do what their reason demands. It is only necessary that this thought should become public opinion; and in order that it may become public opinion it must be spread abroad and explained. This is just what you are doing, and it is a work with which I sympathize with my whole soul and in which I wish you success.

[*1897.*]

[1] The Emancipation of the Serfs in Russia was decreed in 1861, and was carried out during the following few years.—A. M.

'THOU SHALT NOT KILL'

'Thou shalt not kill.' EXOD. xx. 13.
'The disciple is not above his master: but every one when he is perfected shall be as his master.' LUKE vi. 40.
'For all they that take the sword shall perish with the sword.' MATT. xxvi. 52.
'Therefore all things whatsoever ye would that men should do to you, do ye even so to them.' MATT. vii. 12.

WHEN Kings are executed after trial, as in the case of Charles I, Louis XVI, and Maximilian of Mexico; or when they are killed in Court conspiracies, like Peter III, Paul, and various Sultans, Shahs, and Khans—little is said about it. But when they are killed without a trial and without a Court conspiracy—as in the case of Henry IV of France, Alexander II, the Empress of Austria, the late Shah of Persia, and, recently, Humbert—such murders excite the greatest surprise and indignation among Kings and Emperors and their adherents, just as if they themselves never took part in murders, or profited by them, or instigated them. But in fact the mildest of the murdered Kings (Alexander II or Humbert, for instance), were instigators of and accomplices and partakers in the murder of tens of thousands of men who perished on the field of battle, not to speak of executions in their own countries; while more cruel Kings and Emperors have been guilty of hundreds of thousands, and even millions, of murders.

The teaching of Christ repeals the law, 'An eye for an eye, and a tooth for a tooth'; but those who have always clung to that law, and still cling to it, and who apply it to a terrible degree—not only claiming an eye for an eye, but without provocation decreeing the slaughter of thousands, as they do when they declare war—have no right to be indignant at the application of that same law to themselves in so small and insignificant a degree that hardly one King or Emperor is killed for each hundred thousand, or perhaps even for each million, who are killed by the order and with the consent of Kings and Emperors. Kings and Emperors not only should not be indignant at such murders as those of Alexander II and Humbert, but they should be surprised that such murders are so rare, considering the continual and universal example of murder that they give to mankind.

The crowd are so hypnotized that they do not understand the meaning of what is going on before their eyes. They see what constant care Kings, Emperors, and Presidents devote to their disciplined armies; they see the reviews, parades, and manœuvres the rulers hold, about which they boast to one another; and the people crowd to see their own brothers, dressed up in the bright clothes of fools, turned into machines to the sound of drum and trumpet, and all making one and the same movement at one and the same moment at the shout of one man—but they do not understand what it all means. Yet the meaning of this drilling is very clear and simple: it is nothing but a preparation for killing.

It is stupefying men in order to make them fit instruments for murder. And those who do this, who chiefly direct it and are proud of it, are the Kings, Emperors, and Presidents. And it is just these men—who are specially occupied in organizing murder and who have made murder their profession, who wear military uniforms and carry murderous weapons (swords) at their sides—who are horrified and indignant when one of themselves is murdered.

The murder of Kings—the murder of Humbert—

is terrible, but not on account of its cruelty. The things done by command of Kings and Emperors—not only past events such as the massacre of St. Bartholomew, religious butcheries, the terrible repressions of peasant rebellions, and Paris *coups d'état*, but the present-day government executions, the doing-to-death of prisoners in solitary confinement, the Disciplinary Battalions, the hangings, the beheadings, the shootings and slaughter in wars—are incomparably more cruel than the murders committed by Anarchists. Nor are these murders terrible because undeserved. If Alexander II and Humbert did not deserve death, still less did the thousands of Russians who perished at Plevna, or of Italians who perished in Abyssinia.[1] Such murders are terrible not because they are cruel or unmerited, but because of the unreasonableness of those who commit them.

If the regicides act under the influence of personal feelings of indignation evoked by the sufferings of an oppressed people for which they hold Alexander or Carnot or Humbert responsible, or if they act from personal feelings of revenge, then however immoral their conduct may be it is at least intelligible. But how is it that a body of men (Anarchists, we are told) such as those by whom Bresci was sent, and who are now threatening another Emperor—how is it that they cannot devise any better means of improving the condition of humanity than by killing people whose destruction can be of no more use than the decapitation of that mythical monster on whose neck a new head appeared as soon as one was cut off? Kings and Emperors have long ago arranged for themselves a system like that of a magazine-rifle: as soon as one bullet has been discharged another takes its

[1] In the war of 1896.—A. M.

place. *Le roi est mort, vive le roi!* So what is the use of killing them?

Only on a most superficial view can the killing of these men seem a means of saving the nations from oppression and from wars destructive of human life.

One only need remember that similar oppressions and similar wars went on no matter who was at the head of the government—Nicholas or Alexander, Frederick or Wilhelm, Napoleon or Louis, Palmerston or Gladstone, McKinley or anyone else—in order to understand that it is not any particular person who causes these oppressions and these wars from which the nations suffer. The misery of nations is caused not by particular persons but by the particular order of society under which the people are so tied up together that they find themselves all in the power of a few men, or more often in the power of one single man: a man so perverted by his unnatural position as arbiter of the fate and lives of millions, that he is always in an unhealthy state, and always suffers more or less from a mania of self-aggrandizement, which only his exceptional position conceals from general notice.

Apart from the fact that such men are surrounded from earliest childhood to the grave by the most insensate luxury and an atmosphere of falsehood and flattery which always accompanies them, their whole education and all their occupations are centred on one object: learning about former murders, the best present-day ways of murdering, and the best preparations for future murder. From childhood they learn about killing in all its possible forms. They always carry about with them murderous weapons—swords or sabres; they dress themselves in various uniforms; they attend parades, reviews, and manœuvres; they visit one another, presenting one another with Orders and nominating one another to the command of regiments—and not only does no one tell them plainly what they are doing, or say that to busy oneself with preparations for killing is revolting and criminal, but from all sides they hear nothing but approval and enthusiasm for all this activity of theirs. Every time they go out, and at each parade and review, crowds of people flock to greet them with enthusiasm, and it seems to them as if the whole nation approves of their conduct. The only part of the Press that reaches them, and that seems to them the expression of the feelings of the whole people, or at least of its best representatives, most slavishly extols their every word and action, however silly or wicked they may be. Those around them, men and women, clergy and laity—all people who do not prize human dignity—vying with one another in refined flattery, agree with them about anything and deceive them about everything, making it impossible for them to see life as it is. Such rulers might live a hundred years without ever seeing one single really independent man or ever hearing the truth spoken. One is sometimes appalled to hear of the words and deeds of these men; but one need only consider their position in order to understand that anyone in their place would act as they do. If a reasonable man found himself in their place there is only one reasonable action he could perform, and that would be to get away from such a position. Anyone remaining in it would behave as they do.

What indeed must go on in the head of some Wilhelm of Germany—a narrow-minded, ill-educated, vain man, with the ideals of a German Junker—when nothing he can say, however stupid or horrid, will not be met by an enthusiastic *'Hoch!'* and be commented on by the Press of the entire world as though it were something highly important. When he says that at his word soldiers should be ready to kill their own fathers, people shout 'Hurrah!' When he says that the Gospel must be introduced with an iron fist—'Hurrah!' When he says the army is to take no prisoners in China but to slaughter everybody, he is not put into a lunatic asylum but people shout 'Hurrah!' and set sail for China to execute his commands. Or Nicholas II (a man naturally modest) begins his reign by announcing to venerable old men who had expressed a wish to be allowed to discuss their own affairs that such ideas of self-government were 'insensate dreams'—and the organs of the Press he sees and the people he meets praise him for it. He proposes a childish, silly, and hypocritical project of universal peace while at the same time ordering an increase in the army—and there are no limits to the laudations of his wisdom and virtue. Without any need, he foolishly and mercilessly insults and oppresses a whole nation, the Finns, and again he hears nothing but praise. Finally, he arranges the Chinese slaughter— terrible in its injustice, cruelty, and incompatibility with his peace projects—and people applaud him from all sides, both as a victor and as a continuer of his father's peace policy.

What indeed must be going on in the heads and hearts of these men?

So it is not the Alexanders and Humberts, nor the Wilhelms, Nicholases, and Chamberlains[1]— though they decree these oppressions of the nations

[1] In Russia and indeed generally throughout Europe Chamberlain was considered responsible for the Boer War.— A. M.

and these wars—who are really most guilty of these sins; it is rather those who place and support them in the position of arbiters over the lives of their fellow men. And therefore the thing to do is not to kill the Alexanders, Nicholases, Wilhelms, and Humberts, but to cease to support the arrangement of society of which they are a result. And the present order of society is supported by the selfishness and stupefaction of the people, who sell their freedom and honour for insignificant material advantages.

People who stand on the lowest rung of the ladder—partly as a result of being stupefied by a patriotic and pseudo-religious education and partly for the sake of personal advantages—cede their freedom and sense of human dignity at the bidding of these who stand above them and offer them material advantages. In the same way—in consequence of stupefaction, but chiefly for the sake of advantages—those who are a little higher up the ladder cede their freedom and manly dignity, and the same thing repeats itself with those standing yet higher, and so on to the topmost rung —to those who, or to him who, standing at the apex of the social cone have nothing more to obtain, for whom the only motives of action are love of power and vanity, and who are generally so perverted and stupefied by the power of life and death which they hold over their fellow men, and by the consequent servility and flattery of those who surround them, that without ceasing to do evil they feel quite assured that they are benefactors to the human race.

It is the people who sacrifice their dignity as men for material profit who produce these men who cannot act otherwise than as they do act, and with whom it is useless to be angry for their stupid and wicked actions. To kill such men is like whipping children whom one has first spoilt.

That nations should not be oppressed, and that there should be none of these useless wars, and that men should not be indignant with those who seem to cause these evils and should not kill them—it seems that only a very small thing is necessary. It is necessary that men should understand things as they are, should call them by their right names, and should know that an army is an instrument for killing, and that the enrolment and management of an army—the very things which Kings, Emperors, and Presidents occupy themselves with so self-confidently—is a preparation for murder.

If only each King, Emperor, and President understood that his work of directing armies is not an honourable and important duty, as his flatterers persuade him it is, but a bad and shameful act of preparation for murder—and if each private individual understood that the payment of taxes wherewith to hire and equip soldiers, and above all army service itself, are not matters of indifference, but are bad and shameful actions by which he not only permits but participates in murder—then this power of Emperors, Kings, and Presidents, which now arouses our indignation and which causes them to be murdered, would disappear of itself.

So the Alexanders, Carnots, Humberts, and others should not be murdered, but it should be explained to them that they are themselves murderers, and above all they should not be allowed to kill people: men should refuse to murder at their command.

If people do not yet act in this way it is only because governments, to maintain themselves, diligently exercise an hypnotic influence upon the people. And therefore we may help to prevent people killing either Kings or one another, not by killing—murder only increases the hypnotism—but by arousing people from their hypnotic condition.

And it is this I have tried to do by these remarks.

[*August 8, o.s., 1900.*]

Prohibited in Russia, an attempt was made to print this article in the Russian language in Germany; but the edition was seized in July, 1903, and after a trial in the Provincial Court of Leipzig (August, 1903) it was pronounced to be insulting to the German Kaiser, and all copies were ordered to be destroyed.—A. M.

BETHINK YOURSELVES!

(Concerning the Russo-Japanese War)

'This is your hour and the power of darkness.' LUKE xxii. 53.

... Your iniquities have separated between you and your God, and your sins have hid his face from you, and he will not hear. For your hands are defiled with blood, and your fingers with iniquity; your lips have spoken lies, your tongue muttereth wickedness. None sueth in righteousness, and none pleadeth in truth: they trust in vanity, and speak lies; they conceive mischief and bring forth iniquity . . . their works are works of iniquity, and the act of violence is in their hands. Their feet run to evil, and they make haste to shed innocent blood; their thoughts are thoughts of iniquity; desolation and destruction are in their paths. The way of peace they know not; and there is no judgement in their goings; they have made themselves crooked paths; whosoever goeth therein doth not know peace. Therefore is judgement far from us, neither doth righteousness overtake us: we look for light, but behold darkness, for brightness, but we walk in obscurity. We grope for the wall like the blind, yea, we grope as they that have no eyes: we stumble at noonday as in the twilight; among them that are lusty we are as dead men. ISAIAH lix. 2-11.

War is held in greater esteem than ever. A skilled proficient in this business, that murderer of genius, von Moltke, once replied to some Peace delegates in the following terrible words:

'War is sacred, it is instituted by God, it is one of the divine laws of the world, it upholds in men all the great and noble sentiments—honour, self-sacrifice, virtue, and courage. It is War alone that saves men from falling into the grossest materialism.'

To assemble four hundred thousand men in herds, to march night and day without rest, with no time to think, read, or study, without being of the least use to anybody, wallowing in filth, sleeping in the mud, living like animals in continual stupefaction, sacking towns, burning villages, ruining the whole population, and then meeting similar masses of human flesh and falling upon them, shedding rivers of blood, strewing the fields with mangled bodies mixed with mud and blood; losing arms and legs and having brains blown out for no benefit to anyone and dying somewhere on a field while your old parents and your wife and children are perishing of hunger—that is called saving men from falling into the grossest materialism! GUY DE MAUPASSANT.

We will content ourselves with reminding you that the different states of Europe have accumulated a debt of a hundred and thirty milliards (about a hundred and ten within the last century), and that this colossal debt has arisen almost exclusively from the expenses of war; that in time of peace they maintain standing armies of four million men, which they can increase to ten million in times of war;[1] that two-thirds of their budgets are absorbed by interest on these debts and by the maintenance of land and sea forces. G. DE MOLINARI.

Again there is war! Again there is needless and quite unnecessary suffering, together with fraud and a general stupefaction and brutalization of men.

Men who are separated from each other by thousands of miles—Buddhists whose law forbids the killing not only of men but even of animals, and Christians professing a law of brotherhood and love—hundreds of thousands of such men seek one another out on land and sea like wild beasts, to kill, torture, and mutilate one another in the cruellest possible way. Can this really be happening, or is it merely a dream? Something impossible and unbelievable is taking place, and one longs to believe that it is a dream and to awaken from it.

[1] Now, in 1936, these figures have enormously increased and continue to expand.—A. M.

But it is no dream. It is a dreadful reality.

It is understandable that a poor, uneducated Japanese who has been torn from his field and taught that Buddhism consists not in having compassion for all that lives, but in offering sacrifices to idols; and a similar poor illiterate fellow from the neighbourhood of Túla or Nízhni-Nóvgorod who has been taught that Christianity consists in bowing before icons of Christ, the Mother of God, and the Saints—it is understandable that these unfortunate men, taught by centuries of violence and deceit to regard the greatest crime in the world (the murder of their fellow men) as a noble deed, can commit these dreadful crimes without regarding themselves as guilty. But how can so-called enlightened men support war, preach it, participate in it, and, worst of all, without being exposed to its dangers themselves, incite their unfortunate, defrauded brothers to take part in it? For these so-called enlightened men cannot help knowing, I do not say the Christian law (if they recognize themselves to be Christians), but all that has been and is being written and said about the cruelty, futility, and senselessness of war. They are regarded as enlightened just because they know all this. Most of them have themselves written and spoken about it. Not to mention the Hague Conference which evoked universal praise, and all the books, pamphlets, newspaper articles, and speeches concerning the possibility of solving international misunderstandings by international courts—no enlightened man can help knowing that universal competition in the armaments of different states must inevitably result in endless wars and general bankruptcy, or in both of these together. They cannot help knowing that besides the insensate and useless expenditure of milliards of rubles (that is of human labour) on preparations for war, millions of the most energetic and vigorous men perish in wars at the time of their life best for productive labour. (During the past century fourteen million men have so perished.) Enlightened men cannot but know that the grounds of a war are never worth a single human life or a hundredth part of what is spent on it. (In fighting for the emancipation of the negroes much more was spent than would have bought all the slaves in the Southern States.)

Above all, everyone knows and cannot but know that wars evoke the lowest animal passions and deprave and brutalize men. Everyone knows how unconvincing are the arguments in favour of war (such as those brought forward by de Maistre,[1] von Moltke, and others)—all based on the sophistry that in every human calamity it is possible to find a useful side, or on the quite arbitrary assertion that as wars have always existed they must always exist—as if the evil actions of men can be justified by the advantages they bring or by the fact that they have long been committed. Every so-called enlightened man knows all this. But suddenly a war begins and it is all instantly forgotten, and the very men who only yesterday were proving the cruelty, futility, and senselessness of wars, now think, speak, and write only of how to kill as many men as possible, of how to ruin and destroy as much of the produce of human labour as possible, and how to inflame the passion of hatred to the utmost in those peaceful, harmless, industrious men who by their labour feed, clothe, and maintain the pseudo-enlightened men who force them to commit these dreadful deeds, contrary to their conscience, welfare, and faith.

[1] Joseph de Maistre, an ardent Roman Catholic who acted as Sardinian ambassador at Petersburg from 1803 to 1817.—A.M.

II

And Micromegas said:

'O intelligent atoms in whom the Eternal Being has been pleased to manifest his dexterity and his might, the joys you taste on your globe are doubtless very pure, for as you are so immaterial and seem to be all spirit, your lives must be passed in Love and in Thought: that indeed is the true life of spirits. Nowhere yet have I found real happiness, but that you have it here I cannot doubt.'

At these words all the philosophers shook their heads and one of them, more frank than the rest, candidly admitted that apart from a small number of people who were held in little esteem, the rest of the inhabitants of the world were a crowd of madmen, miscreants, and unfortunates. 'If evil be a property of matter,' he said, 'we have more matter than is necessary for the doing of much evil, and too much spirit if evil be a property of the spirit. Do you realize, for instance, that at this moment there are a hundred thousand madmen of our species wearing hats, killing or being killed by a hundred thousand other animals wearing turbans, and that over almost the whole face of the earth this has been the custom from time immemorial?'

The Sirian shuddered and asked what could be the ground for these horrible quarrels between such puny beasts.

'The matter at issue,' replied the philosopher, 'is some mud-heap as large as your heel. It is not that any single man of all these millions who slaughter each other claims one straw on the mud-heap. The point is—shall the mud-heap belong to a certain man called the "Sultan", or to another called, I know not why, "Caesar"? Neither of them has ever seen or will ever see the little bit of land in dispute, and barely one of these animals which slaughter each other has ever seen the animal for which he is slaughtered.'

'Wretches!' cried the Sirian indignantly. 'Such a riot of mad fury is inconceivable! I am tempted to take three steps and with three blows of my foot crush out of existence this ant-hill of absurd cut-throats.'

'Do not trouble,' answered the philosopher, 'they wreak their own ruin. Know that after ten years not a hundredth part of these miscreants is ever left. Know that even when they have not drawn the sword, hunger, exhaustion, or debauchery carries them nearly all off. Besides it is not they who should be punished, but the stay-at-home barbarians who, after a good meal, order from their remote closets the massacre of a million men, and then have solemn prayers of gratitude for the event offered up to God.'   VOLTAIRE, *Micromegas*, Ch. vii.

The folly of modern wars is excused on grounds of dynastic interests, nationality, European equilibrium, and honour. This last is perhaps the most extravagant excuse of all, for there is not a nation in the world that has not polluted itself by all sorts of crimes and shameful actions, nor is there one that has not experienced every possible humiliation. If indeed there still exists a sense of honour among nations, it is strange to support it by making war—that is, by committing all the crimes by which a private person dishonours himself: arson, rape, outrage, murder. . . .   ANATOLE FRANCE.

The savage instinct of murder-in-war has very deep roots in the human brain, because it has been carefully encouraged and cultivated for thousands of years. One likes to hope that a humanity superior to ours will succeed in correcting this original vice, but what will it then think of this civilization calling itself refined and of which we are so proud? Even as we now think of ancient Mexico and of its cannibalism, at one and the same time pious, warlike, and bestial.

CH. LETOURNEAU.

Sometimes out of fear one ruler attacks another in order that the latter should not fall upon him. Sometimes war is begun because the foe is too strong, and sometimes because he is too weak; sometimes our neighbours desire our possessions, or they possess what we want. Then begins war, which lasts until they seize what they may require or surrender the possession which is demanded by us.   JONATHAN SWIFT.

Something incomprehensible and impossible in its cruelty, falsehood, and stupidity is taking place. The Russian Tsar, the very man who summoned all the nations to peace,[1] publicly announces that despite his efforts to maintain the peace so dear to his heart (efforts expressed by the seizure of other peoples' lands, and the strengthening of the army for the defence of these stolen lands)—he is compelled in consequence of attacks by the Japanese to order the same to be done to them as they have begun doing to the Russians, that is, that they should be killed; and announcing this call to murder he mentions God, evoking a Divine blessing on the most dreadful crime in the world. The Japanese Emperor has proclaimed the same thing in regard to the Russians.

Learned jurists, Messieurs Muravèv and Martens, are assiduous in demonstrating that there is no contradiction at all between the former general call to universal peace and the present incitement to war, because other peoples' lands have been seized. Diplomatists publish and send out circulars in the refined French language, proving circumstantially and diligently (though they know that no one believes them) that after all its efforts to establish peaceful relations (in reality after all its efforts to deceive other countries) the Russian government has been compelled to have recourse to the only means for a rational solution of the question, that is, by the murder of men. And the same thing is written by the Japanese diplomatists. Learned men for their part, comparing the present with the past and deducing profound conclusions from these comparisons, argue interminably about the laws

[1] This refers to the Hague Conference of 1899, organized at the instance of Nicholas II, and aiming at an agreement not to increase the armed forces that then existed.—A. M.

of the movements of nations, about the relation of the yellow to the white race, and about Buddhism and Christianity, and on the basis of these deductions and reflections justify the slaughter of the yellow race by Christians. And in the same way the Japanese learned men and philosophers justify the slaughter of the white race. Journalists with unconcealed joy, trying to outdo one another and not stopping at any falsehood however impudent and transparent, prove in various ways that the Russians alone are right and strong and good in every respect, and that all the Japanese are wrong and weak and bad in every respect, and that all those who are inimical or who may become inimical towards the Russians (the English and the Americans) are bad too. And the Japanese and their supporters prove just the same regarding the Russians.

Quite apart from the military people whose profession it is to prepare for murder, crowds of supposedly enlightened people—professors, social reformers, students, gentry, and merchants—of their own accord express most bitter and contemptuous feelings towards the Japanese, the English, and the Americans, towards whom only yesterday they were well disposed or indifferent; and of their own accord express most abject and servile feelings towards the Tsar (to whom they are to say the least completely indifferent) assuring him of their unbounded love and readiness to sacrifice their lives for him.

And that unfortunate and entangled young man, acknowledged as ruler of a hundred and thirty million people, continually deceived and obliged to contradict himself, believes all this, and thanks and blesses for slaughter the troops he calls his, in defence of lands he has even less right to call his. They all present hideous icons to one another (in which no enlightened people now believe and which even uneducated peasants are beginning to abandon) and they all bow to the ground before these icons, kiss them, and pronounce pompous and false speeches which nobody believes.

Wealthy people contribute insignificant portions of their immorally acquired riches to this cause of murder, or to the organization of assistance in the work of murder, while the poor, from whom the government annually collects two milliards, deem it necessary to do likewise, offering their mites also. The government incites and encourages crowds of idlers who walk about the streets with the Tsar's portrait, singing and shouting hurrah and under pretext of patriotism committing all kinds of excesses. All over Russia from the capital to the remotest village the priests in the churches, calling themselves Christians, appeal to the God who enjoined love of one's enemies, the God of love, for help in the devil's work—the slaughter of men.

And stupefied by prayers, sermons, exhortations, processions, pictures, and newspapers, the cannon-fodder—hundreds of thousands of men dressed alike and carrying various lethal weapons—leave their parents, wives, and children, and with agony at heart but with a show of bravado, go where at the risk of their own lives they will commit the most dreadful action, killing men whom they do not know and who have done them no harm. And in their wake go doctors and nurses who for some reason suppose that they cannot serve the simple, peaceful, suffering people at home, but can serve only those who are engaged in slaughtering one another. Those who remain behind rejoice at the news of the murder of men, and when they learn that a great many Japanese have been killed they thank someone whom they call God.

And not only is all this considered a manifestation of elevated feeling, but those who refrain from such manifestations and attempt to bring people to reason are considered traitors and enemies to their nation, and are in danger of being abused and beaten by a brutalized crowd which possesses no other weapon but brute force in defence of its insanity and cruelty.

III

War organizes a body of men who lose the feelings of the citizen in the soldier; whose habits detach them from the community; whose ruling passion is devotion to a chief; who are inured in camp to despotic sway; who are accustomed to accomplish their ends by force and to sport with the rights and happiness of their fellow beings; who delight in tumult, adventure, and peril, and turn with disgust and scorn from the quiet labours of peace. . . . It (war) tends to multiply and perpetuate itself endlessly. The successful nation, flushed by victory, pants for new laurels, whilst the humbled nation, irritated by defeat, is impatient to redeem its honour and repair its losses. . . .

The slaughter of thousands of fellow beings instead of awakening pity flushes them with delirious joy, illuminates the city, and dissolves the whole country in revelry and riot. Thus the heart of man is hardened and his worst passions are nourished. He renounces the bonds and sympathies of humanity.   CHANNING.

The age for military service has arrived, and every young man has to submit to the arbitrary orders of some rascal or ignoramus; he must believe that nobility and greatness consist in renouncing his own will and becoming the tool of another's will, in slashing and in getting himself slashed, in suffering from hunger, thirst, rain, and cold; in being mutilated without knowing why and without any other reward than a glass of brandy on the day of battle and the promise of something impalpable and fictitious—immortality after death, and glory given or refused by the pen of some journalist in his warm room.

A gun is fired. He falls wounded, his comrades finish him off by trampling over him. He is buried half alive and then he may enjoy immortality. He for whom he had given his happiness, his sufferings, and his very life, never knew him. And years later someone comes to collect his whitened bones, out of which they make paint and English blacking for cleaning his General's boots.

ALPHONSE KARR.

They take a man in the bloom of his youth, they put a gun into his hands, a knapsack on his back, and a cockaded hat on his head, and then they say to him: 'My brother-ruler of so-and-so has treated me badly. You must attack his subjects. I have informed them that on such and such a date you will present yourselves at the frontier to slaughter them. . . .

'Perhaps at first you will think that our enemies are men; but they are not men, they are Prussians or Frenchmen. You will distinguish them from the human race by the colour of their uniform. Try to do your duty well, for I am looking on. If you gain the victory, they will bring you to the windows of my palace when you return. I will come down in full uniform and say: "Soldiers, I am satisfied!" . . . Should you remain on the battlefield (which may easily happen) I will communicate the news of your death to your family that they may mourn for you and inherit your share of things. If you lose an arm or a leg I will pay you what they are worth; but if you remain alive and are no longer fit to carry your knapsack I will dismiss you, and you can go and die where you like. That will no longer concern me.'

CLAUDE TILLIER.

But I learnt discipline, namely, that the corporal is always right when he addresses a private, the sergeant when he addresses a corporal, the sub-lieutenant when he addresses a sergeant-major, and so on up to the Field-Marshal—even should they say that twice two is five!

It is at first difficult to grasp this, but there is something which will help you to understand it. It is a notice stuck up in the barracks, and which is read to you from time to time in order to clear your ideas. This notice sets out all that a soldier may wish to do: to return to his village, to refuse to serve, to disobey his commander, and so on—and for all this the penalty is mentioned: capital punishment, or five years' penal servitude.

ERCKMANN-CHATRIAN.

I have bought a negro, he is mine. He works like a horse. I feed him badly, I clothe him similarly, he is beaten when he disobeys. Is there anything surprising in that? Do we treat our soldiers any better? Are they not deprived of liberty like this negro? The only difference is that the soldier costs much less. A good negro is now worth at least five hundred écus, a good soldier is hardly worth fifty. Neither the one nor the other may quit the place where he is confined. Both are beaten for the slightest fault. Their salary is about the same. But the negro has this advantage over the soldier: he does not risk his life but passes it with his wife and children.

Questions sur l'Encyclopédie, par des amateurs, Art. *Esclavage*.

It is as if neither Voltaire, nor Montaigne, nor Pascal, nor Swift, nor Kant, nor Spinoza, had ever existed, nor the hundreds of other writers who have very forcibly exposed the madness and futility of war, and described its cruelty, immorality, and savagery. Above all it is as if Jesus and his teaching of human brotherhood and love of God and man had never existed.

Recalling all this and looking around on what is happening now, one experiences horror less at the abominations of war than at that most horrible of all horrors, the consciousness of the impotence of human reason.

Reason, which alone distinguishes man from the brutes and constitutes his true dignity, is now regarded as an unnecessary, useless, and even pernicious attribute, which simply impedes action, like a bridle dangling from a horse's head, merely entangling his legs and irritating him.

It is understandable that a pagan, a Greek, a Roman, or even a medieval Christian ignorant of the Gospel and blindly believing all the prescriptions of the Church, might fight and while fighting pride himself on his military calling. But how can a believing Christian, or even a sceptic involuntarily permeated by the Christian ideals of human brotherhood and love which have inspired the works of the philosophers, moralists, and artists of our time—how can such a man take a gun or stand by a cannon and aim at a crowd of his fellow men, desiring to kill as many of them as possible?

The Assyrians, Romans, or Greeks might be convinced that when fighting they not only acted according to their conscience but even performed a good action. But we are Christians whether we wish it or not, and the general spirit of Christianity (however it may have been distorted) has lifted us to a higher plane of reason, whence we cannot but feel with our whole being not only the senselessness and cruelty of war but its complete contrast to all that we regard as good and right. And so we cannot quietly do as they did with assurance and firmness. We cannot do it without a consciousness of our criminality, without the desperate feeling of a murderer who having begun to kill his victim and aware in the depths of his soul of his guilt, tries to stupefy or infuriate himself in order to be able to complete his dreadful deed. All the unnatural, feverish, hot-headed, insane excitement that has now seized the idle upper ranks of Russian society, is merely a symptom of their consciousness of the criminality of what is being done. All these swaggering mendacious speeches about devotion to, and worship of, the monarch, all this readiness to sacrifice their lives (they should say other people's lives); all these promises to defend with their breasts land that does not belong to them; all these senseless blessings of one another with various banners and monstrous icons; all these Te Deums; all this preparation of blankets and bandages; all these detachments of nurses; all these contributions to the fleet and to the Red Cross presented to the government—whose direct duty it is, having declared war (and being able to collect as much money as it requires from the people), to organize the necessary fleet and necessary means for attending the wounded—all these pompous, senseless, and blasphemous Slavonic prayers, the utterance of which in various towns the papers report as important news; all these processions, calls for the national anthem, and shouts of hurrah; all this desperate newspaper mendacity which has no fear of exposure, because it is so general; all this stupefaction and brutalization in which Russian society is now plunged, and which is transmitted by degrees to the masses—all this is merely a symptom of the consciousness of guilt in the dreadful thing which is being done.

Spontaneous feeling tells men that what they are doing is wrong, but as a murderer who has begun to assassinate his victim cannot stop, so the fact of the deadly work having been begun seems to Russian people an unanswerable reason in its favour. War has begun, and so it must go on. So it seems to simple, benighted, unlearned men under the influence of the petty passions and stupefaction to which they have been subjected. And in the same way the most learned men of our time demonstrate that man has no free will, and that therefore, even if he understands that the thing he has begun is evil, he cannot stop doing it.

And so dazed and brutalized men continue the dreadful work.

IV

It is amazing to what an extent the most insignificant disagreement can become a sacred war, thanks to diplomacy and the newspapers. When England and France declared war on Russia in 1853 it came about from such insignificant reasons that a long search among the diplomatic archives is necessary to discover it. . . . The death of five hundred thousand good men, and the expenditure of from five to six milliards of money, were the consequences of that strange misunderstanding.

Motives existed. But they were such as were not acknowledged. Napoleon the Third wished by an alliance with England and a successful war to consolidate his power which was of criminal origin. The Russians hoped to obtain possession of Constantinople. The English wished to assure the triumph of their commerce, and to hinder Russian influence in the East. In one shape or another it is always the spirit of conquest or of violence.   CHARLES RICHET.

Can anything be stupider than that a man has the right to kill me because he lives on the other side of a river and his ruler has a quarrel with mine, though I have not quarrelled with him?   PASCAL.

The inhabitants of the planet Earth are still in such a ridiculous state of unintelligence and stupidity that we read every day in the newspapers of the civilized countries a discussion of the diplomatic relations of the chiefs of states aiming at an alliance against a supposed enemy and preparations for war, and that the nations allow their leaders to dispose of them like cattle led to the slaughter, as though never suspecting that the life of each man is his personal property.

The inhabitants of this singular planet have been reared in the conviction that there are nations, frontiers, and standards, and they have such a feeble sense of humanity that that feeling is completely effaced by the sense of the Fatherland. . . . It is true that if those who think could come to an agreement this situation would change, for individually no one desires war. . . . But there exist these political combinations which furnish livelihood for a legion of parasites. FLAMMARION.

When we study, not superficially but fundamentally, the various activities of mankind, we cannot avoid this sad reflection: How many lives are expended for the perpetuation of the power of evil on earth, and how this evil is promoted most of all by permanent armies.

Our astonishment and feeling of sadness increase when we consider that this is all unnecessary, and that this evil complacently accepted by the immense majority of men comes about merely through their stupidity in allowing a comparatively small number of agile and perverted people to exploit them. PATRICE LARROQUE.

Ask a soldier—a private, a corporal, or a non-commissioned officer—who has abandoned his old parents, his wife and children, why he is preparing to kill men he does not know, and he will at first be surprised at your question. He is a soldier, has taken the oath, and must fulfil the orders of his commanders. If you tell him that war, that is the slaughter of men, does not conform to the command 'Thou shalt not kill', he will say: 'But how if our people are attacked?' . . . 'For the Tsar and the Orthodox Faith!' (In answer to my question one of them said: 'But how if he attacks what is sacred?' 'What do you mean?' I asked. 'Why,' said he, 'the flag.') If you try to explain to such a soldier that God's command is more important than the flag, or than anything in the world, he will become silent or will get angry and report you to the authorities.

Ask an officer or a general why he goes to the war. He will tell you that he is a military man, and that military men are indispensable for the defence of the Fatherland. It does not trouble him that murder is not in agreement with the spirit of the Christian law, because he either does not believe in that law or, if he does, he does not believe in that law itself but in some explanation that has been given of it. Above all (like the soldier) he always puts a general question about the State or the Fatherland, instead of the personal question what he himself should do. 'At the present time when the Fatherland is in danger one must act and not argue,' he will say.

Ask the diplomatists who by their deceptions prepare wars why they do it? They will tell you that the object of their activity is the establishment of peace among nations, and that this object is attained not by ideal, unrealizable theories, but by diplomatic activity and being prepared for war. And just as military men put a general question instead of a personal one affecting their own life, so the diplomatists will speak of the interests of Russia, of the perfidy of other Powers, or of the balance of power in Europe, instead of about their own life and activity.

Ask journalists why they incite men to war by their writings. They will say that in general wars are necessary and useful, especially the present one, and they will confirm this by misty patriotic phrases, and (like the military men and the diplomatists) will talk about the general interests of the nation, the State, civilization, and the White Race, instead of saying why they themselves—particular individuals and living men—act in a certain way.

And all those who prepare war will explain their participation in that work in just the same way. They will perhaps agree that it would be desirable to abolish war, but at present, they say, that is impossible; at present—as Russians, and as men occupying certain positions: marshals of the gentry, members of local government, doctors, workers in the Red Cross—they are called on to act and not to argue. 'There is no time to argue and think about ourselves,' they will say, 'while there is a great common work to be done.'

The Tsar, apparently responsible for the whole affair, will say the same. Like the soldier he will be astonished at being asked whether war is now necessary. He does not even admit the idea that it might yet be stopped. He will say that he cannot fail to fulfil what is demanded of him by the whole nation, that—though he recognizes war to be a great evil and has used and is ready to use every possible means to abolish it—in the present case he could not help declaring war and cannot but go on with it. It is necessary for the welfare and glory of Russia.

Every one of these men, to the question why he, Iván, Peter, or Nicholas, recognizing the Christian law as binding on him—the law forbidding the killing of one's neighbour and demanding that one should love and serve him—permits himself to take part in war (that is in violence, loot, and murder) will always answer that he does so for his Fatherland or his faith or his oath or his honour or for civilization or for the future welfare of all mankind—in general for something abstract and indefinite. Moreover, all these men are always so urgently occupied, either by preparation for war or its organization or by discussions about it, that their leisure is taken up in resting from their labours, and they have no time for discussions about their life, and regard such discussions as idle.

V

The mind revolts at the inevitable catastrophe awaiting us, but it is necessary to prepare for it. For twenty years all the powers of knowledge have been exhausted in inventing engines of destruction, and soon a few cannon shots will suffice to destroy a whole army.

It is no longer as formerly a few thousand mercenary wretches who are under arms, but whole nations are preparing to kill one another. . . . And in order to fit them for murder their hatred is excited by assurances that they themselves are hated. And kind-hearted men will believe this, and peaceful citizens having received an absurd order to slay one another for God knows what ridiculous boundary incident or commercial colonial interests, will soon fling themselves at one another with the ferocity of wild beasts.

And they will go to the slaughter like sheep, but with a knowledge of where they are going, and that they are leaving their wives and that their children will be hungry. But they will be so deceived and inebriated by false, highflown words, that they will call on God to bless their bloody deeds. And they will go with enthusiastic songs, cries of joy and festive music, trampling down the harvest they have sown and burning towns they have built—go without indignation, humbly and submissively, despite the fact that the strength is theirs and that if they could only agree, they could establish common-sense and fraternity in place of the savage frauds of diplomacy. EDOUARD ROD.

An eye-witness relates what he saw when he stepped on to the deck of the Varyág during the present Russo-Japanese war. The sight was dreadful. Headless trunks, arms that had been torn off, and fragments of flesh, were lying about in profusion, and everywhere there was blood, and a smell of blood which nauseated even those most accustomed to it. The conning-tower had suffered most—a shell had exploded on it and had killed a young officer who was directing the sighting of the guns. All that was left of that unfortunate young man was a clenched hand holding an instrument; two men who were with the captain were blown to pieces, and two others were severely wounded (both had to have their legs amputated, and then had to undergo a second amputation higher up). The captain escaped with a blow on the head from the splinter of a shell.

And this is not all. The wounded cannot be taken on board neutral ships because of the infection from gangrene and fever.

Gangrene and suppurating wounds, together with hunger, fire, ruin, typhus, small-pox, and other infectious diseases, are also incidental to military glory. Such is war.

And yet Joseph de Maistre sang the praises of the beneficence of war: 'When the human soul loses its resilience owing to effeminacy, when it becomes unbelieving and contracts those rotten vices which accompany the superfluities of civilization, it can only be re-established in blood.'

M. de Vogue, the academician, says much the same thing, and so does M. Brunetiere.

But the unfortunates of whom cannon-fodder is made have a right to disagree with this.

Unfortunately, however, they have not the courage of their convictions. Therein lies the whole evil. Accustomed from of old to allow themselves to be killed on account of questions they do not understand, they continue to let this be done, imagining all to be well.

That is why corpses are now lying beneath the water and are being devoured by crabs.

When everything around them was being demolished by grapeshot, these unfortunates can hardly have consoled themselves by the thought that all this was being done for their good and to re-establish the soul of their contemporaries which had lost its resilience from the superfluities of civilization. They had probably not read Joseph de Maistre.

I advise the wounded to read him between two dressings, and they will learn that war is as necessary as the executioner, because like him it is a manifestation of the justice of God.

This great thought may serve them as consolation while the surgeons are sawing their bones!

HARDOUIN.

In the *Russian News* I read the opinion that Russia's advantage lies in her inexhaustible store of human material.

For children whose father is killed, for a wife whose husband is killed, for a mother whose son is killed—this material is quickly exhausted.

(*From a private letter from a Russian mother, March 1904.*)

You ask whether war is *still* necessary between civilized nations?

I reply that not only is it no longer necessary, but that it never has been necessary. It has always violated the historical development of humanity, infringed human rights, and hindered progress.

If some of the consequences of war have been advantageous to civilization in general, its harmful consequences have been much greater. We are misled because only a part of these harmful consequences is immediately apparent. The greater part and the most important we do not notice. So we must not accept the word 'still'. Its acceptance gives the advocates of war the opportunity to assert that the difference between them and us is only one of temporary expediency or personal appraisal, and our disagreement is then reduced to the fact that we consider war to be useless, while they consider it still useful. They readily concede that it may become unnecessary and even harmful—but only to-morrow and not to-day. To-day they consider it necessary to perform on people these terrible blood-lettings which are called wars, and which are made only to satisfy the personal ambitions of a very small minority—to ensure power, honours, and riches, to a small number of men to the detriment of the masses whose natural credulity and superstitions these men exploit, together with the prejudices created and upheld by them.

CAPITAINE GASTON MOCH.

Men of our Christian world in our time are like a man who has missed the right turning and becomes more and more convinced, the farther he goes, that he is going the wrong way. Yet the greater his doubts the quicker and more desperately does he hurry on, consoling himself with the thought that he must arrive somewhere. But the time comes when it is quite clear that the way along which he is going leads only to a precipice which he begins to discern before him.

That is where Christian humanity stands in our time. It is quite evident that if we continue to live as we are doing—guided in our private lives and in the lives of our separate states solely by desire for personal welfare for ourselves or our states, and think, as we now do, to ensure this welfare by violence—then the means for violence of man against man and state against state will inevitably increase, and we shall first ruin ourselves more and more by expending a major portion of our productivity on armaments; and then become more and more degenerate and depraved by killing the physically best men in wars.

If we do not change our way of life this is as certain as it is mathematically certain that two non-parallel straight lines must meet. And not only is it certain theoretically, but in our time our feeling as well as our intelligence becomes convinced of it. The precipice we are approaching is already visible, and even the most simple, naive, and uneducated people cannot fail to see that by arming ourselves increasingly against one another and slaughtering one another in war, we must inevitably come to mutual destruction, like spiders in a jar.

A sincere, serious, and rational man can now no longer console himself with the thought that matters can be mended, as was formerly supposed, by a universal empire such as that of Rome, or Charlemagne, or Napoleon, or by the medieval, spiritual power of the Pope, or by alliances, the political balance of a European concert and peaceful international tribunals, or as some have thought by an increase of military forces and the invention of new and more powerful weapons of destruction.

The organization of a universal empire or republic of European states is impossible, for the different peoples will never wish to unite into one state. Shall we then organize international tribunals for the solution of international disputes? But who would impose obedience to the tribunal's decision on a contending party that had an army of millions of men? Disarmament? No one desires to begin it, or is able to do so. Shall we perhaps invent even more dreadful means of destruction—balloons with bombs filled with suffocating gases which men will shower on each other from above? Whatever may be invented, every state would furnish itself with similar weapons of destruction. And as the human cannon-fodder faced the bullets that succeeded sword and spear, and the shells, bombs, long-range guns, shrapnel, and torpedoes that succeeded bullets—so it will submit to bombs charged with suffocating gases scattered down upon it from the air.

The speeches of M. Muravëv and Professor Martens as to the Japanese war not conflicting with the Hague Peace Conference, show more obviously than anything else to what an extent speech—the organ for the transmission of thought—is distorted amongst men of our time, and the capacity for clear, rational thinking completely lost. Thought and speech are used not to guide human activity but to justify any activity however criminal it may be. The late Boer war and the present Japanese war (which may at any moment expand into universal slaughter) have proved this beyond all doubt. All anti-war discussions are as useless as an attempt to stop a dog-fight by an eloquent and convincing speech—pointing out to the dogs that it would be better to share the piece of meat they are struggling over, rather than to bite one another and lose the piece of meat which is bound to be carried off by some passing non-combatant dog.

We are rushing on towards the precipice, and cannot stop but are tumbling over it.

No rational man who reflects on the present position of humanity and on what its future must inevitably be, can help seeing that there is no practical way out; that it is impossible to devise any alliance or organization that can save us from the destruction into which we are uncontrollably rushing.

Quite apart from the economic problems which become more and more complex, the mutual relations of states arming against one another and the wars that are ready at any moment to break out, clearly indicate the unavoidable destruction awaiting so-called civilized humanity.

Then what is to be done?

VI

Towards the close of his mission Jesus proclaimed a new society. Before his time nations belonged to one or several masters and were their property like so many herds. Princes and grandees crushed the world with all the weight of their pride and their rapacity. Then Jesus came to put an end to this extreme disorder. He came to lift the bowed heads, to emancipate the slaves. He taught them that as they are equal before God, so men are free in regard to each other, and that no one has any intrinsic power over his brothers, that the divine laws of the human race—equality and liberty—are inviolable; that power cannot be a right, but is a social duty, a service, a kind of bondage freely accepted for the welfare of all. Such is the society which Jesus establishes.

Is that what we now see in the world? Is that the doctrine which reigns on earth? Has it conquered the Gentiles? Are the rulers of the nations the servants, or the masters, of their people? For eighteen centuries generation after generation passes on the teaching of Christ and says that it believes in it. But what change is there in the world? The nations—crushed and suffering—are still awaiting the promised liberation not because Christ's words were untrue or unreal, but because the people either did not understand that the fruits of the teaching must be secured by an effort of their own will, or because numbed by their humiliations they did not do the one thing that brings victory—they were not ready to die for the truth. But they will awaken; something is already stirring within them; they have heard as it were a voice that cries: 'Salvation draws nigh.' LAMENNAIS.

To the glory of humanity it must be said that the nineteenth century tends to approach a new path. It has learned that laws and tribunals should exist for nations, and that, because they are accomplished on a larger scale, crimes committed by nations against nations are not less hateful than crimes committed amongst individuals. QUETELET.

All men are one in origin, one in the law that governs them, and one in the goal they are destined to attain.

Your faith must be one, your actions one, and one the banner under which you contend. Acts, tears, and martyrdoms, form a language common to all men and which all men understand. J. MAZZINI.

No, I appeal to the revolt of the conscience of every man who has seen, or made, the blood of his fellow citizens flow; it is not enough that one single head should carry a burden as heavy as that of so many murders; as many heads as there are combatants would not be too many. In order to be responsible for the law of blood which they execute, it would be just that they should at least have understood it. But the best organizations which I advocate would in themselves be only temporary; for I repeat once more, that armies and war will only last awhile; as, notwithstanding the words of a sophist which I have elsewhere controverted, it is not true that war, even against the foreigner, is *divine*; it is not true that *the earth is thirsting for blood*. War is accursed of God and even of those men who make it and who have a secret horror of it; and the earth cries to heaven praying for fresh water in its rivers, and for the pure dew of its clouds. ALFRED DE VIGNY.

Men are made as little to coerce as to obey, and mutually deprave one another by those two habits. Here stultification, there insolence, nowhere true human dignity. V. P. CONSIDERANT.

If my soldiers were to begin to think, not one of them would remain in the army. FREDERICK THE GREAT.

Two thousand years ago John the Baptist, and after him Jesus, said to the people: 'The time is fulfilled, and the Kingdom of God is at hand. Bethink yourselves ($\mu\epsilon\tau\alpha\nu o\epsilon\hat{\iota}\tau\epsilon$) and believe in the Gospel.' (Mark i. 15.) 'And if you do not bethink yourselves you will all perish.' (Luke xiii. 5.)

But men did not listen, and the destruction foretold is already near at hand, as men of our time cannot but see. We are already perishing, and therefore we cannot close our ears to that means of salvation given of old, but new to us. We cannot but see that besides all the other calamities that flow from our evil and irrational life, military preparations alone and the wars resulting from them must inevitably destroy us. We cannot but see that all the practical means devised for escape from these evils are and must be ineffectual, and that the disastrous plight of nations arming themselves one against another must continually become worse. Therefore the words of Jesus apply to us and our time more than to anyone else or any other time.

He said, 'Bethink yourselves!'—that is, let every man interrupt his work and ask himself: Who am I? Whence have I come? And what is my vocation? And having answered these questions let him decide, according to the answer, whether what he does is in accord with his vocation. It is only necessary for each man of our world and time (that is each man acquainted with the essence of the Christian teaching) to interrupt his activity for a minute, forget what people consider him to be—emperor, soldier, minister, or journalist—and seriously ask himself who he is and what is his vocation, and he will at once doubt the utility, rightfulness, and reasonableness of his activity. 'Before I am emperor, soldier, minister, or journalist,' every man of our Christian world should say to himself, 'before all else I am a man, that is, an organic being sent by the higher will into a universe endless in time and space, where after staying in it for an instant, I shall die—that is disappear from it. Therefore all those personal, social, or even universal human aims which I set before myself and which are set before me by men, are insignificant because of the brevity of my life as well as the illimitability of the life of the universe, and should be subordinated to that higher aim for the attainment of which I am sent into the world.

That ultimate aim, owing to my limitations, is not apprehended by me, but it exists (as there must be a purpose in everything that exists), and my business is to be its tool. My vocation therefore is to be God's workman, fulfilling His work.' And having understood his vocation in this way, every man of our world and time, from emperor to soldier, cannot help seeing with different eyes the duties which he has taken upon himself or which others have laid upon him.

'Before I was crowned and recognized as Emperor,' the Emperor should say to himself, 'before I undertook to fulfil the duties of head of the state, I promised by the very fact that I am alive, to fulfil what is demanded of me by that higher will which sent me into life. I not only know those demands but I feel them in my heart. They consist, as is said in the Christian law which I profess, in submitting to the will of God and fulfilling what it requires of me, namely, that I should love my neighbour, serve him, and do to him as I would wish him to do to me. Am I doing this by ruling men, ordering violence, executions, and most dreadful of all—wars?

'Men tell me that I ought to do this. But God says that I ought to do something quite different. And therefore, however much I may be told that as head of the state I must order deeds of violence, the levying of taxes, executions, and above all war —that is the killing of my fellow men—I do not wish to, and cannot, do these things.'

And the soldier who is instigated to kill men should say the same thing to himself, and so should the minister who deems it his duty to prepare for war and the journalist who incites men to war, and every man who has put to himself the question who he is and what is his vocation in life.

And as soon as the head of the state ceases to direct war, the soldier to fight, the minister to prepare means for war, and the journalist to incite men thereto—then without any new institutions, devices, balance of power, or tribunals, that hopeless position in which people have placed themselves not only as regards war but as regards all their other self-inflicted calamities will cease to exist.

So that, strange as this may seem, the surest and most certain deliverance for men from all their self-inflicted calamities, even the most dreadful of them—war—is attainable not by any external general measures but by that simple appeal to the consciousness of each individual man which was presented by Jesus nineteen hundred years ago—that every man should bethink himself and ask himself who he is, why he lives, and what he should and should not do.

VII

There is a widespread impression abroad that religion may not be a permanent element in human nature. Many are telling us that it is a phase of thought, of feeling, of life, peculiar to the early and comparatively uncultivated stages of man's career, that it is something which civilized man will progressively outgrow and at last leave behind.... I do not think we need be specially troubled over this problem. We ought to be able to look at it dispassionately, because if religion is only superstition, why then of course it ought to be outgrown. ... If on the other hand religion is divine, if it is essential to the highest and noblest human life, then criticism and question will only verify this fact.... If you find some mark on a coin, if you find it on every one of the coins, you feel perfectly certain that there is some reality in the die that stamps the coin, which accounts for that mark. It was not there for nothing, it did not simply happen.

So wherever you find any universal or permanently characteristic quality in human nature, or any other nature for that matter, you may feel perfectly certain that there is something real in the universe that corresponds to it and called it out.

You find man, then, universally a religious being. You find him everywhere believing that he is confronted with an invisible universe. On any theory you choose to hold about this universe, it has made us what we are; and there must be—unless the universe is a lie—a reality corresponding to that which is universal and permanent and real in ourselves, because this universe has called these things into being and has made them what they are.

MINOT J. SAVAGE, *The Passing and the Permanent in Religion.*

The religious element, contemplated from that elevated standpoint, becomes thus the highest and noblest factor in man's education, the greatest potency in his civilization, while effete creeds and political selfishness are the greatest obstacles to human advance. Statecraft and priestcraft are the very opposite of religion. . . . Our study here has shown the religious substance everywhere to be identical, eternal, and divine, permeating the human heart wherever it throbs, feels, and meditates. . . . The logical results of our researches all point to the identical basis of the great religions, to the one doctrine unfolding since the dawn of humanity to this day. . . . Deep at the bottom of all the creeds flows the stream of the one eternal revelation, *the one religion,* the 'word of God to the mind of man'.

Let the Parsee wear his taavids, the Jew his phylacteries, the Christian his cross, and the Moslem his crescent; but let them all remember that these are forms and emblems, while the practical essence is: 'Thou shalt love thy neighbour as thyself'—equally emphasized and accentuated by Manu, Zoroaster, Buddha, Abraham, Moses, Socrates, Hillel, Jesus, Paul, and Mohammed.

MAURICE FLEUGEL.

No true society can exist without a common faith and common purpose. Political activity is their application, and religion supplies their principle. Where this common faith is lacking the will of the majority rules, showing itself in constant instability and the oppression of others. Without God it is possible to coerce, but not to persuade. Without God the majority will be a tyrant, but not an educator of the people.

What we need, what the people need, what the age is crying for that it may find an issue from the slough of selfishness, doubt, and negation in which it is submerged—is faith, in which our souls, ceasing to wander in search of individual ends, can march together in consciousness of one origin, one law, one goal. Every strong faith that arises on the ruins of old and outlived beliefs, changes the existing social order, for every strong faith inevitably influences all departments of human activity.

In different forms and different degrees, humanity repeats the words of the Lord's prayer: 'Thy kingdom come on earth as in heaven.' MAZZINI.

A man may regard himself as an animal among animals, living for the passing day, or he may consider himself as a member of a family, a society, or a nation, living for centuries; or he may and even must (for reason irresistibly prompts him to this) consider himself as part of the whole infinite universe existing eternally. And therefore a reasonable man, besides his relation to the immediate facts of life, must always set up his relation to the whole immense Infinite in time and space, conceived as one whole. And such establishment of man's relation to that whole of which he feels himself to be a part and from which he draws guidance for his actions, is what has been called and is called religion. And therefore religion always has been, and cannot cease to be, a necessary and indispensable condition of the life of a reasonable man and of all reasonable humanity.

LEO TOLSTÓY, *What is Religion?*

Religion (regarded objectively) is the recognition of all our duties as the commands of God. . . .

There is only one true religion, though there may be various faiths. KANT.

The evil from which men of our time are suffering comes from the fact that the majority of them live without what alone affords a rational guidance for human activity, namely religion—not a religion that consists in a belief in dogmas, the fulfilment of rites affording a pleasant diversion, consolation, or stimulant, but a religion which establishes the relation of man to the All, to God, and therefore gives a general higher direction to all human activity, and without which people stand on the plane of animals, or even lower than they. This evil, leading men to inevitable destruction, has shown itself with particular strength in our time, because men, having lost a rational guidance in life and having directed all their efforts to discoveries and improvements chiefly in the sphere of technical knowledge, have developed enormous power over the forces of nature, but lacking guidance for its rational application have naturally used it for the satisfaction of their lower animal impulses.

Bereft of religion, men possessing enormous power over the forces of nature are like children to whom gunpowder or explosive gas has been given as a plaything. Considering this power that men of our time possess, and the way they use it, one feels that their degree of moral development does not really qualify them to use railways, steampower, electricity, telephones, photography, wireless telegraphy, or even to manufacture iron and steel—for they use all these things merely to satisfy their desires, amuse themselves, become dissipated, and destroy one another.

Then what is to be done? Discard all these improvements, all this power mankind has acquired? Forget what it has learnt? That is impossible! However harmfully these mental acquisitions are used, they are still acquisitions, and men cannot forget them. Alter those combinations of nations which have been formed during centuries and establish new ones? Invent new institutions which would prevent the minority from deceiving and exploiting the majority? Diffuse knowledge? All this has been tried and is being tried with great fervour. All these supposed improvements supply a chief means to distract and divert men's attention from the consciousness of inevitable destruction. The boundaries of states are altered, institutions are changed, knowledge is disseminated, but with these other boundaries, other organizations, and increased knowledge, men remain the same beasts ready at any moment to tear each other to pieces, or the same slaves they always have been and will be as long as they continue to be guided not by religious consciousness but by passions, theories, and external suggestions.

Man has no choice: he must be the slave of the most unscrupulous and insolent among slaves, or else a servant of God, because there is but one way for man to be free—by uniting his will with the will of God. Some people bereft of religion repudiate religion itself, others regard as religion those external perverted forms that have superseded it, and guided only by their personal desires—by fear, human laws, or chiefly by mutual hypnotism—they cannot cease to be animals or slaves, and no external efforts can release them from this state, for religion alone makes man free.

And most men of our time lack it.

VIII

Do not that which thy conscience condemns, and say not that which does not agree with truth. Fulfil this, the most important duty, and thou wilt have fulfilled all the object of thy life.

No one can coerce thy will, it is accessible neither to thief nor robber; desire not that which is unreasonable, desire general welfare, and not personal as do the majority of men. The object of life is not to be on the side of the majority, but to escape finding oneself in the ranks of the insane. . . .

Remember that there is a God who desires not praise nor glory from men created in his image, but rather that they, guided by the understanding given them, should in their actions become like unto him. A fig tree is true to its purpose, so is the dog, so also are bees. Then is it possible that man shall not fulfil his vocation? But, alas, these great and sacred truths vanish from thy memory, the bustle of daily life, war, unreasonable fear, spiritual debility, and the habit of being a slave, stifle them. . . .

A small branch cut from the main branch has become thereby separated from the whole tree. A man in emnity with another man is severed from the whole of mankind. But a branch is cut off by another's hand, whereas man estranges himself from his neighbour by hatred and spite, without it is true knowing that thereby he tears himself away from the whole of mankind. But the Divinity having called men into common life as brothers, has endowed them with freedom to become reconciled to each other after dissension. MARCUS AURELIUS.

Enlightenment is the escape of man from his own childishness, which he himself maintains. The *childishness* consists in his incapacity to use his reason without another's guidance. *He himself maintains this childishness* when it is the result of an insufficiency, not of reason but of the decision and manliness to use it without another's guidance. 'Sapere aude!'

Have the manliness to use thine own reason. This is the motto of enlightenment. KANT.

One must extricate the religion Jesus professed from the religion of which Jesus is the object. And when we have laid our finger upon the state of conscience which is the original cell, the basis of the eternal Gospel, we must hold on to it.

As the faint illuminations of a village festival, or the miserable candles of a procession, disappear before the great marvel of the sun's light, so also small local miracles, accidental and doubtful, will flicker out before the law of the world of the Spirit, before the incomparable spectacle of human history guided by God.

AMIEL, *Fragments d'un journal intime.*

I recognize the following proposition as needing no proof: all by which man thinks he can please God, save a good life, is merely religious error and superstition. KANT.

In reality there is only one means of worshipping God—it is by the fulfilment of one's duties, and by acting in accord with the laws of reason.
G. C. LICHTENBERG.

'But in order to abolish the evil from which we are suffering,' those who are preoccupied by various practical activities will say, 'it would be necessary not for a few men only, but all men, to bethink themselves, and having done so to understand the vocation of their lives to lie in the fulfilment of the will of God and the service of their neighbour. Is that possible?'

Not only is it possible, I reply, but it is impossible that it should not be so.

It is impossible for men not to bethink themselves —impossible, that is, for each man not to put to himself the question who he is, and why he lives; for man as a rational being cannot live without a knowledge of why he lives, and has always put that question to himself, and according to the degree of his development has always answered it in his religious teaching. In our time the inner contradiction men feel themselves to be in, presents this question with particular insistence and demands an answer. It is impossible for men of our time to answer this question otherwise than by recognizing the law of life to lie in love to men and the service of them, for this for our time is the only rational answer as to the meaning of human life, and this answer was expressed nineteen hundred years ago in the Christian religion and is known in the same way to the great majority of all mankind.

This answer lives in a latent state in the consciousness of all people of the Christian world of our time. It does not openly express itself and serve as guidance for our life, only because on the one hand those who enjoy the greatest authority—the so-called scientists—being under the coarse delusion that religion is a temporary stage in the development of mankind which they have outgrown, and that men can live without religion, impress this error on those of the masses who are beginning to be educated, and on the other hand because those in power consciously or unconsciously (being themselves under the delusion that the Church faith is the Christian religion) try to support and promote in people the crude superstitions that are given out as the Christian religion.

If only these two deceptions were destroyed, true religion, which is already latent in people of our time, would become evident and obligatory.

To bring this about it is necessary that, on the one hand, men of science should understand that the principle of the brotherhood of all men and the rule of not doing to others what one does not wish for oneself, is not a casual conception, one of a multitude of human theories that can be subordinated to other considerations, but is an indubitable principle standing higher than other perceptions and flowing from the unalterable relations of man to the eternal—to God—and is religion, all religion, and therefore always obligatory.

On the other hand it is necessary that those who consciously or unconsciously preach crude superstitions under the guise of Christianity, should understand that all these dogmas, sacraments, and rites which they support and preach, are not harmless as they suppose, but are in the highest degree harmful, concealing from men that one religious truth which is expressed in the fulfilment of God's will—the brotherhood of man and service of man—and that the rule of doing to others as you wish others to do to you is not one of the prescriptions of the Christian religion but is the whole of practical religion, as is said in the Gospels.

That men of our time should uniformly place before themselves the question of the meaning of life, and uniformly answer it, it is only necessary for those who regard themselves as enlightened to cease to think and impress on others that religion is atavistic—the survival of a savage past—and that for the good life of men a spreading of education is sufficient, that is, the spread of very miscellaneous knowledge which is somehow to bring men to justice and a moral life.[1] These men should understand instead that for the good life of humanity religion is vital, and that this religion already exists and lives in the consciousness of the men of our time; and people who are intentionally and unintentionally stupefying the people by Church superstitions should cease to do so, and should recognize that what is important and

[1] See in the essay *Religion and Morality* (vol. xii of the Centenary Edition, p. 192) Tolstóy's reply to Thomas Huxley's Romanes Lecture in 1894.—A. M.

obligatory in Christianity is not baptism, or the sacraments, or the profession of dogmas, and so forth, but only love to God and one's neighbour, and the fulfilment of the command to act towards others as you wish others to act towards you, and that in this is all the law and the prophets.

If only this were understood both by pseudo-Christians and by men of science, and these simple, clear, and necessary truths were preached to children and to the uneducated, as they now preach their complicated, confused, and unnecessary theories, all men would understand the meaning of their lives uniformly and recognize the same duties as flowing therefrom.

IX

(A letter from a Russian peasant who refused Military Service)

On October 15th, 1895, I was called up for conscription. When my turn came to draw the lot I said I would not do so. The officials looked at me, consulted together, and asked me why I refused.

I answered that it was because I was not going either to take the oath or to carry a gun.

They said that that would be seen to later, but now I must draw the lot.

I refused once more. Then they told the village Elder to draw the lot. He did so and number 674 came out. It was written down.

The military commander entered, called me into his office, and asked: 'Who taught you all this—that you don't want to take the oath?'

'I learnt it myself by reading the Gospel,' I answered.

'I don't think you are able to understand the Gospel,' he replied. 'Everything there is incomprehensible. To understand it one has to learn a great deal.'

To this I said that Jesus did not teach anything

incomprehensible, for even the simplest uneducated people understood his teaching.

Then he told a soldier to take me to the barracks. I went to the kitchen with him and we had dinner there.

After dinner they asked me why I had not taken the oath.

'Because it is said in the Gospel: Swear not at all,' I replied.

They were astonished. Then they asked me: 'Is that really in the Gospel? Find it for us.'

I found the passage, read it out, and they listened.

'But even if it is there,' they said, 'you can't refuse to take the oath or you'll be tortured.'

'Who loses his earthly life will inherit eternal life,' I replied. . . .

On the 20th I was placed in a row with other young soldiers, and the military rules were explained to us. I told them that I would fulfil nothing of this. They asked why.

I said: 'Because as a Christian I will not bear arms or defend myself from enemies, for Christ commanded us to love even our enemies.'

'But are you the only Christian?' they asked. 'Why, we are all Christians!'

'I know nothing about others,' I replied. 'I only know for myself that Jesus told us to do what I am now doing.'

The commander said: 'If you won't drill, I'll let you rot in prison.'

To this I replied: 'Do what you like with me, but I won't serve.'

To-day a commission examined me. The general said to the officers: 'What opinions has this suckling got hold of that he refuses service? Millions serve, and he alone refuses. Have him well flogged, then he will change his views. . . .'

Olkhovík was transported to the Amur. On the steamer everybody fasted during Lent, but he refused. The soldiers asked him why. He explained. Another soldier (Sereda) joined in the conversation. Olkhovík opened the Gospel and began to read the fifth chapter of Matthew. Having read it, he said: 'Jesus forbids the oath, courts of justice, and war, but all this is done among us and is considered legitimate.' A crowd of soldiers had collected around, and remarked that Seredá was not wearing a cross on his neck. 'Where is your cross?' they asked.

'In my box,' he answered.

They asked again: 'Why don't you wear it?'

'Because I love Jesus,' he replied, 'and so I can't wear the thing on which he was crucified.'

Then two non-commissioned officers came up and began talking to Seredá. They said: 'How is it that not long ago you used to fast, but now you have taken off your cross?'

He replied: 'Because I was then in the dark and did not see the light, but now I have begun to read the Gospel and have learnt that a Christian need not do all that.'

Then they said: 'Does this mean that like Olkhovík you won't serve?'

'Yes,' he replied.

They asked why, and he answered: 'Because I am a Christian, and Christians must not take arms against men.'

Seredá was arrested, and together with Olkhovík was exiled to the province of Yakútsk, where they now are.

From *The Letters of P. V. Olkhovík.*

On January 27th, 1894, in the Vorónezh prison hospital, a man named Drozhín, formerly a village teacher in Kursk province, died of pneumonia. His body was thrown into a grave in the prison cemetery like the bodies of all the criminals who die in the prison. Yet he was one of the saintliest, purest, and most truthful men that ever lived.

In August 1891 he was called up for conscription, but, considering all men to be his brothers and regarding murder and violence as the greatest sins against conscience and the will of God, he refused to be a soldier and to bear arms. Also, considering it a sin to surrender his will into the power of others who might demand evil actions of him, he refused to take the oath. Men whose lives are founded on violence and murder condemned him first to one year's solitary confinement in Khárkov, but later he was transferred to the Vorónezh penal battalion where for fifteen months he was tortured by cold, hunger, and solitary confinement. Finally, when consumption developed from his incessant sufferings and privations and he was recognized as unfit for military service, he was transferred to the civil prison where he was to remain confined for another nine years. But while being transferred from the penal battalion to the prison on an extremely frosty day, the police officials neglected to furnish him with a warm coat. The party remained for a long time in the street in front of the police station, and this caused him to catch such a cold that pneumonia set in from which he died twenty-two days later.

The day before his death Drozhín said to the doctor: 'Though I have not lived long, I die with a consciousness of having acted in accord with my convictions and my conscience. Others of course may judge about this better than I can. Perhaps . . . no, I think that I am right,' he concluded.

From *The Life and Death of Drozhín*.

Put on the whole armour of God that ye may be able to stand against the wiles of the devil. For our wrestling is not against flesh and blood, but against the principalities, against the powers, against the world-rulers of this darkness, against the spiritual hosts of wickedness in high places.

Wherefore take up the whole armour of God, that ye may be able to withstand in the evil day, and, having done all, to stand.

Stand therefore, having girded your loins with truth, and having put on the breastplate of righteousness.

EPHESIANS vi. 11–14.

But I shall be asked, how are we to act now—immediately, among ourselves in Russia at this moment when our foes are already attacking us, are killing our people and threatening us? How is a Russian soldier, officer, general, tsar, or private individual, to act? Are we really to let our enemies ruin our dominions, seize the products of our labour, carry off prisoners, and kill our men? What are we to do now that this thing has begun?

'But before the work of war began,' every man who has reflected should reply, 'before all else, the work of my life had begun.' And the work of my life has nothing to do with recognition of the rights of the Chinese, Japanese, or Russians, to Port Arthur. The work of my life consists in fulfilling the will of Him who sent me into this life. And that will is known to me. That will is that I should love my neighbour and serve him. Then why should I —following temporary, casual demands that are cruel and irrational—deviate from the eternal and changeless law of my whole life? If there is a God, He will not ask me when I die (which may happen at any moment) whether I retained Chinnampo with its timber stores, or Port Arthur, or even that conglomeration which is called the Russian Empire, which He did not entrust to my care. He will ask me what I have done with that life which He has put at my disposal. Did I use it for the purpose for which it was intended and under whose conditions it was entrusted to me? Have I fulfilled His law?

So that to this question as to what is to be done now that war has begun, for me, a man who understands his vocation, whatever position I may occupy, there can be no other answer than this— that whatever the circumstances may be, whether the war has begun or not, whether thousands of Russians or Japanese have been killed, whether not only Port Arthur but St. Petersburg and

Moscow have been captured—I cannot act otherwise than as God demands of me, and that therefore I as a man cannot either directly or indirectly, whether by organizing, helping, or inciting to it, take part in war. *I cannot, I do not wish to, and I will not.* What will happen immediately or later from my ceasing to do what is contrary to the will of God I do not and cannot know, but I believe that from fulfilling the will of God nothing can follow but what is good for me and for all men.

You speak with horror of what would happen if we Russians at once ceased to fight and yielded to the Japanese all that they wish of us.

But if it be true that the salvation of mankind from brutalization and self-destruction lies solely in the establishment among men of true religion, demanding that we should love our neighbour and serve him (with which it is impossible to disagree) then every war, every hour of war, and my participation in it, only renders the realization of this only possible means of salvation more difficult and remote.

So that even looking at it from your precarious point of view—appraising actions by their presumed consequences—even so, a yielding by the Russians to the Japanese of all that they desire of us, apart from the unquestionable advantage of ending the ruin and slaughter, would be an approach to the only means of saving mankind from destruction, whereas the continuance of the war, however it may end, would hinder that only means of salvation.

'But even if this be so,' people reply, 'wars can cease only when all men, or the majority of them, refuse to participate in them. The refusal of one man, whether he be Tsar or soldier, would only unnecessarily ruin his life, without the least advantage to anyone. If the Russian Tsar were now to renounce the war he would be dethroned, perhaps killed to get rid of him. If an ordinary man were to refuse military service he would be sent to a penal battalion, or perhaps shot. Why then uselessly throw away one's life, which might be of use to society?' is usually said by those who do not think of the vocation of their whole life and therefore do not understand it.

But this is not what is said and felt by a man who understands the purpose of his life, that is, by a religious man. Such a one is guided in his activity not by the conjectural consequences of his actions but by the consciousness of the purpose of his life. A factory workman goes to the factory and in it does the work allotted to him without considering what will be the consequence of his work. In the same way a soldier acts, carrying out the will of his commanders. So acts a religious man, doing the work prescribed to him by God without arguing as to just what will come of his work. And so for a religious man there is no question as to whether many or few men act as he does, or of what may happen to him if he does what he should do. He knows that besides life and death nothing can happen, and that life and death are in the hands of God whom he obeys.

A religious man acts so and no otherwise not because he wishes to act thus or because it is advantageous to him or to others, but because, believing that his life is in the hands of God, he cannot do otherwise.

In this lies the speciality of the activity of religious men.

And so the salvation of men from the ills they inflict upon themselves will be accomplished only to the extent to which they are guided in their lives not by advantages or arguments, but by religious consciousness.

X

... Men of God are that hidden salt which conserves the world, for the things of the world are conserved only in so far as the Divine salt does not lose its power. 'But if the salt have lost his savour, wherewith can it be salted? It is thenceforth good for nothing, but to be cast out, and to be trodden under foot of men. ... He that has ears to hear, let him hear.' As for us, we are persecuted when God gives the tempter the power to persecute, but when He does not wish to subject us to sufferings we enjoy wonderful peace even in this world which hates us, and we rely on the protection of Him who said: 'Be of good cheer, I have overcome the world.'

Celsus also says that: 'It is impossible that all the inhabitants of Asia, Europe, and Libia, Greeks as well as barbarians, should follow one and the same law. To think so,' he says, 'means to understand nothing.' But we say that not only is it possible, but that the day will come when all reasonable beings will unite under one law. For the Word or Reason will subdue all reasonable beings and transform them into its own perfection.

There are bodily diseases and wounds which no doctoring can cure, but it is not so with the ailments of the soul. There is no evil the cure of which is impossible for supreme Reason, which is God.

ORIGEN, Origen against Celsus.

I feel the force stirring within me which in time will reform the world.

It does not push or obtrude, but I am conscious of it drawing gently and irresistibly at my vitals.

And I see that as I am attracted, so I begin unaccountably to attract others.

I draw them and they in turn draw me, and we recognize a tendency to group ourselves anew. Get in touch with the great central magnet, and you will yourself become a magnet. And as more and more of us find our bearings and exert our powers, gradually the new world will take shape. We become indeed legislators of the divine law, receiving it from God Himself, and human laws shrink and dry up before us.

And I asked the force within my soul: 'Who art thou?'

And it answered and said: 'I am Love, the Lord of Heaven, and I would be called Love, the Lord of Earth. I am the mightiest of all the heavenly hosts, and I am come to create the state that is to be.'

ERNEST CROSBY, *Plain Talk in Psalm and Parable.*

One can say with certainty that the kingdom of God has come to us when the principle of the gradual transformation of the church faith into a universal rational religion is found openly established anywhere, though the complete realization of that kingdom may still be infinitely far from us—for this principle, like a developing and then multiplying germ, already contains all which must enlighten and take possession of the world.

In the life of the universe a thousand years are as one day. We must labour patiently for this realization, and wait for it. KANT.

When I speak to thee about God, do not think that I am speaking to thee about some object made of gold or silver. The God of whom I speak to thee, thou feelest in thy soul. Thou bearest Him in thyself, and by thy impure thoughts and loathsome acts thou defilest His image in thy soul. In the presence of a golden idol which thou regardest as God, thou refrainest from doing aught that is unseemly, but in the presence of that God who in thee thyself sees and hears all, thou does not even blush when thou yieldest thyself to thy disgusting thoughts and actions.

If only we remembered that God in us is the witness of all that we do and think, we should cease to sin, and God would constantly abide in us. Let us then remember God, and think and talk of Him as often as possible.

EPICTETUS.

'But how about the enemies that are attacking us?'

'Love your enemies and you will have none,' is said in the *Teaching of the Twelve Apostles*. And this answer is not mere words as those may imagine who are accustomed to think that the injunction to love one's enemies is something parabolical and signifies not what it says but something else. It is the indication of a very clear and definite activity and of its consequences.

To love one's enemies—the Japanese, the Chinese, those Yellow peoples towards whom erring men are now trying to excite our hatred—to love them does not mean to kill them in order to have a right to poison them with opium, as was done by the English,[1] or to kill them in order to seize their land, as was done by the French, the Russians, and the Germans; or to bury them alive as punishment for injuring roads, or to tie them together by their hair and drown them in the Amur, as the Russians did.

'A disciple is not above his master. . . . It is enough for a disciple that he be as his master.'

To love the Yellow people, whom we call our foes, does not mean to teach them, under the name of Christianity, absurd superstitions about the fall of man, redemption, resurrection, and so on; or to teach them the art of deceiving and killing people, but to teach them justice, unselfishness, compassion, love, and that not in words but by the example of our own good life.

But what have we done and are doing to them?

If we did indeed love our enemies, if even now we began to love our enemies the Japanese, we should have no enemy.

---

[1] 'The public conscience was wounded by a war with China in 1839 on its refusal to allow the smuggling of opium into its dominions.' J. R. Green (*Short History of the English People*).—A. M.

So, strange as it may appear to people occupied with military plans, preparations, diplomatic considerations, administrative, financial, economic measures, revolutionary and socialistic sermons, and various unnecessary sciences by which they think to free mankind from its calamities—the delivery of man not only from the calamities of war, but from all his self-inflicted ills—will be effected, not through emperors or kings instituting peace unions, not by those who would dethrone emperors or kings, or limit them by constitutions, or replace monarchies by republics, not by peace conferences, not by the accomplishment of socialistic programmes or by victories or defeats on land or sea, or by libraries or universities, or by those futile mental exercises which are now called science, but only by there being more and more of those simple men like the Doukhobors, Drozhín, and Olkhovík in Russia, the Nazarines in Austria, Condatier in France, Tervey in Holland, and others who set themselves the aim not of external alterations of life but of their own most faithful fulfilment of the will of Him who sent them into life, and direct all their powers to that fulfilment. Only such people, realizing the kingdom of God in themselves, in their souls, will without aiming directly at that purpose, establish that external kingdom of God which every human soul desires.

Salvation will come about only in this one way and not by any other. And what is now being done by those who, ruling others, instil into them religious and patriotic superstitions, exciting them to exclusiveness, hatred, and murder—as well as by those who to free men from enslavement and oppression invoke them to violent external revolution, or think that the acquisition by men of very much incidental, and for the most part unnecessary, knowledge, will of itself bring them to a good life—all this, distracting men from what alone they need, merely removes them farther from the possibility of salvation.

The evil from which people of the Christian world suffer is that they are temporarily deprived of religion.

Some people, convinced of the discord between existing religion and the state of mental, scientific development attained by humanity in our time, have decided in general that no religion whatever is necessary. They live without religion and preach the uselessness of any religion whatever. Others, holding to the distorted form of the Christian religion in which it is now preached, also live without religion, professing empty external forms which cannot serve as guidance for men's lives.

Yet a religion which answers to the demands of our time exists, is known to all men, and lives in a latent state in the hearts of men of the Christian world. And that this religion should become evident to and binding upon all men, it is only necessary that educated men—the leaders of the masses—should understand that religion is necessary to man, that without religion men cannot live good lives, and that what they call science cannot replace religion. And men in power who support the old empty forms of religion should understand that what they support and preach as religion, is not only not religion, but is the chief obstacle to people's assimilating the true religion, which they already know and which alone can save them from their miseries.

So that the only true means of man's salvation consists in merely ceasing to do what hinders men from making the true religion which lives in their consciousness their own.

XI

A wonderful and horrible thing is come to pass in the land; the prophets prophesy falsely, and the priests bear rule by their means; and my people love to have it so; and what will ye do in the end thereof?
JEREMIAH V. 30, 31.

He hath blinded their eyes, and he hardened their heart; lest they should see with their eyes, and perceive with their heart, and should turn, and I should heal them.
JOHN xii. 40.

If a traveller were to see a people on some far-off island whose houses were protected by loaded cannon and around those houses sentinels patrolled night and day, he could not help thinking that the island was inhabited by brigands. Is it not thus with the European states? How little influence has religion on people, or how far we still are from true religion. LICHTENBERG.

I was finishing this article when news came of the destruction of six hundred innocent lives near Port Arthur. It would seem that the useless suffering and death of these unfortunate, deluded men, who have uselessly suffered a dreadful death, ought to bring to their senses those who were the cause of this destruction. I am not alluding to Makárov and other officers—all those men knew what they were doing and why, and voluntarily, for personal advantage or for ambition, did what they did, screening themselves under the lie of patriotism, which is obvious but is not exposed merely because it is universal. I mention those unfortunate men drawn from all parts of Russia who by the help of religious fraud and under fear of punishment were torn from their honest, reasonable, useful, and laborious family life and driven to the other end of the earth, placed on a cruel and senseless slaughtering machine, and torn to bits or drowned in a distant sea together with that stupid machine, without any need or any possibility of receiving any advantage from all their privations, efforts, and sufferings, and the death that overtook them.

In 1830, during the Polish war, Adjutant Vilejinsky, sent to St. Petersburg by Klopitsky, in a conversation carried on in French with Dibitch, replied to the latter's demands that the Russian troops should enter Poland:

'Monsieur le Maréchal, I think that it is quite impossible for the Polish nation to accept the manifesto with such a condition.'

'Believe me, the Emperor will make no concession.'

'Then I foresee that unhappily there will be war, much blood will be shed and there will be many unfortunate victims.'

'Don't believe it! At most ten thousand men will perish on the two sides, that is all,'[1] said Dibitch in his German accent, quite confident that he, together with another man as cruel and alien to Russian and Polish life as himself (Nicholas I) had a right to condemn or not to condemn to death ten or a hundred thousand Russians and Poles.

One hardly believes that this could have been, so senseless and dreadful is it, and yet it was. Sixty thousand supporters of families perished by the will of those men. And the same thing is taking place now.

[1] Vilejinsky adds: 'The Field Marshal did not then think that more than sixty thousand of the Russians alone would perish in that war, not so much from the enemy's fire as from disease, and that he himself would be among the number.'

To keep the Japanese out of Manchuria and to drive them out of Korea, not ten but fifty and more thousands will in all probability be required. I do not know whether Nicholas II and Kuropátkin say in so many words, as Dibitch did, that *not more than fifty thousand lives* will be needed for this on the Russian side alone, *and only that*; but they think it and cannot but think it, because what they are doing speaks for itself. That unceasing flow of unfortunate, deluded Russian peasants now being transported by thousands to the Far East, are those same *not more than fifty thousand* living Russians whom Nicholas Románov and Alexéy Kuropátkin have decided to sacrifice, and who will be killed in support of those stupidities, robberies, and nastinesses of all kinds which were being committed in China and Korea by immoral, ambitious men, now quietly sitting in their palaces and awaiting fresh glory and fresh advantage and profit from the slaughter of those fifty thousand unfortunate defrauded Russian working men who are guilty of nothing and gain nothing by their sufferings and death. For other people's land, to which the Russians have no right, which has been stolen from its legitimate owners and which in reality the Russians do not need—as well as for certain shady dealings undertaken by speculators who wished to make money in Korea out of other people's forests —enormous sums are spent, that is, a great part of the labour of the whole Russian people, while future generations of that people are being bound by debts, its best workmen withdrawn from labour, and scores of thousands of its sons mercilessly doomed to death. And the destruction of these unfortunate men has already begun. More than this: those who have hatched the war manage it so badly, so carelessly, all is so unexpected, so unprepared, that, as one paper remarks, Russia's chief chance of success lies in the fact that it has inexhaustible human material. It is on this that those rely who send scores of thousands of Russian men to their death!

It is plainly said that the regrettable reverses of our fleet must be compensated for on land. In plain language this means, that if the authorities have managed things badly on sea and by their carelessness have wasted not only the nation's milliards but thousands of lives, we must make up for this by condemning to death several more scores of thousands on land!

Crawling locusts cross rivers in this way: the lower layers are drowned till the bodies of the drowned form a bridge over which those above can pass. So now are the Russian people disposed of.

Thus the first lower layer is already beginning to drown, showing the way for other thousands who will likewise perish.

And do the originators, the instigators and directors of this dreadful business begin to understand their sin, their crime? Not in the least. They are fully persuaded that they have fulfilled and are fulfilling their duty, and they are proud of their activity.

They talk of the loss of the brave Makárov, who as all agree was able to kill men very cleverly, and they deplore the loss of an excellent machine of slaughter that cost so many millions of rubles and has now been sunk, and they discuss how to find another murderer as capable as poor misguided Makárov, and they invent new and even more efficacious tools of slaughter, and all the guilty people engaged in this dreadful work, from the Tsar to the humblest journalist, call with one voice for new insanities and cruelties, and for an intensification of brutality and hatred of one's fellow men.

'Makárov was not alone in Russia and every admiral placed in his position will follow in his steps and will continue the plan and the idea of him who has perished nobly in the strife,' writes the *Novoe Vremya*.

'Let us earnestly pray God for those who have laid down their lives for the sacred Fatherland, not doubting for one moment that the Fatherland will give us fresh sons equally valorous for the further struggle, and will find in them an inexhaustible supply of strength for a worthy completion of the work,' writes the *Petersburg Vedomosti*.

'A virile nation will form no other conclusion from the defeat, however unprecedented, than that we must continue, develop, and conclude the strife. We shall find in ourselves fresh strength, new heroes of the spirit will appear,' writes the *Russ*. And so on.

So murder and every kind of crime continue with yet greater fury. People are enthusiastic about the martial spirit of the volunteers who having unexpectedly come upon fifty of their fellow men, cut them all to pieces, or occupied a village and massacred its whole population, or hung or shot those accused of spying—that is, of doing the very thing which is regarded as indispensable and is constantly being done on our side. News of these crimes is reported in pompous telegrams to their chief director, the Tsar, who sends his valorous troops his blessing for the continuation of such deeds.

Is it not clear that if there is a salvation from this state of things, it is only one—that one which Jesus teaches?

'Seek ye first the kingdom of God and his righteousness' (that which is within you), and all the rest—that is, all the practical welfare for which man is striving—will be realized of itself.

Such is the law of life: practical welfare is attained not when man strives for it—on the contrary, such striving for the most part removes man from the attainment of what he seeks—but only when, without thinking of the attainment of practical welfare, he strives towards the most perfect fulfilment of that which he regards as right before God, before the Source and Law of his life. Only then, incidentally, is practical welfare also attained.

So that there is only one true salvation for men: the fulfilment of the will of God by each individual within himself, that is, in that portion of the universe which alone is subject to his power. In this is the chief, the sole, vocation of every individual, and at the same time the only means by which every individual can influence others, and so to this, and only to this, all the efforts of every man should be directed.

[*April 17th, o.s., 1904.*]

XII

I had only just sent off the last pages of this article on war, when the terrible news arrived of a fresh iniquity committed against the Russian people by those men who, crazed by power and lacking any sense of responsibility, have assumed the right to dispose of them. Again those coarse and servile slaves of slaves—the various generals—decked out in a variety of motley garments, have (either to distinguish themselves, or to spite one another, or to earn the right to add another little star, decoration, or ribbon, to their ridiculous and ostentatious dress, or from sheer stupidity and carelessness) destroyed thousands of those honourable, kindly, laborious working men who provide them with food—and destroyed them with terrible sufferings. And once again this iniquity not only fails to make its perpetrators reflect or repent, but they only tell us how still more men and still more families (both Russian and Japanese) may be killed and mutilated, or ruined, with the greatest speed.

More than this, those guilty of these evil deeds—wishing to prepare people for still more of them—not only do not confess (what is evident to everybody) that even from their patriotic, military point of view, the Russians have suffered a shameful defeat, but they even try to instil into frivolous minds a belief that those unfortunate Russian peasants—who were led into a trap like cattle into a slaughter-house, and of whom several thousands were killed and maimed simply because one general did not understand what another general had said—have performed an heroic feat, since those who could not run away were killed and those who did run away remained alive.

The drowning of many peaceful Japanese by one of those terrible, immoral, and cruel men extolled as generals and admirals, is also described as a great and valorous achievement which must gladden the hearts of the Russian people. And in all the papers appears this horrible incitement to murder:

'Let the two thousand Russians killed on the Yalu, together with the maimed *Retvizán* and her sister ships, and our lost torpedo-boats, teach our cruisers what devastating destruction they must wreak upon the shores of base Japan. She has sent her soldiers to shed Russian blood and no mercy must be shown her. It is impossible to sentimentalize now, it would be sinful. We must fight! We must deal such heavy blows that their memory will freeze the treacherous hearts of the Japanese. Now is the time for our cruisers to put to sea and reduce their towns to ashes, and to rush like a terrible calamity along their beautiful shores.

'There has been enough of sentimentality!'

So the frightful work goes on: loot, violence, murder, hypocrisy, theft, and, above all, the most fearful deceit, and the perversion of both the Christian and the Buddhist teaching.

The Tsar, the man chiefly responsible, continues to hold reviews of his troops, thanks them, rewards and encourages them, and issues an edict calling up the reserves. Again and again his loyal subjects humbly lay their possessions and their lives at the feet of their adored monarch, but these are only words. In reality, desiring to distinguish themselves before each other in actual deeds, they tear fathers and bread-winners away from orphaned families and prepare them for slaughter. And the worse the position of the Russians becomes, the more unconscionably do the journalists lie, converting shameful defeats into victories, conscious that no one will contradict them, and quietly gathering in money from subscriptions and the sales of their papers. The more money and labour is spent on the war the more do all the chiefs and contractors steal, knowing that no one will expose them since everyone is doing the same. The military, trained for murder, and having spent decades in a school of brutality, coarseness, and idleness, rejoice (poor fellows) because, besides getting an increase of pay, the casualties among their superiors create vacancies for them. Christian ministers continue to incite men to the greatest of crimes, hypocritically calling upon God to help in the work of war; and instead of condemning the pastor who, cross in hand and at the very scene of the crime, encourages men to murder, they justify and acclaim him. The same thing goes on in Japan. The benighted Japanese fling themselves into murder with even greater ardour because of their victories, imitating all that is worst in Europe. The Mikado also holds reviews and bestows rewards. Different generals boast themselves, imagining that they have acquired Western culture by having learnt to kill. Their poor unfortunate labouring people, torn from their useful work and from their families, groan as ours do. Their journalists tell lies and rejoice at an increased circulation. And probably (for where murder is acclaimed as heroism, every vice is bound to flourish) all the commanders and contractors make money. Nor do the Japanese theologians and religious teachers lag behind our European ones. As their military men are up to date in the technique of armaments, so are their theologians up to date in the technique of deception and hypocrisy—not merely tolerating but justifying murder, which Buddha forbade.

The learned Buddhist Soyen-Shaku, who rules over eight hundred monasteries, explains that though Buddha forbade manslaughter, he also said that he could not be at peace till all beings are united in the infinitely loving heart of all things; and that to bring the discordant into harmony it is necessary to fight and kill people.[1]

[1] In his article it is said: 'The triune world is my own possession. All things therein are my children. . . . All are but reflections of myself. They are all from the one source. . . . All partake of the one body. Therefore I cannot be at rest

And it is as though the Christian and the Buddhist teaching of the oneness of the human spirit, the brotherhood of man, love, compassion, and the inviolability of human life, had never existed. Men already enlightened by the truth, both Japanese and Russian, fly at one another like wild beasts and worse than wild beasts, with the sole desire to destroy as many lives as possible. Thousands of unfortunates already groan and writhe in cruel suffering and die in agony in Japanese and Russian field-hospitals, asking themselves in perplexity why this fearful thing was done to them; and other thousands are rotting in the earth or on the earth, or floating in the sea, bloated and decomposing. And tens of thousands of fathers, mothers, wives, and children weep for the bread-winners who have perished so uselessly.

But all this is not enough, and more and more

until every being, even the smallest possible fragment of existence, is settled down to its proper appointment. . . .
'This is the position taken by the Buddha, and we, his humble followers, are but to walk in his wake.
'Why then do we fight at all.
'Because the world is not as it ought to be. Because there are here so many perverted creatures, so many wayward thoughts, so many ill-directed hearts, due to ignorant subjectivity. For this reason Buddhists are never tired of combatting all the products of ignorance, and their fight must be continued *to the bitter end. They will give no quarter.* They will mercilessly destroy the very root from which arises the misery of this life. To accomplish this they will never be afraid of sacrificing their lives. . . .'
The quotation continues (as among us) with confused reflections about self-sacrifice and about absence of malice, about the transmigration of souls, and much else—all merely to conceal Buddha's clear and simple command not to kill.
It is further said: 'The hand that is raised to strike, and the eye which is fixed to take aim, do not belong to the individual but are the instruments utilized by the Source which stands above our transient existence.' (From *The Open Court*, May 1904. *Buddhist Views of War*, by the Right Rev. Soyen-Shaku.)

fresh victims are continually being prepared. The chief concern of the Russian organizers of the slaughter is that the supply of cannon-fodder (three thousand men a day doomed to destruction) should not cease for a single day. The Japanese are similarly preoccupied. The locusts are being driven into the river incessantly, so that the later comers may pass over the bodies of the drowned. . . .

When will it end? When will the deceived people come to themselves and say: 'Well, go yourselves, you heartless and Godless tsars, mikados, ministers, metropolitans, abbots, generals, editors, and contractors, or whatever you are entitled. Go yourselves and face the shells and bullets! We don't want to go, and won't go. Leave us in peace to plough, sow, build, and feed you—our parasites!' To say that would be so natural now in Russia, amid the weeping and wailing of hundreds of thousands of mothers, wives, and children from whom their bread-winners—the so-called Reservists—are being taken. Those same Reservists are for the most part able to read. They know what the Far East is. And they know that the war is carried on not for anything at all necessary for the Russian people, but on account of dealings in some alien 'leased land' (as they call it) where it seemed advantageous to some contractors to build a railway and engage on other affairs for profit. They also know, or can know, that they will be killed like sheep in a slaughter-house, for the Japanese have the newest and most perfect instruments of murder and we have not—for the Russian authorities who are sending our people to death did not think in time of procuring such weapons as the Japanese have. Knowing all this, it would be so natural to say: 'Go yourselves, you who started this affair—all of you to whom the war seems necessary and who justify it! *You* go and expose yourselves to the Japanese bullets and torpedoes. We will no longer go, because it is not only unnecessary for us, but we cannot understand why it should be necessary for anyone.'

But they do not say this. They go, and will go, and cannot but go, as long as they fear that which destroys the body, and not that which destroys both body and soul.

'Whether they will kill or mutilate us in some Chinnampos or whatever they are called, where we are being driven, is uncertain,' they argue. 'Perhaps we may get away alive, and even with rewards and glory, like those sailors who are being so fêted all over Russia just now because the Japanese bombs and bullets hit someone else instead of them. But if we refuse we shall certainly be put in prison, starved and beaten, exiled to the province of Yakútsk, or perhaps even killed immediately.' And so with despair in their hearts they go, leaving their wives and children and their rational lives.

Yesterday I met a reservist accompanied by his mother and his wife. They were all three riding in a cart. He was rather tipsy, and his wife's face was swollen with weeping. He addressed me:

'Good-bye, Lëv Nikoláevich! I'm off to the Far East.'

'What! Are you going to fight?'

'Well, someone has to fight!'

'No one should fight!'

He considered. 'But what can I do? *Where can I escape to?*'

I saw that he understood me and had understood that the affair on which he was being sent was a bad one.

'*Where can I escape to?*' It is the precise expression

of the mental condition which in the official and journalistic world is rendered by the words: 'For the Faith, the Tsar, and the Fatherland!' Those who go to suffering and death, abandoning their hungry families, say what they feel: 'Where can I escape to?' While those who sit in safety in their luxurious palaces say that all Russians are ready to lay down their lives for their adored monarch, and for the glory and greatness of Russia.

Yesterday I received two letters, one after the other, from a peasant I know.

This was the first:

'Dear Lèv Nikoláevich—

'Well, to-day I have received the official announcement summoning me to serve, and to-morrow I must present myself at the place appointed. That is all, and then to the Far East to meet Japanese bullets.

'I will not tell you of my own and my family's grief, for you will not fail to understand all the horror of my position and of war. You have painfully realized that long ago and understand it all. I have all the time wished to come to see you and talk with you. I wrote you a long letter in which I described the torments of my soul, but I had not had time to make a clean copy of it when I received this summons. What is my wife to do now, with our four children? Of course you, being an old man, cannot do anything for my family yourself, but you might ask some one of your friends to visit them, just for the sake of a walk. If my wife finds herself unable to bear the agony of her helplessness with all the children, and makes up her mind to go to you for help and advice, I beg you earnestly to receive her and console her. Though she does not know you personally she believes in you, and that means a great deal.

'I cannot resist the summons, but I say beforehand that not one Japanese family shall be orphaned by me. O God, how dreadful all this is! How grievous and painful it is to abandon all that one lives by and with which one is concerned.'

The second letter was this:

'Kind Lëv Nikoláevich,

'Only one day of actual service has passed, but I have already lived through an eternity of most desperate torments. From eight o'clock in the morning till nine in the evening we were crowded and pushed about in the barrack yard like a herd of cattle. The comedy of a medical examination was repeated three times, and all who reported themselves ill did not receive even ten minutes' attention before they were marked 'Fit'. When we, two thousand fit men, were driven from the military commander's at the barracks, a crowd of relations, mothers, and wives with children in their arms, stretched out for nearly a verst along the road, and you should have seen how they clung to their sons and husbands and fathers, and heard how desperately they wailed as they did so! Usually I behave with restraint and can control my feelings, but I could not hold out this time, and I too wept!' (In journalistic language this is expressed by: 'The patriotic emotion displayed was immense.') 'How can one measure the wholesale woe that is now spreading over almost a third of the world? And we, we are now food for cannon, which in the near future will be offered up in sacrifice to a God of revenge and horror. . . .

'I am quite unable to maintain my inner balance. Oh, how I hate myself for this double-mindedness which prevents my serving one Lord and God. . . .'

That man does not yet believe sufficiently that what destroys the body is not terrible, but that is terrible which destroys both body and soul. And so he cannot refuse the service. But yet while leaving his family he promises in advance that not one Japanese family shall be orphaned through him. He believes in the chief law of God, the law of all religions—to do to others as you wish them to do to you. And in our time there are not thousands but millions of men who more or less consciously recognize that law, not Christians only but Buddhists, Mohammedans, Confucians, and Brahmins as well.

True heroes really exist—not those who are now fêted because, having wished to kill others, they themselves escaped—but true heroes who are now confined in prisons and in the province of Yakútsk for having categorically refused to enter the ranks of the murderers, and have preferred martyrdom to that renunciation of the law of Christ. There are also men like the one who wrote to me, and who will go but will not kill. And even the majority who go without thinking, or trying not to think, of what they are doing, feel in the depths of their souls that they are doing wrong to obey the authorities who tear men from their work and their families and send them needlessly to slaughter, a thing repugnant to their souls and to their faith. They only go because they are so entangled on all sides that—'*Where can I escape to?*'

And those who remain at home not only feel but know this, and express it. Yesterday on the high road I met some peasants returning from Túla. One of them walking beside his empty cart, was reading a leaflet.

'What is that?' I asked. 'A telegram?'

He stopped. 'This is yesterday's, but I have to-day's as well.'

He took another out of his pocket. We stopped and I read it.

'You should have seen what it was like at the station yesterday,' he said. 'It was terrible. Wives and children—more than a thousand of them—all crying and sobbing. They surrounded the train but could not board it. Even strangers looking on were in tears. One Túla woman cried out and died on the spot. She had five children. The children were shoved into different asylums, but the father was sent on all the same. . . . And what do we want with this Manchuria or whatever it is called? We have much land of our own. And what a lot of people have been killed and what a lot of money wasted. . . .'

Yes, the people's attitude to war is quite different now from what it used to be, even in '77.[1] People never reacted then as they do now.

The papers write that at receptions of the Tsar (who is travelling about Russia to hypnotize the people who are being sent off to slaughter) indescribable enthusiasm is shown among the populace. In reality something quite different is happening. One hears on all sides reports of how in one place three Reservists hung themselves, in another two more, and how a woman whose husband had been taken brought her three children to the recruiting office and left them there, while another woman hanged herself in the yard of the military commander's home. Everybody is dissatisfied, gloomy, and embittered. People no longer react to the words: 'For the Faith, the Tsar, and the Fatherland!', the national anthem, and shouts of 'Hurrah!' as they used to do. A war of a different kind, a struggling consciousness of the wrongfulness and sin of the thing to which men are being called, is taking place.

Yes, the great strife of our time is not that now

[1] The Russo-Turkish War of 1877-8.—A. M.

taking place between the Japanese and the Russians, nor that which may blaze up between the White and the Yellow races. It is not the strife carried on by torpedoes, bullets, and bombs, but that spiritual strife which has unceasingly gone on, and is now going on, between the enlightened consciousness of mankind—now awaiting its manifestation—and the darkness and oppression which surrounds and burdens mankind.

In his own time Christ yearned in expectation, and said: 'I came to cast fire upon the earth, and how I wish that it were already kindled.' (Luke xii. 49.)

What Christ longed for is being accomplished. The fire is kindling. Let us not check it, but promote it.

April 30th, 1904.

I should never finish this article if I continued to add to it all that confirms its chief thought. Yesterday news was received of the sinking of Japanese battleships; and in what are called the higher circles of Russian fashionable society, wealthy and intelligent people are rejoicing, with no prickings of conscience, at the destruction of thousands of human lives. And to-day I have received from a simple seaman, a man of the lowest rank of society, the following letter:[1]
'Letter from seaman (here follows his Christian name, patronymic, and family name).
'Much respected Lëv Nikoláevich,
'I greet you with a low bow and with love, much respected Lëv Nikoláevich. I have read your book. It was very pleasant reading for me. I am

[1] This letter in the Russian is ungrammatical, ill-spelt, ill-punctuated, and with capital letters constantly misused.—A. M.

very fond of reading what you write, and as we are now in military action, Lev Nikoláevich, will you please tell me whether or not it is pleasing to God that our commanders compel us to kill. I beg you to write me, Lev Nikoláevich, please, whether or not truth exists now on earth. At the church service the priest speaks of the Christ-loving army. Is it true or not that God loves war? Please, Lèv Nikoláevich, have you any books showing whether truth exists on earth or not? Send me such books and I will pay what they cost. I beg you not to neglect my request, Lèv Nikoláevich. If there are no such books, then write to me. I shall be very glad to receive a letter from you and shall await it with impatience.

'Now farewell. I remain alive and well and wish you the same from the Lord God. Good health and good success in your work.'

[Then follows the address, Port Arthur, the name of his ship, his rank, and his Christian name, patronymic, and family name.]

I cannot reply directly to that good, serious, and truly enlightened man. He is in Port Arthur, with which there is no longer any communication either by post or by telegraph. But we still have a means of mutual intercourse—God, in whom we both believe and concerning whom we both know that military 'action' displeases him. The doubt which has arisen in the man's soul is at the same time its own solution.

And that doubt has now arisen and lives in the souls of thousands and thousands of men, not Russians and Japanese only, but all those unfortunate people who are forcibly compelled to do things most repugnant to human nature.

The hypnotism by which the rulers have stupefied and still try to stupefy people soon passes off and its effect grows ever weaker and weaker; whereas the doubt *'whether or not it is pleasing to God that our commanders compel us to kill'* grows stronger and stronger. It can in no way be extinguished and is spreading more and more widely.

The doubt 'whether or not it is pleasing to God that our commanders compel us to kill' is that spark which Christ brought down upon earth, and which begins to kindle.

And to know and feel this is a great joy.

[*Yásnaya Polyána. May 8th, 1904.*]

A GREAT INIQUITY

Russia is passing through an important period destined to have tremendous results.

The nearness and inevitability of the approaching revolution is as usual felt most keenly by those classes of society which by their position are exempt from the necessity of devoting their whole time and strength to physical labour and who can therefore pay attention to politics. These people—the gentry, merchants, officials, medical men, technicians, professors, teachers, artists, students, and lawyers (belonging for the most part to the so-called intelligentsia of the towns)—are now directing the movement that is taking place in Russia, and are devoting their efforts to replacing the existing political order by another which this or that party considers best adapted to securing the liberty and welfare of the Russian folk.

These people—continually suffering all sorts of restrictions and coercions at the hands of the government; arbitrary exile, imprisonment, prohibitions of meetings, suppression of books and newspapers, and the prohibition of strikes and trades unions, as well as restriction of the rights of subject nationalities, and who at the same time are living a life quite estranged from the majority of the agricultural Russian people—naturally regard the restrictions imposed on them as the chief evil the nation is suffering from, and liberation from them as the thing most to be desired.

So think the Liberals and the Social Democrats, who hope that popular representation will enable them to utilize the power of the State to establish a new social order in accord with their theory. So also think the Revolutionaries, who after replacing the present government by a new one, intend to establish laws securing the greatest freedom and welfare for the whole people.

Yet one need only free oneself for a while from the idea which has taken root among our intelligentsia (that the work now before Russia is the introduction of the forms of political life established in Europe and America, and supposed to ensure the liberty and welfare of all their citizens) and simply consider what is morally wrong in our life, to see clearly that the chief evil from which the Russian people are cruelly and unceasingly suffering (an evil of which they are keenly conscious and of which they continually complain)—cannot be removed by any political reforms, just as it has not till now been removed by political reforms in Europe or America. That evil—the fundamental evil from which the Russian people suffer in common with the peoples of Europe and America—is that the majority of the people are deprived of the indubitable and natural right of every man to have the use of a portion of the land on which he was born. It is only necessary to understand the criminality and wickedness of this deprivation to realize that until this atrocity, continually committed by landowners, has ceased, no political reforms will give freedom and welfare to the people; but that on the contrary only the emancipation of the mass of the people from the land-slavery in which they are now held can render political reform a real expression of the people's will, and not a plaything and tool in the hands of politicians.

That is the thought I wish to communicate in this article to those who, at the present important moment for Russia, sincerely wish to serve not their personal aims but the true welfare of the Russian people.

A GREAT INIQUITY

I

The other day I was walking on the high road to Túla. It was the Saturday before Palm Sunday. Peasants were driving to market in their carts with calves, hens, horses, and cows (some of the cows in such poor condition that they were being taken in the carts). A wrinkled old woman was leading a lean and wretched cow. I knew her, and asked why she was taking the animal to market.

'She has no milk,' said the old woman. 'I must sell her and buy one that has. I daresay I shall have to pay another ten rubles in addition, but I've only got five. Where could I get it? In winter we had to spend eighteen rubles on flour, and we have only one breadwinner. I live with my daughter-in-law and four grandchildren. My son is a house-porter in town.'

'Why doesn't your son live at home?'

'There's nothing for him to do. What land have we? Barely enough for kvas.'[1]

A lean and sallow peasant tramped by, his trousers spattered with mine-clay.

'What's taking you to town?' I asked him.

'I want to buy a horse. It's time to begin ploughing and I haven't got one. But they say horses are dear!'

'How much do you want to give?'

'As much as I have.'

'And how much is that?'

'I've scraped together fifteen rubles.'

'What can you buy nowadays for fifteen rubles? Barely a hide!' put in another peasant. 'Whose mine are you at?' he added, looking at the man's trousers stretched at the knees and smeared with red clay.

---

[1] A non-intoxicating drink usually made from rye-malt and rye-flour.—A. M.

'Komaróv's—Iván Komaróv's.'
'How is it you've earned so little?'
'I worked on half-shares. He took half.'
'How much did you earn?' I asked.
'I got two rubles a week, or even less. But what's to be done? We hadn't enough grain to last till Christmas. There isn't enough to buy necessaries.'

A little farther on a young peasant was taking a sleek, well-fed horse to sell.

'A good horse!' said I.

'You might look for a better but you wouldn't find one,' said he, taking me for a buyer. 'Good for ploughing or driving.'

'Then why are you selling it?'

'I can't use it. I have only two allotments of land and can work them with one horse. I kept two through the winter, but I'm sorry I did. The cattle have eaten up everything, and we need money for the rent.'

'Who is your landlord?'

'Márya Ivánovna—thanks to her for letting us have some land, else we might just as well have hung ourselves.'

'How much do you pay her?'

'She fleeces us of fourteen rubles. But where else can we go? We have to hire it.'

A woman drove up with a little boy wearing a small cap. She knew me and got down and offered me her boy for service. The boy was just a mite, with quick intelligent eyes. 'He looks small, but he can do anything,' she said.

'But why do you want to hire out such a little fellow?'

'Why sir, at least it'll be one less to feed. I have four besides myself, and only one allotment of land. God knows we've nothing to eat. They ask for bread and I have nothing to give them.'

Everyone with whom one talks complains of want, and all alike, from one side or other, come back to the cause of it. They have not enough bread, and that is so because of their lack of land.

These were casual encounters on the road; but go through the peasant world all over Russia and see the horrors of want and suffering obviously caused by the fact that they are deprived of land. Half the Russian peasantry live in such a manner that the question for them is not how to improve their lot, but simply how to keep themselves and their families alive—and all because they are short of land.

Go all through Russia and ask the working people why their life is hard, and what they want, and all of them with one voice will name one and the same thing; which they all unceasingly desire and expect, and unceasingly hope for and think about.

And they cannot help thinking and feeling thus, for apart from the chief thing—their insufficiency of land whereon to maintain themselves—most of them cannot but feel themselves to be in slavery to the landed gentry, landowners, and merchants, whose estates surround their small and insufficient allotments. They cannot but think and feel this, for they are constantly suffering fines, blows, and humiliations, because they have taken a sack of grass or an armful of wood (without which they cannot live) or because a horse has strayed from their land on to the landowner's.

Once on the high road I began talking with a blind peasant beggar. Recognizing me by my conversation to be a literate man who read the papers, but not taking me for one of the gentry, he suddenly stopped and gravely asked: 'Well, is there any rumour?'

A GREAT INIQUITY

'What about?' I asked.

'Why, about the gentry's land.'

When I said that I had heard nothing, the blind man shook his head and did not ask me anything more.

I recently said to one of my former pupils, a prosperous, steady, intelligent, and literate peasant: 'Well, are they talking about the land?'

'It's true the people are talking about it,' he replied.

'And what do you think about it yourself?'

'Well, it will probably come over to us,' said he.

Of all that is happening, this question alone is interesting and important to the whole people. And they believe, and cannot help believing, that it will 'come over'.

They cannot help believing this, because it is plain to them that an increasing population living by agriculture cannot continue to exist when they are allowed only a small portion of the land to feed themselves and all the parasites who have fastened on them and are crawling about them.

II

'What is man?' says Henry George in one of his speeches.

'In the first place he is an animal, a land animal who cannot live without land. All that man produces comes from land; all productive labour, in the final analysis, consists in working up land or materials drawn from land, into such forms as fit them for the satisfaction of human wants and desires. Why, man's very body is drawn from the land. Children of the soil, we come from the land, and to the land we must return. Take away from man all that belongs to the land, and what have you but a disembodied spirit? Therefore he who holds the land on which and from which another man must live, is that man's master; and the man is his slave. The man who holds the land on which I must live can command me to life or to death just as absolutely as though I were his chattel. Talk about abolishing slavery—we have not abolished slavery—we have only abolished one rude form of it, chattel slavery. There is a deeper and a more insidious form, a more cursed form yet before us to abolish, in this industrial slavery that makes a virtual slave, while taunting him and mocking him with the name of freedom.'[1]

'Did you ever think,' says Henry George in another part of the same speech, 'of the utter absurdity and strangeness of the fact that, all over the civilized world, the working classes are the poor classes? . . . Think for a moment how it would strike a rational being who had never been on the earth before, if such an intelligence could come down, and you were to explain to him how we live on earth, how houses, and food and clothing, and all the many things we need, are all produced by work, would he not think that the working people would be the people who lived in the finest houses and had most of everything that work produces? Yet, whether you took him to London or Paris or New York, or even to Burlington, he would find that those called working people were the people who lived in the poorest houses.'[2]

The same thing, I would add, occurs to a still greater extent in the country. Idle people live in luxurious palaces, in large and handsome dwellings, while the workers live in dark and dirty hovels.

'All this is strange—just think of it. We naturally

[1] *The Crime of Poverty* (Henry George Foundation of Great Britain), p. 10.
[2] Ibid., p. 12.

despise poverty; and it is reasonable that we should. . . . Nature gives to labour, and to labour alone; there must be human work before any article of wealth can be produced; and, in a natural state of things, the man who toiled honestly and well would be the rich man, and he who did not work would be poor. We have so reversed the order of nature that we are accustomed to think of a working-man as a poor man. . . . The primary cause of this is that we compel those who work to pay others for permission to do so. You buy a coat, a horse, a house; there you are paying the seller for labour exerted, for something that he has produced, or that he has got from the man who did produce it; but when you pay a man for land, what are you paying him for? You are paying for something that no man has produced; you pay him for something that was here before man was, or for a value that was created, not by him individually, but by the community of which you are a part.'[1]

That is why he who has seized land and possesses it is rich, whereas he who works on it or on its products is poor.

'We talk about over-production. How can there be such a thing as over-production while people want? All these things that are said to be over-produced are desired by many people. Why do they not get them? They do not get them because they have not the means to buy them; not that they do not want them. Why have they not the means to buy them? They earn too little. When great masses of men have to work for an average of $1.40 a day, it is no wonder that great quantities of goods cannot be sold.

'Now why is it that men have to work for such

[1] Ibid., p. 13.

low wages? Because, if they were to demand higher wages, there are plenty of unemployed men ready to step into their places. It is this mass of unemployed men who compel that fierce competition that drives wages down to the point of bare subsistence. Why is it that there are men who cannot get employment? Did you ever think what a strange thing it is that men cannot find employment? Adam had no difficulty in finding employment; neither had Robinson Crusoe; the finding of employment was the last thing that troubled them.

'If men cannot find an employer, why can they not employ themselves? Simply because they are shut out from the element on which human labour can alone be exerted. Men are compelled to compete with each other for the wages of an employer, because they have been robbed of the natural opportunities of employing themselves; because they cannot find a piece of God's world on which to work without paying some other human creature for the privilege.'[1]

'Men pray to the Almighty to relieve poverty. But poverty comes not from God's laws—it is blasphemy of the worst kind to say that; it comes from man's injustice to his fellows. Supposing the Almighty were to hear the prayer, how could He carry out the request, so long as His laws are what they are? Consider—the Almighty gives us nothing of the things that constitute wealth; He merely gives us the raw material which must be utilized by man to produce wealth. Does He not give us enough of that now? How could He relieve poverty even if He were to give us more? Supposing, in answer to these prayers, He were to increase the

[1] *The Crime of Poverty* (Henry George Foundation of Great Britain), p. 14.

power of the sun, or the virtues of the soil? Supposing he were to make plants more prolific, or animals to produce after their kind more abundantly? Who would get the benefit of it? Take a country where land is completely monopolized, as it is in most of the civilized countries—who would get the benefit of it? Simply the landowners. And even if God, in answer to prayer, were to send down out of the heavens those things that men require, who would get the benefit?

'In the Old Testament we are told that when the Israelites journeyed through the desert, they were hungered, and that God sent down out of the heavens—manna. There was enough for all of them, and they all took it and were relieved. But, supposing that desert had been held as private property, as the soil of Great Britain is held, as the soil even of our new States is being held; supposing that one of the Israelites had a square mile, and another one had twenty square miles, and another one had a hundred square miles, and the great majority of the Israelites did not have enough to set the soles of their feet upon, which they could call their own—what would become of the manna? What good would it have done to the majority? Not a whit. Though God had sent down manna enough for all, that manna would have been the property of the landholders; they would have employed some of the others, perhaps, to gather it up in heaps for them, and would have sold it to their hungry brethren. Consider it; this purchase and sale of manna might have gone on until the majority of the Israelites had given up all they had, even to the clothes off their backs. What then? Well, then they would not have had anything left with which to buy manna, and the consequence would have been that while they went hungry the manna would have lain in great heaps, and the landowners would have been complaining of the over-production of manna. There would have been a great harvest of manna and hungry people, just precisely the phenomenon that we see to-day.'[1]

'I do not mean to say that, even after you had set right this fundamental injustice, there would not be many things to do; but this I do mean to say, that our treatment of land lies at the bottom of all social questions. This I do mean to say, that, do what you please, reform as you may, you never can get rid of widespread poverty so long as the element on which, and from which, all men must live is made the private property of some men. It is utterly impossible. Reform government—get taxes down to the minimum—build railroads; institute co-operative stores; divide profits, if you choose, between employers and employed—and what will be the result? The result will be that land will increase in value—that will be the result—that and nothing else. Experience shows this. Do not all improvements simply increase the value of land—the price that some must pay others for the privilege of living?'[2]

Let me add that we constantly see the same thing in Russia. All the landowners complain that their estates are unprofitable and are run at a loss, but the price of land is continually rising. It cannot but rise, for the population is increasing and land is a matter of life and death to it.

And so the people give all they can, not only their labour but even their lives, for the land which is being withheld from them.

[1] *The Crime of Poverty* (Henry George Foundation of Great Britain), p. 15.
[2] Ibid., p. 14.

III

There used to be cannibalism, there used to be human sacrifices, there used to be religious prostitution and the killing of weakly children and girls; there used to be blood vengeance and the slaughter of whole populations, judicial tortures, quarterings, burnings at the stake, the lash, and—a thing that has disappeared within our own memory—the *spitzruten*[1] and slavery.

But if we have outlived those dreadful customs and institutions, that does not prove the non-existence among us of institutions and customs which have become as abhorrent to enlightened reason and conscience as those which in their day were abolished and are now for us only a dreadful memory. The path of mankind towards perfection is endless, and at every moment of history there are superstitions, deceptions, and pernicious and evil institutions that men have already outlived and that belong to the past, as well as others that present themselves to us as in the mists of a distant future, and some that we have with us now and the supersession of which forms the problem of our life. Capital punishment and punishment in general is such a case in our day, so also is prostitution, flesh-eating, and the business of militarism and war, and so—nearest and most urgent case of all—is private property in land.

But as people have never freed themselves suddenly from customary injustices nor done so immediately their harmfulness was recognized by the more sensitive people, but have freed themselves in jerks, with stoppages and reactions and then again by fresh leaps towards freedom, comparable

[1] *Spitzruten*—rods used on soldiers who had to run the gauntlet, from which they sometimes died.—A. M.

to the pangs of birth—as was the case with the recent abolition of serfdom—so it is now with the abolition of private property in land.

Prophets and sages of old pointed out the evil and injustice of private property in land thousands of years ago, and the evil of it has been pointed out more and more frequently ever since by the progressive thinkers of Europe. It was specially clearly expressed by those active in the French revolution. Subsequently, owing to the increase of population and the seizure by the rich of a great deal of what had been free land, and also owing to the spread of education and the decreasing harshness of manners, that injustice has become so obvious that progressive people, and even very ordinary people, cannot help seeing and feeling it. But men, especially those who profit by landed property—both the owners themselves and others whose interests are bound up with that institution—are so accustomed to this order of things and have profited by it so long, that they often do not see its injustice and use every possible means to conceal the truth from themselves and from others. The truth is continually appearing more and more clearly, but they try to distort it, suppress it, or extinguish it, and if they cannot succeed in this, then they try to hush it up.

Very striking in this respect is the fate of the activity of the remarkable man who appeared towards the end of the last century—Henry George—who devoted his immense mental powers to elucidating the injustice and cruelty of the institution of landed property and to indicating means of rectifying that injustice under the forms of government now existing in all countries. He did this by his books, articles, and speeches, with such extraordinary force and lucidity that no unprejudiced

A GREAT INIQUITY

person reading his works could fail to agree with his arguments and to see that no reforms can render the condition of the people satisfactory until this fundamental injustice has been abolished, and that the means he proposes for its abolition are reasonable, just, and practicable.

But what has happened? Notwithstanding the fact that when Henry George's works first appeared in English they spread rapidly throughout the Anglo-Saxon world and their high quality could not fail to be appreciated, so that it seemed as if the truth must prevail and find its way to accomplishment—it very soon appeared that in England (and even in Ireland where the crying injustice of private property in land was very clearly manifest) the majority of the most influential and educated people—despite the convincing force of the argument and the practicability of the methods proposed—were opposed to his teaching. Radicals like Parnell, who had at first sympathized with Henry George's projects, soon drew back from it, regarding political reform as more important. In England all the aristocrats were opposed to it, and among others the famous Toynbee, Gladstone, and Herbert Spencer. This latter, after having at first in his *Statics* very definitely expounded the injustice of landed property, afterwards withdrew that opinion and bought up the first edition of his book in order to eliminate all that he had said about it.

At Oxford when Henry George was lecturing, the students organized a hostile demonstration, and the Roman Catholic party regarded his teaching as simply sinful, immoral, dangerous, and contrary to Christ's teaching. The orthodox science of political economy rose up against Henry George's teaching in the same way. Learned professors from the height of their superiority refuted it without understanding it, chiefly because it did not recognize the fundamental principles of their pseudo-science. The Socialists were also inimical—considering the most important problem of the period to be not the land question, but the complete abolition of private property. The chief method of opposing Henry George was, however, the method always employed against irrefutable and self-evident truths. This, which is still being applied to Henry George's teaching, was that of ignoring it. This method of hushing up was practised so successfully that Labouchere, a British Member of Parliament, could say publicly and without contradiction that he 'was not such a visionary as Henry George, and did not propose to take the land from the landlords in order afterwards to rent it out again, but that he only demanded the imposition of a tax on the value of the land'. That is, while attributing to Henry George what he could not possibly have said, Labouchere corrected that imaginary fantasy by putting forward Henry George's actual proposal.[1]

So that thanks to the collective efforts of all those interested in defending the institution of landed property, the teaching of Henry George (irrefutably convincing in its simplicity and lucidity) remains almost unknown, and as years go by attracts ever less and less attention.

Here and there in Scotland, Portugal, or New Zealand, he is remembered, and among hundreds of scientists one is found who knows and defends his teaching. But in England and the United States the number of his adherents dwindles more and more; in France his teaching is almost

[1] See *The Life of Henry George* by his son (Doubleday Doran & Co., New York, 1900), p. 516.

unknown; in Germany it is preached in a very small circle; and everywhere it is stifled by the noisy teaching of Socialism. So that among the majority of supposedly educated people it is known only by name.

IV

They do not argue with Henry George's teaching, they simply do not know it. (There is no other way of dealing with it, for a man who becomes acquainted with it cannot help agreeing with it.)

If it is sometimes referred to, people either attribute to it what it does not say or reassert what Henry George has refuted, or else contradict him simply because he does not conform to the pedantic, arbitrary, and superficial principles of so-called political economy which they recognize as irrefutable truths.

But for all that, the truth that land cannot be private property has so elucidated itself by the actual experience of contemporary life, that there is only one way of continuing to maintain an order of things in which the rights of private property in land are recognized—namely, not to think about it, to ignore the truth, and to occupy oneself with other absorbing affairs. And that is what is being done by the men of our contemporary Christian world.

The political workers of Europe and America occupy themselves with all sorts of things for the welfare of their peoples: tariffs, colonies, income-tax, military and naval budgets, socialistic assemblies, unions and syndicates, the election of presidents, diplomatic relations—anything except the one thing without which there cannot be any true improvement in the people's condition—the re-establishment of the infringed right of all men to use the land. And though the political workers of the Christian world feel in their souls, and cannot but feel, that all they are doing both in the industrial strife and the military strife into which they put all their energies, can result in nothing but the general exhaustion of the strength of the nations; still without looking ahead they yield to the demands of the moment and continue to whirl around as if with a sole desire to forget themselves in an enchanted circle from which there is no issue.

Strange as is this temporary blindness of the political workers of Europe and the United States, it can be explained by the fact that in both continents the people have already gone so far along a wrong road that the majority of them are already torn from the land (or in the United States have never lived on the land) and get their living in factories or as hired agricultural labourers, and desire and demand only one thing—an improvement of their position as hired labourers. It is therefore understandable that to the politicians of Europe and America, attending to the demands of the majority, it may seem that the chief means of improving the position of the people consists in tariffs, trusts, and colonies. But to Russian people —in Russia where the agricultural population forms eighty per cent. of the whole nation and where all these people ask only one thing, that opportunity be given them to remain on the land—it should be clear that something else is needed.

The people of Europe and the United States are in the position of a man who has already gone so far along a road which at first seemed to him the right one, that he is afraid to recognize his mistake although the farther he goes the farther he is removed from his goal. But Russia is still standing at the cross-roads, and can still, as the wise saying has it, 'ask her way while still on the road'.

And what are those Russians doing who wish, or at least say they wish, to arrange a good life for the people?

In everything they imitate what is done in Europe and America.

To arrange a good life for the people they are concerned about freedom of the Press, religious toleration, freedom for trade unions, tariffs, conditional punishments, the separation of the Church from the State, Co-operative Associations, a future socialization of the implements of labour, and above all representative government—that same representative government which has long existed in the European and American countries, but whose existence has never conduced in the least, nor is now conducing, either to the solution of that land question which alone solves all difficulties, or even to its presentation. If Russian politicians do speak about land abuses, which for some reason they call 'the agrarian question' (possibly imagining that this stupid phraseology will conceal the substance of the matter) they do not suggest that private property in land is an evil that should be abolished, but merely suggest various patchings and palliatives to plaster up, hide, and avoid the recognition of this essential, ancient, cruel, obvious, and crying injustice—which awaits its turn to be abolished not only in Russia but in the whole world.

In Russia, where the hundred-million mass of the people continually suffers from the holding up of land by private owners and unceasingly cries about it, the conduct of those who pretend to search everywhere (except where it lies) for means of improving the condition of the people, reminds me exactly of what takes place on the stage when the spectators can all see perfectly well the man who has hidden himself, and the actors can also see him but pretend not to, purposely diverting each other's attention and looking at everything except what it is important for them to see.

V

People have driven into an enclosure a herd of cows on the milk products of which they live. The cows have eaten up and trampled down the forage in the enclosure, they are famished and have chewed each other's tails, they are lowing and struggling to get out of that enclosure into the pasture lands beyond. But the people who live on the milk of these cows have surrounded the enclosure with fields of mint, dye-yielding plants, and tobacco plantations. They have cultivated flowers, and laid out a race-course, a park, and lawn-tennis courts; and they will not let the cows out lest they should spoil these things. But the cows bellow and grow thin, and people begin to fear that they will have no milk. So they devise various means of improving the condition of the cows. They arrange to put awnings over them, they have them rubbed down with wet brushes, they gild their horns, and alter the hours of milking. They concern themselves with the supervision and doctoring of the old and sick cows; they invent new and improved methods of milking and expect that some kind of extraordinarily nutritious grass which they have planted in the enclosure will grow up. They argue about these and many other matters, but do not (and cannot without disturbing all the surroundings of the enclosure) do the one simple thing necessary for the cows as well as for themselves—that is, take down the fence and set the cows free to enjoy naturally the abundant-pastures that surround them.

People who act in this way behave unreasonably, but there is an explanation of their conduct: they are sorry to sacrifice the things with which they have surrounded the enclosure. But what can be said of those who have planted nothing round their enclosure but who (imitating those who keep their cows enclosed for the sake of what they have planted around the enclosure) also keep their cows enclosed, and affirm that they do it for the cows' welfare?

But that is just what Russians—whether for or against the government—do, who arrange all sorts of European institutions for the Russian people who are suffering constantly from want of land, and who forget and deny the chief thing, the one thing the Russian people require—the freeing of the land from private ownership and the establishment of equal rights to the land for everybody.

It is understandable that European parasites who do not draw their subsistence either directly or indirectly from the labour of their own English, French, or German working men, but whose bread is produced by colonial workers in exchange for factory products, and who do not see the labour and sufferings of the workers who feed and support them—may devise a future Socialistic organization for which they are supposedly preparing mankind, and with untroubled conscience amuse themselves meanwhile by electoral campaigns, party struggles, parliamentary debates, the establishment and overthrow of ministries, and various other pastimes which they call science and art.

The real people who feed these European parasites are the labourers they do not see in India, Africa, Australia, and to some extent Russia. But it is not so for us Russians. We have no colonies where slaves we never see provide food for us in exchange for our manufactures. Our breadwinners, hungry and suffering, are always before our eyes, and we cannot transfer the burden of our unjust life to distant colonies, that invisible slaves should feed us.

Our sins are always before us. . . .

And here—instead of entering into the needs of those who support us, listening to their cry and endeavouring to answer it—under pretence of serving them, we prepare for the future a Socialist organization in the European manner, occupying ourselves meanwhile with what amuses and distracts us and professes to be directed to the benefit of the people from whom we are squeezing the last ounce of strength that they may support us, their parasites.

For the welfare of the people we endeavour to abolish the censorship of books, to get rid of arbitrary banishment, to establish primary and agricultural schools everywhere, to increase the number of hospitals, to abolish passports, to cancel arrears of taxes, to establish a strict inspection of factories and compensation for injured workers, to survey the land, to provide assistance through the Peasant Bank for the purchasing of land by the peasants, and much else.

Once realize the unceasing sufferings of millions of people: the dying of old men, women, and children from want, as well as the mortality caused by overwork and insufficient food—once realize the enslavement, the humiliations, all the useless expenditure of strength, the perversion, and the horrors of the needless sufferings of the Russian rural population which arise from lack of land—and it becomes quite clear that all such measures as the abolition of the censorship, of arbitrary banishment, and so on, which are sought for by the pseudo-defenders of the people would (even were they realized) amount to an insignificant drop in the sea of want from which the people are suffering.

But the men concerned with the welfare of the people, while devising insignificant changes that are unimportant both in quality and quantity, not only leave the hundred-million workers in the unceasing slavery caused by the seizure of the land, but many of these men—and the most advanced of them—would like the sufferings of the people to be still more intensified, that they may be driven to the necessity (after leaving on their way millions of victims who will perish of want and depravity) of exchanging the happy agricultural life to which they are accustomed and to which they are attached, for the improved factory life they have devised for them.

The Russian people, owing to their agricultural environment, their love of this form of life, and their Christian trend of character, and also because, almost alone among European nations, they continue to be an agricultural people and wish to remain so—are as it were providentially placed by historic conditions in the forefront of the truly progressive movement of mankind in regard to what is called the labour question.

Yet this Russian people is invited by its fancied representatives and leaders to follow in the wake of the decadent and entangled European and American nations, and to pervert itself and renounce its calling as quickly as possible, in order to become like the Europeans in general.

Astonishing as is the poverty of thought of those men who do not think with their own minds but slavishly repeat what is said by their European models, the hardness of their hearts and their cruelty is still more astonishing.

VI

'Woe unto you, scribes and Pharisees, hypocrites! for ye are like unto whited sepulchres, which outwardly appear beautiful, but inwardly are full of dead men's bones, and of all uncleanness. Even so ye also outwardly appear righteous unto men, but inwardly ye are full of hypocrisy and iniquity.' MATT. xxiii. 27-8.

There was a time when in the name of God and of true faith in Him, men were destroyed, tortured, executed, and slaughtered by tens and hundreds of thousands. And now, from the height of our superiority, we look down on the men who did those things.

But we are wrong. There are just such people among us; the difference is only that the men of old did these things in the name of God and His true service, while those who do similar evil among us now, do it in the name of 'the people' and for their true service. And as among those men of old there were some who were insanely and confidently convinced that they knew the truth, and others who were hypocrites making careers for themselves under pretence of serving God, and the masses who unreasoningly followed the most dexterous and bold—so now those who do evil in the name of service of the people are composed of men insanely and confidently convinced that they alone know what is right, of hypocrites, and of the masses. Much evil was done in their time by the self-proclaimed servants of God, thanks to the teaching they called theology; but if the servants of the people have done less evil by a teaching they call scientific, that is only because they have not yet had time, though their conscience is already burdened by rivers of blood and a great dividing and embittering of the people.

The features of both these activities are alike.

First there is the dissolute and bad life of the majority of these servants both of God and of the people. (Their dignity as the chief servants of God, or of the people, frees them in their opinion from any necessity to restrain their conduct.)

The second feature is the utter lack of interest, attention, or love for that which they desire to serve. God has been and is merely a banner for those servants of His. In reality they did not love Him or seek communion with Him, and neither knew Him nor wished to know Him. So also with many of the servants of the people. 'The people' were and are only a banner, and far from loving them or seeking intercourse with them they did not know them, but in the depths of their souls regarded them with contempt, aversion, and fear.

The third feature is that while they are preoccupied, the former with the service of one and the same God, the latter with the service of one and the same people, they not only disagree among themselves as to the means of their service, but regard the activity of all who do not agree with them as false and pernicious, and call for its forcible suppression. From this, in the former case, came burnings at the stake, inquisitions, and massacres; and in the latter, executions, imprisonments, revolutions, and assassinations.

And finally, the chief and most characteristic feature of both is their complete indifference to, and absolute ignorance of, what is demanded by the One they serve, and of what is proclaimed and announced by Him. God, whom they serve and have served so zealously, has directly and clearly expressed in what they recognize as a Divine revelation, that He is to be served only by men loving their neighbours and doing to others as they wish them to do to them. But they have not recognized this as the means of serving God. They demand something quite different, which they themselves have invented and announced as the demands of God. The servants of the people do just the same. They do not at all recognize what the people express, desire, and clearly ask for. They choose to serve them by what the people not only do not ask of them but have not the least conception of. They serve them by means they have invented, and not by the one thing for which the people never cease to look and for which they unceasingly ask.

VII

Of all the essential changes in the forms of social life there is one that is ripest the world over, and without which no single step forward can be accomplished in the life of man. The necessity of this alteration is obvious to every man who is free from preconceived theories; and it is the concern not of Russia alone, but of the whole world. All the sufferings of mankind in our time are connected with it. We in Russia are fortunate in that the great majority of our people, living by agricultural labour, do not recognize the right o. private property in land, but desire and demand the abolition of that ancient abuse, and express their desire unceasingly.

But no one sees this or wants to see it.

What is the cause of this perversity?

Why do good, kind, intelligent men, of whom many can be found among the liberals, the socialists, the revolutionaries, and even among government officials—why do these men, who desire the people's welfare, not see the one thing they are in need of, for which they unceasingly strive, and without which they constantly suffer? Why are they concerned instead with most various things, the realization of which cannot contribute to the people's welfare without the realization of that which the people desire?

The whole activity of these servants of the people—both governmental and anti-governmental—resembles that of a man who, wishing to help a horse that has stuck in a bog, sits in the cart and shifts the load from place to place, imagining he is helping matters thereby.

Why is this?

The answer is the same as to all inquiries why the people of our time, who might live well and happily, are living badly and miserably.

It is because these men—both governmental and anti-governmental—who are organizing the welfare of the people, lack religion. Without religion man cannot live a reasonable life himself; still less can he know what is good and what is bad, what is necessary and what is unnecessary, for others. That alone is why the men of our time in general, and the Russian intelligentsia in particular (who are completely bereft of religious consciousness and proudly announce that fact), so perversely misunderstand the life and demands of the people they wish to serve—claiming for them many different things, but not the one thing they need.

Without religion it is impossible really to love men, and without love it is impossible to know what they need, and what is more and what less needed. Only those who are not religious and therefore do not truly love, can devise trifling and unimportant improvements in the condition of the people without seeing the chief evil from which the people suffer, and that is to some extent caused by those who wish to help them. Only such people can preach more or less cleverly devised abstract theories concerning the people's future happiness, and not see their present sufferings which call for an immediate alleviation that is quite possible. It is as if someone who has deprived a hungry man of food should give him advice (and that of a very doubtful character) as to how to get food in future—without deeming it necessary to share with him the food he has taken from him.

Fortunately the great and beneficent movements of humanity are accomplished not by parasites feeding on the people's marrow—whatever they may call themselves: government officials, revolutionaries, or liberals—but by religious men, that is by serious, simple, industrious people, who live not for their own profit, vanity, or ambition, and not to attain external results, but for the fulfilment before God of their human vocation.

Such men, and only such, move mankind forward by their quiet but resolute activity. They do not try to distinguish themselves in the eyes of others by devising this or that improvement in the condition of the people (such improvements can be innumerable and are all insignificant if the chief thing is left undone) but they try to live in accord with the law of God and their conscience, and in that endeavour naturally come across the most obvious infringement of God's law and seek means of deliverance both for themselves and others.

A few days ago an acquaintance of mine, a doctor, was waiting for a train in the third-class waiting-room of a large railway station and was reading a paper, when a peasant sitting by him asked about the news. There was an article in that paper about the 'agrarian' conference. The doctor translated the ridiculous word 'agrarian' into Russian, and when the peasant understood that the matter concerned the land, he asked him to read the article. The doctor began to read and other peasants came up. A group collected, some pressed on the backs of others and some sat on the floor, but the faces of all wore a look of solemn concentration. When the reading was over, an old man at the back sighed deeply and crossed himself. He certainly had not understood anything of the confused jargon in which the article was written (which even men who could themselves talk that jargon could not readily understand). He understood nothing of what was written in that article, but he did understand that the matter concerned the great and longstanding sin from which his ancestors had suffered and from which he himself still suffered, and he understood that those who were committing this sin were beginning to be conscious of it. Having understood this he mentally turned to God, and crossed himself. And in that movement of his hand there was more meaning and content than in all the prattle that now fills the columns of our papers. He understood, as all the people understood, that the seizure of the land by those who do not work on it is a great sin, from which his ancestors suffered and perished physically and he himself and his neighbours continue to suffer physically, while those who committed this sin in the past, and those who now commit it, suffer spiritually all the time—and that this sin like every sin (like the sin of serfdom within his own memory) must inevitably come to an end. He knew and felt this, and therefore could not but turn to God at the thought of an approaching solution.

VIII

'Great social reforms,' says Mazzini, 'always have and always will result only from great religious movements.'

Such a religious movement now awaits the Russian people—the whole Russian people, both the workers deprived of land and even more the landowners (large, medium, and small) and all the hundreds of thousands of men who though not actually possessed of land, occupy advantageous positions thanks to the compulsory labour of those who are deprived of it.

The religious movement now due among the Russian people consists in cancelling the great sin that has for so long tormented and divided people not only in Russia but in the whole world.

That sin cannot be undone by political reforms or socialist systems planned for the future, or by a revolution now. Still less can it be undone by philanthropic contributions, or government organizations for the purchase and distribution of land among the peasants.

Such palliative measures only divert attention from the essence of the problem and thus hinder its solution. No artificial sacrifices are necessary, nor concern about the people—what is needed is simply that all who are committing this sin or taking part in it should be conscious of it, and desire to be free from it.

It is only necessary that the undeniable truth which the best of the people know and have always known—that the land cannot be anyone's exclusive property, and that to refuse access to it to those who are in need of it is a sin—should be recognized by all men; that people should become ashamed of withholding the land from those who need it for their subsistence; and that it should be felt to be shameful to participate in any way in withholding the land from those who need it—that it should be felt to be shameful to possess land, and shameful to profit by the labour of men who are forced to work merely because they are refused their legitimate right to the land.

What happened in regard to serfdom (when the landholding nobility and gentry became ashamed of it, when the government became ashamed to maintain those unjust and cruel laws, and when it became evident to the peasants themselves that a wrong for which there was no justification was being done them) should come about in regard to property in land. And this is necessary not for any one class, however numerous, but for all classes, and not merely for all classes and all men of any one country, but for all mankind.

IX

'Social reform is not to be secured by noise and shouting, by complaints and denunciation, by the formation of parties or the making of revolutions,' wrote Henry George, 'but by the awakening of thought and the progress of ideas. Until there be correct thought there cannot be right action, and when there is correct thought right action will follow. . . .

'The great work of the present for every man and every organization of men who would improve social conditions is the work of education, the propagation of ideas. It is only as it aids this that anything else can avail. And in this work everyone who can think may aid, first by forming clear ideas himself and then by endeavouring to arouse the thought of those with whom he comes in contact.'[1]

That is quite right, but to serve that great cause there must be something else besides thought—a religious feeling, that feeling in consequence of which the serf-owners of the last century acknowledged that they were in the wrong, and sought means—in spite of personal losses and even ruin—to free themselves from the guilt that oppressed them.

If the great work of freeing the land is to be accomplished, that same feeling must arise among people of the possessing classes, and must arise to such an extent that people will be ready to sacrifice everything simply to free themselves from the sin in which they have lived and are living.

To talk in various assemblies and committees about improving the condition of the people while possessing hundreds, thousands, and tens of thousands of acres, trading in land, and benefiting in this or that way from landed property, and living luxuriously thanks to the oppression of the people that arises from that evident and cruel injustice—without being willing to sacrifice one's own exceptional advantages obtained from that same injustice—is not only not a good thing, it is both harmful and horrid, and is condemned by common sense, honesty, and Christianity.

It is not necessary to devise cunning means of improving the position of men who are deprived of their legitimate right to the land, but that those who deprive them of it should understand the sin they commit, and cease to participate in it whatever this may cost. Only such moral activity of every man can and will contribute to the solution of the question now confronting humanity.

[1] *Social Problems* (Henry George Foundation of Great Britain), p. 209.

A GREAT INIQUITY

The emancipation of the serfs in Russia was accomplished not by Alexander II, but by those men who understood the sin of serfdom and tried to liberate themselves from it regardless of their personal advantage. It was effected chiefly by Novikóv, Radíshchev, and the Decembrists[1]—those men who (without causing others to suffer) were ready to suffer themselves, and who did suffer for the sake of loyalty to what they felt to be the truth.

The same ought to occur in relation to the emancipation of the land. And I believe there are men living who will accomplish that great work which now faces not only the Russian people but the whole world.

The land question in our time has reached such a stage of ripeness as legalized serfdom had reached fifty years ago. Exactly the same thing is being repeated. As people then sought means of remedying the general uneasiness and dissatisfaction that society felt, and all sorts of external, governmental means were applied, but nothing helped or could help while the ripening question of personal slavery remained unsolved—so now no external measures will help, or can help, until the ripe question of landed property is settled.

Just as measures are now proposed for adding slices to the peasants' land, and for the Peasant Bank to aid them in the purchase of land, and so on, so palliative measures were then proposed and enacted—the so-called 'inventories', rules restricting work for the proprietor to three days a week, and much else. Just as now the owners of land talk about the injustice of terminating the wrongful

[1] Russian radicals of the late eighteenth and early nineteenth century, who suffered exile and other penalties for their reformist efforts.—A. M.

ownership of land, so they then talked of the wrongfulness of depriving the owners of their serfs. Just as the Church then justified serfdom, so now science (which has taken the place of the Church) justifies property in land. As then the serf-owners, more or less realizing their sin, endeavoured to mitigate it in various ways without freeing the slaves, and allowed serfs to pay ransom to free themselves from compulsory work for their masters, or lessened the labour demanded of them, so now the more sensitive landowners, feeling their guilt, try to redeem it by renting their land to the peasantry on easier terms, by selling it through the Land Banks, and organizing for the people schools, ridiculous amusement houses, magic lanterns, and theatres.

And the indifferent attitude of the government is also similar. But as then the question was solved not by those who devised ingenious methods of relieving and improving the condition of the serfs, but by those who—acknowledging the urgent necessity of a solution—did not postpone it to the future, did not anticipate special difficulties, but tried to end the evil at once, not admitting the idea that there could be circumstances in which an acknowledged wrong could continue, and who took the course which appeared best under the existing conditions—so it is now with the land question.

That question will be solved not by men who try to mitigate the evil, or devise alleviations for the people, or postpone the task to the future, but by those who understand that however much a wrong may be mitigated, it remains a wrong—that it is senseless to devise alleviations for a man whom we are torturing, and that one cannot delay when people are suffering, but must at once adopt the best means of ending that suffering.

A GREAT INIQUITY

This is the more easily accomplished in that the method of solving the land question has been worked out by Henry George so thoroughly that even under the existing State organization and compulsory taxation it is impossible to reach any more practical, just, and peaceful decision.

'To beat down and cover up the truth that I have tried to-night to make clear to you,' said Henry George, 'selfishness will call on ignorance. But it has in it the germinative force of truth, and the times are ripe for it. . . .

'The ground is ploughed; the seed is set; the good tree will grow. So little now; only the eye of faith can see it.'[1]

And I think Henry George is right that the removal of the sin of property in land is near, that the movement evoked by him was the last birth-throe, and that the birth itself is imminent—the liberation of men from sufferings they have borne so long. I also think (and I should like to contribute to this in however small a degree) that the removal of this great and world-wide sin—the cessation of which will be an era in the history of mankind—awaits our Russian Slavonic people predestined by its spiritual and economic character for this great and world-wide task. I think that the Russian people should not be proletarianized in imitation of the peoples of Europe and America, but should on the contrary solve the land question at home by the abolition of private ownership, and should show other people the path to a reasonable, free, and happy life (outside industrial, factory, and capitalistic violence and slavery)—in which its great and historic vocation lies.

I should like to think that we Russian parasites, reared by and having received leisure for mental

[1] *Life of Henry George* (by his son) p. 296.

work through the people's labour, shall understand our sin and (independently of personal advantage) try to undo it for the sake of the truth that condemns us.

[*June 1905.*]

SHAKESPEARE AND THE DRAMA

I

An article by Ernest Howard Crosby[1] on Shakespeare's attitude towards the people has suggested to me the idea of expressing the opinion I formed long ago about Shakespeare's works, an opinion quite contrary to that established throughout the European world. Recalling the struggle with doubts, the pretences, and the efforts to attune myself to Shakespeare that I went through owing to my complete disagreement with the general adulation, and supposing that many people have experienced and are experiencing the same perplexity, I think it may be of some use definitely and frankly to express this disagreement of mine with the opinion held by the majority, especially as the conclusions I came to on examining the causes of my disagreement are it seems to me not devoid of interest and significance.

My disagreement with the established opinion about Shakespeare is not the result of a casual mood or of a light-hearted attitude towards the subject, but it is the result of repeated and strenuous efforts extending over many years to harmonize my views with the opinions about Shakespeare accepted throughout the whole educated Christian world.

[1] E. H. Crosby was for some time a member of the New York State Legislature; subsequently he went to Egypt as a judge in the Mixed Tribunals. While there he began reading the works of Tolstóy, which influenced him strongly. He visited Tolstóy, and afterwards co-operated with him in various ways. In an essay on 'Shakespeare and the Working Classes' he drew attention to the anti-democratic tendency of that poet's plays, and Tolstóy began his own essay intending it as a preface to Crosby's.—A. M.

I remember the astonishment I felt when I first read Shakespeare. I had expected to receive a great aesthetic pleasure, but on reading one after another the works regarded as his best, *King Lear, Romeo and Juliet, Hamlet,* and *Macbeth,* not only did I not experience pleasure but I felt an insuperable repulsion and tedium, and a doubt as to whether I lacked sense—since I considered as insignificant or even simply bad, works which are regarded as the summit of perfection by the whole educated world —or whether the importance attributed to Shakespeare's works by that educated world lacks sense. My perplexity was increased by the fact that I have always keenly felt the beauties of poetry in all its forms: why then did Shakespeare's works, recognized by the whole world as works of artistic genius, not only fail to please me but even seem detestable? For a long time I distrusted my judgement, and to check my conclusions I have repeatedly, during the past fifty years, set to work to read Shakespeare in all possible forms—in Russian, in English, and in German in Schlegel's translation, as I was advised to. I read the tragedies, comedies, and historical plays several times over, and I invariably experienced the same feelings—repulsion, weariness, and bewilderment. Now, before writing this article, as an old man of seventy-five,[1] wishing once more to check my conclusions, I have again read the whole of Shakespeare, including the historical plays, the *Henrys, Troilus and Cressida, The Tempest,* and *Cymbeline,* &c., and have experienced the same feeling still more strongly, no longer with perplexity but with a firm and unshakable conviction that the undisputed fame Shakespeare enjoys as a great

[1] Tolstóy was born in 1828. This essay appeared in 1906, so that he began his re-reading of Shakespeare three years before this article was published.—A. M.

genius—which makes writers of our time imitate him, and readers and spectators, distorting their aesthetic and ethical sense, seek non-existent qualities in him—is a great evil, as every falsehood is.

Although I know that the majority of people have such faith in Shakespeare's greatness that on reading this opinion of mine they will not even admit the possibility of its being correct and will not pay any attention to it, I shall nevertheless try as best I can to show why I think Shakespeare cannot be admitted to be either a writer of great genius or even an average one.

For this purpose I will take one of the most admired of Shakespeare's dramas—*King Lear*, in enthusiastic praise of which most of the critics agree.

'The tragedy of Lear is deservedly celebrated among the dramas of Shakespeare,' says Dr. Johnson. 'There is perhaps no play which keeps the attention so strongly fixed, which so much agitates our passions and interests our curiosity.'

'We wish that we could pass this play over and say nothing about it,' says Hazlitt. 'All that we can say must fall far short of the subject, or even of what we ourselves conceive of it. To attempt to give a description of the play itself or of its effect upon the mind is mere impertinence; yet we must say something. It is then the best of Shakespeare's plays, for it is the one in which he was most in earnest.'

'If the originality of invention did not so much stamp almost every play of Shakespeare that to name one as the most original seems a disparagement to others,' says Hallam, 'we might say that this great prerogative of genius was exercised above all in Lear. It diverges more from the model of regular tragedy than *Macbeth* or *Othello*, or even more than *Hamlet*, but the fable is better constructed than in the last of these and it displays full as much of the almost superhuman inspiration of the poet as the other two.'

'King Lear may be recognized as the perfect model of the dramatic art of the whole world,' says Shelley.

'I am not minded to say much of Shakespeare's Arthur;' says Swinburne. 'There are one or two figures in the world of his work of which there are no words that would be fit or good to say. Another of these is Cordelia. The place they have in our lives and thoughts is not one for talk. The niche set apart for them to inhabit in our secret hearts is not penetrable by the lights and noises of common day. There are chapels in the cathedral of man's highest art, as in that of his inmost life, not made to be set open to the eyes and feet of the world. Love and Death and Memory keep charge for us in silence of some beloved names. It is the crowning glory of genius, the final miracle and transcendant gift of poetry that it can add to the number of these and engrave on the very heart of our remembrance fresh names and memories of its own creation.'

'Lear, c'est l'occasion de Cordelia,' says Victor Hugo. 'La maternité de la fille sur le père; sujet profonde; la maternité vénérable entre toutes, si admirablement traduite par la légende de cette romaine, nourrice, au fond d'un cachot, de son père vieillard. La jeune mamelle près de la barbe blanche, il n'est point de spectacle plus sacré. Cette mamelle filiale c'est Cordelia.

'Une fois cette figure rêvée et trouvée Shakespeare a créé son drame.... Shakespeare, portant Cordelia dans sa pensée, a créé cette tragédie comme un dieu, qui ayant une aurore à placer, ferait tout exprès un monde pour l'y mettre.'[1]

'In *Lear* Shakespeare's vision sounded the abyss of horror to its very depths, and his spirit showed neither fear, nor giddiness, nor faintness at the sight,' says Brandes. 'On the threshold of this work a feeling of awe comes over one as on the threshold of the Sistine Chapel with its ceiling-frescoes by Michael Angelo, only that the suffering here is far more intense, the wail wilder, the harmonies of beauty more definitely shattered by the discords of despair.'

Such are the judgements of the critics on this drama, and therefore I think I am justified in choosing it as an example of Shakespeare's best plays.

I will try as impartially as possible to give the contents of the play, and then show why it is not the height of perfection, as it is said to be by the learned critics, but something quite different.

II

The tragedy of Lear begins with a scene in which two courtiers, Kent and Gloucester, are talking. Kent, pointing to a young man who is present, asks Gloucester whether that is his son. Gloucester says that he has often blushed to acknowledge the young man as his son but has

[1] 'Lear is Cordelia's play. The maternal feeling of the daughter towards the father—profound subject—a maternity venerable among all other maternities—so admirably set forth in the legend of that Roman girl who nursed her old father in the depths of a prison. There is no spectacle more holy than that of the young breast near the white beard. That filial breast is Cordelia.

'Once this figure was dreamed and found Shakespeare created his drama . . . Shakespeare, carrying Cordelia in his thoughts, created that tragedy like a god who having an aurora to place makes a world expressly for it.'

now ceased to do so. Kent says: 'I cannot conceive you.' Then Gloucester, in the presence of his son, says: 'Sir, this young fellow's mother could; whereupon she grew round-wombed, and had, indeed, sir, a son for her cradle ere she had a husband for her bed. . . .' He goes on to say that he had another son who was legitimate, but 'though this knave came somewhat saucily before he was sent for, yet was his mother fair, there was good sport at his making, and the whoreson must be acknowledged.'

Such is the introduction. Not to speak of the vulgarity of these words of Gloucester, they are also out of place in the mouth of a man whom it is intended to represent as a noble character. It is impossible to agree with the opinion of some critics that these words are put into Gloucester's mouth to indicate the contempt for illegitimacy from which Edmund suffered. Were that so, it would in the first place have been necessary to make the father express the contempt felt by people in general, and secondly Edmund, in his monologue about the injustice of those who despise him for his birth, should have referred to his father's words. But this is not done, and therefore these words of Gloucester's at the very beginning of the piece were merely for the purpose of informing the public in an amusing way of the fact that Gloucester has a legitimate and an illegitimate son.

After this trumpets are blown, King Lear enters with his daughters and sons-in-law, and makes a speech about being aged and wishing to stand aside from affairs and divide his kingdom between his daughters. In order to know how much he should give to each daughter he announces that to the daughter who tells him she loves him most he will give most. The eldest daughter, Goneril, says that there are no words to express her love, that she loves him 'dearer than eyesight, space, and liberty', and she loves him so much that it 'makes her breath poor'. King Lear immediately allots on the map to this daughter her share, with fields, woods, rivers, and meadows, and puts the same question to his second daughter. The second daughter, Regan, says that her sister has correctly expressed her own feelings, but insufficiently. She, Regan, loves her father so that everything is abhorrent to her except his love. The King rewards this daughter also, and asks his youngest, favourite daughter, in whom, according to his expression, 'the wine of France and milk of Burgundy strive to be interess'd'—that is, who is courted by the King of France and the Duke of Burgundy—asks Cordelia how she loves him. Cordelia, who personifies all the virtues as the two elder sisters personify all the vices, says quite inappropriately, as if on purpose to vex her father, that though she loves and honours him and is grateful to him, yet, if she marries, not all her love will belong to him, but she will love her husband also.

On hearing these words the King is beside himself, and immediately curses his favourite daughter with most terrible and strange maledictions, saying, for instance, that he will love a man who eats his own children as much as he now loves her who was once his daughter.

> The barbarous Scythian,
> Or he that makes his generation messes
> To gorge his appetite, shall to my bosom
> Be as well neighbour'd, pitied, and reliev'd,
> As thou, my sometime daughter.

The courtier, Kent, takes Cordelia's part, and wishing to bring the King to reason upbraids him with his injustice and speaks reasonably about the evil of flattery. Lear, without attending to Kent, banishes him under threat of death, and calling to him Cordelia's two suitors, the King of France and the Duke of Burgundy, proposes to each in turn to take Cordelia without a dowry. The Duke of Burgundy says plainly that he will not take Cordelia without a dowry, but the King of France takes her without dowry and leads her away. After this the elder sisters, there and then conversing with one another, prepare to offend their father who had endowed them. So ends the first scene.

Not to mention the inflated, characterless style in which King Lear—like all Shakespeare's kings—talks, the reader or spectator cannot believe that a king, however old and stupid, could believe the words of the wicked daughters with whom he had lived all their lives, and not trust his favourite daughter, but curse and banish her; therefore the reader or spectator cannot share the feeling of the persons who take part in this unnatural scene.

Scene II begins with Edmund, Gloucester's illegitimate son, soliloquizing on the injustice of men who concede rights and respect to a legitimate son but deny them to an illegitimate son, and he determines to ruin Edgar and usurp his place. For this purpose he forges a letter to himself, as from Edgar, in which the latter is made to appear to wish to kill his father. Having waited till Gloucester appears, Edmund, as if against his own desire, shows him this letter, and the father immediately believes that his son Edgar, whom he tenderly loves, wishes to kill him. The father goes away, Edgar enters, and Edmund suggests to him that his father for some reason wishes to kill him. Edgar also at once believes him, and flees from his father.

The relations between Gloucester and his two

sons, and the feelings of these characters, are as unnatural as Lear's relation to his daughters, if not more so; and therefore it is even more difficult for the spectator to put himself into the mental condition of Gloucester and his sons and to sympathize with them, than it was in regard to Lear and his daughters.

In Scene IV the banished Kent, disguised so that Lear does not recognize him, presents himself to the King who is now staying with Goneril. Lear asks who he is, to which Kent, one does not know why, replies in a jocular tone quite inappropriate to his position: 'A very honest-hearted fellow and as poor as the King.' 'If thou be'st as poor for a subject as he's for a King, thou art poor enough,' replies Lear. 'How old art thou?' 'Not so young, sir, to love a woman for singing, nor so old as to dote on her for anything,' to which the King replies that if he likes him not worse after dinner he will let him remain in his service.

This talk fits in neither with Lear's position nor with Kent's relation to him, and is evidently put into their mouths only because the author thought it witty and amusing.

Goneril's steward appears and is rude to Lear, for which Kent trips him up. The King, who still does not recognize Kent, gives him money for this and takes him into his service. After this the fool appears, and a talk begins between the fool and the King, quite out of accord with the situation, leading to nothing, prolonged, and intended to be amusing. Thus, for instance, the fool says, 'Give me an egg, and I'll give thee two crowns.' The King asks what crowns they shall be. 'Why, after I have cut the egg i'the middle and eat up the meat, the two crowns of the egg. When thou clovest thy crown i'the middle, and gavest away both parts, thou borest thine ass on thy back o'er the dirt; thou hadst little wit in thy bald crown when thou gavest thy golden one away. If I speak like myself in this, let him be whipped that first finds it so.'

In this manner prolonged conversations go on, producing in the spectator or reader a sense of wearisome discomfort such as one experiences when listening to dull jokes.

This conversation is interrupted by the arrival of Goneril. She demands that her father should diminish his retinue: instead of a hundred courtiers he should be satisfied with fifty. On hearing this proposal Lear is seized with terrible, unnatural rage, and asks:

Does any here know me? This is not Lear!
Does Lear walk thus? Speak thus? Where are his eyes?
Either his notion weakens, his discernings
Are lethargied. Ha! Waking? 'tis not so,
Who is it that can tell me who I am?

and so forth.

Meanwhile the fool unceasingly interpolates his humourless jokes. Goneril's husband appears and wishes to appease Lear, but Lear curses Goneril, invoking sterility upon her, or the birth of such a child as would repay with ridicule and contempt her maternal cares, and would thereby show her all the horror and suffering caused by a child's ingratitude.

These words, which express a genuine feeling, might have been touching had only this been said, but they are lost among long high-flown speeches Lear continually utters quite inappropriately. Now he calls down blasts and fogs on his daughter's head, now desires that curses should 'pierce every sense about thee', or, addressing his own eyes, says that if they weep he will pluck them out and cast them, with the waters that they lose, 'to temper clay'.

After this Lear sends Kent, whom he still does not recognize, to his other daughter and notwithstanding the despair he has just expressed he talks with the fool and incites him to jests. The jests continue to be mirthless, and besides the unpleasant feeling akin to shame that one feels at unsuccessful witticisms, they are so long-drawn-out as to be wearisome. So, for instance, the fool asks the King, 'Canst thou tell why one's nose stands i' the middle of one's face?' Lear says he does not know.

'Why, to keep one's eyes of either side one's nose: that what a man cannot smell out he may spy into.'

'Canst tell how an oyster makes his shell?' the fool asks.

'No.'

'Nor I neither; but I can tell why a snail has a house.'

'Why?'

'Why, to put his head in; not to give it away to his daughters, and leave his horns without a case.'

'Be my horses ready?' asks Lear.

'Thy asses are gone about 'em. The reason why the seven stars are no more than seven is a pretty reason.'

'Because they are not eight?' says Lear.

'Yes, indeed; thou wouldst make a good fool,' says the fool, and so forth.

After this long scene a gentleman comes and announces that the horses are ready. The fool says:

> She that's a maid now and laughs at my departure,
> Shall not be a maid long, unless things be cut shorter,

and goes off.

Scene I of Act II begins with the villain Edmund

318 SHAKESPEARE AND THE DRAMA

persuading his brother, when his father enters, to pretend that they are fighting with their swords. Edgar agrees, though it is quite incomprehensible why he should do so. The father finds them fighting. Edgar runs away, and Edmund scratches his own arm to draw blood, and persuades his father that Edgar was using charms to kill his father and had wanted Edmund to help him, but that he had refused to do so and Edgar had then thrown himself upon him and wounded him in the arm. Gloucester believes everything, curses Edgar, and transfers all the rights of his elder and legitimate son to the illegitimate Edmund. The Duke of Cornwall, hearing of this, also rewards Edmund.

In Scene II, before Gloucester's castle, Lear's new servant Kent, still unrecognized by Lear, begins without any reason to abuse Oswald (Goneril's steward), calling him 'a knave, a rascal, an eater of broken meats; a base, proud, shallow, beggarly, three-suited, hundred-pound, filthy, worsted-stocking knave; . . . the son and heir of a mongrel bitch', and so on. Then, drawing his sword, he demands that Oswald should fight him, saying that he will make of him a 'sop o' the moonshine', words no commentator has been able to explain, and when he is stopped he continues to give vent to the strangest abuse, saying, for instance, that he, Oswald, has been made by a tailor, because 'a stone-cutter, or a painter, could not have made him so ill, though they had been but two hours at the trade'. He also says that if he is allowed he will tread this unbolted villain into mortar, and daub the wall of a privy with him.

And in this way Kent, whom nobody recognizes —though both the King and the Duke of Cornwall, as well as Gloucester who is present, should know him well—continues to brawl in the character of a new servant of Lear's, until he is seized and put in the stocks.

Scene III takes place on a heath. Edgar, flying from his father's pursuit, hides himself in a tree, and he tells the audience what kinds of lunatics there are, beggars who go about naked, thrust pins and wooden pricks into their bodies, and scream with wild voices and enforce charity, and he says that he intends to play the part of such a lunatic in order to escape from the pursuit. Having told the audience this he goes off.

Scene IV is again before Gloucester's castle. Lear and the fool enter. Lear sees Kent in the stocks and, still not recognizing him, is inflamed with anger against those who have dared so to treat his messenger, and he calls for the Duke and Regan. The fool goes on with his queer sayings. Lear with difficulty restrains his anger. The Duke and Regan enter. Lear complains of Goneril, but Regan justifies her sister. Lear curses Goneril, and when Regan tells him he had better go back to her sister he is indignant and says: 'Ask her forgiveness?' and goes on his knees, showing how improper it would be for him abjectly to beg food and clothing as charity from his own daughter, and he curses Goneril with the most terrible curses, and asks who has dared to put his messenger in the stocks. Before Regan can answer Goneril arrives. Lear becomes yet more angry and again curses Goneril, and when he is told that the Duke had ordered the stocks he says nothing, for at this moment Regan tells him that she cannot receive him now and that he had better return with Goneril, and in a month's time she will herself receive him but with only fifty followers instead of a hundred. Lear again curses Goneril and does not want to go with her, still hoping that Regan will receive him with all his hundred followers, but Regan now says she will only allow him twenty-five, and then Lear decides to go back with Goneril who allows fifty. Then, when Goneril says that even twenty-five are too many, Lear utters a long discourse about the superfluous and sufficient being conditional conceptions, and says that if a man is allowed only as much as is necessary he is no different from a beast. And here Lear, or rather the actor who plays Lear, addresses himself to a finely dressed woman in the audience, and says that she too does not need her finery, which does not keep her warm. After this he falls into a mad rage, says that he will do something terrible to be revenged upon his daughters, but will not weep, and so he departs. The noise of a storm that is commencing is heard.

Such is the second Act, full of unnatural occurrences and still more unnatural speeches not flowing from the speaker's circumstances, and finishing with the scene between Lear and his daughters which might be powerful if it were not overloaded with speeches most naively absurd and unnatural, and quite inappropriate moreover, put into Lear's mouth. Lear's vacillations between pride, anger, and hope of concessions from his daughters would be exceedingly touching were they not spoilt by these verbose absurdities which he utters about being ready to divorce Regan's dead mother should Regan not be glad to see him, or about evoking 'fensucked fogs' to infect his daughter, or about the heavens being obliged to protect old men as they themselves are old, and much else.

Act III begins with thunder, lightning, and storm—a special kind of storm such as there never was before, as one of the characters in the play says. On the heath a gentleman tells Kent that Lear, expelled by his daughters from their houses, is wandering about the heath alone tearing his hair and throwing it to the winds, and that only the fool is with him. Kent tells the gentleman that the Dukes have quarrelled and that a French army has landed at Dover, and having communicated this he dispatches the gentleman to Dover to meet Cordelia.

Scene II of Act III also takes place on the heath. Lear walks about the heath and utters words intended to express despair: he wishes the winds to blow so hard that they (the winds) should crack their cheeks, and that the rain should drench everything, and that the lightning should singe his white head and thunder strike the earth flat and destroy all the germs 'that make ingrateful man!' The fool keeps uttering yet more senseless words. Kent enters. Lear says that for some reason all criminals shall be discovered and exposed in this storm. Kent, still not recognized by Lear, persuades Lear to take shelter in a hovel. The fool thereupon utters a prophecy quite unrelated to the situation and they all go off.

Scene II is again transferred to Gloucester's castle. Gloucester tells Edmund that the French king has already landed with an army and intends to help Lear. On learning this Edmund decides to accuse his father of treason in order to supplant him.

Scene IV is again on the heath in front of the hovel. Kent invites Lear to enter the hovel, but Lear replies that he has no reason to shelter himself from the storm, that he does not feel it, as the tempest in his mind aroused by his daughters' ingratitude overpowers all else. This true feeling, if expressed in simple words, might evoke sympathy, but amid his inflated and incessant ravings it is hard to notice it, and it loses its significance.

The hovel to which Lear is led turns out to be the same that Edgar has entered disguised as a madman, that is to say, without clothes. Edgar comes out of the hovel and, though they all know him, nobody recognizes him any more than they recognize Kent; and Edgar, Lear, and the fool, begin to talk nonsense which continues with intervals for six pages. In the midst of this scene Gloucester enters (who also fails to recognize either Kent or his own son Edgar), and tells them how his son Edgar wished to kill him.

This scene is again interrupted by one in Gloucester's castle, during which Edmund betrays his father and the Duke declares he will be revenged on Gloucester. The scene again shifts to Lear. Kent, Edgar, Gloucester, Lear, and the fool are in a farm-house and are talking. Edgar says: 'Frateretto calls me and tells me, Nero is an angler in the lake of darkness. . . .' The fool says: 'Nuncle, tell me, whether a madman be a gentleman, or a yeoman?' Lear, who is out of his mind, says that a madman is a king. The fool says: 'No, he's a yeoman, that has a gentleman to his son; for he's a mad yeoman, that sees his son a gentleman before him.' Lear cries out: 'To have a thousand with red burning spits come hissing in upon them.' And Edgar shrieks that the foul fiend bites his back. Then the fool utters an adage that one cannot trust 'the tameness of a wolf, a horse's health, a boy's love, or a whore's oath'. Then Lear imagines that he is trying his daughters. 'Most learned justicer,' says he addressing the naked Edgar. 'Thou, sapient sir, sit here. Now, you she foxes!' To this Edgar says:

> Look, where he stands and glares!
> Wantonest thou eyes at trial, madam?
> Come o'er the bourn, Bessy, to me!

and the fool sings:

> Her boat hath a leak,
> And she must not speak
> Why she dares not come over to thee.

Edgar again says something, and Kent begs Lear to lie down, but Lear continues his imaginary trial.

> Bring in the evidence.
> Thou robed man of justice, take thy place; *(to Edgar)*
> And thou, his yoke-fellow of equity, *(to the fool)*
> Bench by his side. You are of the commission, *(to Kent)*
> Sit you too.

'Pur! the cat is grey,' cries Edgar.

'Arraign her first; 'tis Goneril,' says Lear. 'I here take my oath before this honourable assembly, she kicked the poor King her father.'

Fool: Come hither, mistress Is your name Goneril?
  (addressing a joint-stool)
Lear: And here's another. . . . Stop her there!
  Arms, arms, sword, fire! Corruption in the place!
  False justicer, why hast thou let her 'scape?

and so on.

This raving ends by Lear falling asleep and Gloucester persuading Kent, still without recognizing him, to take the King to Dover. Kent and the fool carry Lear off.

The scene changes to Gloucester's castle. Gloucester himself is accused of treason, and is brought in and bound. The Duke of Cornwall tears out one of his eyes and stamps on it. Regan says that one eye is still whole and that this healthy eye is laughing at the other eye, and urges the Duke to crush it too. The Duke is about to do so, but for some reason one of the servants suddenly takes Gloucester's part and wounds the Duke. Regan kills the servant. The servant dies and tells Gloucester that he has still one eye to see that the

evil-doer is punished. The Duke says: 'Lest it see more, prevent it: out, vile jelly!' and tears out Gloucester's other eye and throws it on the floor. Here Regan mentions that Edmund has denounced his father, and Gloucester suddenly understands that he has been deceived and that Edgar did not wish to kill him.

This ends the third Act. Act IV is again in the open country. Edgar, still in the guise of a maniac, talks in artificial language about the perversities of fate and the advantages of a humble lot. Then, curiously enough, to the very spot on the open heath where he is, comes his father, blind Gloucester, led by an old man, and he too talks about the perversities of fate in that curious Shakespearian language the chief peculiarity of which is that the thoughts arise either from the sound of the words, or by contrast. He tells the old man who leads him to leave him. The old man says that without eyes one cannot go alone, because one cannot *see* the way. Gloucester says:

'I have no way, and therefore want no *eyes*.'

And he argues that he stumbled when he *saw* and that our defects often save us.

'Ah! dear son Edgar,' adds he,

> The food of thy abused father's wrath.
> Might I but live to *see* thee in my touch,
> I'd say I had eyes again!

Edgar, naked, in the character of a lunatic, hears this, but does not disclose himself; he takes the place of the old man who had acted as guide, and talks with his father who does not recognize his voice and believes him to be a madman. Gloucester takes the opportunity to utter a witticism about 'when madmen lead the blind', and insists on driving away the old man, obviously not from motives which might be natural to him at that moment, but merely to enact an imaginary leap over the cliff when left alone with Edgar. And though he has only just seen his blinded father and learned that he repents of having driven him away, Edgar utters quite unnecessary sayings which Shakespeare might know, having read them in Harsnet's book,[1] but which Edgar had no means of becoming acquainted with, and which, above all, it is quite unnatural for him to utter in his then condition. He says:

'Five fiends have been in poor Tom at once: of lust, as Obidicut; Hobbididence, prince of dumbness; Mahu, of stealing; Modo, of murder; and Flibbertigibbet, of mopping and mowing, who since possesses chamber-maids and waiting-women.'

On hearing these words, Gloucester gives Edgar his purse, saying:

That I am wretched
Makes thee the happier. Heavens, deal so still!
Let the superfluous and lust-dieted man
That braves your ordinance, that will not see
Because he doth not feel, feel your power quickly;
So distribution should undo excess,
And each man have enough.

Having uttered these strange words, the blind Gloucester demands that Edgar should lead him to a cliff that he does not himself know, but that hangs over the sea, and they depart.

Scene II of Act IV takes place before the Duke of Albany's palace. Goneril is not only cruel but also dissolute. She despises her husband, and discloses her love to the villain Edmund, who has obtained his father's title of Gloucester. Edmund

[1] *A Declaration of egregious popish impostures*, etc., by Dr. Samuel Harsnet, London, 1603, which contains almost all that Edgar says in his feigned madness.—A. M.

goes away and a conversation takes place between Goneril and her husband. The Duke of Albany, the only character who shows human feelings, has already grown dissatisfied with his wife's treatment of her father, and now definitely takes Lear's part, but he expresses himself in words which destroy one's belief in his feelings. He says that a bear would lick Lear's reverence, and that if the heavens do not send their visible spirits to tame these vile offences, humanity must prey on itself like monsters, and so forth.

Goneril does not listen to him, and he then begins to denounce her.
He says:
> See thyself, devil!
> Proper deformity seems not in the fiend
> So horrid, as in woman.

'O vain fool!' says Goneril, but the Duke continues:

> Thou changed and self-cover'd thing, for shame,
> Be-monster not thy feature. Were it my fitness
> To let these hands obey my blood,
> They are apt enough to dislocate and tear
> Thy flesh and bones:—Howe'er thou art a fiend,
> A woman's shape doth shield thee.

After this a messenger enters and announces that the Duke of Cornwall, wounded by a servant while he was tearing out Gloucester's eyes, has died. Goneril is glad, but already anticipates with fear that Regan, being now a widow, will snatch Edmund from her. This ends the second scene.

Scene III of Act IV represents the French camp. From a conversation between Kent and a gentleman, the reader or spectator learns that the King of France is not in the camp, and that Cordelia has received a letter from Kent and is greatly grieved by what she learns about her father. The gentleman says that her face reminded one of sunshine and rain.

> Her smiles and tears
> Were like a better day: Those happy smilets,
> That play'd on her ripe lip, seem'd not to know
> What guests were in her eyes; which parted thence,
> As pearls from diamonds dropp'd,

and so forth. The gentleman says that Cordelia desires to see her father, but Kent says that Lear is ashamed to see the daughter he has treated so badly.

In Scene IV Cordelia, talking with a physician, tells him that Lear has been seen, and that he is quite mad, wearing on his head a wreath of various weeds and roaming about, and that she has sent soldiers to find him, and she adds the wish that all secret medicinal virtues of the earth may spring to him in her tears, and so forth.

She is told that the forces of the Dukes are approaching; but she is only concerned about her father, and goes off

In Scene V of Act IV, which is in Gloucester's castle, Regan talks with Oswald, Goneril's steward, who is carrying a letter from Goneril to Edmund, and tells him that she also loves Edmund and that as she is a widow it is better for her to marry him than for Goneril to do so, and she asks Oswald to persuade her sister of this. Moreover she tells him that it was very unwise to put out Gloucester's eyes and yet to let him live, and therefore she advises Oswald if he meets Gloucester to kill him, and promises him a great reward if he does so.

In Scene VI Gloucester again appears with his unrecognized son Edgar, who, now dressed as a peasant, is leading his father to the cliff. Gloucester is walking along on level ground, but Edgar assures him that they are with difficulty ascending a steep hill. Gloucester believes this. Edgar tells his father that the noise of the sea is audible; Gloucester believes this also. Edgar stops on a level place and assures his father that he has ascended the cliff and that below him is a terrible abyss, and he leaves him alone. Gloucester, addressing the gods, says that he shakes off his affliction as he could not bear it longer without condemning them, the gods, and having said this he leaps on the level ground and falls, imagining that he has jumped over the cliff. Edgar thereupon utters to himself a yet more confused phrase:

> And yet I know not how conceit may rob
> The treasury of life, when life itself
> Yields to the theft; had he been where he thought,
> By this had thought been past,

and he goes up to Gloucester pretending to be again a different man, and expresses astonishment at the latter not having been killed by his fall from such a dreadful height. Gloucester believes that he has fallen and prepares to die, but he feels that he is alive and begins to doubt having fallen. Then Edgar assures him that he really did jump from a terrible height, and says that the man who was with him at the top was a fiend, for he had eyes like two full moons, and a thousand noses, and wavy horns.

Gloucester believes this, and is persuaded that his despair was caused by the devil, and therefore decides that he will despair no longer but will quietly await death. Just then Lear enters, for some reason all covered with wild flowers. He has gone mad and utters speeches yet more meaningless than before. He talks about coining money, about a bow, calls for a clothier's yard, then he cries out that he sees a mouse which he wishes to entice with a piece of cheese, and then he suddenly asks the password of Edgar, who at once replies with the words, 'Sweet Marjoram'. Lear says, 'Pass!' and the blind Gloucester, who did not recognize his son's or Kent's voice, recognizes the King's.

Then the King, after his disconnected utterances, suddenly begins to speak ironically about flatterers who said 'ay and no' like the theologians and assured him that he could do everything, but when he got into a storm without shelter he saw that this was not true; and then he goes on to say that as all creatures are wanton, and as Gloucester's bastard son was kinder to his father than Lear's daughters had been to theirs (though, according to the course of the play, Lear could know nothing of Edmund's treatment of Gloucester), therefore let copulation thrive, especially as he, a King, lacks soldiers. And thereupon he addresses an imaginary, hypocritically virtuous lady who acts the prude while at the same time, like an animal in heat, she is addicted to lust. All women 'but to the girdle do the gods inherit. Beneath is all the fiend's . . .', and saying this Lear screams and spits with horror. This monologue is evidently meant to be addressed by actor to audience, and probably produces an effect on the stage, but is quite uncalled for in the mouth of Lear—as is his desire to wipe his hand because it 'smells of mortality' when Gloucester wishes to kiss it. Then Gloucester's blindness is referred to, which gives an opportunity for a play of words on eyes and Cupid's blindness, and for Lear to say that Gloucester has 'no eyes in your head, nor no money in your purse? Your eyes are in a *heavy* case, your purse in a *light*.' Then Lear declaims a monologue on the injustice of legal judgement, which is quite out of place in his mouth seeing that he is insane. Then a gentleman enters with attendants, sent by Cordelia to fetch her father. Lear continues to behave madly and runs away. The gentleman sent to fetch Lear does not run after him but continues to tell Edgar lengthily about the position of the French and the British armies.

Oswald enters, and seeing Gloucester and wishing to obtain the reward promised by Regan, attacks him; but Edgar, with his stave, kills Oswald, who when dying gives Edgar (the man who has killed him) Goneril's letter to Edmund, the delivery of which will earn a reward. In this letter Goneril promises to kill her husband and marry Edmund. Edgar drags out Oswald's body by the legs, and then returns and leads his father away.

Scene VII of Act IV takes place in a tent in the French camp. Lear is asleep on a bed. Cordelia enters with Kent, still in disguise. Lear is awakened by music, and seeing Cordelia does not believe she is alive but thinks her an apparition, and does not believe that he is himself alive. Cordelia assures him that she is his daughter and begs him to bless her. He goes on his knees before her, begs forgiveness, admits himself to be old and foolish, and says he is ready to take poison, which he thinks she probably has prepared for him as he is persuaded that she must hate him.

> For your sisters
> Have, as I do remember, done me wrong;
> You have some cause, they have not.

Then little by little he comes to his senses and ceases to rave. His daughter suggests that he should take a little walk. He consents, and says:

> You must bear with me:
> Pray you now, forget and forgive: I am old and foolish.

They go off. The gentleman and Kent, who remain on the scene, talk in order to explain to the audience that Edmund is at the head of the forces and that a battle must soon begin between Lear's defenders and his enemies. So Act IV ends.

In this Fourth Act the scene between Lear and his daughter might have been touching had it not been preceded in three previous acts by the tedious monotonous ravings of Lear, and also had it been the final scene expressing his feelings, but it is not the last.

In Act V Lear's former cold, pompous, artificial ravings are repeated, destroying the impression the preceding scene might have produced.

Scene I of Act V shows us Edmund and Regan (who is jealous of her sister and offers herself to Edmund). Then Goneril comes on with her husband and soldiers. The Duke of Albany, though he pities Lear, considers it his duty to fight against the French who have invaded his country, and so prepares himself for battle.

Then Edgar enters, still disguised, and hands the Duke of Albany the letter, and says that if the Duke wins the battle he should let a herald sound a trumpet, and then (this is 800 years B.C.) a champion will appear who will prove that the contents of the letter are true.

In Scene II Edgar enters leading his father, whom he seats by a tree, and himself goes off. The sounds of a battle are heard, Edgar runs back and says that the battle is lost; Lear and Cordelia are prisoners. Gloucester is again in despair. Edgar, still not disclosing himself to his father, tells him that he should not despair, and Gloucester at once agrees with him.

Scene III opens with a triumphal progress of Edmund the victor. Lear and Cordelia are prisoners. Lear, though he is now no longer insane, still utters the same sort of senseless, inappropriate words, as, for instance, that in prison with Cordelia,

> We two alone will sing like birds i' the cage,
> When thou dost ask me blessing, I'll kneel down,
> And ask of thee forgiveness.

(This kneeling down comes three times over.) He also says that when they are in prison they will wear out poor rogues and 'sects of great ones that ebb and flow by the moon', that he and she are sacrifices upon which 'the gods throw incense', that 'he that parts them shall bring a brand from heaven, and fire us hence like foxes', and that

> The good years shall devour them, flesh and fell,
> Ere they shall make us weep,

and so forth.

Edmund orders Lear and his daughter to be led away to prison, and having ordered a captain to do them some hurt, asks him whether he will fulfil it. The captain replies, 'I cannot draw a cart, nor eat dried oats; but if it be man's work I will do it.' The Duke of Albany, Goneril, and Regan enter. The Duke wishes to take Lear's part, but Edmund opposes this. The sisters intervene and begin to abuse each other, being jealous of Edmund. Here everything becomes so confused that it is difficult to follow the action. The Duke of Albany wants to arrest Edmund, and tells Regan that Edmund had long ago entered into guilty relations with his wife and that therefore Regan must give up her claim on Edmund, and if she wishes to marry should marry him, the Duke of Albany.

Having said this, the Duke challenges Edmund and orders the trumpet to be sounded, and if no one appears intends himself to fight him.

At this point Regan, whom Goneril has evidently

poisoned, writhes with pain. Trumpets are sounded and Edgar enters with a visor which conceals his face, and without giving his name challenges Edmund. Edgar abuses Edmund; Edmund casts back all the abuse on Edgar's head. They fight and Edmund falls. Goneril is in despair.

The Duke of Albany shows Goneril her letter. Goneril goes off.

Edmund, while dying, recognizes that his opponent is his brother. Edgar raises his visor and moralizes to the effect that for having an illegitimate son, Edmund, his father has paid with the loss of his sight. After this Edgar tells the Duke of Albany of his adventures and that he has only now, just before coming to this combat, disclosed himself to his father, and his father could not bear it and died of excitement. Edmund, who is not yet dead, asks what else happened.

Then Edgar relates that while he was sitting by his father's body a man came, embraced him closely, cried out as if he would burst heaven, threw himself on his father's corpse, and told a most piteous tale about Lear and himself, and having told it 'the strings of life began to crack', but just then the trumpet sounded twice and he, Edgar, left him 'tranced'. And this was Kent. Before Edgar has finished telling this story a gentleman runs in with a bloody knife, shouting, 'Help!' To the question 'Who has been killed?' the gentleman says that Goneril is dead, who had poisoned her sister. She had confessed this. Kent enters, and at this moment the bodies of Regan and Goneril are brought in. Edmund thereupon says that evidently the sisters loved him greatly, as the one had poisoned the other and then killed herself for his sake. At the same time he confesses that he had given orders to kill Lear and hang

Cordelia in prison, under the pretence that she had committed suicide; but that he now wishes to prevent this, and, having said so, he dies and is carried out.

After this Lear enters with Cordelia's dead body in his arms (though he is over eighty years of age and ill). And again there begin his terrible ravings which make one feel as ashamed as one does when listening to unsuccessful jokes. Lear demands that they should all howl, and alternately believes that Cordelia is dead and that she is alive. He says:

> Had I your tongues and eyes, I'd use them so
> That heaven's vault should crack.

Then he recounts how he has killed the slave who hanged Cordelia. Next he says that his eyes see badly, and thereupon recognizes Kent whom all along he had not recognized.

The Duke of Albany says that he resigns his power as long as Lear lives, and that he will reward Edgar and Kent and all who have been true to him. At that moment news is brought that Edmund has died; and Lear, continuing his ravings, begs that they will undo one of his buttons, the same request that he made when roaming about the heath. He expresses his thanks for this, tells them all to look somewhere, and with these words he dies.

In conclusion the Duke of Albany, who remains alive, says:

> The weight of this sad time we must obey;
> Speak what we feel, not what we ought to say.
> The oldest hath borne most: we that are young
> Shall never see so much, nor live so long.

All go off to the sound of a dead march. This ends Act V of the play.

III

Such is this celebrated play. Absurd as it may appear in this rendering (which I have tried to make as impartial as possible), I can confidently say that it is yet more absurd in the original. To any man of our time, were he not under the hypnotic influence of the suggestion that this play is the height of perfection, it would be enough to read it to the end, had he patience to do so, to convince himself that far from being the height of perfection it is a very poor, carelessly constructed work, which if it may have been of interest to a certain public of its own day, can evoke nothing but aversion and weariness in us now. And any man of our day free from such suggestion would receive just the same impression from the other much praised dramas of Shakespeare, not to speak of the absurd dramatized tales, *Pericles*, *Twelfth Night*, *The Tempest*, *Cymbeline*, and *Troilus and Cressida*.

But such free-minded people not predisposed to Shakespeare worship, are no longer to be found in our time and in our Christian society. The idea that Shakespeare is a poetic and dramatic genius, and that all his works are the height of perfection, has been instilled into every man of our society and time from an early period of his conscious life. And therefore, superfluous as it would seem, I will try to indicate, in the play of *King Lear* which I have chosen, the defects characteristic of all Shakespeare's tragedies and comedies, as a result of which they not only fail to furnish models of dramatic art but fail to satisfy the most elementary and generally recognized demands of art.

According to the laws laid down by those very critics who extol Shakespeare, the conditions of every tragedy are that the persons who appear should, as a result of their own characters, actions, and the natural movement of events, be brought into conditions in which, finding themselves in opposition to the world around them, they should struggle with it and in that struggle display their inherent qualities.

In the tragedy of *King Lear* the persons represented are indeed externally placed in opposition to the surrounding world and struggle against it. But the struggle does not result from a natural course of events and from their own characters, but is quite arbitrarily arranged by the author and therefore cannot produce on the reader that illusion which constitutes the chief condition of art. Lear is under no necessity to resign his power, and has no reason to do so. And having lived with his daughters all their lives he also has no reason to believe the words of the two elder, and not the truthful statement of the youngest; yet on this the whole tragedy of his position is built.

Equally unnatural is the secondary and very similar plot: the relation of Gloucester to his sons. The position of Gloucester and Edgar arises from the fact that Gloucester, like Lear, immediately believes the very grossest deception, and does not even try to ask the son who had been deceived, whether the accusation against him is true, but curses him and drives him away.

The fact that the relation of Lear to his daughters is just the same as that of Gloucester to his sons, makes one feel even more strongly that they are both arbitrarily invented and do not flow from the characters or the natural course of events. Equally unnatural and obviously invented is the fact that all through the play Lear fails to recognize his old courtier, Kent; and so the relations of Lear and

Kent fail to evoke the sympathy of reader or hearer. This applies in an even greater degree to the position of Edgar, whom nobody recognizes, who acts as guide to his blind father and persuades him that he has leapt from a cliff when he has really jumped on level ground.

These positions in which the characters are quite arbitrarily placed are so unnatural that the reader or spectator is unable either to sympathize with their sufferings or even to be interested in what he reads or hears. That in the first place.

Secondly there is the fact that both in this and in Shakespeare's other dramas all the people live, think, speak, and act, quite out of accord with the given period and place. The action of *King Lear* takes place 800 years B.C., and yet the characters in it are placed in conditions possible only in the Middle Ages: Kings, dukes, armies, illegitimate children, gentlemen, courtiers, doctors, farmers, officers, soldiers, knights in armour, and so on, appear in it. Perhaps such anachronisms (of which all Shakespeare's plays are full) did not infringe the possibility of illusion in the 16th century and the beginning of the 17th, but in our time it is no longer possible to be interested in the development of events that could not have occurred in the conditions the author describes in detail.

The artificiality of the positions, which do not arise from a natural course of events and from the characters of the people engaged, and their incompatibility with the period and the place, is further increased by the coarse embellishments Shakespeare continually makes use of in passages meant to be specially touching. The extraordinary storm during which Lear roams about the heath, the weeds which for some reason he puts on his head, as Ophelia does in *Hamlet*, Edgar's attire—all these effects, far from strengthening the impression, produce a contrary effect. '*Man sieht die Absicht und man wird verstimmt*'[1] as Goethe says. It often happens—as for instance with such obviously intentional effects as the dragging out of half a dozen corpses by the legs, with which Shakespeare often ends his tragedies—that instead of feeling fear and pity one feels the absurdity of the thing.

IV

Not only are the characters in Shakespeare's plays placed in tragic positions which are quite impossible, do not result from the course of events, and are inappropriate to the period and the place, they also behave in a way that is quite arbitrary and not in accord with their own definite characters. It is customary to assert that in Shakespeare's dramas character is particularly well expressed and that with all his vividness his people are as many-sided as real people, and that while exhibiting the nature of a certain given individual they also show the nature of man in general. It is customary to say that Shakespeare's delineation of character is the height of perfection. This is asserted with great confidence and repeated by everyone as an indisputable verity, but much as I have tried to find confirmation of this in Shakespeare's dramas I have always found the reverse.

From the very beginning of reading any of Shakespeare's plays I was at once convinced that it is perfectly evident that he is lacking in the chief, if not the sole, means of portraying character, which is individuality of language—that each person should speak in a way suitable to his own character. That is lacking in Shakespeare. All his characters speak not a language of their own but always one

[1] 'One sees the intention and is put off.'

and the same Shakespearian, affected, unnatural language, which not only could they not speak, but which no real people could ever have spoken anywhere.

No real people could speak, or could have spoken, as Lear does—saying that, 'I would divorce me from thy mother's tomb' if Regan did not receive him, or telling the winds to 'crack your cheeks', or bidding 'the wind blow the earth into the sea', or 'swell the curl'd waters 'bove the main', as the gentleman describes what Lear said to the storm, or that it is easier to bear one's griefs and 'the mind much sufferance doth o'erskip, when grief hath mates, and bearing fellowship' ('bearing' meaning suffering), that Lear is 'childed, as I father'd', as Edgar says, and so forth—unnatural expressions such as overload the speeches of the people in all Shakespeare's dramas.

But it is not only that the characters all talk as no real people ever talked or could talk; they are also all afflicted by a common intemperance of language.

In love, preparing for death, fighting, or dying, they all talk at great length and unexpectedly about quite irrelevant matters, guided more by the sounds of the words and by puns than by the thoughts.

And they all talk alike. Lear raves just as Edgar does when feigning madness. Kent and the fool both speak alike. The words of one person can be put into the mouth of another, and by the character of the speech it is impossible to know who is speaking. If there is a difference in the speech of Shakespeare's characters, it is only that Shakespeare makes different speeches for his characters, and not that they speak differently.

Thus Shakespeare always speaks for his kings

in one and the same inflated, empty language. Similarly all his women who are intended to be poetic, speak the same pseudo-sentimental Shakespearian language: Juliet, Desdemona, Cordelia, and Miranda. In just the same way also it is Shakespeare who always speaks for his villains: Richard, Edmund, Iago, and Macbeth—expressing for them those malignant feelings which villains never express. And yet more identical is the talk of his madmen, with their terrible words, and the speeches of his fools with their mirthless witticisms.

So that the individual speech of living people —that individual speech which in drama is the chief means of presenting character—is lacking in Shakespeare. (If gesture is also a means of expressing character, as in the ballet, it is only a subsidiary means.) If the characters utter whatever comes to hand and as it comes to hand and all in one and the same way, as in Shakespeare, even the effect of gesture is lost; and therefore whatever blind worshippers of Shakespeare may say, Shakespeare does not show us characters.

Those persons who in his dramas stand out as characters, are characters borrowed by him from earlier works which served as the bases of his plays, and they are chiefly depicted, not in the dramatic manner which consists of making each person speak in his own diction, but in the epic manner, by one person describing the qualities of another.

The excellence of Shakespeare's depiction of character is asserted chiefly on the ground of the characters of Lear, Cordelia, Othello, Desdemona, Falstaff, and Hamlet. But these characters, like all the others, instead of belonging to Shakespeare, are taken by him from previous dramas, chronicles, and romances. And these characters were not merely not strengthened by him, but for the most part weakened and spoilt. This is very evident in the drama of King Lear which we are considering, and which was taken by Shakespeare from the play of *King Leir* by an unknown author. The characters of this drama, such as Lear himself and in particular Cordelia, were not only not created by Shakespeare, but have been strikingly weakened by him and deprived of personality as compared with the older play.

In the older play Leir resigns his power because, having become a widower, he thinks only of saving his soul. He asks his daughters about their love for him in order to keep his youngest and favourite daughter with him on his island by means of a cunning device. The two eldest are betrothed, while the youngest does not wish to contract a loveless marriage with any of the neighbouring suitors Leir offers her, and he is afraid she may marry some distant potentate.

The device he has planned, as he explains to his courtier Perillus (Shakespeare's Kent), is this: that when Cordelia tells him that she loves him more than anyone, or as much as her elder sisters do, he will say that in proof of her love she must marry a prince he will indicate on his island.

All these motives of Lear's conduct are lacking in Shakespeare's play. In the older play, when Leir asks his daughters about their love for him, Cordelia does not reply (as Shakespeare has it) that she will not give her father all her love but will also love her husband if she marries—to say which is quite unnatural—she simply says that she cannot express her love in words but hopes her actions will prove it. Goneril and Regan make remarks to the effect that Cordelia's answer is not an answer and that their father cannot quietly accept such indifference. So that in the older play there is an explanation, lacking in Shakespeare, of Leir's anger at the youngest daughter's reply. Leir is vexed at the non-success of his cunning device, and the venomous words of his elder daughters add to his irritation. After the division of his kingdom between the two elder daughters in the older play comes a scene between Cordelia and the King of Gaul which, instead of the impersonal Shakespearian Cordelia, presents us with a very definite and attractive character in the truthful, tender, self-denying youngest daughter. While Cordelia, not repining at being deprived of a share in the inheritance, sits grieving that she has lost her father's love, and looking forward to earning her bread by her own toil, the King of Gaul enters, who in the disguise of a pilgrim wishes to choose a bride from among Leir's daughters. He asks Cordelia the cause of her grief and she tells him. Having fallen in love with her, he woos her for the King of Gaul in his pilgrim guise, but Cordelia says she will only marry a man she loves. Then the pilgrim offers her his hand and heart, and Cordelia confesses that she loves him and agrees to marry him, notwithstanding the poverty and privation that she thinks await her. Then the pilgrim discloses to her that he is himself the King of Gaul, and Cordelia marries him.

Instead of this scene Lear, according to Shakespeare, proposes to Cordelia's two suitors to take her without dowry, and one cynically refuses, while the other takes her without our knowing why.

After this in the older play, as in Shakespeare, Leir undergoes insults from Goneril to whose house he has gone, but he bears these insults in a very different way from that represented by Shakespeare: he feels that by his conduct to Cordelia he has deserved them and he meekly submits. As in Shakespeare so also in the older play, the courtier, Perillus (Kent), who has taken Cordelia's part and has therefore been punished, comes to Leir; not disguised, but simply as a faithful servant who does not abandon his King in a moment of need, and assures him of his love. Leir says to him what in Shakespeare Lear says to Cordelia in the last scene—that if his daughters whom he has benefited hate him, surely one to whom he has done evil cannot love him. But Perillus (Kent) assures the King of his love, and Leir, pacified, goes on to Regan. In the older play there are no tempests or tearing out of grey hairs, but there is a weakened old Leir, overpowered by grief and humbled, and driven out by his second daughter also, who even wishes to kill him. Turned out by his elder daughters, Leir in the older play, as a last resource, goes with Perillus to Cordelia. Instead of the unnatural expulsion of Leir during a tempest and his roaming about the heath, in the old play Leir with Perillus during their journey to France very naturally come to the last degree of want. They sell their clothes to pay for the sea-crossing, and exhausted by cold and hunger they approach Cordelia's house in fishermen's garb. Here again, instead of the unnatural conjoint ravings of the fool, Lear, and Edgar, as presented by Shakespeare, we have in the older play a natural scene of the meeting between the daughter and father. Cordelia—who notwithstanding her happiness has all the time been grieving about her father and praying God to forgive her sisters who have done him so much wrong—meets him, now in the last stage of want, and wishes immediately to disclose herself to him, but her husband advises her not to do so for fear of agitating the weak old man. She agrees and takes Leir into her house, and without revealing herself to him takes care of him. Leir revives little by little, and then the daughter asks him who he is, and how he lived formerly. If, says Leir,

> ... from the first I should relate the cause,
> I would make a heart of adamant to weep.
> And thou, poor soul,
> Kind-hearted as thou art,
> Dost weep already ere I do begin.

Cordelia replies:

> For God's love tell it, and when you have done,
> I'll tell the reason why I weep so soon.

And Leir relates all he has suffered from his elder daughters and says that he now wishes to find shelter with the one who would be right should she condemn him to death. 'If, however,' he says, 'she will receive me with love, it will be God's and her work and not my merit!' To this Cordelia replies, 'Oh, I know for certain that thy daughter will lovingly receive thee!' 'How canst thou know this without knowing her?' says Leir. 'I know,' says Cordelia, 'because not far from here, I had a father who acted towards me as badly as thou hast acted towards her, yet if I were only to see his white head, I would creep to meet him on my knees.' 'No, this cannot be,' says Leir, 'for there are no children in the world so cruel as mine.' 'Do not condemn all for the sins of some,' says Cordelia, falling on her knees. 'Look here, dear father,' she says, 'look at me: I am thy loving daughter.' The father recognizes her and says: 'It is not for thee but for me to beg thy pardon on my knees for all my sins towards thee.'

Is there anything approaching this charming scene in Shakespeare's drama?

Strange as the opinion may appear to Shakespeare's devotees, the whole of this older play is in all respects beyond compare better than Shakespeare's adaptation. It is so, first because in it those superfluous characters—the villain Edmund and the unnatural Gloucester and Edgar, who only distract one's attention—do not appear. Secondly, it is free from the perfectly false 'effects' of Lear's roaming about on the heath, his talks with the fool, and all those impossible disguises, non-recognitions, and wholesale deaths—above all because in this play there is the simple, natural, and deeply touching character of Leir, and the yet more touching and clearly defined character of Cordelia, which are lacking in Shakespeare. And also because in the older drama, instead of Shakespeare's daubed scene of Lear's meeting with Cordelia and her unnecessary murder, there is the exquisite scene of Leir's meeting with Cordelia, which is unequalled by anything in Shakespeare's drama.

The older play also terminates more naturally and more in accord with the spectators' moral demands than does Shakespeare's, namely, by the King of the Gauls conquering the husbands of the elder sisters, and Cordelia not perishing, but replacing Leir in his former position.

This is the position as regards the drama we are examining, borrowed from the old play *King Leir*.

It is the same with *Othello*, which is taken from an Italian story, and it is the same again with the famous *Hamlet*. The same may be said of Antony, Brutus, Cleopatra, Shylock, Richard, and all Shakespeare's characters; they are all taken from antecedent works. Shakespeare, taking the characters already given in previous plays, stories, chronicles, or in Plutarch's *Lives*, not only fails to make them more true to life and more vivid as his adulators assert, but on the contrary always weakens and often destroys them, as in *King Lear*: making his characters commit actions unnatural to them, and making them above all talk in a way natural neither to them nor to any human being. So in *Othello*, though this is—we will not say the best, but the least bad—the least overloaded with pompous verbosity, of all Shakespeare's dramas, the characters of Othello, Iago, Cassio, and Emilia are far less natural and alive in Shakespeare than in the Italian romance. In Shakespeare Othello suffers from epilepsy, of which he has an attack on the stage. Afterwards in Shakespeare the murder of Desdemona is preceded by a strange vow uttered by Othello on his knees, and besides this, Othello in Shakespeare's play is a negro and not a Moor. All this is unusual, inflated, unnatural, and infringes the unity of the character. And there is none of all this in the romance. In the romance also the causes of Othello's jealousy are more naturally presented than in Shakespeare. In the romance Cassio, knowing whose the handkerchief is, goes to Desdemona to return it, but when approaching the back door of Desdemona's house he sees Othello coming and runs away from him. Othello perceives Cassio running away, and this it is that chiefly confirms his suspicion. This is omitted in Shakespeare, and yet this casual incident explains Othello's jealousy more than anything else. In Shakespeare this jealousy is based entirely on Iago's machinations, which are always successful, and on his crafty speeches, which Othello blindly believes. Othello's monologue over the sleeping Desdemona, to the effect that he wishes that she when killed should look as she is when alive, and that he will love her when she is dead and now wishes to inhale her 'balmy breath' and so forth, is quite impossible. A man who is preparing to murder someone he loves cannot utter such phrases, and still less after the murder can he say that the sun and the moon ought now to be eclipsed and the globe to yawn, nor can he, whatever kind of a nigger he may be, address devils, inviting them to roast him in sulphur, and so forth. And finally, however effective may be his suicide (which does not occur in the romance) it quite destroys the conception of his firm character. If he really suffers from grief and remorse then, when intending to kill himself, he would not utter phrases about his own services, about a pearl, about his eyes dropping tears '*as fast as the Arabian trees their medicinable gum*', and still less could he talk about the way a Turk scolded a Venetian, and how '*thus*' he punished him for it! So that despite the powerful movement of feeling in Othello, when under the influence of Iago's hints jealousy rises in him, and afterwards in his scene with Desdemona, our conception of his character is constantly infringed by false pathos and by the unnatural speeches he utters.

So it is with the chief character—Othello. But notwithstanding the disadvantageous alterations he has undergone in comparison with the character from which he is taken in the romance, Othello still remains a character. But all the other personages have been quite spoilt by Shakespeare.

Iago in Shakespeare's play is a complete villain, a deceiver, a thief, and avaricious; he robs Roderigo, succeeds in all sorts of impossible designs, and is therefore a quite unreal person. In Shakespeare the motive of his villainy is, first, that he is offended at Othello not having given him a place he desired; secondly, that he suspects Othello of an intrigue with his wife; and thirdly that, as he says, he feels a strange sort of love for Desdemona. There are many motives, but they are all vague. In the romance there is one motive, and it is simple and clear: Iago's passionate love for Desdemona, changing into hatred of her and of Othello after she had preferred the Moor to him and had definitely repulsed him. Yet more unnatural is the quite unnecessary figure of Roderigo, whom Iago deceives and robs, promising him Desdemona's love and obliging him to do as he is ordered: make Cassio drunk, provoke him, and then kill him. Emilia, who utters anything it occurs to the author to put into her mouth, bears not even the slightest resemblance to a real person.

'But Falstaff, the wonderful Falstaff!' Shakespeare's eulogists will say. 'It is impossible to assert that he is not a live person, and that, having been taken out of an anonymous comedy, he has been weakened.'

Falstaff, like all Shakespeare's characters, was taken from a play by an unknown author, written about a real person, a Sir John Oldcastle who was the friend of some Duke. This Oldcastle had once been accused of heresy and had been saved by his friend the Duke, but was afterwards condemned and burnt at the stake for his religious beliefs, which clashed with Catholicism. To please the Roman Catholic public an unknown author wrote a play about Oldcastle, ridiculing this martyr for his faith and exhibiting him as a worthless man, a boon companion of the Duke's, and from this play Shakespeare took not only the character of Falstaff but also his own humorous attitude towards him. In the first plays of Shakespeare's in which this character appears he was called Oldcastle; but afterwards, when under Elizabeth Protestantism had again triumphed, it was awkward to mock at this martyr of the struggle with

Catholicism, and besides, Oldcastle's relatives had protested, and Shakespeare changed the name from Oldcastle to Falstaff—also an historical character, notorious for having run away at the battle of Agincourt.

Falstaff is really a thoroughly natural and characteristic personage, almost the only natural and characteristic one depicted by Shakespeare. And he is natural and characteristic because, of all Shakespeare's characters, he alone speaks in a way proper to himself. He speaks in a manner proper to himself because he talks just that Shakespearian language, filled with jests that lack humour and unamusing puns, which while unnatural to all Shakespeare's other characters is quite in harmony with the boastful, distorted, perverted character of the drunken Falstaff. That is the only reason why this figure really presents a definite character. Unfortunately the artistic effect of the character is spoilt by the fact that it is so repulsive in its gluttony, drunkenness, debauchery, rascality, mendacity, and cowardice, that it is difficult to share the feeling of merry humour Shakespeare adopts towards it. Such is the case with Falstaff.

But in none of Shakespeare's figures is, I will not say his inability but his complete indifference, to giving his people characters, so strikingly noticeable as in the case of *Hamlet*, and with no other of Shakespeare's works is the blind worship of Shakespeare so strikingly noticeable—that unreasoning hypnotism which does not even admit the thought that any production of his can be other than a work of genius, or that any leading character in a drama of his can fail to be the expression of a new and profoundly conceived character.

Shakespeare takes the ancient story—not at all

bad of its kind—relating: *avec quelle ruse Amlet qui depuis fut Roy de Dannemarch, vengea la mort de son père Horwendille, occis par Fengon, son frère, et autre occurrence de son histoire*, or a drama that was written on the same theme fifteen years before him; and he writes his play on this subject introducing inappropriately (as he constantly does) into the mouth of the chief character all such thoughts of his own as seem to him worthy of attention. Putting these thoughts into his hero's mouth— about life (the grave-diggers); about death ('To be or not to be'); those he had expressed in his sixty-sixth sonnet about the theatre and about women—he did not at all concern himself as to the circumstances under which these speeches were to be delivered, and it naturally results that the person uttering these various thoughts becomes a mere phonograph of Shakespeare, deprived of any character of his own; and his actions and words do not agree.

In the legend Hamlet's personality is quite intelligible: he is revolted by the conduct of his uncle and his mother, wishes to be revenged on them, but fears that his uncle may kill him as he had killed his father, and therefore pretends to be mad, wishing to wait and observe all that was going on at court. But his uncle and his mother, being afraid of him, wish to find out whether he is feigning or is really mad, and send a girl he loves to him. He keeps up his role and afterwards sees his mother alone, kills a courtier who was eavesdropping, and convicts his mother of her sin. Then he is sent to England. He intercepts letters, returns from England, and revenges himself on his enemies, burning them all.

This is all intelligible and flows from Hamlet's character and position. But Shakespeare, by putting into Hamlet's mouth speeches he wished to publish, and making him perform actions needed to secure effective scenes, destroys all that forms Hamlet's character in the legend. Throughout the whole tragedy Hamlet does not do what he might wish to do, but what is needed for the author's plans: now he is frightened by his father's ghost and now he begins to chaff it, calling it 'old mole'; now he loves Ophelia, now he teases her, and so on. There is no possibility of finding any explanation of Hamlet's actions and speeches, and therefore no possibility of attributing any character to him.

But as it is accepted that Shakespeare, the genius, could write nothing bad, learned men devote all the power of their minds to discovering extraordinary beauties in what is an obvious and glaring defect—particularly obvious in Hamlet—namely, that the chief person in the play has no character at all. And, lo and behold, profound critics announce that in this drama, in the person of Hamlet, a perfectly new and profound character is most powerfully presented: consisting in this, that the person has no character; and that in this absence of character lies an achievement of genius—the creation of a profound character! And having decided this, the learned critics write volumes upon volumes, until the laudations and explanations of the grandeur and importance of depicting the character of a man without a character fill whole libraries. It is true that some critics timidly express the thought that there is something strange about this person, and that Hamlet is an unsolved riddle; but no one ventures to say, as in Hans Andersen's story, that the king is naked; that it is clear as day that Shakespeare was unable, and did not even wish, to give Hamlet any character and did not even understand that this was necessary! And learned critics continue to study and praise this enigmatical production, which reminds one of the famous inscribed stone found by Pickwick at a cottage doorstep—which divided the scientific world into two hostile camps.

So that neither the character of Lear, nor of Othello, nor of Falstaff, and still less of Hamlet, at all confirms the existing opinion that Shakespeare's strength lies in the delineation of character.

If in Shakespeare's plays some figures are met with that have characteristic traits (mostly secondary figures such as Polonius in *Hamlet*, and Portia in *The Merchant of Venice*), these few life-like figures —among the five hundred or more secondary figures, and with the complete absence of character in the principal figures—are far from proving that the excellence of Shakespeare's dramas lies in the presentation of character.

That a great mastery in the presentation of character is attributed to Shakespeare arises from his really possessing a peculiarity which when helped out by the play of good actors may appear to superficial observers to be a capacity to manage scenes in which a movement of feeling is expressed. However arbitrary the positions in which he puts his characters, however unnatural to them the language he makes them speak, however lacking in individuality they may be, the movement of feeling itself, its increase and change and the combination of many contrary feelings, are often expressed correctly and powerfully in some of Shakespeare's scenes. And this when performed by good actors evokes, if but for a while, sympathy for the persons represented.

Shakespeare, himself an actor and a clever man, knew not only by speeches, but by exclamations, gestures, and the repetition of words, how to express the state of mind and changes of feeling occurring in the persons represented. So that in many places Shakespeare's characters instead of speaking, merely exclaim, or weep, or in the midst of a monologue indicate the pain of their position by gesture (as when Lear asks to have a button undone), or at a moment of strong excitement they repeat a question several times and cause a word to be repeated which strikes them, as is done by Othello, Macduff, Cleopatra, and others. Similar clever methods of expressing a movement of feeling—giving good actors a chance to show their powers—have often been taken by many critics for the expression of character. But however strongly the play of feeling may be expressed in one scene, a single scene cannot give the character of a person when after the appropriate exclamations or gesture that person begins to talk lengthily not in a natural manner proper to him but according to the author's whim—saying things unnecessary and not in harmony with his character.

V

'Well, but the profound utterances and sayings delivered by Shakespeare's characters?' Shakespeare's eulogists will exclaim. 'Lear's monologue on punishment, Kent's on vengeance, Edgar's on his former life, Gloucester's reflections on the perversity of fate, and in other dramas the famous monologues of Hamlet, Antony, and others?'

Thoughts and sayings may be appreciated, I reply, in prose works, in essays, in collections of aphorisms, but not in artistic dramatic works the aim of which is to elicit sympathy with what is represented. And therefore the monologues and sayings of Shakespeare even if they contained many very profound and fresh thoughts, which is not the case, cannot constitute the excellence of an artistic and poetic work. On the contrary, these speeches, uttered in unnatural conditions, can only spoil artistic works.

An artistic poetic work, especially a drama, should first of all evoke in reader or spectator the illusion that what the persons represented are living through and experiencing is being lived through and experienced by himself. And for this purpose it is not more important for the dramatist to know precisely what he should make his acting characters do and say, than it is to know what he should not make them do and say, so as not to infringe the reader's or spectator's illusion. However eloquent and profound they may be, speeches put into the mouths of acting characters, if they are superfluous and do not accord with the situation and the characters, infringe the main condition of dramatic work—the illusion causing the reader or spectator to experience the feelings of the persons represented. One may without infringing the illusion leave much unsaid: the reader or spectator will himself supply what is needed, and sometimes as a result of this his illusion is even increased; but to say what is superfluous is like jerking and scattering a statue made up of small pieces, or taking the lamp out of a magic lantern. The reader's or spectator's attention is distracted, the reader sees the author, the spectator sees the actor, the illusion is lost, and to recreate it is sometimes impossible. And therefore without a sense of proportion there cannot be an artist, especially a dramatist. And Shakespeare is entirely devoid of this feeling.

Shakespeare's characters continually do and say what is not merely unnatural to them but quite unnecessary. I will not cite examples of this, for

I think that a man who does not himself perceive this striking defect in all Shakespeare's dramas will not be convinced by any possible examples or proofs. It is sufficient to read *King Lear* alone, with the madness, the murders, the plucking out of eyes, Gloucester's jump, the poisonings, and the torrents of abuse—not to mention *Pericles*, *A Winter's Tale*, or *The Tempest*—to convince oneself of this. Only a man quite devoid of the sense of proportion and taste could produce the types of *Titus Andronicus* and *Troilus and Cressida*, and so pitilessly distort the old drama of *King Lear*.

Gervinus tries to prove that Shakespeare possessed a feeling of beauty, *Schonheitssinn*, but all Gervinus's proofs only show that he himself, Gervinus, completely lacked it. In Shakespeare everything is exaggerated: the actions are exaggerated, so are their consequences, the speeches of the characters are exaggerated, and therefore at every step the possibility of artistic impression is infringed.

Whatever people may say, however they may be enraptured by Shakespeare's works, whatever merits they may attribute to them, it is certain that he was not an artist and that his works are not artistic productions. Without a sense of proportion there never was or could be an artist, just as without a sense of rhythm there cannot be a musician. And Shakespeare may be anything you like—only not an artist.

'But one must not forget the times in which Shakespeare wrote,' say his laudators. 'It was a time of cruel and coarse manners, a time of the then fashionable euphuism, that is, an artificial manner of speech—a time of forms of life strange to us, and therefore to judge Shakespeare one must keep in view the times when he wrote. In Homer, as in Shakespeare, there is much that is strange to us, but this does not prevent our valuing the beauties of Homer,' say the laudators. But when one compares Shakespeare with Homer, as Gervinus does, the infinite distance separating true poetry from its imitation emerges with special vividness. However distant Homer is from us we can without the slightest effort transport ourselves into the life he describes. And we are thus transported chiefly because, however alien to us may be the events Homer describes, he believes in what he says and speaks seriously of what he is describing, and therefore he never exaggerates and the sense of measure never deserts him. And therefore it happens that, not to speak of the wonderfully distinct, life-like, and excellent characters of Achilles, Hector, Priam, Odysseus, and the eternally touching scenes of Hector's farewell, of Priam's embassy, of the return of Odysseus, and so forth, the whole of the *Iliad* and still more the *Odyssey*, is as naturally close to us all as if we had lived and were now living among the gods and heroes. But it is not so with Shakespeare. From his first words exaggeration is seen: exaggeration of events, exaggeration of feeling, and exaggeration of expression. It is at once evident that he does not believe in what he is saying, that he has no need to say it, that he is inventing the occurrences he describes, is indifferent to his characters and has devised them merely for the stage, and therefore makes them do and say what may strike his public; and so we do not believe either in the events or in the actions, or in the sufferings of his characters. Nothing so clearly shows the complete absence of aesthetic feeling in Shakespeare as a comparison between him and Homer. The works which we call the works of Homer are artistic, poetic, original works, lived through by their author or authors.

But Shakespeare's works are compositions devised for a particular purpose, and having absolutely nothing in common with art or poetry.

VI

But perhaps the loftiness of Shakespeare's conception of life is such that, even though he does not satisfy the demands of aesthetics, he discloses to us so new and important a view of life that in consideration of its value all his artistic defects become unnoticeable. This is indeed what some laudators of Shakespeare say. Gervinus plainly says that besides Shakespeare's significance in the sphere of dramatic poetry, in which in his opinion he is the equal of 'Homer in the sphere of the epic; Shakespeare, being the greatest judge of the human soul, is a teacher of most indisputable ethical authority, and the most select leader in the world and in life'.

In what then does this indubitable authority of the most select teacher in the world and in life consist? Gervinus devotes the concluding chapter of his second volume (some fifty pages) to an explanation of this.

The ethical authority of this supreme teacher of life, in the opinion of Gervinus, consists in this: 'Shakespeare's moral view starts from the simple point that man is born with powers of activity,' and therefore, first of all, says Gervinus, Shakespeare regarded it as 'an obligation to use our inherent power of action'. (As if it were possible for man not to act!)[1]

'*Die tatkräftigen Männer, Fortinbras, Bolingbroke, Alcibiades, Octavius spielen hier die gegensätzlichen Rollen gegen die verschiedenen Tatlosen; nicht ihre*

[1] This and the quotations in English that follow are taken from *Shakespeare's Commentaries*, by Dr. G. G. Gervinus, translated by F. G. Bennett, London, 1877.—L. T.

Charaktere verdienen ihnen allen ihr Glück und Gedeihen etwa durch eine grosse Ueberlegenheit ihre Natur, sondern trotz ihrer geringern Anlage stellt sich ihre Tatkraft an sich über die Untatigkeit der Anderen hinaus, gleichviel aus wie schoner Quelle diese Passivität, aus wie schlechter jene Tätigkeit fliesse.'[1]

That is to say, Gervinus informs us, that active people like Fortinbras, Bolingbroke, Alcibiades, and Octavius are contrasted by Shakespeare with various characters who do not display energetic activity. And, according to Shakespeare, happiness and success are attained by people who possess this active character, not at all as a result of their superiority of nature. On the contrary, in spite of their inferior talents their energy in itself always gives them the advantage over the inactive people, regardless of whether their inactivity results from excellent impulses, or the activity of the others from base ones. Activity is good, inactivity is evil. Activity transforms evil into good, says Shakespeare, according to Gervinus. 'Shakespeare prefers the principle of Alexander to that of Diogenes,' says Gervinus. In other words, according to him, Shakespeare prefers death and murder from ambition, to self-restraint and wisdom.[2]

According to Gervinus, Shakespeare considers that humanity should not set itself ideals, but that all that is necessary is healthy activity, and a golden mean in everything. Indeed Shakespeare is so imbued with this wise moderation that, in the words of Gervinus, he even allows himself to deny Christian morality which makes exaggerated de-

[1] *Shakespeare*, von G. G. Gervinus, Leipzig, 1872, vol. ii, pp. 550-1.—L. T.

[2] Tolstóy's essay *Non-Acting* deals with a controversy that occurred in 1893 between Zola and Dumas. In it Tolstóy controverts the opinion that activity in itself, lacking moral guidance, is beneficial.—A. M.

mands on human nature. 'How thoroughly penetrated Shakespeare was with this principle of wise moderation', says Gervinus, 'is shown perhaps most strongly in this, that he ventured even to oppose Christian laws which demand an overstraining of human nature; for he did not approve of the limits of duty being extended beyond the intention of nature. He taught therefore the wise and human medium between the Christian and heathen precepts' (p. 917)—a reasonable mean, natural to man, between Christian and pagan injunctions—on the one hand love of one's enemies, and on the other hatred of them!

'That it is possible to do too much in good things is an express doctrine of Shakespeare, both in word and example. . . . Thus excessive liberality ruins Timon, whilst moderate generosity keeps Antonio in honour; the genuine ambition which makes Henry V great overthrows Percy, in whom it rises too high. Exaggerated virtue brings Angelo to ruin; and when in those near him the excess of punishment proves harmful and cannot hinder sin, then mercy, the most Godlike gift that man possesses, is also exhibited in its excess as the producer of sin.'

Shakespeare, says Gervinus, taught that one *may do too much good*. 'He teaches', says Gervinus, 'that morality, like politics, is a matter so complicated with relations, conditions of life, and motives, that it is impossible to bring it to final principles' (p. 918).

'In Shakespeare's opinion (and here also he is one with Bacon and Aristotle) there is no positive law of religion or morals which could form a rule of moral action in precepts ever binding and suitable for all cases.'

Gervinus most clearly expresses Shakespeare's

whole moral theory by saying that Shakespeare does not write for those classes for whom definite religious principles and laws are suitable (that is to say, for nine hundred and ninety-nine people out of every thousand), but for the cultivated, who have made their own a healthy tact in life and such an instinctive feeling as, united with conscience, reason, and will, can direct them to worthy aims of life. But even for these fortunate ones, this teaching may be dangerous if it is taken incompletely. It must be taken whole. 'There are classes', says Gervinus, 'whose morality is best provided for by the positive letter of religion and law; but for such as these Shakespeare's writings are in themselves inaccessible; they are only readable and comprehensible to the cultivated, of whom it can be required that they should appropriate to themselves the healthy measure of life, and that self-reliance in which the guiding and inherent powers of conscience and reason, united with the will, are, when consciously apprehended, worthy aims of life' (p. 919). 'But even for the cultivated also, Shakespeare's doctrine may not always be without danger. . . . The condition on which his doctrine is entirely harmless is this, that it should be fully and completely received and without any expurging and separating. Then it is not only without danger, but it is also more unmistakable and more infallible, and therefore more worthy of our confidence, than any system of morality can be.' (p. 919.)

And in order to accept it all, one should understand that according to his teaching it is insane and harmful for an individual to rise against or 'disregard the bonds of religion and the state' (p. 921). For Shakespeare would abhor a free and independent personality who strong in spirit should oppose any law in politics or morals and should disregard the union of the state and religion 'which has kept society together for centuries' (p. 921). 'For in his opinion the practical wisdom of man should have no higher aim than to carry into society the utmost possible nature and freedom, but for that very reason, and that he might maintain sacred and inviolable the natural laws of society, he would respect existing forms, yet at the same time penetrate into their rational substance with sound criticism, not forgetting nature in civilization, nor, equally, civilization in nature.' Property, the family, the state, are sacred. But the aspiration to recognize the equality of man is insane. 'Its realization would bring the greatest harm to humanity' (p. 925).

'No man has fought more strongly against rank and class prejudices than Shakespeare, but how could his liberal principles have been pleased with the doctrines of those who would have done away with the prejudices of the rich and cultivated only to replace them by the interests and prejudices of the poor and uncultivated? How would this man, who draws us so eloquently to the course of honour, have approved, if in annulling rank, degrees of merit, distinction, we extinguish every impulse to greatness, and by the removal of all degrees, "shake the ladder to all high designs"? If indeed no surreptitious honour and false power were longer to oppress mankind, how would the poet have acknowledged the most fearful force of all, the power of barbarity? In consequence of these modern doctrines of equality he would have apprehended that everything would resolve itself into power; or if this were not the final lot which awaited mankind from these aspirations after equality, if love between nationalities, and endless peace, were not that "nothing" of impossibility, as

Alonso expresses it in the *Tempest*, but could be an actual fruit of these efforts after equality, then the poet would have believed that with this time the old age and decrepitude of the world had arrived, in which it were worthless for the active to live' (p. 925).

Such is Shakespeare's view of life as explained by his greatest exponent and admirer. Another of the recent laudators of Shakespeare, Brandes, adds the following:

'No one, of course, can preserve his life quite pure from injustice, from deception, and from doing harm to others, but injustice and deception are not always vices and even the harm done to other people is not always a vice: it is often only a necessity, a legitimate weapon, a right. At bottom, Shakespeare had always held that there were no such things as unconditional duties and absolute prohibitions. He had never, for example, questioned Hamlet's right to kill the King, scarcely even his right to run his sword through Polonius. Nevertheless he had hitherto been unable to conquer a feeling of indignation and disgust when he saw around him nothing but breaches of the simplest moral laws. Now, on the other hand, the dim divinations of his earlier years crystallized in his mind into a coherent body of thought: no commandment is unconditional; it is not in the observance or non-observance of an external fiat that the merits of an action, to say nothing of a character, consists: everything depends upon the volitional substance into which the individual, as a responsible agent, transmits the formal imperative at the moment of decision.'[1]

[1] *William Shakespeare*, by Georges Brandes, translated by William Archer and Miss Morison, London, 1898, p. 921.— L. T.

In other words Shakespeare now sees clearly that the morality of the aim is the only true, the only possible one; so that, according to Brandes, Shakespeare's fundamental principle, for which he is extolled, is that *the end justifies the means*. Action at all costs, the absence of all ideals, moderation in everything, the maintenance of established forms of life, and the maxim that 'the end justifies the means'.

If one adds to this a Chauvinistic English patriotism, expressed in all his historical plays: a patriotism according to which the English throne is something sacred, the English always defeat the French, slaughtering thousands and losing only scores, Jeanne d'Arc is a witch, Hector and all the Trojans—from whom the English are descended—are heroes, while the Greeks are cowards and traitors, and so forth: this is the view of life of the wisest teacher of life according to his greatest admirer. And anyone who reads attentively the works of Shakespeare cannot but acknowledge that the attribution of this view of life to Shakespeare by those who praise him is perfectly correct.

The value of every poetical work depends on three qualities:

1. The content of the work: the more important the content, that is to say the more important it is for the life of man, the greater is the work.

2. The external beauty achieved by the technical methods proper to the particular kind of art. Thus in dramatic art the technical method will be: that the characters should have a true individuality of their own, a natural and at the same time a touching plot, a correct presentation on the stage of the manifestation and development of feelings, and a sense of proportion in all that is presented.

3. Sincerity, that is to say that the author should

himself vividly feel what he expresses. Without this condition there can be no work of art, as the essence of art consists in the infection of the contemplator of a work by the author's feeling. If the author has not felt what he is expressing, the recipient cannot become infected by the author's feeling, he does not experience any feeling, and the production cannot be classed as a work of art.

The content of Shakespeare's plays, as is seen by the explanations of his greatest admirers, is the lowest, most vulgar view of life which regards the external elevation of the great ones of the earth as a genuine superiority; despises the crowd, that is to say, the working classes; and repudiates not only religious, but even any humanitarian, efforts directed towards the alteration of the existing order of society.

The second condition is also absent in Shakespeare except in his handling of scenes in which a movement of feelings is expressed. There is in his works a lack of naturalness in the situations, the characters lack individuality of speech, and a sense of proportion is also wanting, without which such works cannot be artistic.

The third and chief condition—sincerity—is totally absent in all Shakespeare's works. One sees in all of them an intentional artificiality; it is obvious that he is not in earnest but is playing with words.

VII

The works of Shakespeare do not meet the demands of every art, and, besides that, their tendency is very low and immoral. What then is the meaning of the immense fame these works have enjoyed for more than a hundred years?

To reply to this question seems the more difficult,

because if the works of Shakespeare had any kind of excellence the achievement which has produced the exaggerated praise lavished upon them would be at least to some extent intelligible. But here two extremes meet: works which are beneath criticism, insignificant, empty, and immoral—meet insensate, universal laudation, that proclaims these works to be above everything that has ever been produced by man.

How is this to be explained?

Many times during my life I have had occasion to discuss Shakespeare with his admirers, not only with people little sensitive to poetry but also with those who felt poetic beauty keenly, such as Turgénev, Fet,[1] and others, and each time I have encountered one and the same attitude towards my disagreement with the laudation of Shakespeare.

I was not answered when I pointed out Shakespeare's defects; they only pitied me for my want of comprehension and urged on me the necessity of acknowledging the extraordinary supernatural grandeur of Shakespeare. They did not explain to me in what the beauties of Shakespeare consist, but were merely indefinitely and exaggeratedly enthusiastic about the whole of Shakespeare, extolling some favourite passages: the undoing of Lear's button, Falstaff's lying, Lady Macbeth's spot which would not wash out, Hamlet's address to the ghost of his father, the 'forty thousand brothers', 'none does offend, none, I say none', and so forth.

'Open Shakespeare', I used to say to these admirers of his, 'where you will or as may chance, and you will see that you will never find ten consecutive lines that are comprehensible, natural,

---

[1] A Russian poet of much delicacy of feeling, for many years a great friend of Tolstóy's.—A. M.

characteristic of the person who utters them, and productive of an artistic impression.' (Anyone may make this experiment.) And the laudators of Shakespeare opened pages in Shakespeare's dramas by chance, or at their own choice, and without paying any attention to the reasons I adduced as to why the ten lines selected did not meet the most elementary demands of aesthetics or good sense, praised the very things that appeared to me absurd, unintelligible, and inartistic.

So that in general in response to my endeavours to obtain from the worshippers of Shakespeare an explanation of his greatness, I encountered precisely the attitude I have usually met with, and still meet with, from the defenders of any dogmas accepted not on the basis of reason but on mere credulity. And it was just this attitude of the laudators of Shakespeare—an attitude which may be met with in all the indefinite, misty articles about him, and in conversations—that gave me the key to an understanding of the cause of Shakespeare's fame. There is only one explanation of this astonishing phenomenon: it is one of those epidemic suggestions to which people always have been, and are, liable. Such irrational suggestion has always existed, and still exists in all spheres of life. The medieval Crusades, which influenced not only adults but children, are glaring examples of such suggestion, considerable in scope and deceptiveness, and there have been many other epidemic suggestions astonishing in their senselessness, such as the belief in witches, in the utility of torture for the discovery of truth, the search for the elixir of life, for the philosopher's stone, and the passion for tulips valued at several thousand guilders a bulb, which overran Holland. There always have been and always are such irrational suggestions in all spheres of human life—religious, philosophic, economic, scientific, artistic, and in literature generally, and people only see clearly the insanity of such suggestions after they are freed from them. But as long as they are under their influence these suggestions appear to them such indubitable truths that they do not consider it necessary or possible to reason about them. Since the development of the printing-press these epidemics have become particularly striking.

Since the development of the press it has come about that as soon as something obtains a special significance from accidental circumstances, the organs of the press immediately announce this significance. And as soon as the press has put forward the importance of the matter, the public directs yet more attention to it. The hypnotization of the public incites the press to regard the thing more attentively and in greater detail. The interest of the public is still further increased, and the organs of the press, competing one with another, respond to the public demand.

The public becomes yet more interested, and the press attributes yet more importance to the matter; so that this importance, growing ever greater and greater like a snowball, obtains a quite unnatural appreciation, and this appreciation, exaggerated even to absurdity, maintains itself as long as the outlook on life of the leaders of the press and of the public remains the same. There are in our day innumerable examples of such a misunderstanding of the importance of the most insignificant occurrences, occasioned by the mutual reaction of press and public. A striking example of this was the excitement which seized the whole world over the Dreyfus affair. A suspicion arose that some captain on the French staff had been guilty of treason.

Whether because this captain was a Jew, or from some special internal party disagreements in French society, this event, which resembled others that continually occur without arousing anyone's attention and without interesting the whole world or even the French military, was given a somewhat prominent position by the press. The public paid attention to it. The organs of the press, vying with one another, began to describe, to analyse, to discuss the event, the public became yet more interested, the press responded to the demands of the public and the snowball began to grow and grow, and grew before our eyes to such an extent that there was not a family which had not its disputes about *l'affaire*. So that Caran d'Ache's caricature, which depicted first a peaceful family that had decided not to discuss the Dreyfus affair any more, and then the same family represented as angry furies fighting one another, quite correctly depicted the relation of the whole reading world to the Dreyfus question. Men of other nationalities who could not have any real interest in the question whether a French officer had or had not been a traitor—men moreover who could not know how the affair was going—all divided for or against Dreyfus, some asserting his guilt with assurance, others denying it with equal certainty.

It was only after some years that people began to awaken from the 'suggestion' and to understand that they could not possibly know whether he was guilty or innocent, and that each one of them had a thousand matters nearer and more interesting to him than the Dreyfus affair. Such infatuations occur in all spheres, but they are specially noticeable in the sphere of literature, for the press naturally occupies itself most of all with the affairs of the press, and these are particularly powerful in our day when the press has obtained such an unnatural development. It continually happens that people suddenly begin to devote exaggerated praise to some very insignificant works, and then, if these works do not correspond to the prevailing view of life, suddenly become perfectly indifferent to them and forget both the works themselves and their own previous attitude towards them.

So within my recollection, in the eighteen-forties, there occurred in the artistic sphere the exaltation and laudation of Eugène Sue and George Sand; in the social sphere, of Fourier; in the philosophic sphere, of Comte and Hegel; and in the scientific sphere, of Darwin.

Sue is quite forgotten, George Sand is being forgotten and replaced by the writings of Zola and the Decadents—Baudelaire, Verlaine, Maeterlinck and others. Fourier, with his phalansteries, is quite forgotten, and has been replaced by Karl Marx. Hegel, who justified the existing order, and Comte, who denied the necessity of religious activity in humanity, and Darwin, with his law of struggle for existence, still maintain their places, but are beginning to be neglected and replaced by the teachings of Nietzsche, which though perfectly absurd, unthought-out, obscure, and bad in their content, correspond better to the present-day outlook on life. Thus it sometimes happens that artistic, philosophic, and literary crazes in general, arise, fall rapidly, and are forgotten.

But it also happens that such crazes, having arisen in consequence of special causes accidently favouring their establishment, correspond so well to the view of life diffused in society and especially in literary circles, that they maintain their place for a very long time. Even in Roman times it was remarked that books have their fate, and often a very strange one: failure in spite of high qualities, and enormous undeserved success in spite of insignificance. And a proverb was made: *Pro captu lectoris habent sua fata libelli,* that is, that the fate of books depends on the understanding of those who read them. Such was the correspondence of Shakespeare's work to the view of life of the people among whom his fame arose. And this fame has been maintained, and is still maintained, because the works of Shakespeare continue to correspond to the view of life of those who maintain this fame.

Until the end of the 18th century Shakespeare not only had no particular fame in England, but was less esteemed than his contemporaries: Ben Jonson, Fletcher, Beaumont, and others. His fame began in Germany, and from there passed to England. This happened for the following reason:

Art, especially dramatic art which demands for its realization extensive preparations, expenditure, and labour, was always religious, that is to say, its object was to evoke in man a clearer conception of that relation of man to God attained at the time by the advanced members of the society in which the art was produced.

So it should be by the nature of the case, and so it always had been among all nations: among the Egyptians, Hindus, Chinese, and Greeks—from the earliest time that we have knowledge of the life of man. And it has always happened that with the coarsening of religious forms art diverged more and more from this original aim (which had caused it to be recognized as an important matter —almost an act of worship), and instead of religious aims it adopted worldly aims for the satisfaction of the demands of the crowd, or of the great ones of the earth, that is to say, aims of recreation and amusement.

This deflexion of art from its true and high vocation occurred everywhere, and it occurred in Christendom.

The first manifestation of Christian art was in the worship of God in the temples: the performance of Mass and, in general, of the liturgy. When in course of time the forms of this art of divine worship became insufficient, the Mysteries were produced, depicting those events regarded as most important in the Christian religious view of life. Afterwards, when in the 13th and 14th centuries the centre of gravity of Christian teaching was more and more transferred from the worship of Jesus as God, to the explanation of his teaching and its fulfilment, the form of the Mysteries, which depicted external Christian events, became insufficient and new forms were demanded; and as an expression of this tendency appeared the Moralities, dramatic representations in which the characters personified the Christian virtues and the opposite vices.

But allegories by their very nature, as art of a lower order, could not replace the former religious drama, and no new form of dramatic art corresponding to the conception of Christianity as a teaching of life had yet been found. And dramatic art, lacking a religious basis, began in all Christian countries more and more to deviate from its purpose, and instead of a service of God became a service of the crowd (I mean by 'crowd' not merely the common people, but the majority of immoral or non-moral people indifferent to the higher problems of human life). This deviation was helped on by the fact that just at that time the Greek thinkers, poets, and dramatists, with whom the Christian world had not hitherto been acquainted, were rediscovered and favourably accepted. And therefore, not having yet had time to work out for themselves a clear and satisfactory form of dramatic art suitable to the new conception entertained of Christianity as a teaching of life, and at the same time recognizing the previous Mysteries and Moralities as insufficient, the writers of the 15th and 16th centuries, in their search for a new form, began to imitate the newly discovered Greek models, which were attractive by their elegance and novelty. And as it was chiefly the great ones of the earth who could avail themselves of the drama—the kings, princes, and courtiers—the least religious people, not merely quite indifferent to questions of religion but for the most part thoroughly depraved—it followed that to satisfy the demands of its public the drama of the 15th, 16th, and 17th centuries was chiefly a spectacle intended for depraved kings and the upper classes. Such was the drama of Spain, England, Italy, and France.

The plays of that time, chiefly composed in all these countries according to ancient Greek models, from poems, legends, and biographies, naturally reflected the national characters. In Italy comedies with amusing scenes and characters were chiefly elaborated. In Spain the worldly drama flourished, with complicated plots and ancient historical heroes. The peculiarity of English drama was the coarse effect produced by murders, executions, and battles on the stage, and popular comic interludes. Neither the Italian, nor the Spanish, nor the English drama had European fame, and each of them enjoyed success only in its own country. General fame, thanks to the elegance of its language and the talent of its writers, was enjoyed only by the French drama, which was distinguished by strict adherence to the Greek models, and especially to the law of the three Unities.

So matters continued till the end of the 18th century, but at the end of that century this is what happened: in Germany, which lacked even mediocre dramatists (though there had been a weak and little known writer, Hans Sachs), all educated people, including Frederick the Great, bowed down before the French pseudo-classical drama. And yet at that very time there appeared in Germany a circle of educated and talented writers and poets who, feeling the falsity and coldness of the French drama, sought a newer and freer dramatic form. The members of this group, like all the upper classes of the Christian world at that time, were under the charm and influence of the Greek classics and, being utterly indifferent to religious questions, thought that if the Greek drama depicting the calamities, sufferings, and struggles of its heroes supplied the best model for the drama, then such representation of the sufferings and struggles of heroes would also be a sufficient subject for drama in the Christian world, if only one rejected the narrow demands of pseudo-classicism. These men, not understanding that the sufferings and strife of their heroes had a religious significance for the Greeks, imagined that it was only necessary to reject the inconvenient law of the three Unities, and the representation of various incidents in the lives of historic personages, and of strong human passions in general, would afford a sufficient basis for the drama without its containing any religious element corresponding to the beliefs of their own time. Just such a drama existed at that time among the kindred English people, and the Germans, becoming acquainted with it, decided that just such should be the drama of the new period.

The masterly development of the scenes which constitutes Shakespeare's speciality caused them to select Shakespeare's dramas from among all other English plays, which were not in the least inferior, but often superior, to Shakespeare's.

At the head of the circle stood Goethe, who was then the dictator of public opinion on aesthetic questions. And he it was who—partly from a wish to destroy the fascination of the false French art, partly from a wish to give freer scope to his own dramatic activity, but chiefly because his view of life agreed with Shakespeare's—acclaimed Shakespeare a great poet. When that falsehood had been proclaimed on Goethe's authority, all those aesthetic critics who did not understand art threw themselves upon it like crows upon carrion, and began to search Shakespeare for non-existent beauties and to extol them. These men, German aesthetic critics—for the most part utterly devoid of aesthetic feeling, ignorant of that simple direct artistic impression which for men with a feeling for art clearly distinguishes artistic impression from all other, but believing the authority that had proclaimed Shakespeare as a great poet—began to belaud the whole of Shakespeare indiscriminately, selecting passages especially which struck them by their effects or expressed thoughts corresponding to their own view of life, imagining that such effects and such thoughts constitute the essence of what is called art.

These men acted as blind men would if they tried by touch to select diamonds out of a heap of stones they fingered. As the blind man, long sorting out the many little stones, could finally come to no other conclusion than that all the stones were precious and the smoothest were especially precious, so the aesthetic critics, deprived of artistic feeling, could come to no other result about Shakespeare. To make their praise of the whole of

SHAKESPEARE AND THE DRAMA

Shakespeare more convincing they composed an aesthetic theory, according to which a definite religious view of life is not at all necessary for the creation of works of art in general or for the drama in particular; that for the inner content of a play it is quite enough to depict passions and human characters; that not only is no religious illumination of the matter presented required, but that art ought to be objective, that is to say, it should depict occurrences quite independently of any valuation of what is good or bad. And as this theory was educed from Shakespeare, it naturally happened that the works of Shakespeare corresponded to this theory and were therefore the height of perfection.

And these were the people chiefly responsible for Shakespeare's fame.

Chiefly in consequence of their writings, that interaction of writers and the public came about which found expression, and still finds expression, in the insensate laudation of Shakespeare without any rational basis. These aesthetic critics wrote profound treatises about Shakespeare (eleven thousand volumes have been written about him, and a whole science of Shakespearology has been formulated); the public became more and more interested, and the learned critics explained more and more, that is to say, they added to the confusion and laudation.

So that the first cause of Shakespeare's fame was that the Germans wanted something freer and more alive to oppose to the French drama of which they were tired, and which was really dull and cold. The second cause was that the young German writers required a model for their own dramas. The third and chief cause was the activity of the learned and zealous aesthetic German critics who lacked aesthetic feeling and formulated the theory of objective art, that is to say, deliberately repudiated the religious essence of the drama.

'But,' I shall be asked, 'what do you mean by the words "religious essence of the drama"? Is not what you demand for the drama religious instruction, didactics: what is called a tendency—which is incompatible with true art?' By 'the religious essence of art', I reply, I mean not an external inculcation of any religious truth in artistic guise, and not an allegorical representation of those truths, but the expression of a definite view of life corresponding to the highest religious understanding of a given period: an outlook which, serving as the impelling motive for the composition of the drama, permeates the whole work though the author be unconscious of it. So it has always been with true art, and so it is with every true artist in general and with dramatists especially. Hence, as happened when the drama was a serious thing, and as should be according to the essence of the matter, he alone can write a drama who has something to say to men—something highly important for them —about man's relation to God, to the universe, to all that is infinite and unending.

But when, thanks to the German theories about objective art, an idea had been established that, for drama, this is not wanted at all, then a writer like Shakespeare—who in his own soul had not formed religious convictions corresponding to his period, and who had even no convictions at all, but piled up in his plays all possible events, horrors, fooleries, discussions, and effects—could evidently be accepted as the greatest of dramatic geniuses.

But all these are external reasons: the fundamental inner cause of Shakespeare's fame was, and is, that his plays fitted *pro captu lectoris*, that is to say, responded to the irreligious and immoral attitude of the upper classes of our world.

VIII

A series of accidents brought it about that Goethe at the beginning of the last century, being the dictator of philosophic thought and aesthetic laws, praised Shakespeare; the aesthetic critics caught up that praise and began to write their long foggy erudite articles, and the great European public began to be enchanted by Shakespeare. The critics, responding to this public interest, laboriously vied with one another in writing more and more articles about Shakespeare, and readers and spectators were still further confirmed in their enthusiasm, and Shakespeare's fame kept growing and growing like a snowball, until in our time it has attained a degree of insane laudation that obviously rests on no other basis than suggestion.

'There is no one even approximately equal to Shakespeare either among ancient or modern writers.' 'Poetic truth is the most brilliant gem in the crown of Shakespeare's service.' 'Shakespeare is the greatest moralist of all times.' 'Shakespeare displays such diversity and such objectivity as place him beyond the limits of time and nationality.' 'Shakespeare is the greatest genius that has hitherto existed.' 'For the creation of tragedies, comedies, historical plays, idylls, idyllic comedies, aesthetic idylls, for representation itself, as also for incidental verses, he is the only man. He not only wields unlimited power over our laughter and our tears, over all phases of passion, humour, thought and observation, but he commands an unlimited realm of imagination, full of fancy of a terrifying and amazing character, and he possesses penetration in the world of invention and of reality, and over all this there reigns one and the same truthfulness to character and to nature, and the same spirit of humanity.'

'To Shakespeare the epithet of great applies naturally; and if one adds that independently of his greatness he has also become the reformer of all literature, and moreover has expressed in his works not only the phenomena of the life of his time, but also from thoughts and views that in his day existed only in germ has prophetically foreseen the direction which the social spirit would take in the future (of which we see an amazing example in Hamlet)—one may say without hesitation that Shakespeare was not only a great, but the greatest of all poets that ever existed, and that in the sphere of poetic creation the only rival that equals him is life itself, which in his productions he depicted with such perfection.'

The obvious exaggeration of this appraisement is a most convincing proof that it is not the outcome of sane thought, but of suggestion. The more insignificant, the lower, the emptier, a phenomenon is, once it becomes the object of suggestion, the more supernatural and exaggerated is the importance attributed to it. The Pope is not only holy, but most holy, and so forth. So Shakespeare is not only a good writer, but the greatest genius, the eternal teacher of mankind.

Suggestion is always a deceit, and every deceit is an evil. And really the suggestion that Shakespeare's works are great works of genius, presenting the climax both of aesthetic and ethical perfection, has caused and is causing great injury to men.

This injury is twofold: first, the fall of the drama and the substitution of an empty immoral amusement for that important organ of progress, and secondly, the direct degradation of men by presenting them with false models for imitation.

The life of humanity only approaches perfection by the elucidation of religious consciousness (the only principle securely uniting men one with another). The elucidation of the religious consciousness of man is accomplished through all sides of man's spiritual activity. One side of that activity is art. One part of art, and almost the most important, is the drama.

And therefore the drama, to deserve the importance attributed to it, should serve the elucidation of religious consciousness. Such the drama always was, and such it was in the Christian world. But with the appearance of Protestantism in its broadest sense—that is to say, the appearance of a new understanding of Christianity as a teaching of life—dramatic art did not find a form corresponding to this new understanding of religion, and the men of the Renaissance period were carried away by the imitation of classical art. This was most natural, but the attraction should have passed and art should have found, as it is now beginning to find, a new form corresponding to the altered understanding of Christianity.

But the finding of this new form was hindered by the teaching, which arose among German writers at the end of the 18th and beginning of the 19th centuries, of the so-called objectivity of art—that is to say, the indifference of art to good or evil —together with an exaggerated praise of Shakespeare's dramas, which partly corresponded to the aesthetic theory of the Germans and partly served as material for it. Had there not been this exaggerated praise of Shakespeare's dramas, accepted as the most perfect models of drama, people of the

18th and 19th centuries, and of our own, would have had to understand that the drama, to have a right to exist and be regarded as a serious matter, ought to serve, as always was and cannot but be the case, the elucidation of religious consciousness. And having understood this they would have sought a new form of drama corresponding to their religious perception.

But when it was decided that Shakespeare's drama is the summit of perfection, and that people ought to write as he did without any religious or even any moral content—all the dramatists, imitating him, began to compose plays lacking content, like the plays of Goethe, Schiller, Hugo, and, among us Russians, Púshkin, and the historical plays of Ostróvski, Alexéy Tolstóy, and the innumerable other more or less well-known dramatic works which fill all the theatres and are continually composed by anyone to whom the thought and desire to write plays occurs.

Only thanks to such a mean, petty, understanding of the importance of the drama do there appear among us that endless series of dramatic works presenting the actions, situations, characters, and moods of people, not only devoid of any spiritual content but even lacking any human sense. And let not the reader suppose that I exclude from this estimate of contemporary drama the pieces I myself have incidentally written for the theatre. I recognize them, just like all the rest, to be lacking in that religious content which should form the basis of the future drama.

So that the drama, the most important sphere of art, has become in our time merely an empty and immoral amusement for the empty and immoral crowd. What is worst of all is that to the art of the drama, which has fallen as low as it is possible to fall, people continue to attribute an elevated significance unnatural to it.

Dramatists, actors, theatrical managers, the press—the latter most seriously publishing reports of theatres, operas, and so forth—all feel assured that they are doing something very useful and important.

The drama in our time is like a great man fallen to the lowest stage of degradation, who yet continues to pride himself on his past, of which nothing now remains. And the public of our time is like those who pitilessly get amusement out of this once great man, now descended to the lowest depths.

Such is one harmful effect of the epidemic suggestion of the greatness of Shakespeare. Another harmful effect of that laudation is the setting up of a false model for men's imitation.

If people now wrote of Shakespeare that, for his time, he was a great writer, managed verse well enough, was a clever actor and a good stage-manager, even if their valuation were inexact and somewhat exaggerated, provided it was moderate, people of the younger generations might remain free from the Shakespearian influence. But no young man can now remain free from this harmful influence, for instead of the religious and moral teachers of mankind being held up to him as models of moral perfection, as soon as he enters on life he is confronted first of all by Shakespeare, who learned men have decided (and transmitted from generation to generation as an irrefragable truth) is the greatest of poets and the greatest of life's teachers.

On reading or hearing Shakespeare the question for a young man is no longer whether Shakespeare is good or bad, but only to discover wherein lies that extraordinary aesthetic and ethical beauty of which he has received the suggestion from learned men whom he respects, but which he neither sees nor feels. And perverting his aesthetic and ethical feeling, he tries to force himself to agree with the prevailing opinion. He no longer trusts himself, but trusts to what learned people whom he respects have said (I myself have experienced all this). Reading the critical analyses of the plays and the extracts from books with explanatory commentaries, it begins to seem to him that he feels something like an artistic impression, and the longer this continues the more is his aesthetic and ethical feeling perverted. He already ceases to discriminate independently and clearly between what is truly artistic, and the artificial imitation of art.

But above all, having assimilated that immoral view of life which permeates all Shakespeare's works, he loses the capacity to distinguish between good and evil. And the error of extolling an insignificant, inartistic, and not only non-moral but plainly immoral writer, accomplishes its pernicious work.

That is why I think that the sooner people emancipate themselves from this false worship of Shakespeare the better it will be: first because people when they are freed from this falsehood will come to understand that a drama which has no religious basis is not only not an important or good thing, as is now supposed, but is most trivial and contemptible; and having understood this they will have to search for and work out a new form of modern drama—a drama which will serve for the elucidation and confirmation in man of the highest degree of religious consciousness; and secondly because people, when themselves set free from this hypnotic state, will understand that the insignificant and immoral works of Shakespeare and his imitators, aiming only at distracting and amusing the spectators, cannot possibly serve to teach the meaning of life, but that, as long as there is no real religious drama, guidance for life must be looked for from other sources.

[*1906.*]

WHAT'S TO BE DONE?

ABOUT a month ago I had a visit from two young men, one of whom was wearing a cap and peasant bast shoes, and the other a once fashionable black hat and torn boots.

I asked them who they were, and with unconcealed pride they informed me that they were workmen expelled from Moscow for taking part in the armed rising. Passing our village they had found employment as watchmen on an estate, but had lived there less than a month. The day before they came to see me they had been dismissed, the owner charging them with attempting to persuade the peasants to lay waste the estate. They denied the charge with a smile, saying they had attempted no persuasion but had merely gone into the village of an evening and chatted with their fellows.

They had both read revolutionary literature, particularly the bolder of the two, who had sparkling black eyes and white teeth and smiled a great deal, and they both used foreign words such as 'orator',[1] 'proletariat', 'Social-Democrat', 'exploitation', and so on, in and out of place.

I asked them what they had read, and the darker one replied with a smile that he had read various pamphlets.

'Which?' I asked.

'All sorts. "Land and Liberty" for instance.'

I then asked them what they thought of such pamphlets.

'They tell the real truth,' replied the dark one.

'What is it you find so true in them?' I asked.

[1] Meaning a stump orator for one of the political parties.—A. M.

'Why, that it has become impossible to go on living as we do.'

'Why is it impossible?'

'Why? Because we have neither land nor work, and the government throttles the people without sense or reason.'

And interrupting one another, they began to tell how people who had done nothing wrong were flogged by Cossacks with their heavy whips, seized haphazard by the police, and even shot in their own houses.

On my saying that an armed rebellion was a bad and irrational affair, the dark one smiled and replied quietly: 'We are of a different opinion.'

When I spoke of the sin of murder and the law of God they exchanged glances, and the darker one shrugged his shoulders.

'Does the law of God say the proletariat is to be exploited?' he asked. 'People used to think so, but now they know better, and it can't go on. . . .'

I brought them out some booklets, chiefly on religious subjects. They glanced at the titles and were evidently not pleased.

'Perhaps you don't care for them? If so, don't take them.'

'Why not?' said the darker one, and putting the booklets into their blouses they took their leave.

Though I had not been reading the papers, I knew what had been going on in Russia recently from the talk of my family, from letters I had received, and from accounts given by visitors; and just because I had not read the papers I knew particularly well of the amazing change that had latterly taken place in the views held by our society and by the people, a change amounting to this, that whereas people formerly considered the government to be necessary, now all except a very few looked upon its activity as criminal and wrong and blamed the government alone for all the disturbances. That opinion was shared by professors, postal officials, authors, shopkeepers, doctors, and workmen alike, and the feeling was strengthened by the dissolution of the first Duma and had reached its highest point as a result of the cruel measures lately adopted by the government.

I knew this. But my talk with these two men had a great effect on me. Like the shock which suddenly turns freezing liquid into ice, it suddenly turned a whole series of similar impressions I had previously received into a definite and indubitable conviction.

After my talk with them I saw clearly that all the crimes the government is now committing in order to crush the revolution not only fail to crush it but inflame it all the more, and that if the revolutionary movement appears for a time to die down under the cruelties of the government, it is not destroyed but merely temporarily hidden, and will inevitably spring up again with new and increased strength. The fire is now in such a state that any contact with it can only increase its fierceness. And it became clear to me that the only thing that could help would be for the government to cease any and every attempt to enforce its will, to cease not only executing and arresting, but all banishing, persecuting, and proscribing. Only in that way could this horrible strife between brutalized men be brought to an end.

It became perfectly clear to me that the only means of stopping the horrors that are being committed, and the perversion of the people, was the resignation by the government of its power. I was convinced that that was the best thing the government could do, but I was equally firmly convinced that were I to make any such proposal it would be received merely as an indication that I was quite insane. And therefore, though it was perfectly clear to me that the continuance of governmental cruelty could only make things worse and not better, I did not attempt to write or even to speak about it.

Nearly a month has passed, and unfortunately my supposition finds more and more confirmation. There are more and more executions and more and more murders and robberies. I know this both from conversation and from chance glances at the papers, and I know that the mood of the people and of society has become more and more embittered against the government.

When I was out riding a couple of days ago, a young man wearing a pea-jacket and a curious blue cap with a straight crown was driving in the same direction in a peasant cart, and jumped off his cart and came up to me.

He was a short man with a little red moustache and an unhealthy complexion, and he had a clever, harsh face and a dissatisfied expression.

He asked me for booklets, but this was evidently an excuse for entering into conversation.

I asked him where he came from.

He was a peasant from a distant village, some of the men of which had lately been imprisoned and whose wives had been to see me.

It was a village I knew well and in which it had fallen to my lot to administer the Charter of Liberation,[1] and I had always admired its parti-

[1] The only official position Tolstóy ever held after he left the army was that of 'Arbiter of the Peace' in 1861-2. In that capacity it fell to his lot to regulate the relations between the landlords and the newly emancipated serfs in his district.—A. M.

cularly bold and handsome peasants. Specially talented pupils used to come to my school from that village.

I asked him about the peasants who had been sent to prison, and he told me—with the same assurance and absence of doubt that I had recently encountered in everyone, and the same full confidence that the government alone is to blame—that though they had done no wrong they had been seized, beaten, and imprisoned.

Only with great difficulty could I get him to explain what they were accused of.

It turned out that they were 'orators', and held meetings at which they spoke of the necessity of expropriating the land.

I said that the establishment of an equal right for all to the use of the land cannot be established by violence.

He did not agree.

'Why not?' said he. 'We only need to organize.'

'How will you organize?' I asked.

'That will be seen when the time comes.'

'Do you mean another armed rising?'

'It has become a painful necessity.'

I said (what I always say in such cases) that evil cannot be conquered by evil, but only by refraining from evil.

'But it has become impossible to live like that. We have no work and no land. What's to become of us?' he asked, looking at me from under his brows.

'I am old enough to be your grandfather,' I replied, 'and I won't argue with you. But I will say one thing to you, as to a young man beginning life. If what the government is doing is bad, what you are doing or preparing to do is equally bad. As a young man whose habits are just forming you should do one thing—live rightly, not sinning or resisting the will of God.'

He shook his head with dissatisfaction, and said:

'Every man has his own God. Millions of men —millions of Gods.'

'All the same,' I said, 'I advise you to cease taking part in the revolution.'

'But what's to be done?' he replied. 'We can't go on enduring and enduring. What's to be done?'

I felt that no good would come of our talk and was about to ride away, but he stopped me.

'Won't you help me to subscribe for a newspaper?' he asked.

I refused and rode away from him feeling sad.

He was not one of those unemployed factory hands of whom thousands are now roaming about Russia. He was a peasant agriculturist living in a village, and there are not hundreds or thousands but millions of such peasants. And the infection of such a mood as his is spreading more and more.

On returning home I found my family in the saddest frame of mind. They had just read the newspaper that had come (it was October 6th, old style).

'Twenty-two more executions to-day!' said my daughter. 'It's horrible!'

'Not only horrible, but senseless,' said I.

'But *what's to be done?* They can't be allowed to rob and kill and go unpunished,' said one of those present.

Those words: *What's to be done?* were the very words the two vagabonds from the estate and to-day's peasant revolutionary had used.

'It is impossible to endure these insensate horrors committed by a corrupt government which is ruining both the country and the people. We hate the means we have to employ, but *What's to be done?*' say the revolutionists on the one side.

'One cannot allow some self-appointed pretenders to seize power and rule Russia as they like, perverting and ruining it. Of course, the temporary measures now employed are lamentable, but *What's to be done?*' say the others, the conservatives.

And I thought of people near to me—revolutionists and conservatives—and of to-day's peasant and of those unfortunate revolutionists who import and prepare bombs and murder and rob, and of the equally pitiable, lost men who decree and organize the courts martial, take part in them, and shoot and hang, all alike assuring themselves that they are doing what is necessary and all alike repeating the same words: *What's to be done?*

What's to be done? they all ask, but they do not put it as a question: 'What ought I to do?' They put it as an assertion that it will be much worse for everyone if we cease to do what we are doing.

And everyone is so accustomed to these words which hide an explanation and justification of the most horrible and immoral actions, that it enters no one's head to ask: 'Who are you who ask *What's to be done?* Who are you that you consider yourselves called on to decide other people's fate by actions which all men—even you yourselves—know to be odious and wicked? How do you know that what you wish to alter should be altered in the way that seems to you to be good? Do you not know that there are many men such as you who consider bad and harmful what you consider good and useful? And how do you know that what you are doing will produce the results you expect, for you cannot but be aware that the results attained are generally contrary to those aimed at—especially in affairs relating to the life of a whole nation? And above all, what right have you to do what is contrary to the law of God (if you acknowledge a God), or to the most generally accepted laws of morality (if you acknowledge nothing but the generally accepted laws of morality)? By what right do you consider yourselves freed from those most simple and indubitable human obligations which are irreconcilable with your revolutionary or governmental actions?

If your question *What's to be done?* is really a question and not a justification, and if you put it as you should do to yourselves, a quite clear and simple answer naturally suggests itself. The answer is that you must do not what the Tsar, Governor, police-officers, Duma, or some political party demands of you, but what is natural to you as a man, what is demanded of you by that Power which sent you into the world—the Power most people are accustomed to call God.

And as soon as this reply is given to the question *What's to be done?* it immediately dispels the stupid, crime-begetting fog under whose influence men imagine, for some reason, that they, alone of all men—they who are perhaps the most entangled and the most astray from the true path of life—are called on to decide the fate of millions and for the questionable benefit of these millions to commit deeds which unquestionably and evidently bring disaster to them.

There exists a general law acknowledged by all reasonable men and confirmed by tradition, by all the religions of all the nations, and by true science. This law is that men, to fulfil their destiny and attain their greatest welfare, should help one another, love one another, and in any case not attack each other's liberty and life. Yet strange to say, there are people who assure us that it is quite needless to obey this law, that there are cases in which one may and should act contrary to it, and that such deviations from the eternal law will bring more welfare both to individuals and to societies than the fulfilment of the reasonable, supreme law common to all mankind.

The workmen in a vast complex factory have received and accepted clear instructions from the master as to what they should and should not do, both that the works may go well and for their own welfare. But people turn up who have no idea of what the works produce or of how they produce it, and they assure the workmen that they should cease to do what the master has ordered and should do just the contrary, in order that the works may go properly and the workers obtain the greatest benefit.

Is not that just what these people are doing—unable as they are to grasp all the consequences flowing from the general activity of humanity? They not only do not obey the eternal laws (common to all mankind and confirmed by the human intellect) framed for the success of that complex human activity as well as for the benefit of its individual members, but they break them directly and consciously for the sake of some small one-sided casual aims set up by some of themselves (generally the most erring) under the impression that they will thereby attain results more beneficial than those obtainable by fulfilling the eternal law common to all men and consonant with man's nature—forgetting that others imagine quite the contrary.

I know that to men suffering from that spiritual disease, political obsession, a plain and clear answer to the question *What's to be done?*, an answer telling them to obey the highest law common to all mankind—the law of love to one's neighbour—will appear abstract and unpractical. An answer that would seem to them practical would be one telling them that men, who cannot know the consequences of their actions and cannot know whether they will be alive an hour hence, but who know very well that every murder and act of violence is bad, should nevertheless—under the fanciful pretext that they are establishing other people's future welfare—continually act as if they knew infallibly what consequences their actions will produce, and as if they did not know that to kill and torment people is bad, but only knew that such or such a monarchy or constitution is desirable.

That will be the case with many who are suffering from the spiritual disease of political obsession, but I think the great majority of people suffering from the horrors and crimes committed by men who are so diseased will at last understand the terrible deception under which those lie who regard coercive power used by man to man to be rightful and beneficent, and having understood this will free themselves for ever from the madness and wickedness of either participating in force-using power or submitting to it, and will understand that each man must do one thing—that is, fulfil what is demanded of him by the reasonable and beneficent Source which men call 'God', of whose demands no man possessed of reason can fail to be conscious.

I cannot but think that if all men, forgetting their various positions as ministers, policemen, presidents, and members of various combative or non-combative parties, would only do what is natural to each of them as a human being—not only would those horrors and sufferings cease of which the life of man (and especially of the Russian people) is now full, but the Kingdom of God would have come upon earth.

If only some people would act so, the more of them there were the less evil would there be and the more good order and general welfare.

[*October 1906.*]

I CANNOT BE SILENT

'SEVEN death sentences: two in Petersburg, one in Moscow, two in Pénza, and two in Riga. Four executions: two in Khersón, one in Vílna, one in Odessa.'

This, repeated daily in every newspaper and continued not for weeks, not for months, not for a year, but for years. And this in Russia, that Russia where the people regard every criminal as a man to be pitied and where till quite recently capital punishment was not recognized by law! I remember how proud I used to be of that when talking to Western Europeans. But now for a second and even a third year we have executions, executions, executions, unceasingly!

I take up to-day's paper.

To-day, May 9th, the paper contains these few words: 'To-day in Khersón on the Strelbítsky Field, twenty peasants[1] were hung for an attack, made with intent to rob, on a landed proprietor's estate in the Elisabetgrad district.'

Twelve of those by whose labour we live, the very men whom we have depraved and are still depraving by every means in our power—from the poison of vodka to the terrible falsehood of a creed we impose on them with all our might, but do not ourselves believe in—twelve of these men strangled

---

[1] The papers have since contradicted the statement that twenty peasants were hung. I can only be glad of the mistake, glad not only that eight less have been strangled than was stated at first, but glad also that the awful figure moved me to express in these pages a feeling that has long tormented me. I leave the rest unchanged, therefore, merely substituting the word twelve for the word twenty, since what I said refers not only to the twelve who were hung but to all the thousands who have lately been crushed and killed.—L. T.

with cords by those whom they feed and clothe and house, and who have depraved and still continue to deprave them. Twelve husbands, fathers, and sons, from among those upon whose kindness, industry, and simplicity alone rests the whole of Russian life, are seized, imprisoned, and shackled. Then their hands are tied behind their backs lest they should seize the ropes by which they are to be hung, and they are led to the gallows. Several peasants similar to those about to be hung, but armed, dressed in clean soldiers' uniforms with good boots on their feet and with guns in their hands, accompany the condemned men. Beside them walks a long-haired man wearing a stole and vestments of gold or silver cloth, and bearing a cross. The procession stops. The man in command of the whole business says something, the secretary reads a paper; and when the paper has been read the long-haired man, addressing those whom other people are about to strangle with cords, says something about God and Christ. Immediately after these words the hangmen (there are several, for one man could not manage so complicated a business) dissolve some soap, and, having soaped the loops in the cords that they may tighten better, seize the shackled men, put shrouds on them, lead them to a scaffold, and place the well-soaped nooses round their necks.

And then, one after another, living men are pushed off the benches which are drawn from under their feet, and by their own weight suddenly tighten the nooses round their necks and are painfully strangled. Men, alive a minute before, become corpses dangling from a rope, at first swinging slowly and then resting motionless.

All this is carefully arranged and planned by learned and enlightened people of the upper class.

They arrange to do these things secretly at daybreak so that no one shall see them done, and they arrange that the responsibility for these iniquities shall be so subdivided among those who commit them that each may think and say that it is not he who is responsible for them. They arrange to seek out the most depraved and unfortunate of men, and, while obliging them to do this business planned and approved by themselves, still keep up an appearance of abhorring those who do it. They even plan such a subtle device as this: sentences are pronounced by a military tribunal, yet it is not military people but civilians who have to be present at the execution. And the business is performed by unhappy, deluded, perverted, and despised men who have nothing left them but to soap the cords well that they may grip the necks without fail, and then to get well drunk on poison sold them by these same enlightened upper-class people in order the more quickly and fully to forget their souls and their quality as men. A doctor makes his round of the bodies, feels them, and reports to those in authority that the business has been done properly—all twelve are certainly dead. And those in authority depart to their ordinary occupations with the consciousness of a necessary though painful task performed. The bodies, now grown cold, are taken down and buried.

The thing is awful!

And this is done not once, and not only to these twelve unhappy, misguided men from among the best class of the Russian people; it is done unceasingly for years, to hundreds and thousands of similar misguided men, misguided by the very people who do these terrible things to them.

And it is not this dreadful thing alone that is being done. All sorts of other tortures and violence are being perpetrated in prisons, fortresses, and convict settlements, on the same plea and with the same cold-blooded cruelty.

This is dreadful, but most dreadful of all is the fact that it is not done impulsively under the sway of feelings that silence reason, as occurs in fights, war, or even burglary, but on the contrary it is done at the demand of reason and calculation that silence feeling. That is what makes these deeds so particularly dreadful. Dreadful because these acts—committed by men who, from the judge to the hangman, do not wish to do them—prove more vividly than anything else how pernicious to human souls is despotism; the power of man over man.

It is revolting that one man can take from another his labour, his money, his cow, his horse, nay, even his son or his daughter—but how much more revolting it is that one man can take another's soul by forcing him to do what destroys his spiritual ego and deprives him of spiritual welfare. And that is just what is done by these men who arrange executions, and who by bribes, threats, and deceptions calmly force men—from the judge to the hangman—to commit deeds that certainly deprive them of their true welfare though they are committed in the name of the welfare of mankind.

And while this goes on for years all over Russia, the chief culprits—those by whose order these things are done, those who could put a stop to them—fully convinced that such deeds are useful and even absolutely necessary, either compose speeches and devise methods to prevent the Finns from living as they want to live, and to compel them to live as certain Russian personages wish them to live, or else publish orders to the effect that: 'In Hussar regiments the cuffs and collars of the men's jackets are to be of the same colour as the latter, while those entitled to wear pelisses are not to have braid round the cuffs over the fur.'

What is most dreadful in the whole matter is that all this inhuman violence and killing, besides the direct evil done to the victims and their families, brings a yet more enormous evil on the whole people by spreading depravity—as fire spreads amid dry straw—among every class of Russians. This depravity grows with special rapidity among the simple working folk because all these iniquities—exceeding as they do a hundredfold all that is or has been done by thieves, robbers, and all the revolutionaries put together—are done as though they were something necessary, good, and unavoidable; and are not merely excused but supported by different institutions inseparably connected in the people's minds with justice, and even with sanctity—namely, the Senate, the Synod, the Duma, the Church, and the Tsar.

And this depravity spreads with remarkable rapidity.

A short time ago there were not two executioners to be found in all Russia. In the eighties there was only one. I remember how joyfully Vladímir Solovëv then told me that no second executioner could be found in all Russia and so the one was taken from place to place. Not so now.

A small shopkeeper in Moscow whose affairs were in a bad way offered his services to perform the murders arranged by the government, and, receiving a hundred rubles (£10) for each person hung, soon mended his affairs so well that he no longer required this additional business and has now reverted to his former trade.

In Orël last month, as elsewhere, an executioner was wanted, and a man was immediately found who agreed with the organizers of governmental murders to do the business for fifty rubles per head. But this volunteer hangman, after making the agreement, heard that more was paid in other towns, and at the time of the execution, having put the shroud sack on the victim, instead of leading him to the scaffold, stopped, and, approaching the superintendent, said: 'You must add another twenty-five rubles, your Excellency, or I won't do it!' And he got the increase and did the job.

A little later five people were to be hanged, and the day before the execution a stranger came to see the organizer of governmental murders on a private matter. The organizer went out to him, and the stranger said:

'The other day so-and-so charged you seventy-five rubles a man. I hear five are to be done to-morrow. Let me have the whole job and I'll do it at fifteen rubles a head, and you can rely on its being done properly!'

I do not know whether the offer was accepted or not, but I know it was made.

That is how the crimes committed by the government act on the worst, the least moral, of the people, and these terrible deeds must also have an influence on the majority of men of average morality. Continually hearing and reading about the most terrible inhuman brutality committed by the authorities—that is, by persons whom the people are accustomed to honour as the best of men—the majority of average people, especially the young, preoccupied with their own affairs, instead of realizing that those who do such horrible deeds are unworthy of honour, involuntarily come to the opposite conclusion and argue that if men generally honoured do things that seem to us horrible, these things cannot be as horrible as we suppose.

Of executions, hangings, murders, and bombs, people now write and speak as they used to speak about the weather. Children play at hangings. Lads from the high schools who are almost children go out on expropriating expeditions, ready to kill, just as they used to go out hunting. To kill off the large landed proprietors in order to seize their estates appears now to many people to be the very best solution of the land question.

In general, thanks to the activity of the government which has allowed killing as a means of obtaining its ends, all crimes, robbery, theft, lies, tortures, and murders are now considered by miserable people who have been perverted by that example to be most natural deeds, proper to a man.

Yes! Terrible as are the deeds themselves, the moral, spiritual, unseen evil they produce is incomparably more terrible.

You say you commit all these horrors to restore peace and order.

You restore peace and order!

By what means do you restore them? By destroying the last vestige of faith and morality in men —you, representatives of a Christian authority, leaders and teachers approved and encouraged by the servants of the Church! By committing the greatest crimes: lies, perfidy, torture of all sorts, and this last and most terrible of crimes, the one most abhorrent to every human heart that is not utterly depraved—not just a single murder but murders innumerable, which you think to justify by stupid references to such and such statutes written by yourselves in those stupid and lying books of yours which you blasphemously call 'the laws'.

You say that this is the only means of pacifying the people and quelling the revolution; but that is evidently false! It is plain that you cannot pacify the people unless you satisfy the demand of most elementary justice advanced by Russia's whole agricultural population (that is, the demand for the abolition of private property in land) and refrain from confirming it and in various ways irritating the peasants, as well as those unbalanced and envenomed people who have begun a violent struggle with you. You cannot pacify people by tormenting them and worrying, exiling, imprisoning, and hanging women and children! However hard you may try to stifle in yourselves the reason and love natural to human beings, you still have them within you, and need only come to your senses and think, in order to see that by acting as you do—that is, by taking part in such terrible crimes—you not only fail to cure the disease, but by driving it inwards make it worse.

That is only too evident.

The cause of what is happening does not lie in physical events, but depends entirely on the spiritual mood of the people, which has changed and which no efforts can bring back to its former condition, just as no efforts can turn a grown-up man into a child again. Social irritation or tranquillity cannot depend on whether Peter is hanged or allowed to live, or on whether John lives in Tambóv or in penal servitude at Nerchínsk. Social irritation or tranquillity must depend not on Peter or John alone but on how the great majority of the nation regard their position, and on the attitude of

I CANNOT BE SILENT

this majority to the government, to landed property, to the religion taught them, and on what this majority consider to be good or bad. The power of events does not lie in the material conditions of life at all, but in the spiritual condition of the people. Even if you were to kill and torture a tenth of the Russian nation, the spiritual condition of the rest would not become what you desire.

So that all you are now doing, with all your searchings, spyings, exiling, prisons, penal settlements, and gallows, does not bring the people to the state you desire, but on the contrary increases the irritation and destroys all possibility of peace and order.

'But what is to be done?' you say. 'What is to be done? How are the iniquities that are now perpetrated to be stopped?'

The answer is very simple: 'Cease to do what you are doing.'

Even if no one knew what ought to be done to pacify 'the people'—the whole people (many people know very well that what is most wanted to pacify the Russian people is the freeing of the land from private ownership, just as fifty years ago what was wanted was to free the peasants from serfdom) —if no one knew this, it would still be evident that to pacify the people one ought not to do what only increases its irritation. Yet that is just what you are doing!

What you are doing, you do not for the people but for yourselves, to retain the position you occupy, a position you consider advantageous but which is really a most pitiful and abominable one. So do not say that you do it for the people; that is not true! All the abominations you do are done for yourselves, for your own covetous, ambitious, vain, vindictive, personal ends, in order to continue for a little longer in the depravity in which you live and which seems to you desirable.

However much you may declare that all you do is done for the good of the people, men are beginning to understand you and despise you more and more, and to regard your measures of restraint and suppression not as you wish them to be regarded—as the action of some kind of higher collective Being, the government—but as the personal evil deeds of individual and evil self-seekers.

Then again you say: 'The revolutionaries began all this, not we, and their terrible crimes can only be suppressed by firm measures' (so you call your crimes) 'on the part of the government.'

You say the atrocities committed by the revolutionaries are terrible.

I do not dispute it. I will add that besides being terrible they are stupid, and—like your own actions—fall beside the mark. Yet however terrible and stupid may be their actions—all those bombs and tunnellings, those revolting murders and thefts of money—still all these deeds do not come anywhere near the criminality and stupidity of the deeds you commit.

They are doing just the same as you and for the same motives. They are in the same (I would say 'comic' were its consequences not so terrible) delusion, that men having formed for themselves a plan of what in their opinion is the desirable and proper arrangement of society, have the right and possibility of arranging other people's lives according to that plan. The delusion is the same. These methods are violence of all kinds—including taking life. And the excuse is that an evil deed committed for the benefit of many, ceases to be immoral; and that therefore without offending against the moral law, one may lie, rob, and kill whenever this tends to the realization of that supposed good condition for the many which we imagine that we know and can foresee, and which we wish to establish.

You government people call the acts of the revolutionaries 'atrocities' and 'great crimes'; but the revolutionaries have done and are doing nothing that you have not done, and done to an incomparably greater extent. They only do what you do; you keep spies, practise deception, and spread printed lies, and so do they. You take people's property by all sorts of violent means and use it as you consider best, and they do the same. You execute those whom you think dangerous, and so do they.

So you certainly cannot blame the revolutionaries while you employ the same immoral means as they do for the attainment of your aim. All that you can adduce for your own justification, they can equally adduce for theirs; not to mention that you do much evil that they do not commit, such as squandering the wealth of the nation, preparing for war, making war, subduing and oppressing foreign nationalities, and much else.

You say you have the traditions of the past to guard and the actions of the great men of the past as examples. They, too, have their traditions, also arising from the past—even before the French Revolution. And as to great men, models to copy, martyrs that perished for truth and freedom—they have no fewer of these than you.

So that if there is any difference between you it is only that you wish everything to remain as it has been and is, while they wish for a change. And in thinking that everything cannot always remain as it has been they would be more right than you, had they not adopted from you that curious, destructive delusion that one set of men can know the form of life suitable for all men in the future, and that this form can be established by force. For the rest they only do what you do, using the same means. They are altogether your disciples. They have, as the saying is, picked up all your little dodges. They are not only your disciples, they are your products, your children. If you did not exist neither would they; so that when you try to suppress them by force you behave like a man who presses with his whole weight against a door that opens towards him.

If there be any difference between you and them it is certainly not in your favour but in theirs. The mitigating circumstances on their side are, firstly, that their crimes are committed under conditions of greater personal danger than you are exposed to, and risks and danger excuse much in the eyes of impressionable youth. Secondly, the immense majority of them are quite young people to whom it is natural to go astray, while you for the most part are men of mature age—old men to whom reasoned calm and leniency towards the deluded should be natural. A third mitigating circumstance in their favour is that however odious their murders may be, they are still not so coldly, systematically cruel as are your Schlusselburgs, transportations, gallows, and shootings. And a fourth mitigating circumstance for the revolutionaries is that they all quite categorically repudiate all religious teaching and consider that the end justifies the means. Therefore when they kill one or more men for the sake of the imaginary welfare of the majority, they act quite consistently; whereas you government men—from the lowest hangman to the highest official—all support religion and Christianity, which is altogether incompatible with the deeds you commit.

And it is you elderly men, leaders of other men, professing Christianity, it is you who say, like children who have been fighting, 'We didn't begin —they did!' That is the best you can say—you who have taken on yourselves the role of rulers of the people. And what sort of men are you? Men who acknowledge as God one who most definitely forbade not only judgement and punishment, but even condemnation of others; one who in clearest terms repudiated all punishment, and affirmed the necessity of continual forgiveness however often a crime may be repeated; one who commanded us to turn the other cheek to the smiter, and not return evil for evil; one who in the case of the woman sentenced to be stoned, showed so simply and clearly the impossibility of judgement and punishment between man and man. And you, acknowledging that teacher to be God, can find nothing better to say in your defence than: 'They began it! They kill people, so let us kill them!'

An artist of my acquaintance thought of painting a picture of an execution, and he wanted a model for the executioner. He heard that the duty of executioner in Moscow was at that time performed by a watchman, so he went to the watchman's house. It was Easter-time. The family were sitting in their best clothes at the tea-table, but the master of the house was not there. It turned out afterwards that on catching sight of a stranger he had hidden himself. His wife also seemed abashed, and said that her husband was not at home; but his little girl betrayed him by saying: 'Daddy's in the garret.' She did not know that her father was aware that what he did was evil and therefore could not help being afraid of everybody. The artist explained to the wife that he wanted her husband as a model because his face suited the picture he had planned (of course he did not say what the picture was). Having got into conversation with the wife, the artist, in order to conciliate her, offered to take her little son as a pupil, an offer which evidently tempted her. She went out and after a time the husband entered, morose, restless, frightened, and looking askance. For a long time he tried to get the artist to say why he required just him. When the artist told him he had met him in the street and his face seemed suitable to the projected picture, the watchman asked where had he met him? At what time? In what clothes? And he would not come to terms, evidently fearing and suspecting something bad.

Yes, this executioner at first-hand knows that he is an executioner, he knows that he does wrong and is therefore hated, and he is afraid of men: and I think that this consciousness and this fear before men atone for at least a part of his guilt. But none of you—from the Secretary of the Court to the Premier and the Tsar—who are indirect participators in the iniquities perpetrated every day, seem to feel your guilt or the shame that your participation in these horrors ought to evoke. It is true that like the executioner you fear men, and the greater your responsibility for the crimes the more your fear: the Public Prosecutor feels more fear than the Secretary; the President of the Court more than the Public Prosecutor; the General Governor more than the President; the President of the Council of Ministers more still, and the Tsar most of all. You are all afraid, but unlike the executioner you are afraid not because you know you are doing evil, but because you think other people do evil.

Therefore I think that, low as that unfortunate

watchman has fallen, he is morally immeasurably higher than you participators and part authors of these awful crimes: you who condemn others instead of yourselves and carry your heads so high.

I know that men are but human, that we are all weak, that we all err, and that one cannot judge another. I have long struggled against the feeling that was and is aroused in me by those responsible for these awful crimes, and aroused the more the higher they stand on the social ladder. But I cannot and will not struggle against that feeling any longer.

I cannot and will not. First, because an exposure of these people who do not see the full criminality of their actions is necessary for them as well as for the multitude which, influenced by the external honour and laudation accorded to these people, approves their terrible deeds and even tries to imitate them. And secondly because (I frankly confess it) I hope my exposure of those men will in one way or other evoke the expulsion I desire from the set in which I am now living, and in which I cannot but feel myself a participant in the crimes committed around me.

Everything now being done in Russia is done in the name of the general welfare, in the name of the protection and tranquillity of the people of Russia. And if this be so, then it is also done for me who live in Russia. For me, therefore, exists the destitution of the people deprived of the first and most natural right of man—the right to use the land on which he is born; for me those half-million men torn away from wholesome peasant life and dressed in uniforms and taught to kill; for me that false so-called priesthood whose chief duty it is to pervert and conceal true Christianity; for me all these transportations of men from place to place; for me these hundreds of thousands of hungry migratory workmen; for me these hundreds of thousands of unfortunates dying of typhus and scurvy in the fortresses and prisons which are insufficient for such a multitude; for me the mothers, wives, and fathers of the exiles, the prisoners, and those who are hanged, are suffering; for me are these spies and this bribery; for me the interment of these dozens and hundreds of men who have been shot; for me the horrible work of these hangmen goes on—who were at first enlisted with difficulty but now no longer so loathe their work; for me exist these gallows with well-soaped cords from which hang women, children, and peasants; and for me exists this terrible embitterment of man against his fellow man.

Strange as it seems to say that all this is done for me, and that I am a participator in these terrible deeds, I cannot but feel that there is an indubitable interdependence between my spacious room, my dinner, my clothing, my leisure, and the terrible crimes committed to get rid of those who would like to take from me what I have. And though I know that these homeless, embittered, depraved people—who but for the government's threats would deprive me of all I am using—are products of that same government's actions, still I cannot help feeling that at present my peace really is dependent on all the horrors that are now being perpetrated by the government.

And being conscious of this I can no longer endure it, but must free myself from this intolerable position!

It is impossible to live so! I, at any rate, cannot and will not live so.

That is why I write this and will circulate it by

all means in my power both in Russia and abroad —that one of two things may happen: either that these inhuman deeds may be stopped, or that my connexion with them may be snapped and I put in prison, where I may be clearly conscious that these horrors are not committed on my behalf; or still better (so good that I dare not even dream of such happiness) that they may put on me, as on those twelve or twenty peasants, a shroud and a cap and may push me also off a bench, so that by my own weight I may tighten the well-soaped noose round my old throat.

To attain one of these two aims I address myself to all participators in these terrible deeds, beginning with those who put on their brother men and women and children those caps and nooses—from the prison warders up to you, chief organizers and authorizers of these terrible crimes.

Brother men! Come to your senses, stop and think, consider what you are doing! Remember who you are!

Before being hangmen, generals, public prosecutors, judges, premier or Tsar, are you not men— to-day allowed a peep into God's world, to-morrow ceasing to be? (You hangmen of all grades in particular, who have evoked and are evoking special hatred, should remember this.) Is it possible that you who have had this brief glimpse of God's world (for even if you be not murdered, death is always close behind us all), is it possible that in your lucid moments you do not see that your vocation in life cannot be to torment and kill men; yourselves trembling with fear of being killed, lying to yourselves, to others, and to God, assuring yourselves and others that by participating in these things you are doing an important and grand work for the welfare of millions? Is it possible that—when not intoxicated by your surroundings, by flattery, and by the customary sophistries—you do not each one of you know that this is all mere talk, only invented that, while doing most evil deeds, you may still consider yourself a good man? You cannot but know that you, like each of us, have but one real duty which includes all others—the duty of living the short space granted us in accord with the Will that sent you into this world, and of leaving it in accord with that Will. And that Will desires only one thing: love from man to man.

But what are you doing? To what are you devoting your spiritual strength? Whom do you love? Who loves you? Your wife? Your child? But that is not love. The love of wife and children is not human love. Animals love in that way even more strongly. Human love is the love of man for man—for every man as a son of God and therefore a brother. Whom do you love in that way? No one. Who loves you in that way? No one.

You are feared as a hangman or a wild animal is feared. People flatter you because at heart they despise and hate you—and how they hate you! And you know it and are afraid of men.

Yes, consider it—all you accomplices in murder from the highest to the lowest, consider who you are and cease to do what you are doing. Cease, not for your own sakes, not for the sake of your own personality, not for the sake of men, not that you may cease to be blamed, but for your soul's sake and for the God who lives within you!

1908.

A LETTER TO A HINDU

THE SUBJECTION OF INDIA—ITS CAUSE AND CURE

With an Introduction by M. K. GANDHI

INTRODUCTION

THE letter printed below is a translation of Tolstóy's letter written in Russian in reply to one from the Editor of *Free Hindustan*. After having passed from hand to hand, this letter at last came into my possession through a friend who asked me, as one much interested in Tolstóy's writings, whether I thought it worth publishing. I at once replied in the affirmative, and told him I should translate it myself into Gujarati and induce others to translate and publish it in various Indian vernaculars.

The letter as received by me was a type-written copy. It was therefore referred to the author, who confirmed it as his and kindly granted me permission to print it.

To me, as a humble follower of that great teacher whom I have long looked upon as one of my guides, it is a matter of honour to be connected with the publication of his letter, such especially as the one which is now being given to the world.

It is a mere statement of fact to say that every Indian, whether he owns up to it or not, has national aspirations. But there are as many opinions as there are Indian nationalists as to the exact meaning of that aspiration, and more especially as to the methods to be used to attain the end.

One of the accepted and 'time-honoured' methods to attain the end is that of violence. The assassination of Sir Curzon Wylie was an illustration of that method in its worst and most detestable form. Tolstóy's life has been devoted to replacing the method of violence for removing tyranny or securing reform by the method of non-resistance to evil. He would meet hatred expressed in violence by love expressed in self-suffering. He admits of no exception to whittle down this great and divine law of love. He applies it to all the problems that trouble mankind.

When a man like Tolstóy, one of the clearest thinkers in the western world, one of the greatest writers, one who as a soldier has known what violence is and what it can do, condemns Japan for having blindly followed the law of modern science, falsely so-called, and fears for that country 'the greatest calamities', it is for us to pause and consider whether, in our impatience of English rule, we do not want to replace one evil by another and a worse. India, which is the nursery of the great faiths of the world, will cease to be nationalist India, whatever else she may become, when she goes through the process of civilization in the shape of reproduction on that sacred soil of gun factories and the hateful industrialism which has reduced the people of Europe to a state of slavery, and all but stifled among them the best instincts which are the heritage of the human family.

If we do not want the English in India we must pay the price. Tolstóy indicates it. 'Do not resist evil, but also do not yourselves participate in evil— in the violent deeds of the administration of the law courts, the collection of taxes and, what is more important, of the soldiers, and no one in the world will enslave you', passionately declares the sage of Yásnaya Polyána. Who can question the truth of what he says in the following: 'A commercial company enslaved a nation comprising two hundred millions. Tell this to a man free from superstition and he will fail to grasp what these words mean. What does it mean that thirty thousand people, not athletes, but rather weak and ordinary people, have enslaved two hundred millions of vigorous, clever, capable, freedom-loving people? Do not the figures make it clear that not the English, but the Indians, have enslaved themselves?'

One need not accept all that Tolstóy says—some of his facts are not accurately stated—to realize the central truth of his indictment of the present system, which is to understand and act upon the irresistible power of the soul over the body, of love, which is an attribute of the soul, over the brute or body force generated by the stirring up in us of evil passions.

There is no doubt that there is nothing new in what Tolstóy preaches. But his presentation of the old truth is refreshingly forceful. His logic is unassailable. And above all he endeavours to practise what he preaches. He preaches to convince. He is sincere and in earnest. He commands attention.

M. K. GANDHI.

[*19th November, 1909.*]

A LETTER TO A HINDU

By LEO TOLSTÓY

All that exists is One. People only call this One by different names. .   THE VEDAS.

God is love, and he that abideth in love abideth in God, and God abideth in him.   1 JOHN iv. 16.

God is one whole; we are the parts.
         Exposition of the teaching of the Vedas by Vivekananda.

I

Do not seek quiet and rest in those earthly realms where delusions and desires are engendered, for if thou dost, thou wilt be dragged through the rough wilderness of life, which is far from Me. Whenever thou feelest that thy feet are becoming entangled in the interlaced roots of life, know that thou has strayed from the path to which I beckon thee: for I have placed thee in broad, smooth paths, which are strewn with flowers. I have put a light before thee, which thou canst follow and thus run without stumbling.   KRISHNA.

I have received your letter and two numbers of your periodical, both of which interest me extremely. The oppression of a majority by a minority, and the demoralization inevitably resulting from it, is a phenomenon that has always occupied me and has done so most particularly of late. I will try to explain to you what I think about that subject in general, and particularly about the cause from which the dreadful evils of which you write in your letter, and in the Hindu periodical you have sent me, have arisen and continue to arise.

The reason for the astonishing fact that a majority of working people submit to a handful of idlers who control their labour and their very lives is always and everywhere the same—whether the oppressors and oppressed are of one race or whether, as in India and elsewhere, the oppressors are of a different nation.

This phenomenon seems particularly strange in India, for there more than two hundred million people, highly gifted both physically and mentally, find themselves in the power of a small group of people quite alien to them in thought, and immeasurably inferior to them in religious morality.

From your letter and the articles in *Free Hindustan* as well as from the very interesting writings of the Hindu Swami Vivekananda and others, it appears that, as is the case in our time with the ills of all nations, the reason lies in the lack of a reasonable religious teaching which by explaining the meaning of life would supply a supreme law for the guidance of conduct and would replace the more than dubious precepts of pseudo-religion and pseudo-science with the immoral conclusions deduced from them and commonly called 'civilization'.

Your letter, as well as the articles in *Free Hindustan* and Indian political literature generally, shows that most of the leaders of public opinion among your people no longer attach any significance to the religious teachings that were and are professed by the peoples of India, and recognize no possibility of freeing the people from the oppression they endure except by adopting the irreligious and profoundly immoral social arrangements under which the English and other pseudo-Christian nations live to-day.

And yet the chief if not the sole cause of the enslavement of the Indian peoples by the English lies in this very absence of a religious consciousness and of the guidance for conduct which should flow from it—a lack common in our day to all nations East and West, from Japan to England and America alike.

II

O ye, who see perplexities over your heads, beneath your feet, and to the right and left of you; you will be an eternal enigma unto yourselves until ye become humble and joyful as children. Then will ye find Me, and having found Me in yourselves, you will rule over worlds, and looking out from the great world within to the little world without, you will bless everything that is, and find all is well with time and with you.

KRISHNA.

To make my thoughts clear to you I must go farther back. We do not, cannot, and I venture to say need not, know how men lived millions of years ago or even ten thousand years ago, but we do know positively that, as far back as we have any knowledge of mankind, it has always lived in special groups of families, tribes, and nations in which the majority, in the conviction that it must be so, submissively and willingly bowed to the rule of one or more persons—that is to a very small minority. Despite all varieties of circumstances and personalities these relations manifested themselves among the various peoples of whose origin we have any knowledge; and the farther back we go the more absolutely necessary did this arrangement appear, both to the rulers and the ruled, to make it possible for people to live peacefully together.

So it was everywhere. But though this external form of life existed for centuries and still exists, very early—thousands of years before our time—amid this life based on coercion, one and the same thought constantly emerged among different nations, namely, that in every individual a spiritual element is manifested that gives life to all that exists, and that this spiritual element strives to unite with everything of a like nature to itself, and attains this aim through love. This thought appeared in most various forms at different times and places, with varying completeness and clarity. It found expression in Brahmanism, Judaism, Mazdaism (the teachings of Zoroaster), in Buddhism, Taoism, Confucianism, and in the writings of the Greek and Roman sages, as well as in Christianity and Mohammedanism. The mere fact that this thought has sprung up among different nations and at different times indicates that it is inherent in human nature and contains the truth. But this truth was made known to people who considered that a community could only be kept together if some of them restrained others, and so it appeared quite irreconcilable with the existing order of society. Moreover it was at first expressed only fragmentarily, and so obscurely that though people admitted its theoretic truth they could not entirely accept it as guidance for their conduct. Then, too, the dissemination of the truth in a society based on coercion was always hindered in one and the same manner, namely, those in power, feeling that the recognition of this truth would undermine their position, consciously or sometimes unconsciously perverted it by explanations and additions quite foreign to it, and also opposed it by open violence. Thus the truth—that his life should be directed by the spiritual element which is its basis, which manifests itself as love, and which is so natural to man—this truth, in order to force a way to man's consciousness, had to struggle not merely against the obscurity with which it was expressed and the intentional and unintentional distortions surrounding it, but also against deliberate violence, which by means of persecutions and punishments sought to compel men to accept religious laws authorized by the rulers and conflicting with the truth. Such a hindrance and misrepresentation of the truth—which had not yet achieved complete clarity—occurred everywhere: in Confucianism and Taoism, in Buddhism and in Christianity, in Mohammedanism and in your Brahmanism.

III

My hand has sowed love everywhere, giving unto all that will receive. Blessings are offered unto all My children, but many times in their blindness they fail to see them. How few there are who gather the gifts which lie in profusion at their feet: how many there are, who, in wilful waywardness, turn their eyes away from them and complain with a wail that they have not that which I have given them; many of them defiantly repudiate not only My gifts, but Me also, Me, the Source of all blessings and the Author of their being.

KRISHNA.

I tarry awhile from the turmoil and strife of the world. I will beautify and quicken thy life with love and with joy, for the light of the soul is Love. Where Love is, there is contentment and peace, and where there is contentment and peace, there am I, also, in their midst.

KRISHNA.

The aim of the sinless One consists in acting without causing sorrow to others, although he could attain to great power by ignoring their feelings.

The aim of the sinless One lies in not doing evil unto those who have done evil unto him.

If a man causes suffering even to those who hate him without any reason, he will ultimately have grief not to be overcome.

The punishment of evil doers consists in making them feel ashamed of themselves by doing them a great kindness.

Of what use is superior knowledge in the one, if he

does not endeavour to relieve his neighbour's want as much as his own?

If, in the morning, a man wishes to do evil unto another, in the evening the evil will return to him.

THE HINDU KURAL.

Thus it went on everywhere. The recognition that love represents the highest morality was nowhere denied or contradicted, but this truth was so interwoven everywhere with all kinds of falsehoods which distorted it, that finally nothing of it remained but words. It was taught that this highest morality was only applicable to private life—for home use, as it were—but that in public life all forms of violence—such as imprisonment, executions, and wars—might be used for the protection of the majority against a minority of evil-doers, though such means were diametrically opposed to any vestige of love. And though common sense indicated that if some men claim to decide who is to be subjected to violence of all kinds for the benefit of others, these men to whom violence is applied may, in turn, arrive at a similar conclusion with regard to those who have employed violence to them, and though the great religious teachers of Brahmanism, Buddhism, and above all of Christianity, foreseeing such a perversion of the law of love, have constantly drawn attention to the one invariable condition of love (namely, the enduring of injuries, insults, and violence of all kinds without resisting evil by evil) people continued—regardless of all that leads man forward—to try to unite the incompatibles: the virtue of love, and what is opposed to love, namely, the restraining of evil by violence. And such a teaching, despite its inner contradiction, was so firmly established that the very people who recognize love as a virtue accept as lawful at the same time an order of life based on violence and allowing men not merely to torture but even to kill one another.

For a long time people lived in this obvious contradiction without noticing it. But a time arrived when this contradiction became more and more evident to thinkers of various nations. And the old and simple truth that it is natural for men to help and to love one another, but not to torture and to kill one another, became ever clearer, so that fewer and fewer people were able to believe the sophistries by which the distortion of the truth had been made so plausible.

In former times the chief method of justifying the use of violence and thereby infringing the law of love was by claiming a divine right for the rulers: the Tsars, Sultans, Rajahs, Shahs, and other heads of states. But the longer humanity lived the weaker grew the belief in this peculiar, God-given right of the ruler. That belief withered in the same way and almost simultaneously in the Christian and the Brahman world, as well as in Buddhist and Confucian spheres, and in recent times it has so faded away as to prevail no longer against man's reasonable understanding and the true religious feeling. People saw more and more clearly, and now the majority see quite clearly, the senselessness and immorality of subordinating their wills to those of other people just like themselves, when they are bidden to do what is contrary not only to their interests but also to their moral sense. And so one might suppose that having lost confidence in any religious authority for a belief in the divinity of potentates of various kinds, people would try to free themselves from subjection to it. But unfortunately not only were the rulers, who were considered supernatural beings, benefited by having the peoples in subjection, but as a result of the belief in, and during the rule of, these pseudo-divine beings, ever larger and larger circles of people grouped and established themselves around them, and under an appearance of governing took advantage of the people. And when the old deception of a supernatural and God-appointed authority had dwindled away these men were only concerned to devise a new one which like its predecessor should make it possible to hold the people in bondage to a limited number of rulers.

IV

Children, do you want to know by what your hearts should be guided? Throw aside your longings and strivings after that which is null and void; get rid of your erroneous thoughts about happiness and wisdom, and your empty and insincere desires. Dispense with these and you will know Love. KRISHNA.

Be not the destroyers of yourselves. Arise to your true Being, and then you will have nothing to fear.
KRISHNA.

New justifications have now appeared in place of the antiquated, obsolete, religious ones. These new justifications are just as inadequate as the old ones, but as they are new their futility cannot immediately be recognized by the majority of men. Besides this, those who enjoy power propagate these new sophistries and support them so skilfully that they seem irrefutable even to many of those who suffer from the oppression these theories seek to justify. These new justifications are termed 'scientific'. But by the term 'scientific' is understood just what was formerly understood by the term 'religious': just as formerly everything called 'religious' was held to be unquestionable simply because it was called religious, so now all that is called 'scientific' is held to be unquestionable. In the present case the obsolete religious justification of violence which consisted in the recognition of the supernatural personality of the God-ordained ruler ('there is no power but of God') has been superseded by the 'scientific' justification which puts forward, first, the assertion that because the coercion of man by man has existed in all ages, it follows that such coercion must continue to exist. This assertion that people should continue to live as they have done throughout past ages rather than as their reason and conscience indicate, is what 'science' calls 'the historic law'. A further 'scientific' justification lies in the statement that as among plants and wild beasts there is a constant struggle for existence which always results in the survival of the fittest, a similar struggle should be carried on among human beings—beings, that is, who are gifted with intelligence and love; faculties lacking in the creatures subject to the struggle for existence and survival of the fittest. Such is the second 'scientific' justification.

The third, most important, and unfortunately most widespread justification is, at bottom, the age-old religious one just a little altered: that in public life the suppression of some for the protection of the majority cannot be avoided—so that coercion is unavoidable however desirable reliance on love alone might be in human intercourse. The only difference in this justification by pseudo-science consists in the fact that, to the question why such and such people and not others have the right to decide against whom violence may and must be used, pseudo-science now gives a different reply to that given by religion—which declared that the right to decide was valid because it was pronounced by persons possessed of divine power.

'Science' says that these decisions represent the will of the people, which under a constitutional form of government is supposed to find expression in all the decisions and actions of those who are at the helm at the moment.

Such are the scientific justifications of the principle of coercion. They are not merely weak but absolutely invalid, yet they are so much needed by those who occupy privileged positions that they believe in them as blindly as they formerly believed in the immaculate conception, and propagate them just as confidently. And the unfortunate majority of men bound to toil is so dazzled by the pomp with which these 'scientific truths' are presented, that under this new influence it accepts these scientific stupidities for holy truth, just as it formerly accepted the pseudo-religious justifications; and it continues to submit to the present holders of power who are just as hard-hearted but rather more numerous than before.

V

Who am I? I am that which thou hast searched for since thy baby eyes gazed wonderingly upon the world, whose horizon hides this real life from thee. I am that which in thy heart thou hast prayed for, demanded as thy birthright, although thou hast not known what it was. I am that which has lain in thy soul for hundreds and thousands of years. Sometimes I lay in thee grieving because thou didst not recognize me; sometimes I raised my head, opened my eyes, and extended my arms calling thee either tenderly and quietly, or strenuously, demanding that thou shouldst rebel against the iron chains which bound thee to the earth. KRISHNA.

So matters went on, and still go on, in the Christian world. But we might have hope that in the immense Brahman, Buddhist, and Confucian worlds this new scientific superstition would not establish itself, and that the Chinese, Japanese, and Hindus, once their eyes were opened to the religious fraud justifying violence, would advance directly to a recognition of the law of love inherent in humanity, and which had been so forcibly enunciated by the great Eastern teachers. But what has happened is that the scientific superstition replacing the religious one has been accepted and secured a stronger and stronger hold in the East.

In your periodical you set out as the basic principle which should guide the actions of your people the maxim that: 'Resistance to aggression is not simply justifiable but imperative, non-resistance hurts both Altruism and Egotism.'

Love is the only way to rescue humanity from all ills, and in it you too have the only method of saving your people from enslavement. In very ancient times love was proclaimed with special strength and clearness among your people to be the religious basis of human life. Love, and forcible resistance to evil-doers, involve such a mutual contradiction as to destroy utterly the whole sense and meaning of the conception of love. And what follows? With a light heart and in the twentieth century you, an adherent of a religious people, deny their law, feeling convinced of your scientific enlightenment and your right to do so, and you repeat (do not take this amiss) the amazing stupidity indoctrinated in you by the advocates of the use of violence—the enemies of truth, the servants first of theology and then of science—your European teachers.

You say that the English have enslaved your people and hold them in subjection because the latter have not resisted resolutely enough and have not met force by force.

But the case is just the opposite. If the English have enslaved the people of India it is just because the latter recognized, and still recognize, force as the fundamental principle of the social order. In accord with that principle they submitted to their little rajahs, and on their behalf struggled against one another, fought the Europeans, the English, and are now trying to fight with them again.

A commercial company enslaved a nation comprising two hundred millions. Tell this to a man free from superstition and he will fail to grasp what these words mean. What does it mean that thirty thousand men, not athletes but rather weak and ordinary people, have subdued two hundred million vigorous, clever, capable, and freedom-loving people? Do not the figures make it clear that it is not the English who have enslaved the Indians, but the Indians who have enslaved themselves?

When the Indians complain that the English have enslaved them it is as if drunkards complained that the spirit-dealers who have settled among them have enslaved them. You tell them that they might give up drinking, but they reply that they are so accustomed to it that they cannot abstain, and that they must have alcohol to keep up their energy. Is it not the same thing with the millions of people who submit to thousands, or even to hundreds, of others—of their own or other nations?

If the people of India are enslaved by violence it is only because they themselves live and have lived by violence, and do not recognize the eternal law of love inherent in humanity.

> Pitiful and foolish is the man who seeks what he already has, and does not know that he has it. Yes, pitiful and foolish is he who does not know the bliss of love which surrounds him and which I have given him.
>
> KRISHNA.

As soon as men live entirely in accord with the law of love natural to their hearts and now revealed to them, which excludes all resistance by violence, and therefore hold aloof from all participation in violence—as soon as this happens, not only will hundreds be unable to enslave millions, but not even millions will be able to enslave a single individual. Do not resist the evil-doer and take no part in doing so, either in the violent deeds of the administration, in the law courts, the collection of taxes, or above all in soldiering, and no one in the world will be able to enslave you.

VI

O ye who sit in bondage and continually seek and pant for freedom, seek only for love. Love is peace in itself and peace which gives complete satisfaction. I am the key that opens the portal to the rarely discovered land where contentment alone is found. KRISHNA.

What is now happening to the people of the East as of the West is like what happens to every individual when he passes from childhood to adolescence and from youth to manhood. He loses what had hitherto guided his life and lives without direction, not having found a new standard suitable to his age, and so he invents all sorts of occupations, cares, distractions, and stupefactions to divert his attention from the misery and senselessness of his life. Such a condition may last a long time.

When an individual passes from one period of life to another, a time comes when he cannot go on in senseless activity and excitement as before, but has to understand that although he has outgrown what before used to direct him, this does not mean that he must live without any reasonable guidance, but rather that he must formulate for himself an understanding of life corresponding to his age, and having elucidated it must be guided by it. And in the same way a similar time must come in the growth and development of humanity. I believe that such a time has now arrived—not in the sense that it has come in the year 1908, but that the inherent contradiction of human life has now reached an extreme degree of tension: on the one side there is the consciousness of the beneficence of the law of love, and on the other the existing order of life which has for centuries occasioned an empty, anxious, restless, and troubled mode of life, conflicting as it does with the law of love and built on the use of violence. This contradiction must be faced, and the solution will evidently not be favourable to the outlived law of violence, but to the truth which has dwelt in the hearts of men from remote antiquity: the truth that the law of love is in accord with the nature of man.

But men can only recognize this truth to its full extent when they have completely freed themselves from all religious and scientific superstitions and from all the consequent misrepresentations and sophistical distortions by which its recognition has been hindered for centuries.

To save a sinking ship it is necessary to throw overboard the ballast, which though it may once have been needed would now cause the ship to sink. And so it is with the scientific superstition which hides the truth of their welfare from mankind. In order that men should embrace the truth—not in the vague way they did in childhood, nor in the one-sided and perverted way presented to them by their religious and scientific teachers, but embrace it as their highest law—the complete liberation of this truth from all and every superstition (both pseudo-religious and pseudo-scientific) by which it is still obscured is essential: not a partial, timid attempt, reckoning with traditions sanctified by age and with the habits of the people —not such as was effected in the religious sphere by Guru-Nanak, the founder of the sect of the Sikhs, and in the Christian world by Luther, and by similar reformers in other religions—but a fundamental cleansing of religious consciousness from all ancient religious and modern scientific superstitions.

If only people freed themselves from their beliefs in all kinds of Ormuzds, Brahmas, Sabbaoths, and their incarnation as Krishnas and Christs, from beliefs in Paradises and Hells, in reincarnations and resurrections, from belief in the interference of the Gods in the external affairs of the universe, and above all, if they freed themselves from belief in the infallibility of all the various Vedas, Bibles, Gospels, Tripitakas, Korans, and the like, and also freed themselves from blind belief in a variety of scientific teachings about infinitely small atoms and molecules and in all the infinitely great and infinitely remote worlds, their movements and origin, as well as from faith in the infallibility of the scientific law to which humanity is at present subjected: the historic law, the economic laws, the law of struggle and survival, and so on—if people only freed themselves from this terrible accumulation of futile exercises of our lower capacities of mind and memory called the 'Sciences', and from the innumerable divisions of all sorts of histories, anthropologies, homiletics, bacteriologics, jurisprudences, cosmographies, strategics—their name is legion—and freed themselves from all this harmful, stupifying ballast—the simple law of love, natural to man, accessible to all and solving all questions and perplexities, would of itself become clear and obligatory.

VII

Children, look at the flowers at your feet; do not trample upon them. Look at the love in your midst and do not repudiate it. KRISHNA.

There is a higher reason which transcends all human minds. It is far and near. It permeates all the worlds and at the same time is infinitely higher than they.

A man who sees that all things are contained in the higher spirit cannot treat any being with contempt.

For him to whom all spiritual beings are equal to the highest there can be no room for deception or grief

Those who are ignorant and are devoted to the religious rites only, are in a deep gloom, but those who are given up to fruitless meditations are in a still greater darkness.

UPANISHADS, FROM VEDAS.

Yes, in our time all these things must be cleared away in order that mankind may escape from self-inflicted calamities that have reached an extreme intensity. Whether an Indian seeks liberation from subjection to the English, or anyone else struggles with an oppressor either of his own nationality or of another—whether it be a Negro defending himself against the North Americans; or Persians, Russians, or Turks against the Persian, Russian, or Turkish governments, or any man seeking the greatest welfare for himself and for everybody else —they do not need explanations and justifications of old religious superstitions such as have been formulated by your Vivekanandas, Baba Bharatis, and others, or in the Christian world by a number of similar interpreters and exponents of things that nobody needs; nor the innumerable scientific theories about matters not only unnecessary but for the most part harmful. (In the spiritual realm nothing is indifferent: what is not useful is harmful.)

What are wanted for the Indian as for the

Englishman, the Frenchman, the German, and the Russian, are not Constitutions and Revolutions, nor all sorts of Conferences and Congresses, nor the many ingenious devices for submarine navigation and aerial navigation, nor powerful explosives, nor all sorts of conveniences to add to the enjoyment of the rich, ruling classes; nor new schools and universities with innumerable faculties of science, nor an augmentation of papers and books, nor gramophones and cinematographs, nor those childish and for the most part corrupt stupidities termed art—but one thing only is needful: the knowledge of the simple and clear truth which finds place in every soul that is not stupefied by religious and scientific superstitions—the truth that for our life one law is valid—the law of love, which brings the highest happiness to every individual as well as to all mankind. Free your minds from those overgrown, mountainous imbecilities which hinder your recognition of it, and at once the truth will emerge from amid the pseudo-religious nonsense that has been smothering it: the indubitable, eternal truth inherent in man, which is one and the same in all the great religions of the world. It will in due time emerge and make its way to general recognition, and the nonsense that has obscured it will disappear of itself, and with it will go the evil from which humanity now suffers.

Children, look upwards with your beclouded eyes, and a world full of joy and love will disclose itself to you, a rational world made by My wisdom, the only real world. Then you will know what love has done with you, what love has bestowed upon you, what love demands from you. KRISHNA.

YÁSNAYA POLYÁNA.
December 14th, 1908.

GANDHI LETTERS

To Gandhi.

I HAVE just received your very interesting letter, which gave me much pleasure. God help our dear brothers and co-workers in the Transvaal! Among us, too, this fight between gentleness and brutality, between humility and love and pride and violence, makes itself ever more strongly felt, especially in a sharp collision between religious duty and the State laws, expressed by refusals to perform military service. Such refusals occur more and more often.

I wrote the 'Letter to a Hindu', and am very pleased to have it translated. The Moscow people will let you know the title of the book on Krishna. As regards 're-birth' I for my part should not omit anything, for I think that faith in a re-birth will never restrain mankind as much as faith in the immortality of the soul and in divine truth and love. But I leave it to you to omit it if you wish to. I shall be very glad to assist your edition. The translation and diffusion of my writings in Indian dialects can only be a pleasure to me.

The question of monetary payment should, I think, not arise in connexion with a religious undertaking.

I greet you fraternally, and am glad to have come in touch with you. LEO TOLSTÓY.

(*Undated, but probably written in March 1910.*)

To Count Leo Tolstóy, Yásnaya Polyána, Russia.

JOHANNESBURG,
4th April 1910.

Dear Sir,

You will remember that I wrote to you from London, where I stayed in passing. As your very devoted adherent I send you together with this letter, a little book I have compiled in which I have translated my own writings from Gujarati. It is worth noting that the Indian government confiscated the original. For that reason I hastened to publish the translation. I am afraid of burdening you, but if your health permits and you have time to look through the book I need not say how much I shall value your criticism of it. At the same time I am sending you a few copies of your 'Letter to a Hindu' which you allowed me to publish. It has also been translated into one of the Indian dialects.

Your humble servant,
M. K. GANDHI.

To Mahatma Gandhi.

YÁSNAYA POLYÁNA.
8th May 1910.

Dear friend,

I have just received your letter and your book, *Indian Home Rule*.

I have read the book with great interest, for I consider the question there dealt with—Passive Resistance—to be of very great importance not only for Indians but for the whole of mankind.

I cannot find your first letter, but in looking for it have come upon Doke's biography, which much attracted me and enabled me to know you and understand you better.

I am not very well at present, and therefore refrain from writing all that is in my heart about your book and about your activity in general, which I value highly. I will however do so as soon as I am better.

Your friend and brother,
LEO TOLSTÓY.

To Gandhi, Johannesburg, Transvaal, South Africa.

KOCHETÝ.
7th September 1910.

I received your journal, *Indian Opinion*, and was glad to see what it says of those who renounce all resistance by force, and I immediately felt a wish to let you know what thoughts its perusal aroused in me.

The longer I live—especially now when I clearly feel the approach of death—the more I feel moved to express what I feel more strongly than anything else, and what in my opinion is of immense importance, namely, what we call the renunciation of all opposition by force, which really simply means the doctrine of the law of love unperverted by sophistries. Love, or in other words the striving of men's souls towards unity and the submissive behaviour to one another that results therefrom, represents the highest and indeed the only law of life, as every man knows and feels in the depths of his heart (and as we see most clearly in children), and knows until he becomes involved in the lying net of worldly thoughts. This law was announced by all the philosophies—Indian as well as Chinese, and Jewish, Greek and Roman. Most clearly, I think, was it announced by Christ, who said explicitly that on it hang all the Law and the Prophets. More than that, foreseeing the distortion that has hindered its recognition and may always hinder it, he specially indicated the danger of a misrepresentation that presents itself to men living by worldly interests—namely, that they may claim a right to defend their interests by force or, as he expressed it, to repay blow by blow and recover stolen property by force, etc., etc. He knew, as all reasonable men must do, that any employment of force is incompatible with love as the highest law of life, and that as soon as the use of force appears permissible even in a single case, the law itself is immediately negatived. The whole of Christian civilization, outwardly so splendid, has grown up on this strange and flagrant—partly intentional but chiefly unconscious—misunderstanding and contradiction. At bottom, however, the law of love is, and can be, no longer valid if defence by force is set up beside it. And if once the law of love is not valid, then there remains no law except the right of might. In that state Christendom has lived for 1,900 years. Certainly men have always let themselves be guided by force as the main principle of their social order. The difference between the Christian and all other nations is only this: that in Christianity the law of love had been more clearly and definitely given than in any other religion, and that its adherents solemnly recognized it. Yet despite this they deemed the use of force to be permissible, and based their lives on violence; so that the life of the Christian nations presents a greater contradiction between what they believe and the principle on which their lives are built: a contradiction between love which should prescribe the law of conduct, and the employment of force, recognized under various forms—such as governments, courts of justice, and armies, which are accepted as necessary and esteemed. This contradiction increased with the development of the spiritual life of Christianity and in recent years has reached the utmost tension.

The question now is, that we must choose one of two things—either to admit that we recognize no religious ethics at all but let our conduct of life be decided by the right of might; or to demand that all compulsory levying of taxes be discontinued, and all our legal and police institutions, and above all, military institutions, be abolished.

This spring, at a scripture examination in a Moscow girls' school, first their religious teacher and then an archbishop who was also present, questioned the girls on the ten commandments, especially on the sixth. After the commandments had been correctly recited the archbishop sometimes put a question, usually: 'Is it always and in every case forbidden by the law of God to kill?' And the unfortunate girls, misled by their instructor, had to answer and did answer: 'Not always, for it is permissible in war and at executions.' When, however, this customary additional question—whether it is always a sin to kill—was put to one of these unfortunate creatures (what I am telling you is not an anecdote, but actually happened and was told me by an eyewitness) the girl coloured up and answered decidedly and with emotion: 'Always!' And despite all the customary sophistries of the archbishop, she held steadfastly to it—that to kill is under all circumstances forbidden even in the Old Testament, and that Christ has not only forbidden us to kill, but in general to do any harm to our neighbour. The archbishop, for all his majesty and verbal dexterity, was silenced, and victory remained with the girl.

Yes, we may write in the papers of our progress in mastery of the air, of complicated diplomatic relations, of various clubs, of discoveries, of all sorts of alliances, and of so-called works of art, and we can pass lightly over what that girl said. But we cannot completely silence her, for every Christian feels the same, however vaguely he may do so. Socialism, Communism, Anarchism, Salvation Armies, the growth of crime, freedom from toil, the increasingly absurd luxury of the rich and increased misery of the poor, the fearfully rising number of suicides—are all indications of that inner contradiction which must and will be resolved. And, of course, resolved in such a manner that the law of love will be recognized and all reliance on force abandoned. Your work in the Transvaal, which to us seems to be at the end of the earth, is yet in the centre of our interest and supplies the most weighty practical proof, in which the world can now share, and not only the Christian but all the peoples of the world can participate.

I think it will please you to hear that here in Russia, too, a similar movement is rapidly attracting attention, and refusals of military service increase year by year. However small as yet is with you the number of those who renounce all resistance by force, and with us the number of men who refuse any military service—both the one and the other can say: God is with us, and God is mightier than man.

In the confession of Christianity—even a Christianity deformed as is that taught among us—and a simultaneous belief in the necessity of armies and preparations to slaughter on an ever-increasing scale, there is an obvious contradiction that cries to heaven, and that sooner or later, but probably quite soon, must appear in the light of day in its complete nakedness. That, however, will either annihilate the Christian religion, which is indispensable for the maintenance of the State, or it will sweep away the military and all the use of force bound up with it—which the State needs no less. All governments are aware of this contradiction, your British as much as our Russian, and therefore its recognition will be more energetically opposed by the governments than any other activity inimical to the State, as we in Russia have experienced and as is shown by the articles in your magazine. The governments know from what direction the greatest danger threatens them, and are on guard with watchful eyes not merely to preserve their interests but actually to fight for their very existence.

Yours etc.,
LEO TOLSTÓY.

LETTER TO A JAPANESE

I RECEIVED your very interesting letter and decided at once to answer it fully and fundamentally, but ill health and other things have kept me till now from that, which I regard as a very important matter.

Judging by your mention of your sermon in church, I conclude that you are a Christian. And as I am aware that several religious teachings are current in your country—Shintoism, Confucianism, Taoism, and Buddhism—I conclude that these religions are also known to you.

My supposition that you are acquainted with many religions, makes it possible for me to answer your doubts in the most definite manner. My answer will consist in referring you to the eternal truths of religion: not of this or that religion but of the one appropriate to all mankind, based not on the authority of this or that founder—Buddha, Confucius, Lao-Tsze, Christ, or Mohammed—but on the indubitable nature of the truth that has been preached by all the great thinkers of the world, and that every man not confused by false, perverted teachings, now feels in his heart and accepts with his reason.

The teaching expressed by all the great sages of the world, the authors of the Vedas, Confucius, Lao-Tsze, Buddha, Christ, and Mohammed, as well as by the Greek and Roman sages, Marcus Aurelius, Socrates, and Epictetus—amounts to this: that the essence of human life is not the body, but that spiritual element which exists in our bodies in conditions of time and space—a thing incomprehensible, but of which man is vividly conscious, and which—though the body to which it is bound is continually changing and disintegrates at death —remains independent of time and space and is therefore unchangeable. Life therefore (and this is very clearly expressed in the real, unperverted teaching of Sakya Muni) is nothing but the ever greater and greater liberation of that spiritual element from the physical conditions in which it is confined, and the ever-increasing union, by means of love, of this spiritual element in ourselves with the spiritual element in other beings, and with the spiritual element itself which men call God. That, I think, constitutes the true religious teaching common to all men, on the basis of which I will try to reply to your questions.

The questions you put to me clearly indicate that by 'religion' you do not mean what I consider to be true religious teaching, but that perversion of it which is the chief source of human errors and sufferings.

And strange as it may seem, I am convinced that religion—the very thing that gives man true welfare—is, in its perverted form, the chief source of man's sufferings.

You write that refusal to perform army service may occasion loss of liberty or life to the refusers, and that a refusal to pay taxes will produce various materially harmful consequences. And though it is not given to us men to foresee the consequences of our actions, I will grant that all would happen as you anticipate. But all the same, none of these presumed consequences can have any influence on a truly religious man's perception of the truth or of his duty.

I quite see that non-religious people, revolutionists, anarchists, or socialists, having a definite material aim in view—the welfare of the majority as they understand it—cannot admit the reasonableness of refusals to serve in the army or pay taxes, which in their view can only cause useless suffering or even death to the refusers, without improving the condition of the majority. I quite understand that attitude in non-religious people. But for a religious man, living by the spiritual essence he recognizes in himself, it is different. For such a man there is not and cannot be any question of the consequences (no matter what they may be) of his actions, or of what will happen to his body and his temporal, physical life. Such a man knows that the life of his body is not his own life, and that its course, continuance, and end do not depend on his will. For such a man only one thing is important and necessary: to fulfil what is required of him by the spiritual essence that dwells within him. And in the present case that spiritual essence demands very definitely that he should not participate in actions that are most contrary to love—in murders and in preparation for murders. Very possibly a religious man in a moment of weakness may not feel strong enough to fulfil what is demanded of him by the law he acknowledges as the law of his life, and because of that weakness he may not act as he should. But even so he will always know where the truth lies, and consequently where his duty lies, and if he does not act as he should, he will know that he is guilty and has acted badly, and will try not to repeat the sin when next he is tempted. But he will certainly not doubt the possibility of fulfilling the call of the Highest Will, and will in nowise seek to justify his action or to make any compromise, as you suggest.

Such a view of life is not only not Utopian—as it may appear to people of your nation or of the Christian nations who have lost all reasonable religious understanding of life—but is natural to all mankind.

So that if we were not accustomed to the temporary, almost mad, condition in which all the nations now exist—armed against one another—what is now going on in the world would appear impossibly fantastic, but the refusal of every reasonable man to participate in this madness would certainly not seem so.

The condition of darkness in which mankind now exists would indeed be terrible if in that darkness people did not more and more frequently appear who understand what life should and must be. There are such people, and they recognize themselves to be free in spite of all the threats and punishments the authorities can employ; and they do, not what the insensate authorities demand of them, but what is demanded of them by the highest spiritual essence which speaks clearly and loudly in every man's conscience.

To my great joy now, before my death, I see every day an ever-increasing number of such people, living not by the body but by the spirit, who calmly refuse the demands made by those who form the government to join them in the ranks of murderers, and who joyfully accept all the external, bodily tortures inflicted on them for their refusal. There are many such in Russia—men still quite young who have been kept for years in the strictest imprisonment, but who experience the happiest and most tranquil state of mind, as they recount in their letters or tell those who see them. I have the happiness to be in close touch with many of them and to receive letters from them; and if it interests you I could send you some of their letters.

What I have said about refusals to serve in the army relates also to refusals to pay taxes, about which you write. A religious man may not resist by force those who take any of the fruits of his labour—whether they be private robbers or robbers that are called 'the government'; but he also may not of his own accord help in those evidently evil deeds which are carried out by means of money taken from the people in the guise of taxes.

To your argument about the necessity of forcibly protecting a victim tortured or slain before your eyes, I will reply with an extract from a book, *For Every Day*, which I have compiled, and in which from various points of view I have repeatedly replied to that very objection. This book may interest you I think, for in it are expressed all the fundamentals of that religion which, as I began by saying, are one and the same in all the great religious teachings of the world, as well as in the hearts and minds of all men. Here is the extract:

'It is an astonishing thing that there are people who consider it the business of their lives to correct others. Can it be that these correctors are so good that they have no work left to do in correcting themselves?'

[Tolstóy does not appear to have quoted the extract he meant to give. What he generally said was, that men fond of correcting others are apt to think they can decide who is good and who is bad, and may do violence to those they regard as evil-doers, whereas they ought rather to correct themselves and not rely on, or employ, violence.—A. M.]

I will conclude by saying that there is but one means of improving human life in general: the ever-increasing elucidation and realization of the one religious truth common to all men. And at the same time I will add that I think the Japanese nation, with its external development, 'civilization', 'progress', and military power and glory, is at present in the saddest and most dangerous condition; for it is just that external glitter, and the adoption from depraved Europe of a 'scientific' outlook on life, that more than anything else hinders the manifestation among the Japanese people of that which alone can give welfare—the religious truth that is one for all mankind.

The more in detail you answer me, and the more information you give me—especially about the spiritual condition of the Japanese people—the more grateful I shall be to you.

In spite of all external differences—

Your loving brother,
LEO TOLSTÓY.

YÁSNAYA POLYÁNA.
17th March 1910.

THE WISDOM OF CHILDREN

I

RELIGION

A BOY and his MOTHER

BOY. Why has nurse dressed herself up to-day and put this new shirt on me?

MOTHER. Because to-day is a holiday and we are going to church.

BOY. What holiday is it?

MOTHER. Ascension Day.

BOY. What does 'ascension' mean?

MOTHER. It means that our Lord Jesus Christ ascended into heaven.

BOY. What does 'ascended' mean?

MOTHER. It means that he went up.

BOY. How did he go? On wings?

MOTHER. No, not on wings. He simply went up, because he is God and God can do anything.

BOY. But where did he go to? Papa told me that the sky is really only space. There is nothing there but stars, and beyond the stars other stars, and what we call the sky has no end. So where did he go to?

MOTHER [smiling]. One can't understand everything. One must have faith.

BOY. Faith in what?

MOTHER. What older people say.

BOY. But when I said that someone would die because the salt was spilt, you yourself told me not to believe what is stupid!

MOTHER. Quite right. You should not believe anything stupid.

BOY. But how am I to know what is stupid and what is not?

MOTHER. You must believe the true faith.

BOY. But what is the true faith?

MOTHER. Our faith. [Aside.] I think I am talking nonsense. [Aloud.] Go and tell papa that we are starting, and put on your scarf.

BOY. Shall we have chocolate after the service?

2
WAR

KARLCHEN SCHMIDT, *9 years old.*
PÉTYA ORLÓV, *10 years old.*
MÁSHA ORLÓVA, *8 years old.*

KARLCHEN. Our Prussia won't let the Russians take land from us!

PÉTYA. But we say that the land is ours as we conquered it first.

MÁSHA. Who are 'we'?

PÉTYA. You're only a baby and don't understand. 'We' means the people of our country.

KARLCHEN. It's like that everywhere. Some men belong to one country, some to another.

MÁSHA. Whom do I belong to?

PÉTYA. To Russia, like all of us.

MÁSHA. But if I don't want to?

PÉTYA. Whether you want to or not you are still Russian. And every country has its own tsar or king.

KARLCHEN [interjecting]. Or Parliament. . . .

PÉTYA. Each has its own army and each collects taxes from its own people.

MÁSHA. But why are they so separated?

PÉTYA. What do you mean? Each country is different.

MÁSHA. But why are they so separated?

KARLCHEN. Well, because every man loves his own fatherland.

MÁSHA. I don't understand why they are separate. Wouldn't it be better to be all together?

PÉTYA. To play games it is better to be together, but this is not play, it is an important matter.

MÁSHA. I don't understand.

THE WISDOM OF CHILDREN

KARLCHEN. You'll understand when you grow up.

MÁSHA. Then I don't want to grow up.

PÉTYA. You're little, but you're obstinate already, like all of them.

3

THE FATHERLAND: THE STATE

GAVRÍLA, *a servant and an army reservist.*
MÍSHA, *his master's young son.*

GAVRÍLA. Well, Míshenka, my dear little master, good-bye! I wonder if God will ever let us meet again.

MÍSHA. Are you really going away?

GAVRÍLA. Of course! There's war again, and I'm in the reserve.

MÍSHA. Who is the war with? Who is fighting against whom?

GAVRÍLA. Heaven knows! It's too much for me. I've read about it in the papers but can't understand it all. They say the Austriak is offended that ours has favoured those—what's their names. . . .

MÍSHA. But why do *you* go? If the tsars have quarrelled let them do the fighting.

GAVRÍLA. How can I help going? It's for Tsar, Fatherland, and the Orthodox Faith.

MÍSHA. But you don't want to go?

GAVRÍLA. Who would want to leave wife and children? And why should I want to go from a good place like this?

MÍSHA. Then why do you go? Tell them you don't want to go, and won't go. What would they do to you?

GAVRÍLA [laughs]. What would they do? Drag me off by force!

MÍSHA. But who would drag you off?

GAVRÍLA. Why, men like myself—men under orders!

MÍSHA. But why would they drag you off if they are men like yourself?

GAVRÍLA. It's the order of the commanders. Orders are given, and one is dragged off.

MÍSHA. But if they too refuse?

GAVRÍLA. They can't help themselves.

MÍSHA. Why not?

GAVRÍLA. Why, because . . . because it's the law.

MÍSHA. What sort of law?

GAVRÍLA. You say such queer things! I've been chattering with you too long. It's time for me to set the samovar for the last time.

4

TAXES

ELDER.
GRÚSHKA, *a girl of* 7.

ELDER enters a poor hut. No one is there except seven-year-old GRÚSHKA. The ELDER looks around.

ELDER. Is no one in?

GRÚSHKA. Mámka has gone for the cow, and Fédka is in the master's yard.

ELDER. Well, tell your mother that the Elder has been. Say that this is the third time, and that if she doesn't bring the tax-money without fail by Sunday I shall take the cow.

GRÚSHKA. You'll take our cow? Are you a thief? We won't let you have it!

ELDER [smiling]. What a clever little girl you are! What's your name?

GRÚSHKA. Grúshka.

ELDER. Well, Grúshka, you're a bright little girl. But listen! Tell your mother that I'll take the cow—although I'm not a thief.

GRÚSHKA. But why will you take the cow if you're not a thief?

ELDER. Because what the law requires must be paid. I shall take the cow for taxes.

GRÚSHKA. What do you mean by taxes?

ELDER. There's a clever little girl for you! What are taxes? Why, taxes are what the Tsar orders people to pay.

GRÚSHKA. Who to?

ELDER. Why, to the Tsar of course! And then they'll decide where the money shall go.

GRÚSHKA. But is the Tsar poor? We are poor and he is rich. Why does he take taxes from us?

ELDER. He doesn't take the money for himself, you little silly. He needs it for us, for our needs: for the officials, for the army, for education—for our own good.

GRÚSHKA. What good does it do us if you take our cow? That doesn't do us any good.

ELDER. You'll understand when you grow up. Mind you tell your mother what I've said.

GRÚSHKA. I'm not going to tell her such rubbish. If you and the Tsar need anything, do it for yourselves, and we'll do what we need for ourselves.

ELDER. Ah, when she grows up this girl will be rank poison!

5
CONDEMNATION

MÍTYA, *10 years old.*
ILYÚSHA, *9 years old.*
SÓNYA, *6 years old.*

MÍTYA. I told Peter Semënovich that we could get used to going without clothes. He said we couldn't. Then I told him that Michael Ivánovich says we've accustomed our faces to bearing the cold and could accustom our whole bodies to bearing it in the same way. 'Your Michael Ivánovich is a fool!' says Peter. [Laughs.] And only yesterday Michael Ivánovich said to me: 'Peter Semènovich tells a lot of lies, but what else can one expect from a fool?' [Laughs.]

ILYÚSHA. I should have said: 'You speak badly of him and he speaks badly of you.'

MÍTYA. But seriously, I don't know which of them is the fool.

SÓNYA. They're both fools. A man who says it of another, is a fool himself.

ILYÚSHA. Well, you have just called them both fools, so you must be one yourself!

MÍTYA. I don't like their calling one another 'fool' behind one another's backs. When I grow up I shan't do that, I shall just say what I think to people's faces.

ILYÚSHA. I shall too!

SÓNYA. And I shall be myself.

MÍTYA. What do you mean—'be myself'?

SÓNYA. I mean that I shall say what I think when I wish to, and if I don't wish to I shan't.

ILYÚSHA. Which just shows that you're a fool.

SÓNYA. You said just now that you weren't going to say nasty things about people.

ILYÚSHA. Ah, but I didn't say it behind your back!

6

KINDNESS

MÁSHA
MÍSHA } *two children.*
OLD WOMAN.

MÁSHA and MÍSHA are in front of their house, building a hut for their dolls.

MÁSHA [angrily to MÍSHA]. No, not that way! Take that stick away. You silly!

OLD WOMAN [comes out onto the porch, crosses herself, and exclaims] May Christ bless her, what an angel she is! She's kind to everybody.

[CHILDREN stop playing and look at the OLD WOMAN.]

MÍSHA. Who are you speaking of?

OLD WOMAN. Your mother. She remembers God and has pity on us poor folk. She's just given me a petticoat as well as some tea and money. May God and the Queen of Heaven bless her! She's not like that heathen over there, who says: 'There's a lot of the likes of you prowling about!' And his dogs are so savage I hardly got away from them.

MÁSHA. Who is that?

OLD WOMAN. The man opposite the dram-shop. Ah, he's hard. But let him be! I'm grateful to her—sweet dove—who has helped and comforted me in my sorrow. How could we live at all if there weren't any people like that? [Weeps.]

MÁSHA AND MÍSHA. Yes, she's very kind.

OLD WOMAN. When you children grow up, be like her and don't forget the poor, and then God won't forget you. [Goes away.]

MÍSHA. Poor old woman!

MÁSHA. I'm glad mamma gave her something.

MÍSHA. I don't know why we shouldn't give when there is plenty. We don't need it and she does.

MÁSHA. You remember that John the Baptist said: 'Let him who has two coats give away one'?

MÍSHA. Yes. When I grow up I shall give away everything.

MÁSHA. You can't do that!

MÍSHA. Why not?

MÁSHA. What would become of you?

MÍSHA. That's all the same to me. If we were kind to everyone, everything would be all right.

> [Leaves his play, goes to the nursery, tears a sheet out of a note-book, writes something on it, and puts it in his pocket.
> On the sheet was written: 'We must be kind.']

7

DRUNKENNESS

MAKÁRKA, *aged 12.*
MARFÚTKA, *aged 6.*
PAVLÚSHKA, *aged 10.*
TEACHER.

MAKÁRKA and MARFÚTKA come out of a house into the street.
  MARFÚTKA is crying. PAVLÚSHKA is standing on the doorstep of a neighbouring house.

PAVLÚSHKA. Where the devil are you off to at this time of night?

MAKÁRKA. He's drunk again.

PAVLÚSHKA. Uncle Prokhór?

MAKÁRKA. Who else would it be?

MARFÚTKA. He's beating mammy.

MAKÁRKA. I'm not going in again. He'll be beating me, too. [Sits down on the threshold.] I'll spend the night here. I won't go in.

[Silence. MARFÚTKA cries.]

PAVLÚSHKA. Oh, shut up! It's no use. What can we do? Leave off I tell you!

MARFÚTKA [through her tears]. If I were Tsar I'd thrash those who let him have vodka. I wouldn't let anyone sell vodka!

MAKÁRKA. The idea! The Tsar himself deals in vodka. He forbids others to sell it so as not to lose the profit himself.

PAVLÚSHKA. Rubbish!

MAKÁRKA. Rubbish, indeed! Go and ask why Akulína was sent to prison. Because she sold vodka without a licence and caused loss to the Tsar!

PAVLÚSHKA. Is that what it was for? They said it was for something against the law. . . .

MAKÁRKA. Well, it is against the law to sell vodka without a licence.

MARFÚTKA. I wouldn't let anyone sell it. It's vodka that does all the harm. Sometimes he's all right, but when he's drunk he beats everybody terribly.

PAVLÚSHKA. You do say queer things! I'll ask our teacher to-morrow. He'll know all about it.

MAKÁRKA. All right. Ask him.

Next morning Prokhór, MAKÁRKA's father, having slept off his drunkenness, has gone out to take a hair of the dog that bit him. MAKÁRKA's mother, her eye swollen and blackened, has been kneading bread. PAVLÚSHKA has gone to school. The boys have not yet assembled. The TEACHER is sitting in the porch smoking while the boys enter the school.

PAVLÚSHKA [going up to TEACHER]. Tell me, Evgény Semënich . . . someone told me yesterday that the Tsar trades in vodka but that Akulína was put in prison for doing so. Is that true?

TEACHER. Whoever told you that was a fool, and you were silly to believe him. The Tsar doesn't trade in anything—that's why he's Tsar. And Akulína was put in prison for selling vodka without a licence and so causing a loss to the Treasury.

PAVLÚSHKA. How could she cause a loss?

TEACHER. Because there is an excise-duty on liquor. A vedro [2·7 gallons] costs the Treasury two rubles, and it sells at eight rubles and forty kopéks. The difference goes as revenue for the government. And that revenue is very large—seven hundred millions.

PAVLÚSHKA. So that the more vodka is drunk the bigger the revenue?

TEACHER. Of course. If it weren't for this revenue there wouldn't be enough money for the army and the schools, and all that we need.

PAVLÚSHKA. But if everybody needs these things

why don't they take the money direct from us? Why get it through vodka?

TEACHER. 'Why get it through vodka?' Because that's the law! Well, children, now you're here, take your places!

8

CAPITAL PUNISHMENT

PETER PETRÓVICH, *a Professor.*
MÁRYA IVÁNOVNA, *his wife.*
FÉDYA, *their son, 9 years old.*
IVÁN VASÍLEVICH, *the military public prosecutor.*

MÁRYA IVÁNOVNA is sewing. FÉDYA is listening to his father's conversation.

IVÁN VASÍLEVICH. One cannot deny the lessons of history. The suppression—that is the elimination from circulation of perverted people who are dangerous to society—attains its aim, as we have seen not only in France after the Revolution, but at other times in history, and again here and now in Russia.

PETER PETRÓVICH. No, we cannot be sure of that. We cannot know the ultimate consequences, and that assertion does not justify these exceptional enactments.[1]

IVÁN VASÍLEVICH. But we have no right to presuppose that the results of the exceptional enactments will be harmful either, or that even if harm does result it will have been caused by the application of these enactments. That is one thing! Another is that men who have lost all semblance of humanity and have become wild beasts must be treated with severity. In the case of that man, for instance, who calmly cut the throats of an old woman and her three children just for the sake of three hundred rubles—how could you deal with him except by the extreme penalty?

PETER PETRÓVICH. I don't absolutely condemn

[1] A reference to the State of Enforced Protection (a modified State of Siege) which at that time overrode the common law in Russia.—A. M.

the infliction of the death penalty. I only oppose the courts-martial which inflict it so frequently. If these repeated executions acted only as a deterrent it would be different, but they demoralize people by making them indifferent to the killing of their fellow men.

IVÁN VASÍLEVICH. Again we do not know the ultimate consequences, but we do know the beneficial results. . . .

PETER PETRÓVICH. Beneficial?

IVÁN VASÍLEVICH. Yes, we have no right to deny the immediate benefits. How can society afford not to deal out retribution according to his deeds to such a criminal as. . . .

PETER PETRÓVICH. You mean that society should revenge itself?

IVÁN VASÍLEVICH. Not revenge itself! On the contrary, replace personal revenge by public retribution.

PETER PETRÓVICH. Yes. But surely it should be done in a way prescribed by law once for all—not by exceptional enactment.

IVÁN VASÍLEVICH. Public retribution replaces that fortuitous, exaggerated, unlawful revenge, frequently unfounded and mistaken, that private persons might employ.

PETER PETRÓVICH [becoming heated]. Then in your opinion this public retribution is never applied casually, but is always above suspicion and never mistaken? No, I can never agree to that! Your arguments will never convince me or anyone else that these exceptional enactments under which thousands have been executed and are still being executed are reasonable, legitimate, or beneficial. [Gets up and walks up and down agitatedly.]

FÉDYA [to his mother]. Mamma, what is papa upset about?

MÁRYA IVÁNOVNA. Papa thinks it is wrong that there should be so many executions.

FÉDYA. Do you mean that people are put to death?

MÁRYA IVÁNOVNA. Yes. He thinks it should not be done so often.

FÉDYA [going up to his father]. Papa, doesn't it say in the Ten Commandments: 'Thou shalt not kill'? Then it ought not to be done at all!

PETER PETRÓVICH [smiling]. That doesn't refer to what we are talking about. It means that individuals should not kill one another.

FÉDYA. But when men are executed they are killed just the same, aren't they?

PETER PETRÓVICH. Of course; but you must understand when and why it may be done.

FÉDYA. When may it be done?

PETER PETRÓVICH. Now how can I explain.... Well, in war for instance. And when a criminal kills someone, how can he be allowed to go unpunished?

FÉDYA. But why does the Gospel say we should love everyone and forgive everyone?

PETER PETRÓVICH. It would be well if that could be done—but it can't.

FÉDYA. Why not?

PETER PETRÓVICH. Oh, because it can't! [Turns to IVÁN VASÍLEVICH, who has been smiling as he listened to FÉDYA.] So, my worthy Iván Vasílevich, I do not, and cannot, recognize the exceptional enactments and the courts-martial.

9
PRISONS

SĔMKA, *13 years old.*
AKSÚTKA, *10 years old.*
MÍTKA, *10 years old.*
PALÁSHKA, *9 years old.*
VÁNKA, *8 years old.*

The children are sitting by a well after gathering mushrooms.

AKSÚTKA. What a dreadful state Aunt Matrèna was in! And the children! One began to howl and then they all howled together.

VÁNKA. Why were they so upset?

PALÁSHKA. Why? Because their father was being taken to jail. Enough to make them upset.

VÁNKA. What's he been sent to jail for?

AKSÚTKA. Who knows? They came and told him to get ready, and took him and led him off. We saw it all. . . .

SĔMKA. They took him for stealing horses. Dëmkin's was stolen, and Krasnóvs' was his work, too. Even our gelding fell into his clutches. Do you think they ought to pat him on the head for it?

AKSÚTKA. Yes, I know. But I can't help feeling sorry for the children. There are four of them you know, and they're so poor—they haven't even any bread. They came begging from us to-day.

SĔMKA. But then they shouldn't steal.

MÍTKA. Yes, but it was the father who did the stealing, not the children. So why should they have to go begging?

SĔMKA. To teach them not to steal.

MÍTKA. But it wasn't the children, it was their father.

SĔMKA. Oh, how you keep harping on one string! 'The children—The children!' Why did he do wrong? Is he to be allowed to steal because he has a lot of children?

VÁNKA. What will they do with him in the jail?

AKSÚTKA. Just keep him there—that's all.

VÁNKA. Will they feed him?

SĔMKA. Yes, of course, the damned horse-thief! What is prison to him? Everything provided and he sits there comfortably. If only I was Tsar I'd know how to deal with horse-thieves. I'd teach them not to steal! But what happens now? He sits there at ease with friends of his own kind, and they teach one another how to steal better. My grandfather was telling us how Petrúkha used to be a good lad, but after he had been in jail just once he came out such a thorough scoundrel that it was all up with him. From that time he began....

VÁNKA. Then why do they lock them up?

SĔMKA. Oh, go and ask them!

AKSÚTKA. They lock him up and feed him....

SĔMKA. So that he should learn his job better!

AKSÚTKA. While his children and their mother starve to death! They're neighbours and I'm sorry for them. What'll become of them? They come begging for bread and we can't help giving.

VÁNKA. Then why do they put people in prison?

SĔMKA. What else could be done with them?

VÁNKA. 'What else could be done'? Well, somehow . . . so that . . . .

SĔMKA. You say 'somehow', but how, you don't know yourself! Wiser men than you have thought about it and haven't found a way.

PALÁSHKA. I think if I was the Tsarítsa. . . .

AKSÚTKA [laughs]. Well, what would you do, Tsarítsa?

PALÁSHKA. I'd make it so that no one should steal and the children wouldn't cry.

AKSÚTKA. Yes, but how would you do it?

PALÁSHKA. I'd arrange it so that everyone should have all they need and no one should be wronged, and everything would be all right for everybody.

SÉMKA. Well done, Tsarítsa! But how would you do it all?

PALÁSHKA. I don't know, but I'd do it.

MÍTKA. Let's go through the thick birch wood, shall we? The girls got a lot of mushrooms there the other day.

SÉMKA. That's a good idea. Come on, you others. And you, Tsarítsa, mind you don't spill your mushrooms, you're getting too clever by half!

[They get up and set out.]

10

RICHES

A LANDOWNER.
His WIFE.
Their 6-year-old son, VÁSYA.
A TRAMP.

The LANDOWNER and his WIFE are sitting at tea on a balcony with their daughter and VÁSYA. A young TRAMP approaches.

LANDOWNER [to TRAMP]. What is it?

TRAMP [bowing]. You can see what it is, master! Have pity on a workless man! I'm starving and in rags. I've been in Moscow, and am begging my way home. Help a poor man!

LANDOWNER. Why are you in want?

TRAMP. Because I have no money, master.

LANDOWNER. If you worked you wouldn't be so poor.

TRAMP. I'd be glad to work, but there's no work to be had nowadays. They're shutting down everywhere.

LANDOWNER. Other people get work. Why can't you?

TRAMP. Honest, master, I'd be thankful to get a job, but I can't get one. Have pity on me, master! This is the second day I've had nothing to eat.

LANDOWNER [looks into his purse. To his WIFE]. *Avez-vous de la petite monnaie? Je n'ai que des assignats.*[1]

MISTRESS [to VÁSYA]. Go and look in the bag on the little table by my bed, there's a good boy. You'll find a purse there—bring it to me.

VÁSYA [does not hear what his mother has said, but stares at the TRAMP without taking his eyes off him].

[1] Have you any small change? I have nothing but paper money.

MISTRESS. Vásya, don't you hear? [Pulls him by the sleeve.] Vásya!

VÁSYA. What is it, mamma? [His mother repeats what she had said. VÁSYA jumps up.] All right, mamma. [Goes out, still looking at the TRAMP.]

LANDOWNER [to TRAMP]. Wait a little—in a minute. [TRAMP steps aside. To his WIFE, in French.] It's dreadful what a lot of them are going about without work. It's all laziness—but still it's terrible if he's really hungry.

MISTRESS. They exaggerate. I hear it's just the same abroad. In New York, I see, there are about a hundred thousand unemployed! Would you like some more tea?

LANDOWNER. Yes, please, but a little weaker this time. [He smokes and they are silent.]

> [The TRAMP looks at them, shakes his head, and coughs, evidently wishing to attract their attention. VÁSYA runs in with the purse and immediately looks round for the TRAMP. He gives the purse to his mother and stares at the man.]

LANDOWNER [taking a threepenny bit from the purse]. Here you—what's your name—take this!

> [TRAMP takes off his cap, bows, and takes the coin.]

TRAMP. Thank you for having pity on a poor man.

LANDOWNER. The chief pity to me is that you don't get work. If you worked you wouldn't go hungry. He who works will not want.

TRAMP [putting on his cap and turning away]. It's true what they say:
> 'Work bends your back,
> But fills no sack.'

[Goes off.]

VÁSYA. What did he say?

LANDOWNER. Some stupid peasant proverb: 'Work bends your back, but fills no sack,'

VÁSYA. What does that mean?

LANDOWNER. It means that work makes a man bent without his becoming rich.

VÁSYA. And is that wrong?

LANDOWNER. Of course it is! Those who loaf about like that fellow and don't want to work are always poor. Only those who work get rich.

VÁSYA. But how is it we are rich? We don't work!

MISTRESS [laughing]. How do you know papa doesn't work?

VÁSYA. I don't know. But I do know that we are very rich, so papa ought to have a lot of work to do. Does he work very hard?

LANDOWNER. All work is not alike. Perhaps my work couldn't be done by everyone.

VÁSYA. What is your work?

LANDOWNER. To have you fed, clothed, and taught.

VÁSYA. But he has to do that, too, for his children. Then why does he have to go about so miserably while we are so . . . .

LANDOWNER [laughing]. Here's a natural socialist!

MISTRESS. Yes, indeed: *'Ein Narr kann mehr fragen, als tausend Weise antworten können.'* One fool can ask more than a thousand sages can answer. Only one should say *'ein Kind'* instead of *'ein Narr'*. And it's true of every child.

II

LOVING THOSE WHO INJURE YOU

MÁSHA, *10 years old.*
VÁNYA, *8 years old.*

MÁSHA. I was just thinking how nice it would be if mamma came back now and took us out driving with her—first to the Arcade and then to see Nástya. What would you like to happen?

VÁNYA. Me? I'd like it to be the same as yesterday.

MÁSHA. Why, what happened yesterday? Grísha hit you and then you both cried! There's not much good in that!

VÁNYA. That's just what there was! It was so good that nothing could be better. And that's what I should like to happen again to-day.

MÁSHA. I don't know what you're talking about.

VÁNYA. Well, I'll try to explain what I mean. Do you remember how last Sunday Uncle Pável Ivánovich . . . isn't he a dear?

MÁSHA. Yes, everybody loves him. Mamma says he's a saint. And that's quite true.

VÁNYA. Well . . . do you remember that last Sunday he told a story of a man whom everybody treated badly, and how the worse they treated him the more he loved them? They abused him, but he praised them. They beat him, but he helped them. Uncle said that if people behaved like that they would feel very happy. I liked that story and I wanted to be like that man. So when Grísha hit me yesterday I kissed him. And he cried. And I felt so happy. But I didn't manage so well with nurse. She began scolding me, and I forgot how I ought to behave and was rude to her. And now

I should like to try again and behave as I did to Grísha.

MÁSHA. You mean you'd like someone to hit you?

VÁNYA. I should like it very much. I should do as I did with Grísha, and should feel happy directly.

MÁSHA. What rubbish! You always were stupid and you still are!

VÁNYA. That doesn't matter. I know now what to do to be happy all the time.

MÁSHA. You little idiot! But does it really make you happy to behave like that?

VÁNYA. Very happy!

12

THE PRESS

VOLÓDYA, *a High School pupil, 14 years old.*
SÓNYA, *15 years old.*
MÍSHA, *8 years old.*
A PORTER.

VOLÓDYA is reading and doing homework, SÓNYA is writing. The PORTER comes in with a heavy load on his back, followed by MÍSHA.

PORTER. Where shall I put this load, master? It has almost pulled my arms out of their sockets.

VOLÓDYA. Where were you told to put it?

PORTER. Vasíli Timoféevich said: 'Put it in the lesson-room for the present till the master comes himself.'

VOLÓDYA. Well, then, dump it there in the corner. [Goes on with his reading. The PORTER puts down his load and sighs.]

SÓNYA. What's that he's brought?

VOLÓDYA. A newspaper called *The Truth*.

SÓNYA. Why is there such a lot of it?

VOLÓDYA. It's the file for the whole year. [Goes on reading.]

MÍSHA. People have written all that!

PORTER. True enough! Those who wrote it must have worked hard.

VOLÓDYA. What did you say?

PORTER. I said that those who wrote it all didn't shirk work. Well, I'll be going. Please tell them that I brought the papers. [Goes out.]

SÓNYA [to VOLÓDYA]. Why does papa want all those papers?

VOLÓDYA. He wants to cut out Bolshakóv's articles.

SÓNYA. But Uncle Mikháil Ivánovich says that Bolshakóv's articles make him sick!

VOLÓDYA. Oh, that's what Uncle Mikháil Ivánovich thinks. He reads *Verity for All*.

MÍSHA. And is uncle's *Verity* as big as this?

SÓNYA. Bigger still! But this is only for one year, and it has been coming out for twenty years or more.

MÍSHA. What? Twenty lots like this, and another twenty?

SÓNYA [wishing to astonish MÍSHA]. Well, what of it? Those are only two newspapers. There are thirty or more of them published.

VOLÓDYA [without lifting his head]. Thirty! There are five hundred and thirty in Russia alone, and if you reckon those published abroad—there are thousands.

MÍSHA. You couldn't get them into this room?

VOLÓDYA. This room! They'd fill up our whole street. But please don't keep worrying. I've got an exam to-morrow, and you're hindering me with your nonsense. [Reads again.]

MÍSHA. I think they oughtn't to write so much.

SÓNYA. Why shouldn't they?

MÍSHA. Because if it's the truth, they shouldn't always be repeating the same thing, and if it's not true, they oughtn't to write it at all.

SÓNYA. So that's what you think!

MÍSHA. But why do they write such an awful lot?

VOLÓDYA [looking up from his book]. Because without the freedom of the press we shouldn't know the truth.

MÍSHA. But papa says that the truth is in *Truth*, and Uncle Mikháil says that *Truth* makes him sick. How do they know whether the truth is in *Truth* or in *Verity*?

SÓNYA. He's quite right! There are too many papers, and magazines, and books.

VOLÓDYA. How like a woman—always frivolous!

SÓNYA. No! I say there are so many of them that we can't tell....

VOLÓDYA. Everyone has his reason given him to judge where the truth is.

MÍSHA. Well, if everyone has a reason, then everyone can judge for himself.

VOLÓDYA. So your great mind has pronounced on the matter! But do please go away somewhere and stop interrupting me.

13
REPENTANCE

VÓLYA, *8 years old.*
FÉDYA, *10 years old.*

vólya stands in the passage with an empty plate and is crying. FÉDYA runs in and stops short.

FÉDYA. Mamma told me to see where you were. What are you crying about? Did you take it to nurse? [Sees the empty plate and whistles.] Where is the pudding?

VÓLYA. I ... I ... I wanted ... and suddenly. ... Oh, oh, oh, I didn't mean to, but I ate it. ...

FÉDYA. You didn't take it to nurse but ate it yourself? That was a nice thing to do! And mamma thought you'd like to take it to nurse!

VÓLYA. Yes, I did like taking it ... but all of a sudden ... I didn't mean to ... oh, oh, oh!

FÉDYA. You just tasted it and then ate it all up! That's good! [Laughs.]

VÓLYA. Yes, it's all very well for you to laugh. But how can I tell them.... I can't tell nurse and I can't tell mamma....

FÉDYA. Well, you've done it—ha—ha—ha—so you ate it all up! Now what's the use of crying? You've got to think what to do.

VÓLYA. What can I think of? What am I to do?

FÉDYA. What a fix! [Tries not to laugh. Silence.]

VÓLYA. What shall I do? It's terrible! [Sobs.]

FÉDYA. What are you so upset about? Stop crying, do! Just go and tell mamma you took it.

VÓLYA. That would make it worse.

FÉDYA. Well, then, go and confess to nurse.

VÓLYA. How can I?

FÉDYA. Listen, then! You stay here, and I'll run to nurse and tell her. She won't mind.

VÓLYA. No, don't say anything to her. How can I tell her?

FÉDYA. Oh, rubbish! You've done wrong—but what's to be done? I'll just go and tell her. [Runs off.]

VÓLYA. Fédya! Fédya! Wait! . . . Oh, he's gone. . . . I only meant to taste it, and then—I don't remember how—but I ate it all up! What shall I do? [Sobs]

FÉDYA comes running.

FÉDYA. That's enough crying! I told you nurse would forgive you. She only said: 'Oh, my poor darling!'

VÓLYA. But isn't she angry?

FÉDYA. She didn't think of being angry! 'The Lord be with him and the pudding!' she said. 'I'd have given it him myself.'

VÓLYA. But you see I didn't mean to do it! [Begins to cry again.]

FÉDYA. What's the matter now? We won't tell mamma, and nurse has forgiven you!

VÓLYA. Yes, nurse has forgiven me. She's kind and good. But I'm bad, bad, bad! That's what makes me cry.

14
ART

A FOOTMAN.
The HOUSEKEEPER.
PÁVEL, *the butler's assistant.*
NATÁSHA, *8 years old.*
NÍNA, *a High School girl.*
SÉNECHKA, *a High School boy.*

FOOTMAN [carrying a tray]. Almond-milk with the tea, and some rum!

HOUSEKEEPER [knitting a stocking and counting the stitches]. . . . Twenty-two, twenty-three. . . .

FOOTMAN. Do you hear, Avdótya Vasílevna? Hey, Avdótya Vasílevna!

HOUSEKEEPER. I hear, I hear! Directly! I can't tear myself in half. [To NATÁSHA] I'll get you a plum in a minute, dear. Only give me time. I'll get the milk ready first. [Strains the milk.]

FOOTMAN [sitting down]. Well, I saw quite enough of it! Whatever do they pay their money for?

HOUSEKEEPER. What are you talking about? Did they go to the theatre? It seems to have been a long play to-day.

FOOTMAN. The opera is always long. You sit and sit. . . . They were good enough to let me see it. I was surprised! [PÁVEL comes in bringing some plums, and stops to listen.]

HOUSEKEEPER. Then there was singing?

FOOTMAN. Yes, but what singing! Just stupid shouting—not like anything real at all. 'I love her very much,' he says—and shouts it as loud as he can, not a bit like anything real. And then they quarrel and have a fight, and then start singing again.

HOUSEKEEPER. But a season-ticket for the opera costs a lot they say.

FOOTMAN. For our box they pay three hundred rubles for twelve performances.

PÁVEL [shaking his head]. Three hundred rubles! Who gets the money?

FOOTMAN. Those who sing get a lot, of course. They say that a prima-donna earns fifty thousand rubles in a year.

PÁVEL. Not to speak of thousands—three hundred rubles is a tremendous lot of money to a peasant. Some of us struggle all our lives and can't save three hundred rubles or even a hundred.

NÍNA comes into the pantry.

NÍNA. Is Natásha here? Where have you been? Mamma is asking for you.

NATÁSHA [eating a plum]. I'll come in a minute.

NÍNA [to PÁVEL]. What did you say about a hundred rubles?

HOUSEKEEPER. Semën Nikoláevich [pointing to the FOOTMAN] was telling us about the singing at the opera to-day and how highly the singers are paid, and Pável here was surprised. Is it true, Nína Mikháilovna, that a singer gets as much as twenty-five thousand rubles?

NÍNA. Even more! One singer was offered a hundred and fifty thousand rubles to go to America. And that's not all. In the papers yesterday it was reported that a musician received twenty-five thousand rubles for a finger-nail.

PÁVEL. They'll print anything! Is such a thing possible?

NÍNA [with evident satisfaction]. It's true, I tell you.

PÁVEL. But why did they pay him that for a nail?

NATÁSHA. Yes, why?

NÍNA. Because he was a pianist and was insured, so that if anything happened to his hand and he couldn't play he got paid for it.

PÁVEL. What a business!

SÉNECHKA, a sixth-form High School boy, enters.

SÉNECHKA. What a congress you have here! What's it all about? [NÍNA tells him.]

SÉNECHKA [with even greater satisfaction]. I know a better one than that! A dancer in Paris has insured her legs for two hundred thousand rubles in case she injures them and can't work.

FOOTMAN. Those are the people, if you'll excuse my saying so, who do their work without breeches.

PÁVEL. There's work for you! Fancy paying them money for it!

SÉNECHKA. But not everybody can do it remember, and think how many years it takes them to learn it.

PÁVEL. Learn what? Something good, or how to twirl their legs?

SÉNECHKA. Oh, you don't understand. Art is a great thing.

PÁVEL. Well, I think it's all rubbish! And it's the fat folk who have such mad money to throw away. If they had to earn it as we do, with a bent back, there wouldn't be any of those dancers and singers. The whole lot of them aren't worth a farthing.

SÉNECHKA. What a thing it is to have no education! To him Beethoven, and Viardo, and Raphael are all rubbish.

NATÁSHA. And I think that what he says is true.

NÍNA. Let us go. Come along!

15

SCIENCE

A schoolboy of 15, on the modern side of the school.
A schoolboy of 16, on the classical side.
VOLÓDYA } *8-year-old twins.*
PETRÚSHA

MODERNIST. What good is Latin and Greek to me? Everything good, or of any importance, has been translated into modern languages.

CLASSICIST. You will never understand the *Iliad* unless you read it in Greek.

MODERNIST. But I have no need to read it at all, and I don't want to.

VOLÓDYA. What is the *Iliad*?

MODERNIST. A story.

CLASSICIST. Yes, but there isn't another story like it in the world.

PETRÚSHA. What makes it so good?

MODERNIST. Nothing. It's just a story like any other.

CLASSICIST. You'll never get a real understanding of the past unless you know those stories.

MODERNIST. In my opinion that is just as much a superstition as the superstition called theology.

CLASSICIST [growing heated]. Theology is falsehood and nonsense, but this is history and wisdom.

VOLÓDYA. Is theology really nonsense?

CLASSICIST. What are you joining in for? You don't understand anything about it.

VOLÓDYA AND PETRÚSHA [together, offended]. Why don't we understand?

VOLÓDYA. Perhaps we understand better than you do.

CLASSICIST. Oh, all right, all right! But sit still

and don't keep interrupting our conversation. [To the MODERNIST.] You say the ancient languages have no application to modern life. But the same can be said about bacteriology and chemistry and physics and astronomy. What good is it to know the distances of the stars, and their sizes, and all those details that are of no use to anyone?

MODERNIST. Why do you say such knowledge is no good? It is very useful.

CLASSICIST. What for?

MODERNIST. What for? All sorts of things—navigation, for instance.

CLASSICIST. You don't need astronomy for that!

MODERNIST. Well, how about the practical application of science to agriculture, medicine, and industry. . . .

CLASSICIST. That same knowledge is also utilized in making bombs, and in wars, and is used by the revolutionaries. If it made people live better lives. . . .

MODERNIST. And are people made better by your sort of science?

VOLÓDYA. What sort of science does make people better?

CLASSICIST. I told you not to interrupt the conversation of your elders. You only talk nonsense.

VOLÓDYA AND PETRÚSHA [together]. But nonsense or not, what sciences make people live better?

MODERNIST. There are no such sciences. Everyone must do that for himself.

CLASSICIST. Why do you bother to talk to them? They don't understand anything.

MODERNIST. Why not? [to VOLÓDYA and PETRÚSHA]. They don't teach one how to live in the High School.

VOLÓDYA. If they don't teach that, then there is no need to study.

PETRÚSHA. When we grow bigger we won't learn unnecessary things.

VOLÓDYA. But we will live better ourselves.

CLASSICIST [laughing]. See how these sages have summed it all up!

16

GOING TO LAW

A PEASANT.
His WIFE.
His son's GODFATHER.
FEDOR ⎫ *their sons.*
PÉTKA ⎭

PEASANT [entering hut and taking off his things]. Lord, what weather! I could hardly get there.

WIFE. Yes, it's a long way off! It must be some fifteen versts.

PEASANT. It's quite twenty. [To FEDOR] Go and put up the horse.

WIFE. Well, have they awarded it to us?

PEASANT. The devil of an award! There's no sense in it at all.

GODFATHER. What's it all about, friend? I don't understand.

PEASANT. Well, you see it's like this; Averyán has grabbed my kitchen-garden and says it's his, and I can't get the matter settled.

WIFE. We've been at law about it for two years.

GODFATHER. I know, I know. It was being tried by the local court last Lent. But I heard that it was settled in your favour.

PEASANT. Yes, that's so, but Averyán went to the Land Captain, and he sent the case back for re-trial. So I went before the Judges, and they, too, decided in my favour; that should have settled it. But no, they've reconsidered it now and given it to him. There's fine judges for you!

WIFE. Well, what's going to happen now?

PEASANT. I'm not going to let him take what's mine. I shall take the matter to a higher Court. I've spoken to a lawyer about it already.

GODFATHER. But suppose the higher Court goes his way, too?

PEASANT. Then I'll take it higher still! I won't give way to that fat-bellied devil, if I have to part with my last cow. He shall learn who he's up against.

GODFATHER. What a curse these judges are—a real curse! But what if they also decide in his favour?

PEASANT. I'll take it to the Tsar. . . . But I must go and give the horse his hay. [Goes out.]

PÉTKA. And if the Tsar decides against us, who is there to go to then?

WIFE. Beyond the Tsar there's nobody.

PÉTKA. Why do some of them award it to Averyán and others to daddy?

WIFE. It must be because they don't know themselves.

PÉTKA. Then why do we ask them, if they don't know?

WIFE. Because no one wants to give up what belongs to him.

PÉTKA. When I grow up I know what I'll do. If I disagree with anybody about anything we'll draw lots to see who is to have it. Whoever gets it, that will be the end of it. I always do that with Akúlka.

GODFATHER. And perhaps that's the best way, really! Settle it without sin.

WIFE. So it is. What haven't we spent over that bit of ground—more than it's worth! Oh, it's a sin—a sin!

17
CRIMINAL LAW

GRÍSHKA, *12 years old.*
SEMKA, *10 years old.*
TÍSHKA, *13 years old.*

TÍSHKA. They'll put him in prison so that he doesn't sneak into someone else's corn-bin again. He'll be afraid to do it another time.

SEMKA. It's all right if he really did do it, but Grandpa Mikíta was saying that Mitrofán was sent to jail quite wrongly.

TÍSHKA. What do you mean—wrongly? Won't the man who sentenced him wrongly be punished?

GRÍSHKA. They won't pat him on the head for it if he sentenced him wrongly. He'll be punished, too.

SEMKA. But who will punish him?

TÍSHKA. Those who are above him.

SEMKA. And who is above him?

TÍSHKA. The authorities.

SEMKA. But suppose the authorities make a mistake, too?

GRÍSHKA. There are still higher authorities who will punish them. That's why there is a Tsar.

SEMKA. And if the Tsar makes a mistake who'll punish him?

TÍSHKA. 'Who will punish? Who will punish?' We know. . . .

GRÍSHKA. God will punish him.

SEMKA. Then surely God will punish the man who climbed into the corn-bin? So God and God alone ought to punish anyone who is guilty. God will make no mistakes.

TÍSHKA. But you see it can't be done like that!

SEMKA. Why not?

TÍSHKA. Because. . . .

18

PRIVATE PROPERTY

An old CARPENTER.
A BOY of 7.

The old CARPENTER is mending the rails of a balcony. The son of the owner is watching him and admiring his work.

BOY. How well you do it! What's your name?

CARPENTER. Well, they used to call me Khrólka, but now they call me Khrol. My other name is Sávich.

BOY. How well you work, Khrol Sávich!

CARPENTER. What's worth doing at all is worth doing well. What pleasure is there in bad work?

BOY. Have you got a balcony at your house?

CARPENTER [laughing]. A balcony! Ah, my boy, such a balcony as yours can't compare with! One with neither window nor door, neither roof nor walls nor floor. That's what our balcony is like.

BOY. You're always making jokes! No, but really and truly, have you got a balcony like this? I want to know.

CARPENTER. A balcony? Why, my dear little chap, how could the likes of us have a balcony? It's a mercy if we have as much as a roof over our heads—as for a balcony! I've been trying to build myself a hut ever since the spring. I pulled down the old one, but I can't get the new one finished. It hasn't got a roof on yet and it stands there rotting.

BOY [surprised]. Why is that?

CARPENTER. Simply because I'm not strong enough.

BOY. What do you mean—not strong enough? You work for us, don't you?

What work can she do? There's only me to do all the work—and that crowd around me crying for food....

LADY. Are there really seven children?

OLD WOMAN. May I die if there aren't! The eldest is only just beginning to help a little, the rest are all too small.

LADY. But why has she had so many?

OLD WOMAN. What can you expect? He is living near by in the town—comes home for a visit or on a holiday . . . and they are young people. If only he were taken somewhere far away!

LADY. Yes. Some mourn because they have no children or because their children die, but you mourn because there are so many.

OLD WOMAN. So many, so many! More than we have strength for. But you will give her some hope, lady?

LADY. Very well. I was godmother to the others, and I will be to this one, too. Is it a boy?

OLD WOMAN. A boy, little but healthy. He cries like anything.... Will you fix the time?

LADY. Have it whenever you like.

[OLD WOMAN thanks her and goes away.]

TÁNICHKA. Mamma, why is it some people have children and others not? You have and Matrena has, but Parásha hasn't.

LADY. Parásha isn't married. Children are born when people are married. They marry, become husband and wife, and then children are born.

TÁNICHKA. Always?

LADY. No, not always. Cook has a wife, you know, but they have no children.

TÁNICHKA. But couldn't it be arranged so that people who want children should have them and those who don't want them shouldn't have them?

BOY. What stupid things you ask!

TÁNICHKA. Not stupid at all! I think that if Matrëna's daughter doesn't want children, it would be better to arrange that she shouldn't have them. Can't that be done, mamma?

BOY. You talk nonsense, silly. You don't know anything about it.

TÁNICHKA. Can't it be done, mamma?

LADY. How can I tell you? We don't know.... It depends on God.

TÁNICHKA. But what causes children to be born?

BOY [laughs]. A goat!

TÁNICHKA [offended]. There's nothing to laugh at. I think that if children make it hard for people, as Matrëna says, it ought to be arranged that they shouldn't be born. Nurse hasn't any children and never has had.

LADY. But she isn't married. She has no husband.

TÁNICHKA. So should all be who don't wish to have children. Or else what happens? Children are born and there's nothing to feed them on. [LADY exchanges glances with the boy and is silent.] When I am grown up I will certainly marry and arrange to have just a girl and a boy—and no more. It isn't right that there should be children and they shouldn't be loved! How I shall love my children! Really, mamma! I will go to nurse and ask her about it. [Goes away.]

LADY [to her son]. Yes, how goes the saying? 'Out of the mouths of babes'... how is it? 'there comes truth.' What she said is quite true. If only people understood that marriage is an important matter and not an amusement—that they should marry not for their own sakes but for their children's—we should not have those horrors of abandoned and neglected children, and it would not happen as with Matrëna's daughter, that children are not a joy but a grief.

20

EDUCATION

A PORTER.
NIKOLÁY, *a High School boy of 15.*
KÁTYA, *aged 7.*
Their MOTHER.

The PORTER *is polishing the door-knobs.* KÁTYA *is building a toy house with little bricks.* NIKOLÁY *enters and flings down his books.*

NIKOLÁY. Damn them all and their blasted High School!

PORTER. What's the matter?

NIKOLÁY. They've given me a one[1] again, devil take them! There'll be another row. Much good their damned geography is to me. Where is some Clifornia [California] or other! Why the devil must I know that?

PORTER. And what will they do to you?

NIKOLÁY. Keep me back in the same class again.

PORTER. But why don't you learn your lessons?

NIKOLÁY. Because I can't learn rubbish—that's why. Oh, let them all go to blazes! [*Throws himself into a chair.*] I'll go and tell mamma that I can't go on, and there's an end of it. Let them do what they like, but I can't go on. And if she won't take me out of the school—by God, I'll run away!

PORTER. Where will you run to?

NIKOLÁY. I'll run away from home. I'll hire myself out as a coachman or a yard-porter! Anything would be better than that rot.

PORTER. But a porter's job isn't easy, you know. Getting up early, chopping the wood, carrying it in and stoking the fires.

NIKOLÁY. Phew! [*Whistles.*] That's a holiday!

[1] The lowest mark. The highest was five.—A. M.

Splitting logs is a nice job. You won't put me off with that. It's an awfully nice job. You should just try to learn geography!

PORTER. Really? But why do they make you do it?

NIKOLÁY. You may well ask why! There's no 'why' about it—it's just the custom. They think people can't get along without it.

PORTER But you must learn, or you'll never get into the Service and receive a grade and a salary like your papa and your uncle.

NIKOLÁY. But suppose I don't want to?

KÁTYA. Yes, suppose he doesn't want to?

MOTHER enters with a note in her hand.

MOTHER. The Headmaster writes that you've got a one again! That won't do, Nikólenka. It's one of two things: either you study or you don't.

NIKOLÁY. Of course it's one or the other. I can't, I can't, I can't! Let me leave school for God's sake, mamma! I simply can't learn.

MOTHER. Why can't you?

NIKOLÁY. I just can't! It won't go into my head.

MOTHER. It won't go into your head because you don't concentrate. Stop thinking about rubbish, and think of your lessons.

NIKOLÁY. I'm in earnest, mamma. Do let me leave! I don't ask for anything else, only set me free from this horrible studying—this drudgery. I can't stand it!

MOTHER. But what will you do?

NIKOLÁY. That's my affair.

MOTHER. No, it's not your affair, it's mine. I am answerable to God for you, and I must have you educated.

NIKOLÁY. But supposing I can't be educated?

MOTHER [severely]. What nonsense! I appeal to you as your mother, for the last time, to turn over a new leaf and do what is demanded of you. If you don't listen to me I shall have to take other steps.

NIKOLÁY. I have told you I can't and don't want to.

MOTHER. Take care, Nikoláy!

NIKOLÁY. There's nothing to take care of! Why do you torment me? You don't understand.

MOTHER. Don't dare to speak to me like that! How dare you? Leave this room at once! And take care!

NIKOLÁY. All right, I'll go. I'm not afraid of anything and I don't want anything from you. [Runs out, slamming the door.]

MOTHER [to herself]. He worries me to death. But I know what it all comes from. It's all because he won't concentrate on the necessary things, but fills his head with rubbish—the dogs and the hens.

KÁTYA. But mamma, don't you remember you yourself told me how impossible it was to stand in a corner and not think of a white bear?

MOTHER. I'm not talking about that. I'm saying he must learn what he is told to.

KÁTYA. But he says he can't.

MOTHER. He talks nonsense.

KÁTYA. But he doesn't say he doesn't want to do anything; only he doesn't want to learn geography. He wants to work. He wants to be a coachman or a porter.

MOTHER. If he were a porter's son he might be a porter, but he is your father's son and so he must study.

KÁTYA. But he doesn't want to!

MOTHER. Whether he wants to or not, he must.

KÁTYA. But supposing he can't?

MOTHER. Mind you don't follow his example!

KÁTYA. But that's exactly what I shall do. I won't on any account learn what I don't want to.

MOTHER. Then you will be an ignorant fool. [Silence.]

KÁTYA. When I grow up and have children of my own I won't on any account force them to learn. If they want to study I shall let them, but if they don't I shan't make them.

MOTHER. When you grow up you'll do nothing of the kind.

KÁTYA. I certainly shall.

MOTHER. You won't, when you grow up.

KÁTYA. Yes I shall, I shall, I shall!

MOTHER. Then you'll be a fool.

KÁTYA. Nurse says, God needs fools.

THOUGHTS SELECTED FROM PRIVATE LETTERS

TWO VIEWS OF LIFE

THERE are only two strictly logical views of life: one a false one, which understands life to mean those visible phenomena that occur in our bodies from the time of birth to the time of death; the other a true one, which understands life to be the invisible consciousness which dwells within us. One view is false, the other true, but both are logical.

The first of these views, the false one which understands life to mean the phenomena visible in our bodies from birth till death, is as old as the world. It is not, as many people suppose, a view of life produced by the materialistic science and philosophy of our day; our science and philosophy have only carried that conception to its farthest limits, making more obvious than ever the incompatibility of that view of life with the fundamental demands of human nature, but it is a very old and primitive view, held by men on the lowest level of development. It was expressed by Chinese, by Buddhists, and by Jews, and in the Book of Job.

This view is now expressed as follows: Life is an accidental play of the forces in matter, showing itself in time and space. What we call our consciousness is not life, but a delusion of the senses which makes it seem as if life lay in that consciousness. Consciousness is a spark which under certain conditions is ignited in matter, burns up to a flame, dies down, and at last goes out altogether. This flame (i.e. consciousness), attendant upon matter for a certain time between two infinities of time, is —nothing. And *though consciousness perceives itself and the whole universe, and sits in judgement on itself and on the universe, and sees the play of chance in this universe, and, above all, calls it a play of chance in contradistinction to something which is not chance*—this consciousness itself is only an outcome of lifeless matter—a phantom appearing and vanishing without meaning or result. Everything is the outcome of ever-changing matter, and what we call life is but a condition of dead matter.

That is one view of life. It is a perfectly logical view. According to this view, man's reasonable consciousness is but an accident incidental to a certain state of matter, and therefore what we in our consciousness call life, is but a phantom. Only dead matter exists. What we call life is the play of death.

The other view of life is this. Life is only what I am conscious of in myself. And I am always conscious of my life not as something that has been or will be (that is how I *reflect* on my life), but when I am *conscious* of it I feel that I *am*—never beginning anywhere, never ending anywhere. With the consciousness of my life, conceptions of time and space do not blend. My life manifests itself in time and space, but that is only its *manifestation*. Life itself, as I am conscious of it, is something I perceive apart from time and space. So that in this view of life we get just the contrary result: not that consciousness of life is a phantom, but that everything relating to time and space is of the nature of a phantom.

Therefore, in this view, the cessation of my physical existence in time and space has no reality, and cannot end or even hinder my true life. And according to this view death does not exist.

MATTER IS THE LIMIT OF SPIRIT

The material form in which the awakening of our consciousness of true life finds us in this world is, so to speak, the boundary limiting the free development of our spirit.

Matter is the limit of spirit. But true life is the destruction of this limitation.

In this understanding of life lies the very essence of the understanding of truth—that essence which gives man the consciousness of eternal life.

Materialists mistake that which limits life, for life itself.

THE SCAFFOLDING

We must remind ourselves as often as possible that our true life is not this external, material life that passes before our eyes here on earth, but that it is the inner life of our spirit, for which the visible life serves only as a scaffolding—a necessary aid to our spiritual growth. The scaffolding itself is only of temporary importance, and after it has served its purpose is no longer wanted but even becomes a hindrance.

Seeing before him an enormously high and elaborately constructed scaffolding, while the building itself only just shows above its foundations, man is apt to make the mistake of attaching more importance to the scaffolding than to the building for the sake of which alone this temporary scaffolding has been put up.

We must remind ourselves and one another that the scaffolding has no meaning or importance except to render possible the erection of the building itself.

THE LIFE OF THE SPIRIT

There are moments when one ceases to believe in spiritual life.

This is not unbelief, but rather periods of belief in physical life.

A man suddenly begins to be afraid of death. This always happens when something has befogged him and he once more begins to believe that bodily life is real life, just as in a theatre you may forget yourself and think that what you see on the stage is actually happening, and so may be frightened by what is done there.

That is what happens in life.

After a man has understood that his life is not on the stage but in the stalls—that is, not in his personality but outside it—it sometimes happens that, from old habit, he suddenly succumbs again to the seduction of illusion and feels frightened.

But these moments of illusion are not enough to convince me that what goes on before me (in my physical life) is really happening.

At times when one's spirit sinks one must treat oneself as one treats an invalid—and keep quiet!

THE FEAR OF DEATH

It is generally supposed that there is something mystical in our view of life and death. But there is nothing of the kind.

I like my garden, I like reading a book, I like caressing a child. By dying I lose all this, and therefore I do not wish to die, and I fear death.

It may be that my whole life consists of such temporary worldly desires and their gratification. If so I cannot help being afraid of what will end these desires. But if these desires and their gratification have given way and been replaced in me by another desire—the desire to do the will of God, to give myself to Him in my present state and in any possible future state—then the more my desires have changed the less I fear death, and the less does death exist for me. And if my desires be completely transformed, then nothing but life remains and there is no death. To replace what is earthly and temporary by what is eternal is the way of life, and along it we must travel. But in what state his own soul is—each one knows for himself.

THE WAY TO KNOW GOD AND THE SOUL

God and the Soul are known by me in the same way that I know infinity: not by means of definitions but in quite another way. Definitions only destroy for me that knowledge. Just as I know assuredly that there is an infinity of numbers, so do I know that there is a God and that I have a soul. For me this knowledge is indubitable, simply because I am led to it unavoidably.

To the certainty of the infinity of numbers I am led by addition.

To the certain knowledge of God I am led by the question, 'Whence come I?'

To the knowledge of the soul I am led by the question, 'What am I?'

And I know surely of the infinity of numbers, and of the existence of God and of my soul, when I am led to the knowledge of them by these most simple questions.

To one I add one, and one more, and another one, and another one; or I break a stick in two, and again in two, and again, and again—and I cannot help knowing that number is infinite.

I was born of my mother, and she of my grandmother, and she of my great-grandmother, but the very first—of whom? And I inevitably arrive at God.

My legs are not I, my arms are not I, my head is not I, my feelings are not I, even my thoughts are not I: then what am I? I am I, I am my soul.

From whatever side I approach God it will always be the same. The origin of my thoughts, my reason, is God. The origin of my love is also He. The origin of matter is He, too.

It is the same with the conception of the soul. If I consider my striving after truth, I know that this striving after truth is my immaterial basis—my soul. If I turn to my feelings of love for goodness, I know that it is my soul which loves.

INDEX TO THIS VOLUME

Abraham, Gerald, xiv.
Abyssinia, 197.
Alexander I, 19.
— II, 303.
Amiel, 238.
Anna Karénina, 52.
'Ant Brothers', 42.
Arnold, Matthew, xv, 188.
Ascension, the, 446.

Belshazzar, Feast of, 123.
Birukóv, P. I., 56.
Boer War, 227.
Bóndarev, T., 189.
Boyhood and Youth, 5.
Brandes, G. M., 362.
Bryullóv, K. P., 81.
Buddha, 261.

Carpenter, Edward, xx, 176
Centenary Edition, viii, xxviii.
Channing, W. E., 213.
Chertkóv, V. G., viii, x.
Childhood, 33.
'Christianity of beef-steaks', 123.
Comte, A., 181, 369.
Confession, vii, ix, xix.
Considerant, V. P., 229.
Crosby, Ernest Howard, 249, 307.
Crusades, the, 366.

Daily Telegraph, xvi, xvii.
Decembrists, the, 303.
Dibitch, 254, 255.
Dillon, Dr. E. J., xvii.
Doke, 434.
Dólokhov, 40.
Dostoévski, 81.
Doukhobórs, xxvi.

Dreyfus, 367-8.
Drózhin, 243-4.
Dumas, A., *fils*, 136, 154 et seq., 162, 170.
Durnovó, Minister of Interior, xvii.

Encyclical of Pope Leo XIII, 97.
Engelhardt, Varvára, 10, 12.
Epictetus, 249, 440.
Erckmann-Chatrian, 215.
Érgolski, Tatiána Alexándrovna ('Auntie Tatiána'), 13, 16, 24, 26, 27, 28.
Essays on Art, xxiii.
Ethics of Diet, The, 124, 134, 135.

Fanfarónov Hill, 43.
Fedor Ivánovich, 8, 32, 39, 41, 42, 51.
Fet, A., 365.
Feuillet, Octave, 100, 101.
Final Struggle, The, xiv, xxvii.
Flammarion, 219.
Fleugel, Maurice, 233.
For Every Day, 444.
France, Anatole, 209.
Frederick the Great, 229, 373.

Gandhi, xxv-xxvi, 413-15, 433 et seq.
Garrod, H. W., xv, xxviii.
George, Henry, xxi, 189 et seq., 277 et seq., 284 et seq., 301, 305.
Gervinus, G. G., 355, 357.
Goethe, 338, 374, 377, 380.
Gógol, 52.

Gorchakóv, Prince Alexéy Ivánovich, Minister of War, 17.
—, — Andrew Ivánovich, 17.
Great Iniquity, A, xxi.
Grísha, 28.

Haeckel, Ernst, 64, 65.
Hague Peace Conference, 210, 226.
Hallam, H., 309.
Hardouin, J., 224.
Harsnet, Dr. Samuel, 325.
Hazlitt, William, 309.
Herzen, 105, 106.
Hindu Kural, 421.
Homer, 355.
Hugo, Victor, 310, 380.
Huxley, Thomas, 240.

I Cannot Be Silent, xxiv.
Iliad, The, 479.
Islénev, 30, 31, 36, 55.

John the Baptist, 165, 229
Johnson, Dr., 309.

Kant, 87, 234, 237, 238, 249.
Karr, Alphonse, 214.
Kazán, 18, 44, 46, 47, 48.
Kingdom of God is Within You, The, xix.
Knight, G Wilson, xxii–xxiii.
Kolokóltsev, Grísha, 57, 58, 59, 60, 61, 62.
Krishna, 416, 418, 420, 423, 425, 427, 428, 431, 432.
Kuropátkin, Alexéy, 255.

Labouchere, 286.
Lamennais, 228.
Lao-Tsze, 148.
Larroque, Patrice, 219.
Lessing, G. E., 85.
Letourneau, Ch., 209.

Letters on Henry George, xxi, 189.
Letter to a Hindu, xxv, 413.
Letter to a Japanese, xxvi, 440.
Lichtenberg, 238, 253.
Luther, 430.
Lyubóv Sergéevna, 50, 51.

Maistre, Joseph de, 207, 223.
Makárov, 253, 256, 257.
Manet, 138.
Marcus Aurelius, 29, 113, 237, 440.
Martens, F. F. de, 210, 226.
Marx, Karl, 183, 369.
Másha (Tolstóy's sister), 16, 55, 56.
Maupassant, Guy de, 100, 205.
Mazzini, J., 228, 234, 300.
Milford, Sir Humphrey, xxvii.
Míshenka (Tolstóy's illegitimate brother), 18.
Moch, Capitaine Gaston, 225.
Molinari, G. de, 205.
Moltke, von, 207.
Moore, George, xiii–xiv.
Moralities, the, 371, 372.
Muravev, 210, 226.
Mysteries, the, 371, 372.

Nazároff, A. I., viii.
Nicholas I, 19.
— II, 200, 210, 255.
Nietzsche, 369.
Novikóv, 303.

Obolénski, D. A., 54.
Ocházov, 33.
Ogarev, N. P. (the exile), 104, 105, 106.
Olkhovík, 242.
Onégin, 101.

INDEX TO THIS VOLUME 503

Origen, 248.
Ostróvski, A. N., 380.

Parnell, 285.
Pascal, 218.
Peter the Great, 153.
Pickwick, 352.
Plato, 92.
Plevna, 197.
Pope, The, 378.
Potemkin, 10.
'Priests of Science', 152.
Prophecy, 162.
Pugachev, 34
Púshkin, A., 2, 30, 101, 380.

Quetelet, 228.

Raskólnikov, 81, 82.
Recollections, xix–xx, 1.
Redemption, the, 95, 104.
Richet, Charles, 218.
Rod, Edouard, 222.
Romanes Lecture, 1894, xxi.
Ruskin, John, 188.
Russo-Japanese War, xxii, 204 et seq.

Sacraments, the, 104.
Sakya Muni, 441.
Sand, George, 369.
Savage, Minot J., 233.
Scaevola, Mucius, 24.
Schiller, 47, 380.
Shakespeare, xxii–xxiii, 308 et seq.
Shaw, Bernard, xi, xix.
Shelley, 310.
Shibúnin, 61, 62.
Skóbelev, M. D., 72.
Socrates, 98, 440.
Soviets, 500.
Soyen-Shaku, 261, 262.
Spencer, Herbert, 285.
Stasyulévich, A. M., 57, 58, 60, 61.

Sterne, L., 5.
Stolýpin, P. A., xxv.
Súzdal Monastery, xvii.
Swift, Jonathan, 209.

Taylorian Lecture, xv.
Temyashóv, 30, 31, 39.
— Dúnechka, 29, 31.
Tillier, Claude, 214
Tolstóy, Alexándra Andréevna, 61, 62.
— Alexéy, 380.
— Dmítri (brother), 16, 38, 41, 42, 45, 46, 47, 48, 49, 50, 51, 52, 53, 54, 55, 56.
— Ilyá (grandfather), 15.
— Leo N., vii–xxviii, 46, 234, 387.
— Márya (mother), 11.
— — (Máshenka) (sister), 16, 55, 56.
— Nicholas (brother), viii, 15, 16, 38, 39, 43, 45, 48, 52.
— — (father), 17, 18, 26.
— Count Peter Ivánovich, 24.
— Sergéy (brother), 16, 38, 39, 40, 45, 46, 48, 49, 52.
— Sergius (eldest son), xiv, xxvii.
— Theodore, 40.
Töpffer, R., 5.
Traill, H. D., x.
Trubetskóy, Princess Catherine Dmítrievna (grandmother), 10.
Turgénev, I. S., 13, 365.

Vedas, the, 416, 431.
Vigny, Alfred de, 229.
Vilejínsky, Adjutant, 254.
Vivekananda, 416, 417.

Volkónski, Prince (grandfather), 14.

War and Peace, 21, 25.
West, Rebecca, xiv.
What is Art?, ix–xvi.
What Then Must We Do?, xix.
Wilhelm of Germany, Kaiser, 199.

Yásnaya Polyána, 52.
Yazýkov, 19, 20, 25, 29, 31.
Yúshkov, V. I., 25, 51.
— Pelagéya Ilýnıshna (Tolstóy's aunt), 18, 27, 47, 51.

Zola, E., 136 et seq., 150, 152, 160, 166, 369.

SET IN GREAT BRITAIN
AT THE
UNIVERSITY PRESS, OXFORD,
BY JOHN JOHNSON,
PRINTER TO THE UNIVERSITY.
PRINTED BY
MERRITT AND HATCHER, LTD ,
LONDON.